ENGLISH TRANSPORTED

ENGLISH TRANSPORTED

Essays on Australasian English
edited by
W. S. RAMSON

AUSTRALIAN NATIONAL UNIVERSITY PRESS
CANBERRA 1970

© William Stanley Ramson

This book is copyright. Apart from any fair dealing for the purposes of private study, research, criticism, or review, as permitted under the Copyright Act, no part may be reproduced by any process without written permission. Inquiries should be made to the publisher.

Printed and manufactured in Australia
Registered in Australia for transmission by post as a book

National Library of Australia card no. & ISBN—
0 7081 0626 9 (clothbound)
0 7081 0631 5 (paperbound)
Library of Congress Catalog card no. 72-113946

PREFACE

'Australasian' is a little-used word for a concept repudiated in most senses except the geographical, and it may rightly be asked if its use in the sub-title of a collection of readings such as this does not impose an artificial unity on the contents. Words like 'Austral' (chosen by Morris for the title of his dictionary in 1898), 'Antipodean', or 'Anzac', each with connotations inappropriate to this context, certainly would suggest such a unity: the use of a geographical name, neutral in the social connotations, tolerates both the similarities and the differences between the English of Australia and that of New Zealand, and affirms the logic of studying the two together.

And such a study is logical. Both countries were settled at roughly the same time; both drew, if not on the same social balance, at least on the same population source. Both presented their English-speaking settlers with new environments and different occupational techniques. Both required, as their separate societies emerged, substantially new dialects of English, which in each case reflected a new and individual social balance and coped with new demands.

If the Australian and New Zealand dialects had developed in isolation from each other, their common origin and length of life would have made an integrated study useful. As it is, the contacts between the two countries have been so close that it is doubtful if one dialect can be fully recorded without prior or concurrent knowledge of the other. Both the similarities and the differences are illuminating: conclusions which can already be drawn about one suggest approaches to the other; patterns emerge which may or may not be repeated; individual features gain or lose importance as their uniqueness is confirmed or denied.

'Australasian' covers, of course, more than these two countries, and, once a start has been made on the recording of Australian English and New Zealand English, there is a case to be made for recording, and examining in relation to these two major dialects in the region, the English of Papua-New Guinea, Norfolk Island, and those Pacific islands which have, during their short history of European settlement, been in close touch with Australia and New Zealand. Each of these potential dialect areas demands its own investigation, but each is illuminated if the major interdependent dialects of the region and their subsidiaries are studied together.

This collection assumes the value of such an integrated regional approach but provides, as a cursory glance will show, only an uneven coverage. The bulk of the papers are on aspects of Australian English, two are on New Zealand English, and one on the pidgin used in Papua-New Guinea. Though this balance may seem to argue that Australian English is the major dialect in the region, it is in fact no more than a reflection of the present state of studies.[1] Some aspects of Australian English have been fairly fully recorded; the corresponding aspects of New Zealand English have not. Some attention has been given to Norfolk Island English, but it is only recently that a beginning has been made in describing that of Papua-New Guinea. Not the least of this collection's aims is to draw attention to the neglected areas.

Within Australia there is some reason for optimism. Two research centres, the Australian Language Research Centre in the University of Sydney, and the Queensland Speech Survey, have already accumulated valuable data, and the Australian Academy of the Humanities has recently announced its support for an historical dictionary of Australian English. Also cheering is the fact that the contributors to this collection are drawn from a number of Australian universities, an earnest of the extent to which the work is being pushed forward on several fronts. It is a reasonable assumption that the new universities in Papua-New Guinea and Fiji will bring the English of those countries under scrutiny. But the situation in New Zealand is far from encouraging; both the papers on New Zealand English in this collection were written by expatriates, and, outside Auckland and Victoria, the subject is receiving little attention. The need, there as here, is for a properly supported historical project on which subsequent specific studies can be based.

Two of the papers in this collection are in the nature of pioneer studies. J. A. W. Bennett's paper on New Zealand English was written while he was on service during the war and published in *American Speech* in 1943. As late as 1966 it remained, as G. W. Turner remarked in *The English Language in Australia and New Zealand*, 'the best survey of New Zealand English'.[2] A. G. Mitchell's Australian Humanities Research Council Address of 1960 was delivered some fifteen years after the publication of his *Pronunciation of English in Australia*, and reported in part on the preliminary findings of the Mitchell-Delbridge speech survey. For much of his period as McCaughie Professor of English in the University of Sydney Mitchell was Australian English's only advocate, and the address has

---

[1] See my 'Australian and New Zealand English: The Present State of Studies', *Kivung*, Vol. 2, No. 1, 1969, pp. 42-56.

[2] P. 217. My title, *English Transported*, is borrowed from Turner, this being the title of his first chapter.

Preface

historical value as a statement of an approach which has stimulated and guided later students of both the vocabulary and the pronunciation.

The papers which follow these, Turner's on New Zealand English, and Delbridge's, Gunn's, and my own on Australian English, are intended to provide a more complete picture than either of the early papers was able to do. Drawing on information assembled in the last decade, they follow through tendencies which Bennett and Mitchell suggested, establish more clearly the main lines of development, and serve both to indicate the areas in which research is continuing and the areas in which further research should be encouraged.

In both Australia and New Zealand the English language has come into contact with the languages of indigenous peoples, the Aborigines and the Maoris, and the languages of immigrant European minorities. In both cases the direct effect has been small; lexical borrowings from the Maori and Aboriginal languages have occurred in specific areas, and some account of these is given in Turner's paper and my own. But forms of English have developed in these contact situations which have only recently come under examination. Clyne's paper reports on studies of the speech of European migrants in Australia, and Dutton's, based on work completed as part of the Queensland Speech Survey, on the English used by the Aborigines in one part of Australia. Less has been done on the latter than on the former, but both serve not only as reports on work in progress but as models for further studies. Susan Kaldor's paper examines specifically the language difficulties met by Asian students in Australia: the problem is a recent one, and her findings are of relevance in both Australia and New Zealand.

A similar but more complex situation arises in Papua-New Guinea. Here the 'English transported' is Australian English. A study of the emerging New Guinea English is at present being undertaken at the University of Papua and New Guinea, but the region's major contribution to the language complex of Australasia is the variety of pidgin English which Laycock describes in this volume.

The two remaining papers are those of Flint and Johnston. As Director of the Queensland Speech Survey Flint has initiated a series of research projects on the varieties of English used in parts of Queensland, and his paper is a demonstration, using passages of written and spoken English, of the techniques of linguistic description which he has evolved. Johnston's paper deals with a different subject altogether, that is, with the use of language in literature, and his concern is with relating the emergence of a new dialect to the contemporaneous emergence of a new literature, with establishing the relevance of linguistic studies of Australian English to the use of a distinctively Australian 'voice' in Australian literature.

David Blair's bibliography, which supersedes earlier bibliographies of Australian English, is the fullest available record of the main areas of activity.

Such a collection cannot be read as providing any sort of final statement on the use of English in Australasia. It is our hope that there is sufficient material not otherwise readily accessible assembled here for the book to be used in university and college courses, and for it to be of real interest to those working in related fields and to the general reader. But the book's real purpose will have been served if it acts as a stimulus and encourages a more active interest in recording the many facets of the English language as it is used in Australia, New Zealand, and the Southwest Pacific.

W. S. RAMSON

Australian National University
1969

NOTES ON CONTRIBUTORS

A. G. MITCHELL, now Vice-Chancellor of Macquarie University, formerly Professor of English, University of Sydney, pioneered the academic study of Australian pronunciation with his *The Pronunciation of English in Australia* (1946, rev. ed. A. Delbridge 1965) and, with A. Delbridge, *The Speech of Australian Adolescents* (1965).

A. DELBRIDGE, who collaborated with Professor Mitchell in organising a speech survey of adolescents, and in writing the resulting book, is a Professor in the School of English Studies and Director of the Speech and Language Research Centre, Macquarie University.

W. S. RAMSON is a Senior Lecturer in English at the Australian National University. He is the author of *Australian English* (1966), and has also edited, in 1967, *The Emigrant Family*, by Alexander Harris (1849).

J. S. GUNN, Associate Professor of English and a member of the Australian Language Research Centre in the University of Sydney, is the author of the A.L.R.C. Occasional Papers on the vocabulary of shearing.

J. A. W. BENNETT, now Professor of Mediaeval and Renaissance English in the University of Cambridge, is a New Zealander, and took his first degree in that country.

G. W. TURNER is Reader in English at the University of Adelaide. He comes from New Zealand, and is the author of *The English Language in Australia and New Zealand* (1966).

DON LAYCOCK, at present a Senior Fellow in Linguistics at the Institute of Advanced Studies of the Australian National University, has done eighteen months' field work in the Sepik and Bougainville districts, studying Melanesian Pidgin and the Papuan languages of New Guinea.

MICHAEL G. CLYNE, a Senior Lecturer in German at Monash University, has worked extensively on the speech of migrants, especially German migrants. He is the author of *Transference and Triggering* (1967).

T. E. DUTTON is a Research Fellow in Linguistics, Institute of Advanced Studies, Australian National University.

E. H. FLINT is a Senior Lecturer in English at the University of Queensland and Director of the Queensland Speech Survey.

G. K. W. JOHNSTON, Professor of English at the Royal Military College, Duntroon, is editor of the Australian Writers and Their Work series, and has two books in press, *The Annals of Australian Literature* and a *Bibliography of Australian Literature*.

SUSAN KALDOR is a Lecturer in Anthropological Linguistics in the Department of Anthropology at the University of Western Australia.

DAVID BLAIR is a Research Assistant in the School of English Studies at Macquarie University.

CONTENTS

	Preface	v
	Notes on Contributors	ix
	Acknowledgments	xii
1	The Australian Accent *A. G. Mitchell*	1
2	The Recent Study of Spoken Australian English *A. Delbridge*	15
3	Nineteenth-Century Australian English *W. S. Ramson*	32
4	Twentieth-Century Australian Idiom *J. S. Gunn*	49
5	English as it is Spoken in New Zealand *J. A. W. Bennett*	69
6	New Zealand English Today *G. W. Turner*	84
7	Pidgin English in New Guinea *Don Laycock*	102
8	Migrant English in Australia *Michael G. Clyne*	123
9	Informal English in the Torres Straits *T. E. Dutton*	137
10	A Comparison of Spoken and Written English: Towards an Integrated Method of Linguistic Description *E. H. Flint*	161
11	The Language of Australian Literature *G. K. W. Johnston*	188
12	Asian Students and Australian English *Susan Kaldor*	203
	A Bibliography of Australian English *David Blair*	223
	Index to Bibliography	238
	Index	241

ACKNOWLEDGMENTS

Acknowledgment is made to the following: to the Australian Academy of the Humanities and to Sydney University Press for permission to reprint A. G. Mitchell's 1960 address to the Australian Humanities Research Council; to *American Speech* for permission to reprint J. A. W. Bennett's article from Vol. XVIII (1943) of that journal; to *Australian Literary Studies* for permission to use G. K. W. Johnston's revision of an article published in Vol. 3 (1967) of that journal; to Angus and Robertson Ltd for permission to quote from A. D. Hope's *Collected Poems*, James McAuley's *Selected Poems*, Kenneth Slessor's *Poems*, Judith Wright's *Selected Poems*, and Cecil Mann's *Henry Lawson, Best Stories*; to Faber and Faber Ltd, and Harcourt Brace and World Inc., for permission to quote from T. S. Eliot's *Four Quartets*, 'Little Gidding'; and to the Lothian Publishing Co. Ltd for permission to quote from a poem originally published in Bernard O'Dowd's *The Bush*.

I would like also to thank the editorial staff of the Australian National University Press for their help, the cartographers of the Geography Department of the Australian National University for drawing the map of the Torres Straits Islands, and Joyce Arey and Jane Vaughan of the English Department of the Australian National University for their help in preparing the chapter bibliographies.

W.S.R.

A. G. MITCHELL

THE AUSTRALIAN ACCENT

The history of opinion on this subject deserves attention in that, in all the assertions and speculations that have been put forward, we may discern certain attitudes or bases of judgment.

There has been the bringing of Australian pronunciation, to its detriment, into comparison with one sort of English pronunciation, which was raised to the position of a general standard. Any respect in which Australian pronunciation differed from the educated pronunciation of Southern England was presented not as mere difference but as deterioration or corruption. This was natural at a time when the scientific study of speech was still only beginning, and when almost everything in print took educated Southern English pronunciation as the natural basis of description, so that this sort of pronunciation was taken to be 'English'. This kind of speech had a somewhat adventitious prestige added to it, because it alone was described and codified in grammars and dictionaries in general currency in this country. Although Noah Webster in 1789 had asserted the claim of American English to separate status, it was only thirty years ago that strenuous objections were made when American scholars tentatively and mildly suggested that a distinction might be made between American English and English English. Yet today no form of English has had closer attention from an advanced linguistic scholarship than the American. Though we may readily understand why the shift in point of view was a long time coming, we have lagged a little too far behind the Americans in seeing the common sense of the view that Australian English, in all its characteristics, deserves the same equality with English English as has been accorded to American English.

Another common judgment has been based on traditional beliefs and practices associated with the arts of public speaking and acting. I am not necessarily condemning these beliefs and practices. Their purpose is to make possible the use of the voice to carry well in a large auditorium without strain. They aim at a relaxed control of the vocal apparatus, control of breathing, and reinforcement of the resonance of the voice. They seek to rationalise in a seeming scientific way procedures that have been found by experience to work. Unfortunately, this body of precept has become associated with teachings about purity of vowels, roundness of tone, and other vague notions, and in general has led to an over-careful manner of speech that is quite artificial. Discussion about Australian speech has been confused by a succession of elocutionary examiners who have compared the speech of Australians with an abstract ideal of sonority and controlled phonation. Those who have taken their criticisms seriously have not reflected that almost any form of English pronunciation would fare the same in this sort of comparison. The impression left by many of the visiting and native elocutionary experts is that the Australian pronunciation represents a worse declension from standards of good English than any other kind of English. This is nonsense.

As a result of such comparison, constantly made and too little questioned, we have come to accept some judgments about sound in Australian speech that are quite irrational. When an Australian says H-A-Y we say it contains an unpleasant sound. When someone else says H-I-G-H we say this contains a pure and an agreeable sound. But it is the same sound in both cases. We regard *do* and *see*, as most Australians say them, as pronounced with distorted vowels. Yet these sounds occur in Scottish pronunciation, *down* and *fly*, and pretty certainly existed in Shakespeare's pronunciation. The sound in the Australian pronunciation of *see* is little different from the pronunciation of the French *oeil*—and I do not know of anyone who has described this sound as in itself unmusical or distorted. Judgments like this arise from comparisons of dubious validity, and then have claimed for them, quite wrongly, a musical or aesthetic basis.

In a great deal of this discussion there has been much generalising from insufficient observation and much taking of the abnormal for the typical. Most of the comments of visiting elocutionists have been offhand and superficial, and based on the most hasty and scrappy observation. It is obviously very easy to let pass the great majority that has no very striking characteristics, which indeed, because of its very ordinariness does not register, and to take as evidence those characteristics that register because they are unusual. There has gradually developed from the accumulation of impressions derived in this way a composite image of the Australian speaking that is truly disturbing. He is supposed to speak Cockney, to speak through his nose, to speak through an immobile slit in his face, not making use of his lips, to speak in a dull monotone, to have no rhythm in his speech, flattening vowels and ignoring most consonants. I doubt whether I have heard an Australian to whose speech all these specifications would apply. He is a mere figment.

Yet people go on saying that these are characteristics of Australian speech generally, and these statements have attained the status of truths established merely by repetition. Let us take just one—the statement

The Australian Accent

about nasality. It is constantly being asserted that Australian speech is nasal. Yet a survey shows that the percentage of Australian speakers with noticeable nasality in their speech is about three or four. No figure has been arrived at for British or American English, but I should be very surprised indeed if it were less than three or four per cent. The repeated statement that Australian speech is nasal by comparison with other forms of English is unsupported, meaningless, and almost certainly wrong. Yet people go on repeating it as if it were a truth hardly to be doubted.

I might just refer to one or two of these judgments, quite without foundation, that have now become part of a pseudo-scholarly folklore about Australian speech. They occur in widely read books of some influence, and keep turning up in broadcasts and articles in periodicals and newspapers. Professor Pear in his recent book, *Personality Appearance and Speech*, quotes a B.B.C. broadcast, containing gems like this: 'I have heard an uneducated Australian put about half a dozen vowels into the one word "bread": like this: "brairyard".' In the *Manchester Guardian Weekly* of 12 February 1959, Mr Edwin S. Morrisby, moved apparently by the thought that there are sixty thousand permanent Australian residents in England and thirty thousand transients, wrote an article in which all the old chestnuts were trotted out.

> The accent, according to most people, is flat, thin, ugly and unpleasant. The typical Australian [notice 'typical'] speaks with his lips spread firmly against his teeth, his jaw moving little, and his soft palate lowered. He can, and often does, carry on a conversation without appearing to open his mouth at all. This is, of course, the reason for the distinctive Australian accent. The tongue has much less room to move in, so the vowels are pushed close together and the speech moves forward.

There are four columns of it. Eric Partridge in *British and American English Since 1900* says: 'the natural conditions, the physiography of Australia have . . . tended to produce a certain type of speech organs, to which the dulcet sounds of Southern English are not merely alien but impossible'.[1]

The origin and course of some of these beliefs can be followed. This belief that the physiography of the country has produced organs of speech that in turn necessarily produce the Australian accent seems to have begun in scattered observations (or illusions) that Australians speak without moving their lips, nasally, and without moving their jaws. Some causes or consequences of these assumptions were speculated about from time to time, as, for example, that nasality must mean lazy use of the soft palate or that alleged failure to open the jaw enough must interfere with the resonance or projection of vowels. These speculations were gathered together in a sort of system by S. J. Baker in his book, *The Australian*

[1] *British and American English*, p. 85.

Language, and given an appearance of being scientifically secure. Baker accounts for the characteristics of Australian speech by 'an ingrained tendency to speak through lips spread firmly against the teeth, to resist jaw movements, to lower the soft palate habitually'. From this strange consequences follow, as, for example, a restriction of the space within which the tongue can move, so that 'the vowels are brought more closely together' and 'are more liable to influence one another'.[2] The influence of Mr Baker's speculations can be traced widely in books in which Australian speech is referred to and in various periodical articles. The truth is that there is hardly a bit of evidence to support them. It is unlikely in the extreme that different habits in the use of the vocal structures would be produced by extra-linguistic causes and then produce certain variations in the sounds made. It is more likely that memory of sounds would cause variation in the vocal movements. There exists no evidence at all for saying that the Australian's use of the soft palate differs from the Englishman's use of it. If it is said that we can make deductions about the use of the soft palate from the sounds that the Australian makes, then there is no evidence to justify the statement that Australian speech generally is nasal, or that it is more nasal than other kinds of English.

In trying to see the pattern of Australian speech and its likeness to and difference from other kinds of English speech, we must not start with a non-existent datum called 'the English language' and then see any particular sort of English speech as a declension from or a distortion of this. We must start at the opposite end of particularity and see what larger groupings or layers may appear when we make a properly disciplined observation of sample groups taken from a language community that shows a complicated variety in speech habits. We must begin with observation of what is actually working and functioning.

When we look for form and pattern in this complex variety we must decide what characteristics of pronunciation we are going to take as showing, by their variations, groupings of speakers from which we may deduce a consistent pattern of speech variation. In other words, we must be clear what we understand by an accent. In general we look for those characteristics which might be expected to show stability in large groupings and variation as between groupings, independently of the many habits or qualities of speech peculiar to individuals. There is strictly no identity in speech behaviour because no two human organisms are identical. We look for degrees of resemblance. We begin by eliminating these individual variations. We eliminate voice quality, for example, because in the linguistic system the vowel [a], say, in *heart*, we regard as the same vowel whether the voice that utters it is a low-pitched male or a high-pitched female, whether harsh, or dulcet, or breathy, strong, or weak. We cut off these

[2] *Australian Language*, pp. 342, 341.

The Australian Accent

characteristics as varying independently, and for the greater part unsystematically, in relation to the constant elements of the phonological system. If we say that some Australians say [av] and others say [æv], then that variation is observable independently of individual peculiarities of voice. Vocal differences are physiological or psychological and not linguistic variations.

Then we cut off what have been labelled the *emphatica*—variations in pitch, in loudness, in rhythm, that are not parts of the general phonological system but vary unsystematically from one individual to another. One may say the sentence, 'I'm very pleased indeed', excitedly, loudly, or on a high general pitch, and another may say it slowly, placidly, softly, and on a medium pitch, and we regard it as the same sentence said in the same accent. Or the same person may say it now in one way and now in another, but we take it to be said in the same accent or style. Or these *emphatica*, these devices for emphasis, may be the same in two utterances of the same sentence and we may describe the styles of speech or accents as different.

There is good reason, too, for eliminating those elisions, assimilations, and weakening of consonants that are commonly regarded as signs of careless or illiterate speech. These cover pronunciations like:

jæftə juz ə difrnt beit	you have to use a different bait
srait	that's right
ət tʌfnz jʌp	it toughens you up
las sæddi	last Saturday
hiz ə rait	he's all right
satnun	this afternoon

All of these may be accounted for by pretty regular phonetic tendencies, and there is good reason for believing that these tendencies operate generally wherever English is spoken. There is, at present, no evidence at all to support any assertion that these tendencies are commoner in Australian speech than in any other form of English. We have recorded and we shall try to estimate their extent in the survey,[3] and such an estimate has its educational interest. But until a similar estimate is made for English or American English there is no justification at all for saying that these elided or assimilated pronunciations are particularly characteristic of Australian pronunciation.

By repeated observation we arrive at a set of diagnostic features. We eliminate from our consideration these characteristics, which we think of as in free variation, unrelated to the variations in the general phonological

[3] The survey is reported on fully in Mitchell and Delbridge, *The Speech of Australian Adolescents.*

system. We then look for regular variations, covering large groups in the speech community, in the elements of this system. We try to discover what the pattern of variations is and look for the simplest classification of types of speech that will account for the evidence.

In any language community the ways in which styles of speaking are the same are much more numerous than the ways in which they differ. The extent to which the speech of a Stepney docker and of an old Etonian differ is much less than the extent to which they are the same. The area of variability which is the cause of so much argument is actually very small compared to all that is involved in the phonological system of the language.

It has not been possible until recently to make a systematic sampling of speech that would cover the whole of Australia. It is such a vast country that the cost of covering the field by travel would be prohibitive. But, with the development of the tape-recorder, it has become possible to gather recorded data through the post, and to plan inquiries that are statistically secure. My colleague, Arthur Delbridge, and I have analysed most of the material contained in recordings made by ten thousand pupils in four hundred high schools from all parts of Australia. Although it is premature as yet to speak of conclusions, some general statements would be secure enough.

So far our observation confirms earlier conclusions that we may distinguish at least two, and probably three, styles of speech in Australia, and that there is no need to distinguish more than three. My feeling, based on insufficient bulk of observation, not well enough controlled and disciplined (because this was impossible), has been that we could distinguish three styles, which I have called an Educated Australian, a Broad Australian, and an extreme form of Broad Australian pronunciation. The evidence of our survey indicates that such a classification is sound. The figures, however, have strengthened a doubt I have long had about the names that have been given to these three styles. The proportion of those who speak what has been called Broad Australian is so great that the term is inappropriate, and I am proposing the name 'General Australian' for it. The proportion of speakers, in this sampling, who use this type of speech seems to be over ninety per cent. What has been called the extreme form of Broad Australian would appropriately be called Broad Australian. What to call the third style I am not sure. I have been calling it Educated Australian because it is the Australian style that approximates to the English style commonly referred to as Educated Southern English. But to call it Educated Australian is to suggest a sort of relationship between education and style of speaking which we know not to hold. For many speakers the label 'Modified Australian' would be appropriate, but this term would suggest that this style of speech is not indigenous, and I do not think this is right. 'Cultivated Australian' might be a reasonably satisfactory descriptive label.

It is clear enough, then, that if we distinguish three styles of speech, shading into one another, we shall be able to account adequately for the pattern of speech variation in Australia. The overwhelming proportion of speakers speak General Australian—the proportions speaking Cultivated Australian and Broad Australian are small by comparison.

By working over the data we may arrive at a fuller and a more refined list of the phonological elements which, in related variation, show up the differences between these styles of speech. As I have mentioned before, the resemblances between any two sorts of English pronunciation are much more numerous than the differences, and this is particularly true of styles of speech in the same language community. So much is the same that differences may exist without interfering with communication. If we compare General Australian with Cultivated Australian we shall not find systematic differences in vowels or consonants, but we shall find differences in six diphthongs, those that occur in the words *beat, boot, say, so, high, how*. If we ask Australians to say the sentence, 'Let's pick a good spot near the water and pass the morning sitting in the sun', differences will not appear as between General Australian and Cultivated Australian. But if we ask them to say the sentence, 'The plane flew down low over the runway, then increased speed and circled the aerodrome a second time', differences will show up very clearly. It is clear that these six sounds are the chief indexes of variation. There may be others, and we are constantly watching for them. We have wondered, for example, whether systematic variations in rhythm might appear, but so far have not found any. We have been collecting the evidence about the slow rhythm of the drawl, because it has so constantly been said that the drawl is characteristic of Australian speech that we wanted to know what, at any rate, the gross figures would be. So far they show, in this sampling, that the drawl is uncommon in Australian speech.

One of the remarkable characteristics of Australian speech is its comparative uniformity. In the material examined there is just a suggestion that there may be one or two habits characteristic of some people in South Australia, and we have yet to see how these may be sifted out. Apart from that, there is no suggestion anywhere of any regional variation. Everywhere we find the three recognisable types of speech, varying only in their proportions. Linguistically we have in Australia a continuous population. There are, as far as evidence so far assembled indicates, no clearly defined regional differences. Whether there may be pockets of distinctive usage must remain an open question until more detailed evidence is available.

People keep on saying that they can distinguish, for example, a South

Australian from a Queenslander by his speech. When I ask them what their evidence is they often say that a South Australian has a particular way of saying 'school' and the Queenslander uses the word 'port' where others would say 'case'. We know that there are lexical differences in usage between various parts of Australia, and it may well be that some individual words have different pronunciations in some fairly well-defined areas. But I am not concerned here with lexical differences or with scattered variations in pronunciations of individual words. I am concerned with systematic, pervasive, consistent phonological variations.

Others, thinking of the great variety of speech in England, have felt that in such a large area as Australia there must be regional differences, and that it must be just a matter of finding them. But there is no necessary reason why the English pattern should be repeated in Australia, and, as I hope to show, strong reason why it should not be.

This brings us to the reasons why we have in Australia ways of speaking that may be distinguished from ways of speaking in England and America, and why we have a pattern of speech variation different from those discernible in England or America.

In the speculation about this problem the tendency has been to ask *why* before inquiring *what* or *how*, and to put forward answers to the question *why* before knowing the evidence. We need not complain too much about this. It is generally necessary, I suppose, for man to live by tentative answers to the question *why* while he still labours to find out *what* and *how*.

Theories put forward to answer the question why Australians have distinctive ways of speaking English—theories based on assumptions about things like climate, physiology, and national psychology—are hardly worth spending time on. The question is one of origins and history. We have a great deal of evidence yet to gather and assess, both synchronic, of the patterns of speech variation, and historical, of the social history of Australia. We shall come to the answer to our question (as near as is possible) by inquiring how what we can conclude about the one may be lined up with what we can find out about the other. Some conclusions are fairly secure now, and may provide a broad framework for filling in more precise details.

The principle from which we begin is that speech is a form of human behaviour and something that exists and functions within the nervous system of each speaker. Allowing for individual physical and psychological differences, the extent to which this complex of habits will correspond in any two people will depend on the extent to which they use the language in the same or comparable social groups. Every individual is constantly monitoring his own speech, and adjusting it to the speech of people whom he constantly speaks to and listens to. If we think of the group of people to whom a given person would regularly speak as a sort of area, not every part of equal density, and its boundaries blurred and shifting, and every area for every individual overlapping every other individual area, either actually or by extension through intermediaries, we shall have a model of the constantly interacting monitoring of speech that goes on in a definable speech community, and a model of the stability that is maintained in a speech community. Isolation of communities or stable social divisions will break or attenuate the continuous overlapping. Speech characteristics and the pattern of speech variation are, therefore, a reflection of social history.

To explain how Australian speech developed its distinctive features we need to know the parts of England that the earliest convicts and settlers came from and in what proportion, and then we need to know as much as we can about the social history of Australia.

I do not propose to go into the complexities that we face in interpreting evidence under these two heads, but some general statements may be ventured. Australian speech is in its origins a town speech. The overwhelming number of convicts and early settlers (one estimate is four or five to one) were from the towns. This explains, I think, the loss of many words describing features of the countryside that Sir Keith Hancock has lamented in his book, *Australia*.[4] Town-dwellers would not use words like *brook*, *glade*, *glen*, *dale*. I should imagine that this sort of lexical reduction would be very common in the history of the language in Australia. Many of the vocabularies associated with sheep husbandry and agriculture would have been reduced because the settlers from the towns, even if they heard them from shepherds or farmhands, would not remember all the rich variety of traditional technical words and would reduce them to a basic list of general terms. Generalisation and reduction must have been major tendencies in the history of the language in Australia because the language was in its origins a town speech.

Again, it was in its origins a working-class speech, the language of people who were poor and for the most part unskilled. It had a large component of southeastern English city speech and of Irish. It included ways of speech characteristic of many parts of England, Scotland, and Wales, but every one of these pretty certainly small in comparison with the southeast English and Irish component. The proportion of Irish in the years before 1850 seems to have been higher than in the years after 1850.

All these forms of speech were brought together in Australia in constant interaction, and this had never happened in England. Speech developed in Australia in a society in which there has been constant movement from place to place and social mobility from the beginning. In the society of the beginning years convicts were constantly being moved from place to place.

[4] *Australia*, p. 242.

The area that a man might cover as prisoner, assigned servant, and emancipist was very large. This movement covered the whole of New South Wales, Victoria, and Moreton Bay while these constituted a single administrative area. The free settlers moved from place to place. Judith Wright in *The Generations of Men* describes how her forbears established themselves in New England and then moved on to Queensland to develop another property. It has commonly happened in Australian history that a centre has grown quite rapidly to a large population of ten thousand or more, drawn from many parts of the country, and then has quite quickly declined and dispersed. There have been large population movements following land development, gold discovery, depression, and the petering out of goldfields. After the failure of the goldfields, their mixed, temporary, and unsettled population became a very large mobile work force in constant and extensive movement.

These internal population movements, added to mobility in the social structure itself, have provided the conditions in which speech has developed in Australia. Generalisation must have been a ruling tendency. The psychology of the process is fairly clear. The man who speaks an English dialect that is not often heard does not want to invite attention to himself and so tends to modify his speech, either in a negative way, by changing the characteristics of his speech that are most individual, or in a more positive way, by adapting his habits to those of the majority. Even if those who first came continued with their minority speech little changed during their lifetime, the children's speech would conform to that of the majority. This has clearly been true also of the non-British communities. Absorption, dispersal, interaction, generalisation, and levelling must have been the ruling tendencies. Conditions have never been favourable to the persistence or the origination of minority forms of speech.

Just when a recognisable, distinct Australian speech emerged we can only speculate. One would imagine that a significant date would be when the number of the colonial-born became important, and this was not until the 1830s. Owing to the trebling of the population in the decade following the gold rushes, it was not until the 1860s that those born in the colony equalled the immigrants. But we might guess that the main features of Australian speech were established by the 1830s.

The demographic background to the development of speech in Australia has been similar to that of the great western movement of population in America, in which settlers from all the then established colonies, as well as fresh immigrants, were brought together in a mobile society made up, linguistically, of various interacting groups. It is these demographic conditions that have produced modern General American speech, as they produced General Australian. There was never an Australian settlement anything like that earlier phase of American settlement in which different styles of speech established themselves in the colonies along the Atlantic coast. Australia does not show the regional variation of speech that we find in the United States.

It is not difficult, therefore, to understand why Australian speech should have this remarkable uniformity or why Australia, in spite of its size, its early fragmentary colonisation, and the concentration of its population along discontinuous strips of the coastal fringe, should be linguistically a continuous population.

I think we might sometimes dwell a little on the advantages of this uniformity. Much as we may enjoy the rich variety of language styles in England, much as we may delight in the literary uses to which they may be put, there are social advantages in having gradations in a general pattern rather than sharp regional and social differences. Educationally there are obvious advantages. The Australian teacher does not have to deal with the great variety of language types in teaching the literary language. He works in a very much simpler pattern. The advantage to the pupil is even greater. For the Australian pupil there are not the differences in sound, vocabulary, and morphology that exist for so many pupils in Great Britain, between the language that they have learnt by imitation from parents and associates and the literary language they learn to read and write at school.

Why this should be so is an interesting speculation. It may be in part because a large proportion of the early settlers and convicts came from London and its environs, the area whose language was the historical basis of the literary language. It must be in large part a result of the generalising and interactionary processes in the development of the language in Australia.

Some writers have affected to find in Australian speech habits a dull sameness, a flat colourlessness, corresponding to the subdued monotony of its landscape. This and other such impressionistic comparisons have a neat originality that sometimes persuades people that they may embody intuitive glimpses of the truth. But they have small relation to the truth about this matter, which it is the task of scholarship, through the collection and assessment of evidence of great complexity, patiently to uncover.

So far we have confined our attention to the pattern of speech variations within Australia, and have not adverted to the position of Australian speech in the English-speaking world. Here we move in two realms, the scientific and the impressionistic.

Let us look at the scientific first. As we have said before, in searching for a set of systematic variations we leave out of account individual and, we believe, unsystematic variations in such things as voice quality and psychological qualities reflected in speech. If we compare Cultivated Australian speech with, say, Educated Southern English or Received Pronunciation as it is now called, we shall find many differences on the phonetic level, but few, perhaps no differences on the phonemic level. If we think of the phonological structure of a language as an interconnecting network of contrastive patterns, we shall conclude that no differences appear between Educated Southern English and Cultivated Australian. The phonemic contrasts that separate words like *hurl, heard, hers* from *hill, hid,* and *his* are exactly the same in both forms of pronunciation. Yet there is a clear difference between the more open [ɜ] of English pronunciation and the closer [ɜ] of the Australian. The phonemic contrast that separates *hut, cut, cud, luck,* from *heart, cart, card, lark* is the same for both forms of pronunciation. But in Southern English pronunciation [ʌ] and [a] have retracted resonances and in Australian pronunciation they have front resonances. In Australian pronunciation, again, there is less acoustic difference between [ʌ] and [a] than between [ʌ] and [a] in English pronunciation. The sets of phonemic contrasts in the two forms of English speech are the same, but the exact resonances that show these phonemic contrasts are different. The exact tone or resonance environment in which this contrast is shown is retracted in Educated Southern English but front in Australian. There is a phonetic but not a phonemic difference. When speakers of English make comments on the differences between their own and other sorts of English (whether amused, derisive, or merely puzzled), it is generally the phonetic difference that they have in mind.

At the phonemic level of abstraction hardly any differences would appear between any form of Australian pronunciation and Educated Southern English. One interesting exception is in the nature of the contrasts in *fled—flared*; *lid—leered*. In Educated Southern English and in most sorts of Australian speech the contrast is between a short vowel and a centering diphthong. In some sorts of Australian speech the contrast is simply one of length, the resonance remaining unchanged and only the length changing: *fled—flared*, like the *mettre—maître* contrast in French, and rather uncommon in English.

Because the pattern of interconnecting contrasts, with the smallest of possible exceptions, is the same in the two forms of speech, we say that they are the same language with variations. But it is the actual resonances of the sounds that cumulatively impress themselves upon the listener in the different parts of the English-speaking world. We may say that phonemically the contrast that the Englishman makes when he says *far, fur,* and *fare* is exactly the same as the Australian makes when he says *far, fur,* and *fare*. Because the phonemic contrasts are the same, speakers of different sorts of English can afford the sport of arguing about the differences in resonance of the items that make the same phonemic contrasts.

When we come to impressionistic comparisons of Australian with other sorts of English speech it is a little difficult to keep our bearings. So much depends on preconception and familiarity. In both respects Australian speech is heavily at a disadvantage. We have for a long time been familiar with many styles of English speech and have sorted them out in common acceptance as well-bred and cultured, or outlandish and rustic, as musical and lilting. It was not, however, until 1929 that modern technology brought us the talking film and began to make us familiar with American speech. American books and magazines had been read before then, but it was not till 1930 that in England and Australia people generally could actually hear American speech. The first effects were so shattering that it was only in 1929 that a member of the Federal Parliament said that government action might be desirable to control the baneful influence of the American accent on Australian schoolchildren.

Through films, radio, recordings, and television, however, we have become so familiar with American ways of speaking that we accept them without surprise. But Australian speech is not much known abroad, and some forms of it exported in locally produced films and radio dramas would lend colour to the worst preconceived anxieties about it. For this reason the performance of *Summer of the Seventeenth Doll* in London and New York was an interesting happening. Australian English was heard in London and New York as a living dramatic medium in a play good enough to be taken seriously by serious critics. The interesting thing was that the language was accepted in London. The English critics are a little difficult to reconcile, the *Evening Standard* saying that the accent and the slang melt into one great big yawn of incomprehensibility, the *Observer* saying that Lawler, the star, had a barely perceptible accent of any kind. On the whole the London critics accepted the accent as refreshing, salty, remarkably like Cockney. The New York critics, on the other hand, seem undoubtedly to have killed the play because of their difficulties with the language. They had trouble with the sounds. One said that by the time he realised that *Bonnie* was not a girl but a man called Barney, the plot had moved on so that he could not catch up. Some said they found the accent so exotic as to be virtually unintelligible. Some began uncomfortably to feel that the play was not saying to them the same things that it said to Australians. The contrast in attitude is most interesting. The English accepted the accent and idiom of *The Doll* and felt that they were able to catch the nuances of the play, though they would have caught some wrong impressions by ranging the accent with Cockney. But in America the unfamiliarity of accent and idiom was apparently an insurmountable barrier. One wonders whether the Americans will ever become as familiar with them as we in the last thirty years have become with the American.

We have, then, the attitude of the scholar seeking patterns of order in a complex form of human behaviour manifesting itself in the native language of people in the English-speaking countries, and adopting these days a relativistic approach—that is, accepting as right and good in its own local, social setting and for its own purposes, every form of English speech that is actually functioning and working. Alongside this we have general human attitudes, in the individual based on the natural inclination to be superior or amused (now and again admiring) at speech habits that differ from one's own, and, when held in the mass, based on a linguistic folklore. Such human attitudes are mostly irrational and contradictory. Some Australians admire American speech and imitate it: others dislike it. Some admire and imitate English Received Pronunciation: others dislike forms of speech that they can identify as English. They find disagreeable the speech that they describe as 'very English'. Differences in speech may indicate differences of class, place, or social status in one country and not in another, or may indicate them in different ways or to different extents in different English-speaking countries. Within any one English-speaking community we get to know how far we can go in guessing a man's background from his speech, but when we apply judgments tutored in one context to speakers from other countries we may make serious errors.

This tangle of attitudes, much as we discount them in the pursuit of a scientific analysis, is very much a reality, and we cannot quite ignore them.

Gradually motion pictures, radio, television, and sales of records are spreading some awareness of the types of English speech that may be heard in the various English-speaking countries. With familiarity some of the more extravagant attitudes are being qualified. But Australian speech is still in a much less favourable position than English or American.

REFERENCES CITED

Baker, S. J., *The Australian Language*, Sydney, 1945.
Hancock, W. K., *Australia*, 1930, Aust. ed., Sydney, 1945.
Lawler, R., *Summer of the Seventeenth Doll*, Sydney, 1957.
Mitchell, A. G., and Delbridge, Arthur, *The Speech of Australian Adolescents: A Survey*, Sydney, 1965.
Partridge, E., and Clark, J. W. (eds.), *British and American English Since 1900*, London, 1951.
Pear, T. H., *Personality, Appearance and Speech*, London, 1957.
Wright, Judith, *The Generations of Men*, Melbourne, 1959.

THE RECENT STUDY OF SPOKEN AUSTRALIAN ENGLISH

Two traditions are discernible in the recent study of spoken Australian English, both of them well established in the practice of linguistic scholars the world over. One of them involves the scholar in the systematic investigation of questions which have a popular appeal and an obvious relevance to communication in society; questions of the sort that ordinary people ask (and perhaps more often rather dogmatically answer); questions, for example, about the status and acceptability of the local product, about its history, its efficiency, its power to communicate the fundamental right-mindedness of the people who speak it, about its regional variations, about the impression it makes on strangers. The other tradition pursues the academic business of abstracting from the stream of spoken utterance whatever is linguistically relevant, and deriving from this relevant material a statement of the systematic use of sound elements in the language.

These two traditions overlap at many points, especially since the notion of 'linguistic relevance' requires some test that will expose the limits of relevance by patently going beyond them. Increasing interest in the prosodies and in paralinguistics is making it harder, not easier, to expose the limits of linguistic relevance. The border areas often prove the most interesting to work in, and work there is stimulated by the general interest it excites.

The features of paralanguage are generally excluded from language itself by the current definitions of the science of linguistics. For they are characteristically gradient features, occupying varying stretches of a cline. Linguists, with some exceptions, have preferred not to concern themselves with such features. 'In general . . . if we find continuous-scale contrasts in the vicinity of what we are sure is language, we exclude them from language.'[1] If not actually excluded from language, as defined, they may be somewhat grudgingly admitted as things to be looked at when there is leisure, later on. Because they arise from, and perhaps communicate information about, the individuality of the speaker and the state of his emotions, they are taken to be either devoid of linguistic information, being

---

[1] Hockett, *A Manual of Phonology*, p. 17.

physiologically determined and automatic, or else (in so far as the features are not amenable to analysis in terms of discrete elements) as random and unregulated. They are therefore not of interest to the linguists who search only for discrete microlinguistic forms. But, of course, it is impossible to know that they are either automatic or unregulated without thorough testing. Even if they turn out to be not so well regulated as to permit of some sausage-machine or layer-cake analysis, it may be that they can be shown by their non-random distribution to have conventional value, in that they show a correlation with other aspects of the language in question and yet clearly belong to language, and not to some other concurrent mode of communication. In the words of Jassem, 'Whatever is conventionalized in the language of a speech community is for that very reason essential in that language'.[2] One is reminded of Firth's exclamation in 'Modes of Meaning'[3] that 'Surely it is part of the meaning of an American to sound like one'. The search for definite formal functional relationships 'around the edges of language' (to use Bolinger's phrase) might well show that the edges are not where they have been thought to be, or even that the notion of edges has to be supplanted by a new doctrine.

The existence of a speech convention, the linguistic status and communicative value of which can be confidently stated in terms of high generality, may be attested intuitively by any native speaker of the language. The contrastive elements emerge plainly from the continuum. But, throughout the whole range of convention in Australian English, there are some questions of phonological style, of hard-core prosody, of lexicon, and of dialectology, as these things are now organised, as well as questions in the virtually unstudied areas of articulatory setting and voice quality, in which the inquiring linguist is likely to meet with conflicting intuitions in his informants, even within the same universe of discourse. If there is real doubt about the features of a convention, doubt even about its existence, its place in an account of the structure of the language needs to be worked out from the actual performance of speakers, by experimental or statistical methods. If statistical, the size and the nature of the sample has to meet the strict demands of the relevant techniques; the collecting and processing of data may be arduous; and the results are more likely to be expressed in terms of norms and variances than of categories and units. In any case, variability between speakers and within the speech of the same speaker has to be assessed; and to be assessed, it must first be looked for and taken for what it is.

Along with an interest in experiment and systematic observation there is another aspect of performance in speech which is beginning to appear

---

[2] Jassem, *The Intonation of Conversational English*, pp. 27-8.
[3] *Essays and Studies*, Vol. 4, 1951, p. 120.

in Australian studies. This is the active role of perception. Recent theories of speech perception, as presented by Joos, Ladefoged, Lieberman, and others of the 'motor theory' school, and Chomsky, all incorporate the notion of perception as an active process:

> the dependence of perception on properties physically present in the signal is less than total . . . A person will normally not be aware of many properties manifest in the signal, and, at the same time, his interpretation may involve elements which have no direct physical correlates, since what is perceived depends not only on the physical constitution of the signal but also on the hearer's knowledge of the language as well as on a host of extragrammatical factors.[4]

Though the extant theories of speech perception offer different accounts of what factors mediate between the acoustic signal and the interpretation, it seems that the active role of perception forces linguists to take into account the performance of both speaker and hearer, especially in areas like prosody, in which one has reason to doubt that every native speaker has anything like the same tacit understanding of what the patterns and regularities of the system are.

In 1960 Professor Fry, writing about the place of experiment in linguistics, claimed that

> it is difficult to think of any major modification in a general linguistic theory that has been the outcome of renewed observation of human linguistic behaviour. The general tendency has been to begin operations with a modicum of phonetic observation, to construct a system of categories on the basis of such observations and thereafter to devise theories, to modify them, or to discard them because of inter-relations *within the theory* rather than because of relations between the theory and observations of behaviour.[5]

The present chapter is designed to show what interests have emerged, what observations have been made, and what theories have developed, with respect to the speaking of English in Australia, since Fry's rather gloomy words were written. The main areas of interest have been dialect features, phonology, origins and development, prosodic and paralinguistic features, and speech perception. These will be briefly surveyed, one by one.

DIALECT FEATURES

The early work of Professor A. G. Mitchell, as presented in the first edition of *The Pronunciation of English in Australia*, postulated a regionally homogeneous language in which there were two major types of pronunciation, called Educated Australian and Broad Australian. The Broad variety had an extreme form, which could be called Uneducated Australian.

---

[4] Chomsky and Halle, *The Sound Pattern of English*, p. 294.
[5] Fry, D. B., 'Linguistic Theory and Experimental Research', *Transactions of the Philological Society*, 1960, p. 15.

Another classification in terms of three varieties, corresponding to Mitchell's, appeared in an important article by G. R. Cochrane.[6] In this article, which used Australian vowels to demonstrate the usefulness of some procedures in structural dialectology, Cochrane emphasised that the three varieties 'are not by any means the only ones that can be observed', and reserved his judgment as to whether the three are really separate varieties. Judgment on their separateness rested partly on questions of phonemic structure, and partly on the social meanings of the diaphonic differences between the varieties. Since Cochrane's article appeared, the investigation of both of these aspects of Australian English has been advanced with some vigour.

The survey referred to in Professor Mitchell's paper, *The Australian Accent*, reprinted in this volume,[7] was designed to provide a larger sampling of Australian speech, from which there might emerge a suitable classification of dialects or varieties, based on the relation of speech forms to each other and to an array of socio-economic and educational factors. The results of this survey[8] emerged from the analysis of more than seven thousand recorded conversations between high school students (aged sixteen to eighteen years) and their teachers. The participating pupils were randomly chosen from 327 secondary schools of all types, state and private. Geographically, the survey covered the main population areas of Australia, in town and country. Information about the places of birth and schooling of the pupils, and the place of birth of the parents, gave some indication of the range of regional influences bearing on each child. For light on the relation of home background, and other social influences, to language type, the survey relied on information about the place and nature of schooling, and on the parents' status in the community, in so far as this could be estimated from the father's occupation.

The recorded conversations were assessed, auditorily, for the phonetic quality of vowel nuclei, the rate of speech, the use of assimilation and elision, the strength of consonant articulation, the range and variability of pitch, and nasality. Among these features, vowel quality was taken to be the basis of classification for what might turn out to be speech varieties or even dialects. Preliminary investigation had suggested strongly that the grouping of idiolects into phonetic classes could be achieved most directly by the observation of six particular vowel nuclei as diagnostic features. The six were the vowel nuclei used in the words *beat, boot, say, so, high, how*, though observation was not limited to differences in these alone. It was apparent that for any one nucleus many different phone types would occur, as one moved from speaker to speaker. The differences

---

[6] 'The Australian English Vowels as a Diasystem'.
[7] Pp. 5-7.
[8] Mitchell and Delbridge, *The Speech of Australian Adolescents*.

were not merely of 'personal quality', to use Ladefoged's term,[9] but of 'phonetic quality'. The phonetic differences could be arrayed in a spectrum, between extreme positions. After extensive listening, it was decided that the whole range for each of the key vowel nuclei could conveniently be divided into three groups. This is the basis of the classification which gave rise to the terms Cultivated Australian, General Australian, and Broad Australian. For the language corpus studied, the distribution of speakers was as follows:

        Broad Australian   34 per cent
        General Australian   55 per cent
        Cultivated Australian   11 per cent

These figures ought not to be allowed to obscure a basic difficulty of analysis which has been experienced by all who have worked in this field: the difficulty of reconciling categorical analysis of this sort with the magnitude of the difference between individuals, and the extent of variability within each person.

For this recording, some speakers used a mixed range of diaphones, drawn usually from adjoining categories. Even more of them used a phonetic quality for individual nuclei that was somewhere between the qualities thought to be characteristic of two adjoining categories. As a result, one had a genuine doubt as to whether a given speaker should be assigned, say, to the Broad or to the General category. The percentages given above reflect a decision, not entirely arbitrary, by which borderline instances were assigned to the extreme categories, rather than to the central one. This decision was supported by the observation that the borderline cases patterned significantly with the extreme categories in some of the other phonetic features investigated, particularly with the extent of the use of assimilation and elision, and of nasality.

The problem of variability within the person emerged even in those set-piece recordings: there was variability with context, as one might have expected, and variability arising from changing the mode of utterance—from conversation to reading from a script, for example. One guesses that there would also be variability in phonetic and phonological style from occasion to occasion, though it did not get an opportunity to appear in this investigation. Dr J. R. Bernard has reported, ruefully, that during his search for enough speakers of Broad Australian, suitable speakers, Broad when he first found them, became General by the time he could get them into the laboratory.[10]

A set of relationships was worked out between the phonetic data and the distribution of the speakers by sex, school, social background, and

[9] Ladefoged, *Three Areas of Experimental Phonetics*, p. 56.
[10] Some Measurements of Some Sounds of Australian English, p. 65.

region. As a result, it was possible to postulate for Australian English a single phonemic segmental structure, with a wide range of diaphonic variations that are socially meaningful throughout the continent. The diaphonic distinctiveness of Cultivated Australian is pretty well established, but for General and Broad, although speakers at the centre of each category are clearly separable in auditory judgment, there is a substantial borderline area which makes the investigator acutely aware of the arbitrariness of his decision. He is cutting a continuum, and finds that his sensitivity to difference is greatest at the point where he tries to make the cut.

Statistically, at least, one can say that the choice a person makes of a speech variety is affected by a complex set of factors, chief among which are the sex of the speaker, the type of school attended, his family background, and his residence either in the city or the country. Girls tend towards Cultivated and General forms, boys towards General and Broad. Cultivated speech correlates significantly with the higher occupations, independent schools, and city life. But there emerged no geographical or cultural boundaries for diaphones, and speakers of each of the main varieties could be found anywhere within the same city or town, the same school and even the same family. One feels some confidence in believing that what emerged from the inspection of this limited corpus would reappear in a still wider investigation, were it to be undertaken, though the category proportions would no doubt reflect the altered sample.

What regional features did appear were not purely regional. For example, an unusual range of diaphones of /oʊ/ turned up in South Australian speakers, in words like *no, though, Borneo*. But this proved to be a social feature, rather than a regional one, since it was found only among girls in independent schools. It is occasionally heard in other parts of Australia, but only among women and girls educated in independent schools.

The existence of 'pockets of distinctive usage',[11] so often alleged by casual observers, was neither demonstrated nor disproved by the survey just described. But some attention was given to them in the Queensland Speech Survey, described by E. H. Flint in 'The Question of Language, Dialect, Idiolect, and Style in Queensland English'. He refers to

> communities or areas of distinctive usage which have been found in the Cape York Peninsula and Gulf regions; in Aboriginal communities further south; less certainly in areas of original German and Italian settlement distributed throughout the State; and of course among migrants.[12]

There is still a need for detailed accounts of the language of mature speakers, especially speakers of minimal education, and especially in areas which might be suspected of being 'pockets of distinctive usage'. One of

[11] Mitchell, p. 7 above.
[12] P. 6.

the difficulties, as Flint points out, is that regional isolation does not really exist. Aborigines in settlements and missions 'are free to leave for work periods and return',[13] and their social isolation is not absolute. And Sharwood and Horton, reporting a regional study of phoneme frequencies, found that the informal spoken English of one of the oldest and largest areas of Italian settlement in Queensland, at Innisfail, showed scarcely any traces of Italian influence.

Australia's immigration policy over the last two decades has substantially increased the European element in the population, and there is developing a fertile field for linguistic investigation in the inter-relations of Australian English and the languages and dialects of the immigrants, and their children. Work in this field is described in Dr Clyne's article elsewhere in this volume.

The phonetic and, in some measure, phonemic reality of the three variety classification just described has been examined instrumentally and statistically by Dr J. R. Bernard in 'Some Measurements of Some Sounds of Australian English'.[14] Dr Bernard set out to provide a fuller specification of the vocalic nuclei of Australian English, using acoustic measurement, and to compare the outcome of his objective procedures with the subjective impressions on which the earlier classifications had been based. He recorded and made spectrographic analyses of the voices of 170 mature males. The speakers were classified impressionistically, in the Mitchell-Delbridge manner, and then their individual vowel sounds were typed acoustically from the sonagram measurements. Not the smallest value of this study is that it provides for the first time a body of detailed specifications of the formant frequencies of the voices of a large number of speakers, and an impressive account of the difficulties involved in getting them, including the severe phonetic inconstancy of so many of the speakers. In Bernard's view, his results vindicated the established concept of Australian English as a spectrum, the range of which is consistent with the interpretation of Australian English as 'one and only one dialect'.[15]

In the act of vindicating this notion Bernard added immensely to our detailed knowledge of the phonetics and phonology of Australian English, and threw new light on many assumptions and judgments. Among the nuclei themselves, he gave general confirmation to the spectrum descriptions already offered, throwing doubt principally on the spectral analysis of [u] in terms of a glide running back on to a true target ([əʊ]), with glides of increasing length from General to Broad. He suggested instead a range of central monophthongs varying chiefly in the degree of fronting (Broad [uˑ] General [u] Cultivated [uʼ]).

[13] P. 10.
[14] P. 10.
[15] P. 902.

PHONOLOGY

Most of the accounts that have been given of the pronunciation of English in Australia have attempted more or less seriously to relate the sounds of the language to a set of linguistic elements at the phonemic level, as this has been defined in one or another of the theories of modern linguistics. It is perhaps pertinent to notice here that the most extensive recent account of the sound pattern of English, one long-promised, and long-awaited by linguists, dismisses the phonemic level as something the existence of which has never been demonstrated. The authors refer to 'strong reasons to doubt its existence' and announce that they 'will make no further mention of "phonemic analysis" or "phonemes" in this study and will also avoid terms such as "morphophonemic" which imply the existence of a phonemic level'.[16] What effects this not altogether unexpected manifesto will have on the linguistic study of Australian English one would not like to guess, but it would be surprising if it had no effects.

Meanwhile, Australian studies have reflected and contributed to the theoretical debates on phonemic method that have occupied linguists of the world. Cochrane's article in *Word* tests the application to Australian English of two rival accounts of long vowel segments: one in which they are treated as unit phonemes, and another in which each long vowel is taken to be a sequence of two phonemes—a short vowel phoneme followed by one of three semi-vowels or glides. He finds good reasons to reject the two-phoneme in favour of the unit-phoneme analysis, and in doing so falls in with the practice, one would judge, of most Australian writers in this field. By contrast one finds the advantages of the binary system assumed by Alex I. Jones, who analysed what he called 'Sydney English' in terms of seven simple vowel nuclei and thirteen diphthongs. The simple vowel phonemes are established by the contrasts *pit/pet/pat/po*(tato)*/putt/put/pot*. The diphthongal phonemes in *be/bay/boy/buy* are front gliding, and those in *bared/bad/bird/bard/board/gone* are centre-gliding. It is interesting that Jones's article was intended to

> draw the attention of students of English dialects to the existence of a form for which no more than seven vowel phonemes need be assumed for a complete description in terms analogous to those of Trager and Smith's *Outline*.[17]

Trager himself, as editor, suggested a reworking of the analysis in which, among other alterations, he suggested, apparently on the strength of his listening to 'r-less' dialects in America and England, that Jones's nuclei in *leer, sure, fire, flour* should be written not with an /h/, as Jones had written them, but with an /r/, in the belief that the glide is an allophone of /r/. He symbolised the nuclei as /yr, ɪwr, ayr, æwr/ respectively, and

---

[16] Chomsky and Halle, *Sound Pattern of English*, p. 11.
[17] 'Sydney Australian—a Seven Vowel System', p. 33.

was apparently pleased to be able to show that 'the so-called Trager-Smith analysis is really an overall one into which all the varieties of English so far examined objectively fit without any real problems'.[18]

The problems of establishing and expressing the structural uniformity of the Australian dialect are great, and require that the scholar work at a level of abstractness from the material which the ordinary reader might find it hard to reach. Professor Hammarström, working at the difficulties of this same set of vowel nuclei, has suggested that in *peer, fair, poor*, the diphthongs might well be interpreted as realisations of a vowel plus /r/, so that the diphthong [ɪə] in *here* would realise /ɪr/. He suggested that the difficulty of relating phonemic structure to the phonetic reality could be met with the new terms, *diphthongeme, diphthong*; *monophthongeme, monophthong*.[19] Using this terminology, one could then say that the sequence of monophthongemes /ɪr/ (as in *here*) is realised as the diphthong [ɪə] when pronounced in one syllable and as a sequence of monophthongs when pronounced in two syllables (presumably as in *hero*, my example).

Whatever type of analysis is used, there is continued interest in the components of the list of distinctive vowel segments. The list had already been altered, with general agreement, in the light of Cochrane's evidence that only speakers of A1 (Mitchell's Cultivated) use /uː/ for words like *toured*, and that [ɔ] and [ɔə] are nowhere meaningfully opposed, with the result that the one phonemic symbol can be used, for example, to transcribe *four* and *fought*. The most recent change to be debated is the possibility that long [æ] should be added to the list of phonemes. The contributions made[20] have raised a number of interesting theoretical questions concerning phonological juncture, length measurement, dialect distribution, and dialect history. Jones found that the responses of schoolchildren, asked to indicate whether pairs of words (*pad, sad*; *Pam, jam*; *pad, bad*) rhymed perfectly with each other or not, revealed a non-random distribution in terms of region and sex. The differences were admitted to be 'high order statistical abstractions and probably not observable directly'.[21] 'Some speakers may not have contrasts between [æ] and [æː] but [æː] will still be phonologically distinctive so long as it is lexically determined, [that is] so long as its occurrence is not phonologically predictable.'[22]

---

[18] Ibid., p. 35.

[19] 'Some Remarks on Australian Diphthongs'.

[20] Bernard, 'An Extra Phoneme of Australian English'; Cochrane, 'loŋ [æ] in ostreiljən iŋgliʃ'; Burgess, 'Extra Phonemes in Australian English: A Further Contribution'; Jones, 'A Phonological-Lexical Study of the Distribution of the Sounds [æ] and [æː]'; Laycock, 'lɔŋ "ʃoht vawlz" in əstrəiljən iŋgliʃ'.

[21] 'Phonological-Lexical Study', p. 117.

[22] Jones, *An Outline Word Phonology*, p. 7.

Cochrane, for his part in the debate, explains the phonetic differences between *canna* and *canner*, not in terms of phonemic length in the nucleus, but as an effect of juncture, saying that the more obviously composite member of the pair may be distinguished by the use of juncture.²³ Mr Burgess is suspicious of the whole extra-phoneme enterprise, Dr Laycock takes /æ/ to be just one of four short vowels in Australian English which contrast with the same vowels lengthened, and Dr Bernard concludes that /æ:/ is a 'numerically minor, somewhat unstable, but clearly observable feature of our language. Informal conversation suggests that it exists also in British, Scottish, and, to a smaller extent perhaps, American English.'²⁴

ORIGINS AND DEVELOPMENT

The problem of the origins of the Australian accent has continued to interest scholars, and the 'mixing-bowl' theory, which suggests the rise of a new variety of English out of the amalgamation of dialects brought together in a new community, still stands behind most of the accounts offered. The evidence of historical records, whether direct or indirect, is so meagre as to be incapable of initiating any theory at all. Brother Hill's plan of working through early written records to find evidences of where, when, and how the accent appeared unfortunately brought to light only the unsystematic and often contradictory observations of lay observers.²⁵

Detailed origins for Australian vowel sounds are postulated by G. W. Turner on the principle that 'Australian developments continue the total process of English vowel change'.²⁶ He describes the relationship of Received Standard and Australian pronunciation

> not as parent and daughter languages but as two successive generalizations of English speech based in each case predominantly on the South East Midland variety, the second generalization including the first as its most important component.²⁷

But if the detailing of the actual historical processes strikes the reader as speculative, much the same must be said of explanations using a quite different approach. A. I. Jones offered one technique of reconstruction. He based it on Keyser's claim²⁸ (following Bloomfield and Sapir) that a

---

²³ 'loŋ [æ] in ostreiljən iŋgliʃ', p. 24.

²⁴ 'An Extra Phoneme of Australian English', p. 352.

²⁵ Hill, 'Prospects of the Study of Early Australian Pronunciation'; Early Australian Pronunciation—the Value of Manuscript Evidence.

²⁶ 'On the Origin of Australian Vowel Sounds', p. 37; *The English Language in Australia and New Zealand*, pp. 96-104.

²⁷ 'On the Origin of Australian Vowel Sounds', p. 36.

²⁸ Keyser, review of Kurath and McDavid, *The Pronunciation of English in the Atlantic States*, p. 303.

specific present ordering of a given set of rules may reflect their acquisition through time. Thus, in accounting for city/country distributions of [æ] and [æː], Jones[29] showed that this distribution could plausibly constitute a model of the dialect situation which presumably gave rise to it. But 'in the absence of any systematic comparable information on British dialects this must remain purely speculative'.

The idea of finding in the present an explanation of what has led up to it in the past reappears more generally in the work of J. R. Bernard.[30] His review of the historical evidence leads him to postulate London English 'as the most significant single influence in the new town-based composite form', and to feel 'that the suggestion of a very early evolution of the Australian form is correct'. His explanation of the appearance of this same form in all Australian communities, and in a rather similar form even in New Zealand, is that the Australian accent was 'created' over and over again in 'germinal centres' of the colony, each time producing much the same mixture from the ingredients in the pudding bowl. The concept of mobility of the population seems to him inadequate to explain the appearance, perhaps even earlier than 1830, of the same new accent in a dispersed series of settlements. As to the development of the varieties of Australian English pronunciation, Bernard puts forward a theory suggested and well supported by an observed feature of current speech, namely the ability and the readiness of Australian speakers to 'upgrade' their speech, either on occasions, or for life, from one variety to another, the second being apparently more respect-worthy than the first.[31] He suggests that 'General Australian grows out of the aspirations of the socially successful speakers of Broad Australian'.[32] Cultivated Australian may well have its origins in the groups of upper-class colonists who from the beginning doubtless tried to retain upper-class speech patterns. But Cultivated, in his view, is not the linear descendant of Received Pronunciation, so much as 'the result of modifying Broad forms, past the General, towards what was *believed* to be RP'.[33] And even Cultivated can be 'upgraded' to Modified Australian. If Bernard's suggestions have any prophetic value, it may not be too fanciful to think of Australians going leapfrogging into a future of linguistic refinement in which the principle that 'the last shall be first' will put the cycle of our speech varieties into perpetual motion. Fortunately, good sense is likely to prevail.

[29] 'A Phonological-Lexical Study', p. 112.
[30] Some Measurements of Some Sounds of Australian English, p. 10.
[31] See also Gunn, 'The Influence of Background on the Speech of Teachers' College Students'; Mitchell and Delbridge, *The Speech of Australian Adolescents*, p. 65.
[32] 'Some Measurements of Some Sounds of Australian English', p. 17.
[33] Ibid., p. 648.

PROSODIC AND PARALINGUISTIC FEATURES

There has been no shortage of candid comment on the Australian accent, and the complaints most frequently recurring are directed at our distinctively ugly voice quality, our monotony of tone and stress, our drawl. These features can be placed somewhere along that 'scale of linguisticness' which has prosodic features at one end and paralinguistic features at the other.[34] If voice quality, for example, can be shown to have such a distribution that one can respond to an utterance by saying, 'That's an Australian', there would be some justification for putting voice quality somewhere on this scale of linguisticness. But the strange thing is that the features mentioned above as being frequently commented on have been practically ignored in the academic study of Australian English. Even intonation, the linguistic relevance of which is seldom doubted, has been the subject of no completed major study.[35] Perhaps one reason for this has been the absence of a persuasive theory of phonation and of the factors involved in changes of intensity and fundamental frequency of voice. The linguistic status of these features has only recently been sufficiently well established to divorce the study of them from the pragmatic pedagogical setting in which earlier studies were conducted in England and America. The material itself—pitch, loudness, length, pause, rhythm, tempo—is notoriously hard to examine auditorily. Personal quality is not easily distinguished from phonetic quality, and phonemic relationships are hard to establish. Instrumental analysis is not by itself linguistically discriminating, and tends to raise rather more questions than it settles. Even if some usable results are achieved, by any method, there is a great shortage of comparable information in at least some of these areas for other national forms of English.

Nevertheless, some conclusions have been reported. Some differences in intonation between Australian English and Received Pronunciation were noted in Professor Mitchell's *Pronunciation of English in Australia*, using an Armstrong and Ward type of notation. Postulating a narrower range of pitch for Australians, G. W. Turner also made some interesting comparisons between pitch patterns for Australian and English sentences.[36] The Mitchell-Delbridge survey referred to a 'distinguishable group of pupils whose conversation was marked, relative to the other students, by a narrow range of pitch and a minimum of pitch variability'.[37]

Rate of utterance was observed impressionistically in the Mitchell-

---

[34] Crystal and Quirk, *Systems of Prosodic and Paralinguistic Features in English*, p. 12.

[35] The most substantial study so far was made by Adams, The Intonation of Question and Answer in Australian Speech.

[36] *The English Language in Australia and New Zealand*, p. 92.

[37] *The Speech of Australian Adolescents*, p. 58.

Delbridge survey,[38] and it was noted that Broad speakers tended either towards a low rate of utterance, or to a jerky gabble. The most fluent speakers were children born in an English-speaking country outside Australia (mainly in the British Isles). This observation suggested a point of differentiation between Australian and English norms for rate of utterance. Progress in an instrumental analysis of utterance rates was reported by J. R. Bernard,[39] who concluded, rather tentatively, that Australian speech is 'unusually slow and rhythmically even, at least as compared to RP', and that there is some support in his findings for the notion of a characteristic rate for a particular dialect; but the size of the average divergence from mean figures left him persuaded that rate is more an index of personality than of dialect.

The question of voice quality has generally been discussed as a matter of aesthetic taste, not relevant to linguistic analysis. Without challenging the notion of a biologically determined voice-set which is the individual possession of every speaking person, one may perhaps at least wonder whether there is not a good deal of learning involved in the individual's possession of a range of more favoured and less favoured phonatory and articulatory settings, and whether these come to have dialectal and social meanings. Beatrice Honikman[40] used the term 'articulatory setting' to refer to 'the disposition of the parts of the speech mechanism and their composite action . . . for articulation according to the phonetic substance of the language concerned'. She tried to characterise the articulatory settings of French and English in terms of positions of jaw and lips, muscular tension, characteristic positions of rest in the mouth; in short, of the gross oral posture and mechanics which form a framework for the merging of isolated sounds into 'that harmonious cognizable whole which constitutes the established pronunciation of a language'. There have been no detailed studies of the phonatory and articulatory settings of Australian English, yet the force of popular comment and the inability of scholars to characterise in linguistic terms some of the possibly distinctive perceived features of Australian speech suggest that here is an area where useful research might be done. The development of more refined methods of physiological study, the accessibility of speech synthesisers for relating perception to acoustic and physiological parameters, and the accumulation of comparable data for other varieties of English all offer encouragement.

SPEECH PERCEPTION

The range of phonetic studies that are actually feasible has increased very

[38] Ibid., p. 63.
[39] 'The Rates of Utterance in Australian Dialect Groups'.
[40] 'Articulatory Settings', p. 73.

greatly in the past ten years, thanks to the establishment of research laboratories in phonetics in many Australian universities. At the University of Queensland, the University of Sydney, the University of New South Wales, at Monash, the Australian National University, Macquarie, and others, there are well-established facilities for spectrographic and other types of acoustic analysis of speech. Facilities for parametric synthesis are beginning to appear, and computer analysis for more than statistical use is attracting the attention of scholars.

The sort of work available to post-graduate students can be judged from the titles of theses included in Mr Blair's bibliography, printed in this volume. The range of facilities and techniques available can most easily be shown by describing one of them. The one chosen[41] exemplifies, as well, the increasing interest being shown in perception in relation to the motor and acoustic stages of the speech chain.

The point of origin of the thesis is the claim frequently made that Australians say /aɪ/ when they mean /eɪ/, so that listeners believe that they are saying 'like' or 'die' when they are really saying 'lake' or 'day'. Does this really happen when Australian listeners are listening to Australian speakers? Is the confusion, if it exists, affected by the variety of English spoken by the speaker and by the listener, especially if these are different? Is there one variety the speakers of which are understood most clearly by all listeners? Is there one variety the speakers of which understand all speakers most clearly? Are some Australian vowels, when free of context, more intelligible than others? Are the most intelligible vowels the same for all three varieties of Australian English? These were the sorts of questions to which answers were sought, using experimental methods.

Nine male speakers, three from each of the main varieties, recorded sixteen stressed vowels in a standard carrier phrase, with minimal mean pitch differences between speakers. The vowels were abstracted from their carrier phrase, and the voice quality of the speakers obscured by the accompaniment of flat white noise. A tape was prepared, with the vowels presented in random order and at a specified signal-to-noise ratio. This was played, in two versions, to 150 listeners, each of whom had been tested audiometrically to detect defective hearing, and classified in terms of the variety of Australian English spoken. Fifty speakers in each variety, Cultivated, General, and Broad, were selected as the subjects for the listening experiment. In this experiment, the listeners in groups of nine were asked to identify the vowels heard as the tape was played through a loudspeaker in a sound-treated room. A computer program was written to facilitate the analysis of the results in terms of confusion-matrices. Orders of intelligibility were obtained from the different speaker-listener combinations and for all speakers and all listeners combined. A general

[41] Robertson, Intelligibility of Australian English Vowels.

analysis of variance was carried out, and variations in the scores were related, statistically, to the version of the test tape heard, to the sex of the listener, and to his intelligence quotient. Sonagrams were made for each of the test words for each speaker, and a method investigated for predicting a speaker's intelligibility in noise from an examination of the formant characteristics of the sonagrams.

Some of the objectives of the thesis were not realised because effects due to speech variety became inextricable from effects due to the use of background noise. Nevertheless it did appear that, in the conditions of the experiment, the order of intelligibility for vowels is that found in the list: *hud, had, hod, hid, herd, howed, hade, horde, who'd, head, hood, hoyed, hide, heed, hoad*. The short vowels were heard consistently clearly for all speakers.

> But the order of intelligibility differed according to the speech variety of the speaker: *hade* was progressively less clear from Broad to Cultivated Australian, and *hoyed* was clear only when spoken by Cultivated listeners.[42]

The one confusion which did not occur was the one from which the thesis arose: Broad Australian /eɪ/, which is often heard as /aɪ/ by foreign listeners, was not misheard in this way by Australian listeners. 'The Cultivated /aɪ/ sound, on the other hand, was heard as /eɪ/ a significant number of times. This would seem to indicate that Australians automatically expect to hear fairly broad allophones of the /eɪ/ sound.'[43]

Indeed, in tests without context and without background noise, it appeared that Australians are so conditioned to the broader varieties of Australian speech that they understand General and Broad speakers more readily than they understand Cultivated speakers.

> From this it would seem that a listener does not interpret the vowels he hears in terms of his own articulations. Rather, he seems to interpret them in terms of a generalised vowel chart constructed from the speech of the majority of the community.[44]

This finding is taken to support the interpretation of the speech perception process offered by Joos rather than the motor theory advanced by the Haskins group.

The theoretical interest and the educational and other practical relevance of investigations of this sort offer a strong stimulus to post-graduate research, and it is encouraging to know that there are now facilities available in so many Australian universities. In contrastive studies between English and other languages, in questions of the teaching of English, both as a native and as a foreign language, in sociological aspects of communication,

[42] Ibid., p. 326.
[43] Ibid.
[44] Ibid., p. 332.

in questions of language assimilation by migrants, in the study of disorders of hearing, speech, and language, as well as in the central disciplines of theoretical and descriptive linguistics, there are rich opportunities for useful research.

REFERENCES CITED

Adams, Corinne, The Intonation of Question and Answer in Australian Speech, M.A. thesis, University of Sydney, 1967.
Bernard, J. R. L-B., 'An Extra Phoneme of Australian English', *AUMLA*, Vol. 20, 1963, pp. 346-52.
———, 'The Rates of Utterance in Australian Dialect Groups', University of Sydney, Australian Language Research Centre, *Occasional Paper* No. 7.
———, Some Measurements of Some Sounds of Australian English, Ph.D. thesis, University of Sydney, 1967.
Burgess, O. N., 'Extra Phonemes in Australian English: A Further Contribution', *AUMLA*, Vol. 30, 1968, pp. 180-7.
Chomsky, Noam, and Halle, Morris, *The Sound Pattern of English*, New York, 1968.
Cochrane, G. R., 'The Australian English Vowels as a Diasystem', *Word*, Vol. 15, April 1959, pp. 69-88.
———, 'loŋ [æ] in ostreiljən iŋgliʃ', *Maître Phonétique* No. 124, 1965, pp. 22-6.
Crystal, David, and Quirk, Randolph, *Systems of Prosodic and Paralinguistic Features in English*, The Hague, 1964.
Flint, E. H., 'The Question of Language, Dialect, Idiolect and Style in Queensland English', Linguistic Circle of Canberra, *Bulletin* No. 2, 1965, pp. 1-21.
Gunn, J. S., 'The Influence of Background on the Speech of Teachers' College Students', *Forum of Education*, Vol. 22, No. 1, March 1963, pp. 18-41.
Hammarström, U. G. E., 'Some Remarks on Australian Diphthongs', abstract to be published in *Proceedings of the Twelfth Congress of AULLA*, 1968 (in press).
Hill, Robert, Early Australian Pronunciation—The Value of Manuscript Evidence, M.A. thesis, University of Sydney, 1967.
———, 'Prospects of the Study of Early Australian Pronunciation', *English Studies*, Vol. 48, No. 1, February 1967, pp. 43-52.
Hockett, C. F., *A Manual of Phonology*, Baltimore, 1955.
Honikman, Beatrice, 'Articulatory Settings'. In *In Honour of Daniel Jones*, ed. D. Abercrombie *et al.*, London, 1964.
Jassem, W., *The Intonation of Conversational English*, Travaux de la Société des Sciences et des Lettres, Series A, No. 45, Warsaw, 1952.
Jones, Alex I., *An Outline Word Phonology of Australian English*, University of Sydney, Australian Language Research Centre, *Occasional Paper* No. 8.
———, A Phonological-Lexical Study of the Distribution of the Sounds [æ] and [æ:], in the Speech of Secondary School Children in New South Wales, M.A. thesis, University of Sydney, 1966.
———, 'Sydney Australian—a Seven Vowel System', *Studies in Linguistics*, Vol. 18, 1964-6, pp. 29-35.
Keyser, S. J., Review of H. Kurath and Raven McDavid, *The Pronunciation of English in the Atlantic States, Language*, Vol. 39, 1963, pp. 303-16.
Ladefoged, P., *Three Areas of Experimental Phonetics*, Oxford, 1967.
Laycock, D. C., 'lɔŋ "ʃoht vawlz" in *əstrəiljən* iŋgliʃ', *Maître Phonétique* No. 126, 1966, pp. 22-3.
Mitchell, A. G., *The Pronunciation of English in Australia*, Sydney, 1946, rev. ed. with Arthur Delbridge, Sydney, 1965.

———, and Delbridge, Arthur, *The Speech of Australian Adolescents*, Sydney, 1965.
Robertson, M. A., Intelligibility of Australian English Vowels, M.A. thesis, Macquarie University, 1969.
Sharwood, John, and Horton, Ivor, 'Phoneme Frequencies in Australian English', *AUMLA*, Vol. 26, 1966, pp. 272-302.
Trager, G. L., and Smith, H. L., *An Outline of English Structure*, Washington, 1962.
Turner, G. W., *The English Language in Australia and New Zealand*, London, 1966.
———, 'On the Origin of Australian Vowel Sounds', *AUMLA*, Vol. 13, 1960, pp. 33-45.

NINETEENTH-CENTURY AUSTRALIAN ENGLISH

> Once a jolly swagman camped by a billabong,
> Under the shade of a coolibah tree;
> And he sang as he watched and waited till his billy boiled,
> 'You'll come a-waltzing matilda with me'.

When in 1969 Australia's Prime Minister, John Gorton, pledged his country's willingness to go 'a-waltzing matilda' with Mr Nixon, his intentions were plain enough: yet the literal-minded might have wondered what carrying a swag had to do with international relations, and the curious have asked in vain for the origin of this most Australian of Australianisms. Continued speculation about the derivations of some of the other Australianisms in the song—*swagman, billabong, coolibah, jumbuck, tuckerbag, squatter,* and *trooper*—is further testimony to our ignorance of the language we use and, more particularly, of the language used last century by the first generations of Australians.

Is *swag* derived from the criminal cant word for stolen clothing? Does *billabong* come from two Aboriginal words *billa,* 'water', and *bong,* or *bung,* 'dead'? Is *jumbuck* from an Aboriginal word, *dombar,* 'a white cloud', or is it a corruption of 'jump-up'? Is *billy* a derivative of French *bouilli* (the original *billy* being an old *boeuf bouilli* tin), Aboriginal *billa,* the proper name *William,* or Scots *billy pot*? Does *squatter,* as C. P. Hodgson claimed in *Reminiscences of Australia* (1846), come from a verb meaning 'literally to sit on the haunches', and is it used of Australian sheep-farmers 'from their being obliged frequently to adopt that position'?[1] We have only to think of some of the words used in another song which most Australians learn—'Click Go the Shears'—to realise how familiar many of these early Australianisms are but how much we still have to learn about their use and early history. Young as the Australian vocabulary may be, it is a rich and exciting field to explore.

Twentieth-century Australian English is, as Mr Gunn points out, subject

---

[1] Hodgson, *Reminiscences in Australia,* p. 4. For a fuller discussion of the nineteenth-century vocabulary, see Ramson, *Australian English,* on which this article is based.

to a range of influences of which the nineteenth-century vocabulary was free. At least until the 1850s, until the great influx of miners, traders, travellers, and adventurers drawn by the discovery of gold, the Australian colony, like its trans-Tasman neighbour, was relatively isolated. Instead, therefore, of a vocabulary which, like that of British English in the formative period of the late Middle Ages and Renaissance, was 'at home' to various major influences and expanding through borrowing, we have a vocabulary which, like that of Old English, was expanding largely through the utilisation of its own resources. It was a vocabulary which took its character partly from the early nineteenth-century British English of the settlers, and partly from the innovations that they made when confronted with a new environment and with new occupations. It is likely, therefore, to appear 'conservative', in the sense that words from British regional dialects and from British city slang which had not become part of Standard English were pressed into new service; but likely also to appear inventive, dynamic, young, and vigorous because it created new words freely and easily and was the main vehicle of communication in a new society, and therefore as dynamic in its growth as that society.

It is unwise, in our present state of knowledge, to emphasise one of these sides of the vocabulary at the expense of the other. By far the greater part of the Australian vocabulary is Standard English and, in most areas of usage, the *Concise Oxford Dictionary* is as good a guide for the Australian as it is for the Englishman. But the vocabulary is given its character, its feeling of difference, by the deletions, adaptations, and additions that are made, by a disposition of its main elements that may be different from the pattern of nineteenth-century British English. The reasons for this are historical: a study of the developing Australian vocabulary complements the social historian's record of a developing society, and it is as wrong to neglect the contribution of the British regional dialects as it is to overemphasise the 'Australian-made' innovations.

It is even more unwise to go beyond these generalisations about the Australian's language and use them as a basis for judgments about his character. Sidney J. Baker's *The Australian Language* is the classic example of this, but the doyen of amateur exponents of the gentle art of lexicography, Eric Partridge, slips easily into the same vein. Australian innovations listed in *Slang Today and Yesterday* (1933), he argues,

> bear witness to [the] force and picturesqueness [of Australian English], its richness and variety, qualities due in part to the exhilarating and often romantic occupation of this vast country and in part to the intrepidity and resourcefulness of the early settlers and to the continued need for those moral assets as well as the persisting exhilaration.[2]

[2] Partridge, *Slang Today and Yesterday*, p. 288.

This is the approach which Professor Mitchell once classified as the 'patriotic'.[3] It is essentially misguided—as any comparison of the early writings about American and Australian English will show—and seriously misleading in that it encourages a distortion of the history of Australian English to bring it into line with the supposed emergence of a national ethos at the end of the nineteenth century—an emergence which is associated with the move towards Federation, and manifested through the medium of the *Bulletin* and the school of writers associated with that journal.

In fact there is ample evidence that, before 1850, there was enough difference between Australian and British English—and enough consciousness of the difference—for a writer like Alexander Harris, perhaps 'the first fyndere of our faire langage', to confidently differentiate between standard British English and the several dialects found in the colony. In his novel, *The Emigrant Family*, Harris has, for instance, a Welshman, a Jew, an upper-class Englishman, a 'native' Australian, a group of ex-convicts who are allowed some variety in their speech, and a number of pidgin-speaking Aborigines. His own style uses, naturally and easily, a range of Australianisms and in dialogue he uses others to good dramatic effect. Dispatches to London and journals of travellers or settlers, which before 1850 tended to be written in a conservative, rather literary English, not infrequently relax into Australianisms, often with the rather awkward modifier, 'in colonial parlance', or some similar apology.

One example of the recognition of this difference, from the *Colonial Literary Journal* of 1844, has an anonymous correspondent offer two translations of a German sonnet, one into standard nineteenth-century poetic diction, one into 'Australian': *cottage* is replaced by *bark hut*, *verdant lea* by a *patch of maize*, *brook* by *creek*, *tree* by *wattle*, *nightingale* by *cocky-bird*, and *rising wind* by *brickfielder*. The editorial comment adds patronisingly:

> We insert this at the request of an anonymous correspondent, as we think the Colonial manner in which he has translated the Ode will amuse our country subscribers.[4]

But as early as 1805 these distinctions between Australian and British usage had been remarked by Governor King: *brush* he defines as 'a dark impenetrable thicket consisting of plants and herbacious Shrubs'; *forest land* as 'a local expression', its distinguishing character being its grass rather than its trees; *scrub*, again described as 'a local expression', as 'Shrubs of low growth, Soil of a bad quality with small Iron gravelly Stones'.[5] *Plain*, similarly, was redefined: as an anonymous writer noticed

[3] Mitchell, *The Pronunciation of English in Australia*, p. 3.
[4] *Colonial Literary Journal*, July 1844, p. 62.
[5] King to Camden, *Historical Records of Australia*, Vol. V, p. 586.

in 1839, 'the word *plain* here means *open*, either partially or wholly free from bush'.⁶ And an 1852 description is even more clear:

> 'Plains' in Australia are open, park-like districts, with merely clumps of trees standing at intervals, the undulating ground being covered with fine grass. . . .⁷

Creek and *lagoon* are noted by King in the same dispatch as familiar English words which, as 'local expressions', have been given new meanings by the colonists.

In the light of subsequent usage King's definitions all need amplification, but they indicate an awareness of differences which is early and, as a marker of growth, significant: the creation of new meanings and new words does not wait on abstract conceptions like the emergence of a national consciousness, but occurs when and where a need is felt. King's difficulties in describing to the Colonial Office the sort of terrain he was encountering led him to introduce Camden to new meanings of existing words which, among the colonists, were already 'doing service'; the colonists had also to communicate with the Aborigines, and that they did so in a makeshift and essentially pragmatic form of language can be gauged from David Collins's observation in 1796:

> Language indeed, is out of the question for at the time of writing this, nothing but a barbarous mixture of English with the Port Jackson dialect is spoken by either party; and it must be added that even in that the natives have the advantage, comprehending, with much greater aptness than we can pretend to, everything they hear us say.⁸

It is wrong, therefore, to look for a vocabulary which betrays characteristics peculiar to the Australian—inventiveness, virility, love of wordplay, freedom from linguistic conservatism; we are recording the vocabulary of a predominantly British people transplanted to a new and unfamiliar environment and faced with the immediate necessity of communicating with their fellows. We need to be a little more open-minded than the patriotic commentators, and somewhat less selective than such a traveller as Alexander Marjoribanks, whose only observation was on the currency of *bloody*:

> It is the favourite oath in that country. One may tell you that he married a bloody young wife, another, a bloody old one; and a bushranger will call out 'Stop, or I'll blow your bloody brains out'.

Marjoribanks recalls a bullocky who used *bloody* twenty-five times in fifteen minutes, and calculates that, with eight hours a day off for sleep and six for silence, he would, in the course of the fifty years of his natural

---
⁶ *A Voice from the Bush in Australia*, p. 13.
⁷ J. B. Jukes (ed.), *Lectures on Gold*, p. 20.
⁸ Collins, *An Account of the English Colony in New South Wales*, Vol. I, p. 544.

swearing life, 'have pronounced this disgusting word no less than 18,200,000 times'.[9] Marjoribanks can, incidentally, be compared with contemporary commentators, like John O'Grady in *They're a Weird Mob*, and Afferbeck Lauder in *Strine*, both of whom cash in on the supposed 'Australianness' of a small, often repeated, but largely unrepresentative selection of linguistic features.

How, then, can we define an Australianism? The simplest approach is to take the 'standard' vocabulary of the parent language, British English, as it is recorded in, say, the *Concise Oxford Dictionary*, and see how it accords with the 'standard' vocabulary of Australian English. Some words will have dropped out, like those 'beautiful names of an intimate countryside' Sir Keith Hancock noted in *Australia*—*field, meadow, woods, copse, spinney, thicket, dale, glen, brook, inn,* and *village*;[10] some will have been added—Aboriginal words, and the Australian's replacement for these older English words for the countryside, words like *paddock, bush, scrub, gully, creek,* and *township*, which have been given new meanings here. Some of the additions, the Aboriginal words for instance, will be peculiarly Australian and may never gain currency outside Australia—or even outside one region of Australia; others will be derived from existing standard English words, gaining a new form through composition, or a new meaning through the processes of extension, association, generalisation, and particularisation; others again will be derived from British regional dialects, British slang, or from the vocabulary of another colonial dialect, American or Canadian English for instance, and will have gained a different status from that held in standard British English.

The total picture is difficult to grasp: how does one tally up the British English words not used by Australians? track down the history of words like *shicer* and *spieler*,[11] both German in origin but both with 'records' in American and British slang usage? assess the status and usage of British regional dialect words like *darg, kellick, skillion, smoodger,* and *taws*? For most purposes we can say that our concern is with Australian additions to the standard vocabulary of British English, but the relationship between the two is complex, our knowledge of several levels of usage in British, American, and Australian English remains limited, and the danger of oversimplifying is always present.

As Professor Mitchell first pointed out, 'Australian speech is in its origins a town speech', and further, 'a working-class speech, the language of people who were poor and for the most part unskilled'.[12] This is important in several ways. It suggests, firstly, that we should expect no

[9] Marjoribanks, *Travels in New South Wales*, pp. 57-8.
[10] Hancock, *Australia*, p. 242.
[11] See p. 134 below.
[12] See p. 9 above.

substantial carry-over of rural occupational vocabularies from British regional dialects; secondly, that the contribution of the regional dialects will be most noticeable in the general colloquial vocabulary of the Australian; and thirdly, that, with little access to the rich resources of the dialect vocabularies, Australian English would have to equip itself to handle life of a predominantly rural character through what, since Anglo-Saxon times, have been the normal methods of expansion of English: extension, or generalisation of meaning, and the forming of compounds and derivatives. Borrow it did, of course, where it could. But the Aboriginal languages were not a feasible source for anything but the names of flora and fauna, a handful of colloquialisms, and words limited in their reference to the Aborigines themselves; and the contacts with American English which, given the obvious similarities between the two frontier societies, could have made a substantial contribution to the settlers' vocabulary, were too slight or too late to be effectual.

Regional dialect words, of course, have a habit of remaining much more a part of the spoken than of the written language, of perpetuating their use in families or localities, and it is not at all improbable that, given the increase in immigrants from rural areas that came later in the century— of the Scottish farmers, for instance, whose contribution to the place-names of the New England district suggests that, if The New State Movement ever came to anything, a Scottish Nationalist breakaway would follow[13]—more rural occupational terms from the regional dialects came in than are found in written sources. Again, with the evidence at hand, it is impossible to establish either the dating or status of those words that are recorded; but only a few, like *back o'beyond, bail, claypan, to fall* a a tree (rather than Standard English *fell*), *paddock, poddy,* 'fat, pot-bellied' (used mostly of handfed calves), *poley,* 'a hornless beast', *run, to snig,* 'to drag timber with ropes or chains', and *waterhole,* come to mind. And, though some of these, like *poley* and *snig,* are unchanged in their application, others have been extended in meaning. *Back o'beyond* has now peculiarly Australian connotations; *bail* is used, as Boldrewood pointed out, as freely of Christians as of cows;[14] the Australian *paddock,* with its familiar compound, *home paddock,* is different from the English, as is *run,* with its several compounds, *back run, cattle run, sheep run,* and *stock run.*

A handful of mining terms demonstrate the same processes: *sprag,* 'a timber prop', *stuff,* 'gold bearing ore or dirt', and *tailings,* 'waste', retain their dialect meaning. Others, like *fossick* and *mullock,* have undergone

---

[13] So, in the triangle centred on *Armidale, Inverell,* and *Glen Innes,* are *Ben Lomond* and *Ben Nevis, Glencoe* and *Glen Elgin,* the *Aberfoyle* River, *Dundee,* and *Rob Roy.*

[14] *Robbery Under Arms,* p. 368.

some change of meaning: both had very general application in British regional dialects, were narrowed in meaning to meet the specific context of gold-mining, but subsequently widened as, like *darg*, they have come into general colloquial use.

The dialect words which have made most impact on Australian English, though, are those which suggest no distinct background of specific or occupational use but are very much part of the general colloquial vocabulary, words like *barrack, chiack, dinkum, shivoo*, and *taws*, like *cobber, guiver, larrikin, nark*, and perhaps *pommy* and *wowser*, and the intensives *boomer, flaming, jimbang, ringer*, and *sollicker*. Some of these—*guiver* for instance, meaning 'plausible talk'—are probably obsolete now, as are *carney*, 'to flatter' or 'flattery', *cross*, 'illegal, dishonest', and *fakement*, 'a contrivance or dodge', which seem to have had quite wide use during the nineteenth century.

Cross and *fakement* serve as reminders that the boundary between regional dialect and general urban slang is not easily marked out: both have histories in regional dialect vocabularies but both have moved into criminal cant. James Hardy Vaux, a thrice-transported convict, in a glossary compiled in Newcastle, New South Wales, in 1812, and dedicated to Thomas C. Skottowe, in the pious hope that he would find it amusing because of its novelty and useful in his magisterial capacity[15] (a dedication which recalls Watkin Tench's observation in 1793 that an interpreter was frequently necessary in the law courts), records these, as well as *blunt* and *brads*, both meaning 'money', *family*, 'the fraternity of thieves and others who make their living *on the cross*', *flat*, 'an honest man', *plant*, used either as a verb, 'to hide', or as a noun, and *trap*, 'a policeman'. All of these are used by Alexander Harris in his representation of the speech of convicts and ex-convicts in *The Emigrant Family*. Meanings have, in some cases, changed: *cove*, for instance, in Harris's time refers no longer to a shopkeeper but to the boss of a station; *new chum* and *old chum*, both used originally of fellow convicts, have gained a wider currency; but the provenance of each word is clear, and the transference to a new environment explains the different meanings of these words and, to take another example, of the long-established English slang words, *duff* and *plant*.

Something of the antiquity of this section of the vocabulary was realised by C. J. Dennis, who, seeking to justify his pride as 'arch-protagonist and chief promulgator of an argot hitherto little known in the English-speaking world', discovered to his chagrin that much of what he recorded was derived from Yiddish, from 'the old rhyming slang of London thieves', and from 'the secret tongue of Romany',[16] urban and not rural sources

---

[15] The glossary is accessible in *The Memoirs of James Hardy Vaux*.
[16] Quoted in Chisholm, *The Making of a Sentimental Bloke*, p. 82.

of what many find the most distinctive elements of the late nineteenth-century Australian vocabulary.

But this is, in a sense, the negative side of the picture. These are survivals, non-standard words which, because they have found new or extended uses, have been given new status. More important in every way are the words which the colonists formed for themselves, the adaptations of the standard vocabulary of British English to the new uses with which it was suddenly confronted. This process of adaptation, caused by the inadequacy of the existing vocabulary in the new environment and characterised by the generalisation of meaning of a number of commonly used but unspecific words, and their subsequent particularisation through being compounded, accounts for the greater part of Australian additions to the vocabulary during the nineteenth century.

We can, perhaps, imagine something of the wonder with which the settlers surveyed the strange new land in which they had arrived, a land which was physically far removed from the neatly tailored countryside they had left behind, and rich in exotic flora and fauna; an unfamiliar and apparently inhospitable land in which they had to pursue the unfamiliar activities of pioneering and settling; a land inhabited only by tribes of primitive Aborigines, whose linguistic territories were so small and closely defined that words learnt from the Port Jackson tribe were of no help in communicating with those on the Hawkesbury, or inland towards the Blue Mountains. E. E. Morris, looking back in 1898 on the wealth of new words with which the settlers met the challenge of naming all that they met, guessed

> that there never was an instance in history when so many new names were needed, and that there never will be such an occasion again, for never did settlers come, nor can they ever again come, upon Flora and Fauna so completely different from anything seen by them before.[17]

This is a large, almost certainly an excessive claim, but it serves to remind us that the need for new names in the first twenty or thirty years of settlement was real and urgent: there is no cause to press claims for the vigour and inventiveness of any one branch of the language if it can be shown to be meeting a recurring need in a conventional manner. The early history of American English makes a useful comparison with the early history of Australian, not only because attitudes expressed towards the language are similar, but because the situation is almost exactly parallel: a vocabulary of defined limits was transported to a new environment and new demands made upon it. The American settlers met these demands in the same way as settlers in Australia or, indeed, in any colonial setting. They borrowed where borrowing was possible, but in the main

---

[17] *Austral English*, p. xii.

depended on the extended and varied use of the basic vocabulary with which they came.

Governor King's use of a handful of words for features of the landscape—*brush, creek, forest land, lagoon, plain,* and *scrub*[18]—shows this process at its earliest and simplest. It is at its most dramatic in the naming of flora where, more commonly than in the naming of fauna, the settlers used names which were derived from a supposed resemblance to English trees or plants familiar in their memory. The point is made by an English traveller in 1831:

> The resemblance of what are called apple-trees in Australia, to those of the same name at home, is so striking at a distance in these situations, that the comparisons could not be avoided, although the former bear no fruit, and do not even belong to the same species.[19]

Examples of this which are found before 1810 in reports to the Colonial Office—in a formal English which is slower to adopt new terms than the spoken variety—include *apple-tree, box, cherry-tree, mahogany, native pear,* and *oak*. We notice also the early attachment of particularisers, in *Huon pine* and *Moreton Bay fig*, named after the place where they were first found; in *Callan's stringybark* and *Caley's ironbark*, named after the first to describe the tree. The confusion some English visitors felt is well voiced by G. C. Mundy in 1852:

> Most of the trees, or rather of the timbers, of this colony owe their names to the sawyers who first tested their qualities. They were guided by the colour and character of the wood, knowing and caring nothing about botanical relations. Thus the swamp-oak and the she-oak have rather the exterior of the larch than any quercine aspect. Pomona would indignantly disown the apple-tree for there is not the semblance of a pippin on its tufted branches. A shingle of the beef-wood resembles a cypress, but is of a tenderer green, bearing a worthless little berry, having its stone or seed outside . . . The pear-tree is, I believe, an eucalypt, and bears a pear of solid wood, hard as heart of oak. . . .[20]

Mundy's comments on *cedar* are similarly illuminating:

> Here I saw for the first time the cedar—the most valuable timber in the country for upholstery—the mahogany, in short, of New Holland, a wood which it much resembles in colour and grain, although inferior in solidity. It has no affinity whatever with the cedar of other climes—the foliage nearly resembling the European ash; it is not even a coniferous tree.[21]

This simple process of the extension of a word's meaning to meet a new and in some way not dissimilar need in the colony accounts also for

---

[18] See above, pp. 34-5.
[19] Dawson, *The Present State of Australia*, pp. 195-6.
[20] *Our Antipodes*, Vol. II, pp. 25-6.
[21] Ibid., p. 25.

the transference of a cluster of terms from the context of a convict settlement to the sheep-farming context in which many of the unwilling immigrants later found themselves. The early history of *mob* is not yet adequately documented, but it would seem likely that, being the common English term in the early nineteenth century for a disorderly rabble, it transferred readily to the wilful flocks of sheep settlers had to keep together on unfenced land. *Muster*, similarly, passes from a military context into convict usage, being the word customarily employed by the Governor of the colony when ordering an assembly of the convicts. From the convicts themselves to the sheep they tended is but a further step.

From convict usage also comes the special use of *hut* and *hutkeeper*, as applied first to convict accommodation and its custodian and later to a shepherd's dwelling and his offsider who cleaned, cooked, and sometimes watched the sheep by night. *Assignment* and *ticket-of-leave* retain their early Australian meanings only in historical contexts, as does the interesting pair, *currency*, 'native-born', and *sterling*, 'immigrant', which implies a far earlier concept of devaluation than that faced by Britain this century; but *overseer* and *superintendent*, both used of officers in charge of convict gangs, were, in the twenties and thirties, being used of farm managers: and perhaps *gang*, as used now of shearers in Australia and New Zealand, has followed the same course. *Cove*, recorded by Vaux for 'the master of a house or shop', achieves a usage similar to that of *overseer*, though it is clearly out of an urban slang rather than convict context. The early history of *station* needs more attention than it has had, but its probable development is from the early use referring to a government outpost at which convicts were employed, to one at which convicts were employed specifically to tend stock: individual settlers followed government practice, and the word early acquired its present meaning.

Once the use of *station* became settled the number of compounds and full-word combinations from it multiplied: *back station, cattle station, head station, out sheep station, outstation, sheep station, station-hand, station-house,* and *stock station* were all in use in the nineteenth century. This sort of proliferation is readily managed and gives a vocabulary which is readily comprehensible: in early Australian English a relatively small number of words, like *bush, native, run,* and *stock,* spawned a range of straightforward and indispensable terms. *Bush*, for instance, which had given *bushfire, bush horse, bush hut, bush life, bushman,* and *bush road* before 1850, has led also to the more imaginative *bush-lawyer*, 'one who fancies himself as versed in the law', *bush telegraph*, 'grapevine', and the numerous short-lived but self-explanatory combinations peculiarly associated with the *bush* ethos—*bush breakfast*, 'mutton, damper and tea',[22]

[22] Byrne, *Twelve Years' Wandering in the British Colonies*, Vol. I, p. 170.

bush costume, 'blue shirt, belt, and cabbage tree hat',[23] and *bush language*, 'which may be better imagined than described'.[24]

Bushranger, the most 'Australian' of all of these, is probably, like *bush* itself, a borrowing from American English. We would reasonably expect some of the words used by colonial administrators in reference to practices in the American colony to be similarly used in Australia, and the likelihood of this is increased when we realise that, up to 1821, instructions to the New South Wales Governors regularly referred to settlers as *planters*. *Block*, *location*, *section*, and *township* were all used with specific meanings in the surveying of land for settlement, their Australian meaning either being the same as or derived from the American; and *bush*, *bushranger*, *landshark* (which replaced the older English *landjobber*), and *squatter* seem to be from the same source. Few would now think of *bushranger* as anything but Australian, as it was used very early for what Macquarie called 'banditti': but even this sense may have carried over from American English. Compounds formed from *stock* are more run-of-the-mill, and perhaps a better illustration of the indispensable nature of the vocabulary so built up: *stock keeper* and *stockman* were both in use by 1800, *stock-farm*, *stock-holder*, *stock-house*, *stock-hut*, *stock run*, and *stock station* by 1830.

Many of the names for flora and fauna are similarly straightforward and, despite the occasional picturesqueness, self-explanatory. *Beefwood*, *ironbark*, *lightwood*, and *stringybark* indicate a quality of the wood, as does *raspberry-jam wood*, if J. Capper's explanation that 'it emits, when cut, an odour precisely similar to that of raspberry jam'[25] is to be believed. The *blackboy* is not such a fanciful name, if one thinks of their depiction in early engravings, and *celery-topped pine*, if cumbersome, is not confusing. Others, like *blackbutt*, *bluegum*, *flooded gum*, *saltbush*, and *tea tree*, were all in use in the first half of the century.

Descriptive names for fauna were perhaps more taxing. *Kookaburra* does not seem to have been much used until late in the century, the most common early names being *laughing jackass*, recorded as early as 1798, *bushman's clock*, and *settler's clock*. Early accounts of the *whipbird* refer to it as the *coachman's whipbird* or *coachman*, like *razor-grinder*, a name chosen because of the associations aroused by the bird's call, while in the case of the *lyrebird*, described also as a *pheasant* or *bird of paradise*, it was the bird's arresting appearance that gave rise to the name. Analogies were of course made with northern European species, and it is only later that *native dog* has given way to *dingo* and *native companion* to *brolga*. One interesting but now disguised derivation is that of *rosella*, a Latini-

[23] Banister and Mossman, *Australia Visited and Revisited*, p. 248.
[24] Read, *What I Heard, Saw, and Did*, p. 124.
[25] *Our Gold Colonies*, p. 9.

sation of *rosehiller*, itself an abbreviation of *rosehill parrot*, the name given to a parrot found near the Governor's residence, 'Rosehill', at Parramatta. Linguistically interesting as they are, many of these descriptive compounds have an extra fascination which derives from the glimpses they give of the settler's way of life and his discovery of the world about him.

In the naming of flora and fauna, more than with any other part of the vocabulary, the settlers were able to borrow from the Aboriginal languages. One word, in fact—*kangaroo*—was borrowed some twenty years before the settlers arrived and firmly established in English and French by the time they did: it is the one word surviving in English from the first record ever made of an Aboriginal language—during Cook's visit to the Endeavour River in 1770—and the meaning to those Aborigines, which later visitors to the region were unable to discover, remains something of a mystery. The Port Jackson Aborigines borrowed it back from the first settlers—though they were unsure for a while of the meaning and used it of all animals except dogs.

The early history of *kangaroo* provides the pattern, in fact, for subsequent borrowing, a pattern the same as that followed with borrowings from the Indian languages in the American colony. The first languages met were the first recorded, and it is from these, however limited their territories may have been, that borrowings were made. Thus we find that the number of words borrowed from the Port Jackson language and from those immediately adjacent to it is greater than that from any other single part of the country: Governor Hunter's vocabulary of the Port Jackson language ran to about 250 terms and, of these, almost one-tenth are still current in Australian English today.

Borrowing seems to have taken place on two levels, into the colloquial speech of the convicts and their fellows—where words like *baal* (a negative), *bogey*, 'to bathe', *budgeree*, 'good', *carbon*, 'large', *cooee*, *gibber*, 'rock or boulder', *gunyah*, 'hut', *jerran*, 'afraid', *jumbuck*, and *pyalla*, 'to talk', rub shoulders with slang or 'pidgin' expressions like *boy, gammon, mob, piccaninny, sit down*, 'stay', and *walkabout*.

This 'barbarous mixture', noticed in 1798 by Collins,[26] later became the basis of the Aboriginal pidgin used in Queensland and the Northern Territory; but attempts to use it were not always successful, as T. L. Mitchell noted in 1832, in his description of an attempt to converse with Aborigines on the Liverpool Plains:

> The string of low slang words which the natives nearer the colony suppose to be our language, while our stockmen believe they speak theirs, was of no use here. In vain did Dawkins address them thus: *What for you jerran budgerry whitefellow? Whitefellow brother belongit to blackfellow.*[27]

[26] See above, p. 35.   [27] *Three Expeditions into the Interior*, Vol. I, p. 63.

In Alexander Harris's *The Emigrant Family* there are a number of passages in which the conversations between Aborigines and stockmen are so represented, but it is difficult to tell if this early Aboriginal pidgin developed at all fully, and probable that it remained, as in the early encounters of the English and Maori languages, little more than a limited and casual exchange of vocabulary operating at certain levels only.

More important were the more numerous and more 'serious' borrowings, those deliberately taken over into English to name flora and fauna and label various features of the life of the Aborigines. Thus there were borrowed and in use, before 1850, names for birds like *boobook, budgerigar, currawong, jerryang,* and *wonga wonga*; for animals like *dingo, kangaroo, koala, potoroo, wallaby, wallaroo, warrigal,* and *wombat*; and for trees and plants like *brigalow, burrawang, geebung, kurrajong, mulga, quandong, waratah,* and *yarrah*.

For the dwellings of the Aborigines several alternatives were early available. The oldest, the Port Jackson word *gunyah*, was in fairly wide use by 1830, but other regional terms, like *gundy* from inland New South Wales, *quamby* and *mia mia* from Victoria, *humpy* from Queensland, and *wurley* from South Australia have enjoyed varying periods of use. Perhaps the most interesting of these is *mia mia*, the apparent origin of the New Zealand *mai mai*, 'a duckshooter's blind',[28] but the cluster perhaps also illustrates that, when the borrowing is at the colloquial level, the local term is likely to be preferred to the older term, in this case *gunyah*, which may have already become well established in the written standard.

The names of Aboriginal weapons, like *boomerang, hielamon, nulla nulla, waddy,* and *woomera*, and words associated with Aboriginal ceremonies, like *corroboree*, were borrowed early and achieved a measure of currency in descriptions of Aboriginal life. It is true of most of these, as of Aboriginal borrowings generally, that they have tended to remain 'fixed' labels, with their reference and area of usage clearly defined. There was, inevitably, an aura of novelty and romance about some of the more exotic that led to their wider adoption: there was, as early as 1814, an English brig named the *Kangaroo*, and the novelty of 'the leaping quadruped' sighted by Cook ensured the wider currency which the prevalence of toy koalas at international airports may eventually give that animal. But the number of Aboriginal words which have entered general English is small, and the number which have, like *boomerang, corroboree, dingo,* and *galah*, undergone some change of meaning, smaller still. The Aboriginal languages have made an important contribution to the vocabulary, but a comparison with that made by Maori to New Zealand English is a measure of the initial and continuing differences in

[28] See below, p. 96.

the cultural contact enjoyed by the two native races with their European invaders.

Most of the words that have been mentioned so far have been 'early' —they can be found in use before 1850, in the so-called 'colonial' period, and they represent, in a sense, the basic stock of Australianisms. Extensions in meaning of existing British English words, survivals of British regional dialect or slang usage, compounds, and borrowings from the Aboriginal languages—these demonstrate the main sources of the early nineteenth-century vocabulary and, in doing so, confirm both its provenance and its essential character. Like the vocabulary of early American English, that of early Australian is exactly what the social historian would expect; and this is true also of both its subsequent development during the nineteenth century and its impact on 'general' English.

A. D. Hope's description of an Australia where 'second-hand Europeans pullulate timidly on the edge of alien shores'[29] suggests that, for the greater part of its history, Australian society has been a transplant, and that traffic between it and the parent society has been very much one way. And certainly, in comparison with the American colony, there has not been, even in the twentieth century, much exporting of things so characteristically Australian as to have been named here. Immediate as the spread of *kangaroo* was, it has remained a word usable in limited contexts only; nothing comparable with the *tomato*, the *potato*, or *tobacco* has been found here, nor, though the outback myth may have local validity and Ned Kelly may yet rise to international fame, has there been anything comparable with the literary and mass media exploitation of America's 'Wild West'.

Though methods, and consequently terminology, are sometimes different, Australia's occupations are those pursued first in Britain and America: the combination of new conditions and the complex of social factors making up the background of the settlers meant the development of occupational vocabularies which were partly traditional and partly new, but essentially local. The vocabulary of sheep-farming, for instance, could be passed on to New Zealand, but there was no call for it to be borrowed by British or American English, and little possibility, therefore, of it being found in general English in anything other than a specifically historical or Australian context. Again, the fact that the Californian gold rushes preceded the Australian meant that the Australian miners could draw on the American vocabulary as well as on the traditional dialect vocabulary, but the composite vocabulary which emerged has had a mainly local application.

As far as colloquialisms and slang expressions are concerned, the situation is slightly different: there is always more fluidity in areas of

[29] *Collected Poems*, p. 13.

colloquial speech, and more room for duplication and changes resulting from fashion. But the sort of contact which spreads colloquialisms abroad, that of Australian men and women serving in two world wars or, on a more restricted scale, of Australian radio and television programs and of tourists travelling overseas, is a twentieth-century phenomenon. Australian English in the nineteenth century contributed to New Zealand English, but otherwise gave little to the English used in other parts of the world.

Another important difference from American English accounts for the homogeneity of the Australian vocabulary. Not only were nineteenth-century settlers of predominantly British origin, bringing with them a British English word-stock and the habits of vocabulary expansion outlined above, but they did not, like their American counterparts, have to contend with competition within the colony from other European powers. Australian English has not, as has American, borrowed directly from French, German, Dutch, and Spanish, and has not therefore developed a different 'balance', a different pattern of lexical nuclei, from British English.

Again, as Dr Clyne shows elsewhere in this volume, this situation may change if increasing numbers of European migrants retain a degree of bilingualism and a less one-sided lexical exchange develops; but in the nineteenth century, when the only two immigrant groups which were large enough to have had some effect were the Chinese on the goldfields and the German Lutherans in South Australia, social factors militated against their having any impact at all.[30] Both groups retained their separate identity but neither impinged to any extent on a generally unreceptive Australian majority: restrictive policies were, of course, adopted against Chinese immigration and, early in this century, Australian participation in World War I led to a temporary hardening of Australian attitudes towards the German settlers.

During the second half of the nineteenth century, then, the Australian vocabulary continued to follow the pattern of growth established in the early years of the colony, the major events in its history being the influx of British and American slang and colloquialisms during the gold-rush period and the emergence of Australian English as a written as well as a spoken language during the nineties. It is a reasonable assumption that early usage in the colony approximated to one of two extremes: at one the polite, written, standard form of eighteenth-century English continued to be used by a minority—the military, the governors, and the squattocracy; at the other a strange and undoubtedly barbaric (to the cultivated ear) mixture of urban slang, criminal cant, odd rural dialect survivals, nautical and military slang, and Aboriginal was used by the convicts, ex-convicts, and many of the assisted immigrants. The neologisms occasioned by the new environment were, of course, common to both, but, 'tainted' to some

---

[30] See my *Australian English*, pp. 152-63.

extent with colonial associations, they merged more naturally and fully with the emerging spoken Australian than with the written English which, through till the eighties, remained close to the models provided in contemporary British literary journals.

We find glimpses of the range of colloquial words and occupational terms used in spoken Australian before 1850—in Alexander Harris's novel, for instance—but Harris's natural style is literary and high-flown, and it is only towards the end of the century, in the novels of Rolf Boldrewood and then, of course, in the writing of Lawson and Furphy in the bush, and early in the twentieth century, in the writing of Dennis and Stone in the city, that the problem of classification comes into the open. Literary journals until the time of the *Bulletin* had remained conservative in their use of language—they change little from 1800 to 1870 and draw heavily on British journals for their material and manner. The *Bulletin*'s policy of encouraging the man in the bush to write his own verse, his own anecdotes and stories and titbits of advice, to make the paper a sort of bushman's forum, completely changed the situation: a vast colloquial vocabulary, much of it current back into the fifties, is brought into print, the spoken and the written levels have come together, and the whole question of the relation of Australian English in the nineties to the Queen's English raised. Karl Lentzner, a German lexicographer, pinpointed the problem when he assembled a vocabulary of 'the rich and racy slang of the fifth continent', invented, he said, because the words were 'absolutely needed', or because they expressed some idea 'more ingeniously, sententiously, and amusingly than others had done'.[31] These words, he argues, are not slang, but they are not the Queen's English either; and it is perhaps at this point, on the turn of the century, that Australian English gets its first formal recognition as a separate dialect of English, that it finds its first genuine manifestation in a national literature, and that it becomes possible to think of it in terms of its own sub-categories, of Standard Australian, of written and spoken, formal and colloquial Australian English.[32]

This paper sketches the main outlines of the development of the vocabulary during the nineteenth century. It remains only to point out that, until extensive and long-overdue historical lexicographical work is carried out, no more than an outline of Australian or New Zealand English in either this period or the twentieth century is possible.

---

[31] *Dictionary of the Slang-English of Australia and of Some Mixed Languages*, pp. vii-viii.
[32] See Johnston's chapter in this volume.

REFERENCES CITED

Baker, S. J., *The Australian Language*, Sydney, 1945 (rev. ed. 1966).
Banister, T., and Mossman, S., *Australia Visited and Revisited*, London, 1853.
Boldrewood, R. (pseud. for T. A. Browne), *Robbery Under Arms*, London, 1898.
Byrne, J. C., *Twelve Years' Wandering in the British Colonies*, 2 vols., London, 1848.
Capper, J., *Our Gold Colonies*, London, 1854.
Chisholm, A. H., *The Making of a Sentimental Bloke*, Melbourne, 1946.
Collins, D., *An Account of the English Colony in New South Wales*, 2 vols., London, 1798.
Culotta, Nino (pseud. for J. P. O'Grady), *They're a Weird Mob*, Sydney, 1958.
Dawson, R., *The Present State of Australia*, London, 1831.
Hancock, W. K., *Australia*, 1930, Aust. ed., Sydney, 1945.
Harris, A., *The Emigrant Family, or the Story of an Australian Settler*, London, 1849; ed. W. S. Ramson, Canberra, 1967.
Hodgson, C. P., *Reminiscences of Australia*, London, 1846.
Hope, A. D., *Collected Poems*, Sydney, 1966.
Hunter, J., *An Historical Journal of the Transactions at Port Jackson and Norfolk Island, etc.*, London, 1793.
Jukes, J. B. (ed.), *Lectures on Gold for the Instruction of Emigrants about to Proceed to Australia*, London, 1852.
Lauder, Afferbeck (pseud. for Alistair Morrison), *Let Stalk Strine*, Sydney, 1965.
Lentzner, K., *Dictionary of the Slang-English of Australia and of Some Mixed Languages*, Halle-Leipzig, 1892.
McLachlan, N. (ed.), *The Memoirs of James Hardy Vaux*, London, 1964.
Marjoribanks, A., *Travels in New South Wales*, London, 1847.
Mitchell, A. G., *The Pronunciation of English in Australia*, Sydney, 1946.
Mitchell, T. L., *Three Expeditions into the Interior of Eastern Australia*, 2 vols., London, 1838.
Morris, E. E., *Austral English, A Dictionary of Australasian Words, Phrases and Usages*, London, 1898.
Mundy, G. C., *Our Antipodes*, 2nd rev. ed., 3 vols., London, 1852.
Partridge, E., *Slang Today and Yesterday*, London, 1933.
Ramson, W. S., *Australian English. An Historical Study of the Vocabulary, 1788-1898*, Canberra, 1966.
Read, C. R., *What I Heard, Saw, and Did at the Australian Gold Fields*, London, 1853.
Vaux, James Hardy; see under McLachlan, N.
Anon., *A Voice from the Bush in Australia*, London, 1839.

4 J. S. GUNN

TWENTIETH-CENTURY AUSTRALIAN IDIOM

Twentieth-century Australian English is understandably more complex than that which existed earlier. For nearly a hundred years our idiom has had an identity of its own, yet to study it raises questions about its relationship with other English idioms or Australian of the previous century, and about the attention which should or should not be given to slang and colloquial usage, quite apart from any examination of what is essentially Australian about it. One must regret the absence of any comprehensive established authority; the *Oxford English Dictionary*, *Webster's*, and others often make clear a non-Australian origin of an 'Australianism', but are not always able to establish successfully the characteristic Australian application of a word or phrase. It is the colloquial flavour and extended *use* which are so hard to describe.

Another preliminary observation must be that our present idiom, like that of any expanded English in a new setting, has developed from and with its earlier forms. A surprising number of current Australian expressions go back to the nineteenth century,[1] the period when Aboriginal words also made their greatest impact, one manifested mainly in new and 'local' naming. It was then, too, that the terminologies of gold-mining and various primary industries were established, along with the circulation of what one can only call the idiom of the itinerant worker.

The twentieth century has seen a flow-on from the previous era as such activities continued and the language proved useful, and one might also expect fresh naming in the light of changing experience, new industries, and the appeal of some attractive usage. In addition this century has seen wars and a changing political, social, and cultural outlook which must also have affected the vocabulary, but which have not necessarily meant constant fresh coinages. The patriotic Australian may not like it but there are relatively few words one could call Australian creations, and the trend with the passing of time seems to have been one of growing more mature, more worldly, and less peculiarly Australian in our English.

[1] See Ramson, *Australian English*, Chapter 6 and Turner, *The English Language in Australia and New Zealand*, Chapter 7.

Everyday usage tends to depend mainly on direct acceptance or modification of other English, and even the habits of word formation, which will be mentioned later, are part of English everywhere.

Nevertheless, many words and expressions have been preserved in a special way in this country, and colourful polysemic extensions of English sustain distinctiveness and life in our vocabulary. This is one value of a book like that of S. J. Baker, even if descriptive method is of little concern to him, and terms which are formal or colloquial, local or imported, tend to be mixed. He has paid great attention to the rich body of Australian informal usage and, while appreciating the comments of his critics, one must realise the difficulty of classifying tidily terms which have an Australianness about them but a disturbing habit of not settling down in special groups, areas, or occupations.

Care is essential anywhere in dealing with informal usage, but in Australia there is a special need, because it is here that much of the distinctiveness of our idiom is found. The reputation for colour, irony, and flexibility is often too eagerly seized upon, and many word lists,[2] 'Aussie Englishes', or whatever they may be called, easily give a distorted impression. Some writers give an impression of an average Australian's daily verbal fare which simply does not exist, and which frequently forms the language of people (including Australians) trying to act the part of Australians.

Another warning should be issued against the habit of regarding as Australianisms occasional short-lived, local expressions. These occur in all English, and the Australian version is often colourful, witty, and appealing; but this does not mean that such words are an essential part of the idiom. Some attain generality while others have restricted, popular use, and in the main these are easy to identify for their passing faddishness. Ackroyd[3] mentioned the triviality of *ox-persuader* and *buffalo navigator*, 'whip', and there is no difficulty in adding to her list with terms like *flea-rake*, 'comb', *eggshell blonde*, 'bald', *fly swisher stew*, 'oxtail soup', *honey cart* or *17-door sedan*, 'sanitary cart', *face plaster*, 'alcoholic drink', and dozens of others.[4] In certain areas along the Murray River the kookaburra is also called a *ha-ha duck* because some migrants eat them. I have no doubt that several phrases like these will be claimed as established usage by different people or areas, just as many named later as current colloquial

[2] This is not intended to include valuable dictionary supplements or special occupation word lists.

[3] Ackroyd, 'Lingo-Jingo', p. 100.

[4] E.g. *hen fruit*, 'eggs', *stagger juice*, 'alcohol', *bitumen blonde*, 'brunette', *bushfire blonde*, 'redhead', *passion pit*, 'drive-in theatre', *piccaninny daylight*, 'dawn', *lager lodge*, 'bar', *underground mutton*, 'rabbit', *concertina*, 'side of lamb', *goggle box, idiot box*, 'television set', *laughing sides*, 'elastic-sided boots', *dog's Jew's harp*, 'suet dumpling', *he would skin a flea for its fat*, 'mean person', *play the four-string fiddle*, 'milk the cow', *five-finger discount*, 'pilfering', *leave some dogs tied up*, 'leave debts', *granpa's balls*, a 'crop which won't grow', *four-wheeler*, 'rare church attender'.

idiom will not be accepted everywhere. Some have been in use for a long time, which adds further to the problem of classification, and, of course, the very nature of such English prevents accurate documentation or placement within a particular area or social group.

It is true that in his *Austral English* Morris played down the slang and colloquial side of the Australian vocabulary but, since his time, there has been increasing interest in informal usage. There are obvious dangers in regarding certain verbal peculiarities as general Australian, but one should not ignore established usage even if it sometimes, by being overstressed, gives the erroneous impression that Australian speech is unusually rich and creative. From our very beginnings such idiom has had an important place, probably because it has always provided what was almost a mark of the established, accepted citizen, a distinguishing 'matey' idiom by which one avoided the label 'stranger' or 'new chum'. The colourful and unusual often has considerable generality and may not necessarily be vulgar or slangy. In the discussion which follows no suggestion of Australia-wide currency can be made, though this may sometimes be true, nor is it asserted that Australians are greatly different from other English speakers in their inventiveness: but something of the character of our idiom can be learnt.

There is certainly a vast store of fairly stable colloquial expressions which usually do not require an explanation of meaning for Australians. It does not take much listening to hear familiar, long-standing, and often slangy expressions like *doing one's block, going* or *feeling crook, better than a kick in the tail, over the fence, stir the possum, on the grouter, home and hosed, punch the bundy, put in the nips* (*hooks,* or *fangs*), *Sydney or the bush,* and *starve the crows,* a list which no Australian would have trouble in adding to.[5] Some of these may be local and some may not

[5] E.g. *Lower than a snake's belly in a rut, bust a gut, put in the boot, get stuck into, back o' Bourke, give it a fly, fair crack of the whip, give it the herbs, have a lash (bash) at, on the knocker, do a line, drag the chain, hit the kick, jump the rattler, on the outer, pull your head in, stiffen the lizards, make one's alley good, where the crows fly backwards, this side of the black stump, Pitt Street grazier.* Some are probably just as English as Australian; for example, *couldn't care less, drives me up the wall.*

One rather surprising thing about this idiom is that at times people think it is quite disgusting, by implication if not directly. Some of our excretory imagery, nearly all of English origin, would lose point if cleaned up; could *farting around, pig's arse, up to shit bonzer, up shitter's ditch* (or *creek*) be rephrased; can another pair express opposites as well as *piss poor* and *shit hot*; is there a better way of saying *I wouldn't piss on him if he was on fire?* No more obscenity is intended here than in the country schoolboy's naming of the *piss bush* and the *piss ant.* On the other hand there is an almost priggish *naïveté* in the way we accept some euphemisms from earlier English or American use, or create our own. Cows *slip* their calves rather than 'miscarry' (English); sheep are often *marked* (American), not 'castrated' or 'cut'; and the ridiculous is reached when sheep are *joined*, 'mated', or the activity of cleaning up fly-struck sheep is called *chasing marguerites.*

be peculiarly Australian,[6] especially in their manner of construction, but many have an Australian identity, a particular understatement, vulgarity, or ironical twist which makes them worth recording. We give the language life in such expressions as *put the hard word on, come the raw prawn, tickle the peter, what do you think this is—bushweek?*, the *two-bob millionaire* who *big notes* himself, drought country *you couldn't flog a flea over*, or the weather so hot it is *a hundred in the waterbag*.

There will always be fresh creations which may or may not appeal; recently I heard a friend talk of *jagging a jackpot*, and a slow racehorse which *couldn't run a message*. Many are obsolescent; it is some time since I heard anyone talk of *packing the tweeds* for being scared, *hell, west and crooked* for all directions, or of a person in whom one has doubts, especially in intelligence, being *only fifteen bob in the pound*. Our change of currency may affect this idiom, admirably as it assesses anything from a fraction to the full quantity. Perhaps we may move to estimates such as *only fifty cents in the dollar*, and subtler variants of expressions like the British English *tuppence short*.

Apart from general expressions like these, Australian idiom has other recognisable features which are often shared with English speakers elsewhere. From British English we have adopted *extra* and *pretty* as intensifiers of extreme and moderate force, and *dead* for an absolute notion. There is plenty of vitality in phrases like *dead cert, broke, sure, spit of, nuts on*, etc., or *extra* or *pretty* with adjectives like *lucky* or *grouse*. *A bit* and *fair* have a moderating function in groups such as *a bit off colour, a bit hard to take, a bit of strife*, or *a bit of a kid*, and in *fair go, fair enough, fair game*, and *fair dinkum*.

Colloquial phrases using vivid but sometimes nonsensical journalistic similes seem more popular with Australians than other English speakers, and usually have local or limited use: *fit as a Mallee bull, looking like a consumptive kangaroo, mean as dishwater, awkward as a pig with a serviette, handy as a cow with a musket, buzzing round like a fly in a strange lavatory*. Others we use have often been imported but are popular and perhaps becoming hackneyed (*slow as a wet week, rough as goats' knees, fat as mud, dressed like a sore toe, silly as a two bob watch, dropped like a hot brick, full as a goog, game as Ned Kelly, like a bat out of hell*), but there are many which are very colourful, sometimes quite old, and

---

[6] The following, for example, are British English, often of great age, and perhaps obsolete: *put the kybosh on, get sweet with, give them gyp, go the whole hog, a lick and a promise, dressed to the nines, pay through the nose, more than you can shake a stick at, on the nod, shake the dust of a place, do the dirty on, buy on the never-never*, 'time payment', *put on the dog*, 'swagger, over-dressed', *long in the tooth*, 'old'.

In a similar way some are American: *get the hang of, hit the roof, losing his marbles, stick your neck out, throw your weight around, knock about*.

very Australian (*miserable as a bandicoot, like a rat up a drainpipe, rough as guts, happy as a pig in shit, sticking like shit to a blanket, game as meat ants, hot as Hay, hell and Booligal, lazy as a cut dog, mad as a cut snake, sitting like a shag on a rock, shearing like snow sliding off a log*).

One could not attempt to list all words which have a colloquial Australian flavour about them without producing a small dictionary, nor could any such list give a clear indication of the general currency, usage level, and age of these words. In my own files there are plenty of newcomers to me which would be well known by certain groups or in different areas, for example *hooch*, 'encourage', *fly*, 'argument', *floater*, 'bad cheque', *grobble*, 'beg', *oozle*, 'steal', *jeep*, 'shopping stroller', *flap*, 'banknotes', *growly*, 'excellent', *gumpy*, 'pimple', *moonlighter*, 'cattle duffer', *diced*, 'upset', *hoozle*, 'urge to movement', *grill*, 'Southern European', *alf*, 'heterosexual Australian male', *ampster*, 'one who looks interested to attract other customers', *plod*, 'worker's time sheet', *bandicoot*, 'cut root vegetables below ground'. It only requires a few examples like these for us to realise that some investigation of regional, social, and occupational usage is needed in Australia. While I have deliberately tried to avoid any nineteenth-century terms,[7] there can be little doubt that further research would show an earlier use of some of these words.

There remains in general use that large body of informal words which appears distinctively Australian. In any sample we find that, as with longer expressions, ideas about their Australianness or modern flavour can often be wrong. As an experiment I drew up a list of words which most people would accept as twentieth-century Australian. A large number of these proved to be possible importations from England,[8] and some were of American origin.[9] After eliminating a few words which were older (for example, *barrack, scungy, demon, monty, dummy, smoodge, spruik,*

[7] This raises the difficulty of drawing any line between the nineteenth and twentieth century in this article. I have tried to keep to this century but allow overlap at times because vocabulary, like all aspects of language, is a continuum, and an early citation does not always indicate later frequency, spread, or special use.

[8] *Backbencher, backyard, bank on*, 'rely', *barney, blow-in*, 'newcomer', *bung*, 'put', *cadge*, 'beg', *chouse*, 'deceive', *click*, 'agree', *cock-eyed, con*, 'trick', *conk out, corker*, 'excellent', *dial*, 'face', *doctor*, 'wind', *drop*, 'give birth to', *found*, 'board and lodging', *gee*, 'urge', *goolie*, 'stone', *grotty*, 'unpleasant', *hazed off*, 'sun dried, of land', *hum*, 'beg', *hump*, 'carry', *jake*, 'all right', *job*, 'punch', *joker*, 'person', *kick*, 'pocket', *kitty*, 'pooled finance', *knock*, 'disparage', *knock off*, 'steal', *kokum*, 'real thing', *lean to, let fly*, 'throw', *lug*, 'carry', *lurk*, 'underhand venture', *mingy*, 'mean', *nobble*, 'to dope', *quilting*, 'beating', *reneg*, 'betray one's word', *scarp*, 'run', *scrounge*, 'steal', *spiel*, 'talk', *sponge*, 'live off someone', *sting*, 'beg', *windbag, whinger*.

[9] *Bull*, 'deception', *boner/booboo*, 'mistake', *clap*, 'crouch suddenly', *kangaroo court*, 'mockery of a court', *malarky*, 'nonsense', *stash, flip*, 'irresponsible person', *jerry to*, 'aware of', *gander*, 'look', *kick*, 'buy for the group, shout', *monniker*, 'name', *scalper*, 'sells tickets for a profit', *bite*, 'beg', *scrub*, 'cancel', *fire trail, high rise* (of buildings).

E

stoush), there remained a list of typical Australian terms,[10] some of which could no doubt be placed in the nineteenth century. These are included (for example, *battler*) because they have undergone some change in sense. While there can be little doubt that Australians have a thriving colloquial English, the evidence suggests that we should not be too eager to claim all 'Australianisms' as our own, and that the currency of many terms is often of surprisingly long standing for what is sometimes called slang.

In their ways of constructing idiomatic expressions Australians are little different from other users of English. Thus we have familiar and often long-established compounds like *hard case, bush telegraph, mulga wire, bush lawyer, awake up, bull dust, brown bomber,* and the host of combinations with words like *stock* or *station*. Rhyming slang is also popularly associated with Australian usage, even if many examples are of English origin. Those which appear Australian often have an affectedness and faddishness about them and little of the appositeness noticed in other naming, for example *uncle Willy,* 'silly', *tos and froms,* 'Poms', *Suzie Wongs,* 'thongs', *eau de cologne,* 'phone', *pie and peas,* 'threes', *meat pies,* 'eyes', *magic wand,* 'blond', *ducks and geese,* 'police'.

It is of interest that imposed on many rhyming groups we have the Australian love of the truncated term,[11] so that *Jack McNab,* 'scab', becomes *Jacky; rubbedy dub,* 'pub', *the rubbedy;* a *fiddley did,* 'quid', a *fid* or *fiddley;* the *onkaparinga,* 'finger', an *onka;* and so on. Apparently the rhyme is not always so attractive,[12] and the shortened idiom is often preferred. Familiar part phrases, which are often meaningless unless one knows the jargon, are frequent enough to be called a linguistic habit of

---

[10] *Bagman,* 'swagman', *battler,* 'hard worker', *blow through,* 'depart', *blue,* 'summons', *blue,* 'fight', *bunny,* 'unlucky one', *cashed up,* 'in funds', *chunder,* 'vomit' *cop,* 'receive in payment', *crook,* 'ill, angry', *dag,* 'amusing person', *drum/oil,* 'information', *galah/nong/gig/dill,* 'fool', *dip out,* 'miss, lose', *dob in,* 'inform on', *donga,* 'bush', *front,* 'appear before', *gig,* 'look', *guk,* 'verbal nonsense', *king hit,* 'sudden knockout blow', *light on,* 'short supply', *lob,* 'arrive', *molly dook,* 'left handed', *nick off,* 'leave', *nip,* 'beg', *racehorse,* 'thinly rolled cigarette or swag', *rubbish,* 'pour scorn on', *scaler,* 'does not pay his fare', *sling,* 'pay up', *sling off,* 'speak disparagingly', *snag,* 'sausage', *spin,* 'experience, a go', *talent,* 'girls', *tats,* 'teeth'. With some there will always be doubts; for example, *bobby dazzler,* 'very good thing or person', *blue,* 'spend', *clap out,* 'collapse', *flake out,* 'pass out', *dicey,* 'chancy', *nick,* 'condition,' *cop,* 'what one receives', even when dictionary entries, or lack of them, could appear to clinch an academic argument.

[11] Nevertheless, people being what they are, we hear *dough,* 'money', extended to *doh-ray-me.*

These are also found in English usage, for example, *butcher's hook,* 'look', becomes *butcher's; on my Tod Sloane,* 'alone', is usually *on my Tod.*

[12] In Maurer, 'Australian Rhyming Argot in the American Underworld', an attempt was made to track down the Australian origins of over 350 American rhyming slang groups. Everything pointed to Australia as the possible source, yet a mere nine could be acknowledged as Australian, and only a few of these had any real currency, namely *Captain Cook,* 'look', *Pat Malone,* 'alone', *mad mick,* 'pick', and *Sydney Harbour,* 'barber'.

Australians, hence *fats/stores* sheep, *built in* cupboard, wool *clip*, *fibro* cement, *hargan* saw, *super* phosphate, one-armed *bandit*, picnic races, *poddy* calf, *New South* Wales, *redback* spider, *mantle* shelf, *venetian* blind, cigarette *makings*, *hard earned* cash, bull *dozer*, *combine* harvester-header, *Coff's* Harbour.

Another feature of our idiom, also noted by S. J. Baker,[13] which seems stronger here than in English elsewhere, is the love of the familiar diminutives. New ones are being introduced all the time—for example, *sandie*, 'beach girl', *pinkie*, 'nursing aide'—and those well established would include *swiftie*, *surfie*, *wharfie*, *cocky*, and many others[14] of varying colour, function, and value. Some take a bit of getting used to, for example, *littlies* and *biggies*, 'children', *folkie*, *dustie*, *pokie*, 'poker machine', *wheelie*, 'car addict', *happies*, 'birthday greetings', *dimmies*, 'dull children', *krautie*, 'V.W. car'. A boyhood friend of mine always said *anothery*, and recently I hear *thisie* and *thatie*, which, with some of the others here, is hardly red-blooded Australian.

In a similar way there is something gaily direct about formations like *garbo*, *compo*, *reffo*, *smoko*, *salvo*, *metho*, *kero*, *milko*, and *oppo*, 'child in an opportunity class'. The *chocko*, 'chocolate soldier' of World War II has given way to the present *nasho*, and nothing could be neater than *Paddo*, 'Paddington, Sydney' or *Thomo's*, 'two-up school', but some are trite and could fade away, for example, *spearo*, 'fisherman', *protto*, 'Protestant', and *promo*, 'T.V. promotion'.

In keeping with the desire for short expression is an Australian tendency to use the definite article in a directive way in phrases like *the Alice, the bitumen, the wet, the dry, the cool, the hot, the makings*, 'tobacco and paper'. We also like to associate a person's name with a thing or place, and so we have *Jacky Howe* singlets, *Gympie* hammers, *Buckley's* chance, *Kidman's* joy, 'golden syrup', a *Darling* shower, 'dust storm', *Barcoo* rot, 'skin disease', and the even less general *Pat Mackie* cap and *Mick Kelly* collar (on beer). Here, as elsewhere, streets, bridges, etc., are named after people, and, like the English, we enjoy some fascinating combinations like *Johnny Wood's Crossing, Tumble-down Dick Hill*, or *Happy Jack Creek*. Most have their origins in the nineteenth-century expansion of the early settlements, and the whole subject of place names is one well worthy of investigation, if only to demonstrate further links with Britain.

Australians like to describe jobs by converting compound verbs into nouns. Quite apart from the general English and journalistic *counter*

---

[13] In McLeod (ed.), *Pattern of Australian Culture*, p. 127.

[14] Also *lippie*, *possie*, *shrewdie*, *Tassie*, *conshie*, *mossie*, *blowie*, 'fly', *bullocky*, *frillie*, 'lizard', *sickie*, *Sallie*, 'Salvation Army', *truckie*, *muddie*, 'crab', *premie*, 'baby'. We share many of these with English usage: *postie*, *footie*, *cossie*, *bikie*, *falsie*, *brickie*, *oldie*, *brekkie*, *quickie*, and *clippie*, 'bus conductress'.

jumper, 'salesman', *kid whacker*, 'teacher', *pen pusher*, and similar agent compounds, we have people in specific jobs, like *picker up*, 'shearing hand', *sucker basher*, 'cuts off new growth under a ringbark', *tailer up*, 'drover at the rear of a mob', *tailer out*, 'sawmill hand', and the obsolete *stick-picker* who gathers branches fallen from ringbarked trees. Most of us are familiar with terms like *cleaner upper*, *doer upper*, *kicker out*, and *dobber in*, but only recently I heard a woman refer to herself as a *knocker-alonger* with someone.

So far an attempt has been made to raise issues related to colloquial idiom, which is admittedly often vulgar or slangy. A great deal of it has respectable, valuable usage, quite apart from its picturesque character, and it is not always easy to separate formal or semi-formal practice from the colloquial, especially when specific occupations or activities are being examined. During the twentieth century Australian English has been subject to such external influences as wars outside its borders, a changing relationship with the rest of the world, and an influx of population from Europe. At the same time there has been internal industrial growth which, especially since World War II, has gone along with an increasing consciousness of the American way of life. During all this the idiom established earlier has flourished, especially in farming, grazing, mining, and other primary activities, with normal semantic changes, new acquisitions, and losses.

Like the English, Australians will borrow words when necessary, but it is not surprising that a huge migration plan has not added significantly to our word stock. What British words we have adopted are probably the result of several influences (television, travel, etc.) and other Europeans have given us little beyond specialised fashion and food names. Of far greater interest is the fact that our modern idiom has been strengthened not so much by Australian inventiveness or variation of existing words, as by joining in the adoption of what can only be called 'world English'. We are as familiar as anyone else with this English, and from one or two newspapers it is easy to select such terms as *activist, aerosol, chopper, credibility gap, dropout, gear, gimmick, happening, hawk, dove, hippy, hooked, kinky, mini, module, pacification, pad, pot, psychedelic, rat race, splashdown, transplant, trendsetter, turbojet*. There is nothing special to any particular English-speaking group in the generation of vocabulary like this, but such journalistic terminology is not our main interest.

One Australian study[15] has attempted to examine the vocabulary of a group of workmen who would not be overly concerned with local slang or professional jargon. My impression was that this English was general English; in the first thousand headwords one has to search hard to find

[15] Schonell, Meddleton, Shaw, B. A., *et al.*, *A Study of the Oral Vocabulary of Adults*.

Twentieth-Century Australian Idiom

Australianisms which would require special explanation. The most difficult were *pushbike, joker, blowfly, bloke, blue,* 'fight', *bullocky, earbasher, homestead, lifesaver, offsider, slip-rails, two-up, weatherboard, weekender*; and the first three or four are as much English as Australian. The Australian elements were obviously there, but the frequency was very slight; of the 500 most commonly used words I could not find any which would puzzle the average Englishman or American.

Much of the added vocabulary in this 'world English' has come from or via American usage, an increasing influence ever since the advent of the motion picture. If anything this tendency could be expected to grow, especially as we now have the wholesale buying or aping of American television shows in addition to an increasing interest in the 'American Way' since the establishment of close ties during and since World War II.[16] Nevertheless, as in the last century and the years before 1940 when Australian comment was generally against the adoption of American idiom, it appears that few Australian words have been displaced. Over a long period we have picked up odd terms like *bubbler, median strip, milk bar, quinella,* and even *kangaroo court*, plus a few colloquialisms mentioned earlier, but there is little risk that *alfalfa, hobo, trunk, ranch, grub, slot machine, stag party* will replace *lucerne, swaggie, boot, station, tucker, poker machine, buck's party*.[17] We do adopt American things or ideas with their names, but much of this is the 'world English' already mentioned.

From the opposite point of view an analysis of new words in current British English can be interesting. A recent book on contemporary English had an index of nearly 900 selected modern words and phrases, and few indeed were not known in Australia.[18] The exceptions would have as restricted a use in Australia as Britain, for example, one or two proper names like *Bailey Bridge* (developed in World War II), an occasional borrowed elegancy such as *origami*, 'Japanese paper folding', or *gazpacho*, a Spanish dish, a few special journalistic combinations (*paraflare, paramine; megabirth, megadeath*), some similar creations of more doubtful stability, such as *monokini, huggee, diseconomics, conurbation,* 'concentration of population around cities', several slangy expressions which have

---

[16] The influence of American is slight compared with English, and in World War II any impact would not have been felt much beyond Sydney, Melbourne, Brisbane, and one or two north Queensland cities. As history shows, the 'invaders' usually make the adjustments while those who are invaded simply pick out what they need or are attracted to at the moment.

[17] Baker, in 'The Influence of American Slang on Australia', points out that some of our 'Americanisms' predate the American (*also ran, boomer, buckjumper, brush,* etc.), but this is not very significant, nor am I inclined to pay too much attention to comments about Australian apathy, resentment of outsiders, or pride in its own terminology. These must be present to some degree, but usually run second to the practical naming needs of a language.

[18] Foster, *The Changing English Language.*

variants everywhere (*big boy burger, chance of a cat in hell,* and *bucking the tiger* for gambling), and one or two well known words Australians have little use for (*au pair girl*). This left a handful of terms, usually familiar to Australians, but for which different words are often used, for example, *anorak,* 'parka', *airgraph,* 'aerogramme', *motorway* (for which our 'highway' is an apology), *cheese flaps,* 'ravioli', *elevenses,* 'morning tea', *teamster,* 'road haulier', *knickers,* 'panties'. There is truly little in general English that would present communication difficulty for Australians or other English speakers, in spite of the fact that we use many English words with a different sense; for example, we mean different things for *house, lay-by, creek, vest, robin, public school,* a list any visitor to England could add to. We come back to the impression of an overall traffic in English vocabulary, to this exchangeable, cosmopolitan commodity, even if affectation and fashion do inevitably interfere with the real advantages of its usefulness. For Australian idiom we should first look at things Australian.

Many of our industries and activities have a practical, meaningful terminology which, in spite of some history in English itself, also provides freshness and individuality to the language. Some of this is almost formal or technical, although it could appear quite informal, while other expressions are clear evidence of a love of a wide range of colloquialisms. This inevitably leads to what looks like synonymy, and requires some investigation to see if it is a quick-changing, happy-go-lucky system, an indicator of subtle differences of sense, or the result of different terminologies developing in different areas, especially in those industries which are carried out in places having little contact with each other.

An opal glossary[19] yields terms, several with English origins, which do appear almost synonymous; for example, *angel stone/ steel band/ iron band/ hard band/ bandstone*; *fault/slide*; *front/port,* 'side of a slide'; *shin cracker/grey billy/bully*; *specking/lousing/noodling*; *schnide/sinter/potch*. This work has not been fully field-tested, but it appears reasonably certain that, apart from casual substitution (*steel* or *iron* band), various forms could exist according to geographical area, precise differences in application, or gradual obsolescence of one form for another.

In a pilot study of the same trends noted on shearing terms, a questionnaire survey is being carried out among shearing contractors scattered through New South Wales. The results will be reported very soon and it seems likely that a fuller investigation will show an interesting pattern. The quasi-synonyms are there (*shedhand/rouseabout/bluetongue/loppy*; *wig/wigging/tops/topknot*; *catch/bell-sheep/snob/cobbler*), but research to this moment demonstrates a generality of use, probably the result of

[19] At present being compiled by the author. A much larger work on gold-mining, compiled by the Australian Language Research Centre, shows the same tendency.

the greater centralising and uniformity which has taken place because of union activity and easier transport and communications. There are few isolated pockets and, when one has put the ephemeral slang terms aside (for example, *brownie gorger, leatherneck, lizard, seagull, stealbeak*, all meaning 'shedhand'), the two or three terms remaining appear difficult to identify positively with particular areas or definite levels of usage. This may once have been possible, but the earlier nomadic life of shearers would make it unlikely. At present the luxury (or wastefulness) of synonymous informal terms exists, and the more formal expressions are usually known wherever the work is carried out.

At the moment it appears certain that in most Australian activities any differences in naming are not so great that communication is threatened. Future trends in specific naming might be towards greater uniformity as a result of single administration, union activities, take-overs, and the like, but profitable investigations can be carried out on the colloquial idiom of many industries. Some glossaries[20] are being prepared on several Australian occupations and these should provide information about special function, level of usage, synonymy, and perhaps area of use of the terms. There is certainly a wide field awaiting investigation, and much can be added to what we already know by detailed research of the established terms of various activities, only one or two of which can be touched on here.

There must be a great number of distinctive functional expressions relating to the land, many with quite a history. Some appear very informal, such as *mickey*, 'young bull', *jerker*, 'boundary rider', *long paddock*, 'stock route', *buckrunner*, 'one who rounds up wild horses', *stargazer*, 'horse which stumbles frequently', and *Jillaroo*, 'girl *jackaroo*', but there are plenty of specialised terms, for example, *rotational grazing* as against *set stocking* (for worm control), *soiled* properties, 'good soil cover', *dirty* properties, 'overgrown', *strawberry burn*, 'incomplete burning off', *homestrip*, 'landing strip', *table drain, mulesing operations*, 'fly prevention', *dropping flock*, 'ewes in lamb', *sheep vanners*, 'very young cattle', *the drop*, 'lamb yield'. I have heard of gates described as *pushover* and *cocky's gap*, and of fences with wonderful names like *post and rail* (English), *cockatoo, chock and log*, each specific in its use. Machinery is appropriately named if we are to judge by the *scuffler* (from the English *scuffle*, a type of cultivator), the *forest devil*, 'stump remover', and the *smooger* (which smoothes down earthen banks).

Research on the vocabulary of the dried fruits industry is being conducted, and a mixture of original and adapted uses of words will result, to add to such specialised and general terms as *stays, dip tins, spur*

[20] The Australian Language Research Centre, University of Sydney, is also accumulating informant and reader material on general Australian usage.

pruning, rod pruning, spreader jack, snatching, 'cutting currants', *slasher,* 'topping knife', *silt box,* 'section to keep silt out of drain', *silly plough* (for burrowing close to vines), *liner* (used in cleaning process), *wrap on, tie on, roll on, riddle* (special use of this English word for a sieve), *rack shaker, knifing,* 'weeding below the surface', *cut out,* 'get rid of unwanted wood', *blockie,* 'person who works a block', *green manure,* 'cover crop which is turned in', *gordo,* 'variety of large muscatel', *fruit,* 'measurement of standard fruit tin, about 7½ lbs', *frost pot,* 'crude oil burner', *dip,* 'emulsified oil in solution to remove bloom and crack the grape', *delver,* 'apparatus to cut a clear drain', *delve,* 'clear silt', *crown,* 'grade or quality of fruit, 1 to 6', *traying*.

Communication is well catered for in the less formal idiom of many activities, but the movements are not all the same. The turf provides words with plenty of colour about them when we consider such things as *goers, good things, hoops, mudlarks, ring-ins, groundlarks,* and *trots* which can be good or bad. This, and Australia's own game of *swy* or *two-up* (*toss, kip, spin, micks, keep nit*—English *nix, cockatoo, get set*), must be a rich source for vocabulary investigation. In contrast, the young Australians' sport of surfboarding has usually been content to adopt a great deal of established American terminology, perhaps a sign of the way we are heading in language. Someone may soon document *hand boarding, hanging five, spinner, soup, skeg, shooting the tube, quasimoto, popouts, pearling, wipe out, walk or trim the board, kamikaze, hotdogging, hodad, head dip, hang ten, gremmie, goofy foot, coffin,* and the many other terms associated with this sport. Perhaps it is time that a study was also made of the sources (almost certainly English) of the idiom of younger Australians and their play. As an example, the game of marbles has given *knuckledown, fudging,* and the cry of *mully grubs* to general usage, quite apart from its special references to *stinkies, kellies, tors,* and *connies*. In all their other activities we must not forget those marvellous names for cicadas such as *floury miller, black prince, lamplighter, green Monday,* and *double drummer*.

Quite apart from special word lists which are so often misnamed as a kind of slang instead of a semi-technical useful idiom, Australian vocabulary can also satisfy the requests of many scholars[21] that there should be more concern about useful everyday naming which is distinctively Australian. There is certainly enough 'Australian' usage of the English word stock to make a dictionary for this country. A glance through newspapers and journals and attention to the conversation and comments of colleagues yielded a sample of what could be assembled from a thorough study of everyday English. The variety provided by any such random sampling is usually one of special Australian application, if not always of Australian

[21] E.g. Arthur Delbridge's review, *Australian Literary Studies*, Vol. 2, No. 4, 1966, pp. 300-4; Bernard, 'The Need for a Dictionary of Australian English'.

origin. Within the special area of meaning we should appreciate exact senses, for example a group like *tank*, 'dam', *lagoon, billabong, gilgai, swamp*, each of which refers to non-flowing water in a special way. Many names are known everywhere or have quite a history (*paddock, damper, larrikin, bush, yabbie, property, furphy, wowser, station, gibber, kelpie, outback, swag, black tracker*, and jobs like *sleeper cutting, stump grubbing, brushing, dogging, docking*), often with a flavour of the country about them.

We must not make the mistake of restricting Australianisms to the bush. Some of our words are world terms without any echoes of Waltzing Matilda (*Siroset, Sydney silkie, jindivik, Australian crawl, wobble board*), and others are familiar general Australian, for example, *award wage, total wage, basic wage, grouper, unity ticket, brick veneer, week-ender, beef roads, battle-axe block, stratum title, stubby, traymobile, thongs, shark meshing, pedal wireless, white-ant* (verb), *sleep-out, taxi-truck, home-unit, metal roads, fettler, flying doctor, polocrosse, stock and station agent, stump-jump plough, flow-on, hot mix* (road sealer), *lifesaver, bombora*, and *pie* (commercial sense of collusion on prices).

War is one phenomenon which affects the idiom of any country, and from selected lists which have appeared[22] it is clear that such Australian words are little different in their pattern from other English. We can ignore one group, which seems to be restricted essentially to military use, awaiting revival in another war, or as Turner[23] said, 'to flutter into life at reunions'. A surprising thing about the remainder is that some have had a long history in colloquial usage and many have a place well clear of services slang. World War I 'Australianisms' from earlier American (and Australian) use are *banjo*, 'shovel', *bonzer, bull*, 'trivial or boastful talk', *bite*, 'borrow', and from England we have *binge*, 'drunken spree', *bird*, 'girl', *scrounge*, the sailor's *burgoo* or *bergoo*, 'porridge', *beetle around, snavvle, suck-in, wangle*, and probably *cobber, hum*, 'cadge', and others where documentation is inadequate for guaranteeing one special source. Popular Australian colloquialisms which emerged or were revived in World War I include *bludge*, 'loaf', *joey*, 'military policeman', *stonker*, 'baffle', *string-on*, 'deceive', and perhaps several out of *axle-grease*, 'butter', *babbling brook*, 'cook', *bot*, 'cadge', *breeze-up*, 'fear', *furphy*, 'rumour', *rat*, 'to search', *slushy, stiff*, 'unlucky', *ziff*, 'short beard'. Of passing interest are the journalistic non-generalised slangy expressions relating to army life. Downing provides many which illustrate well the irony and vitality of these, but some could have spread from other allied forces, for example, *Anzac button*, 'nail', *body snatching*, 'raiding party', *branding paddock*, 'parade

[22] Downing, *Digger Dialects*; Mitchell, 'Fighting Words', and 'A Glossary of War-Words'.
[23] Turner, *The English Language in Australia and New Zealand*, p. 22.

ground', *bumbrusher*, 'batman', *christen the squirt*, 'bayonet a man', *comforts fund*, 'shells', *feed bag*, 'gas mask', *grappling irons*, 'spurs', *meat hook*, 'arm', *nail scissors*, 'general's insignia', *parakeet*, 'staff officer', *rainbow*, 'one who joined up after the armistice, that is, after the storm', *reinstoushments*, 'reinforcements', *smudged*, 'blown to bits'.

World War II has provided similar colourful terms. Some of these did not survive because they had little outside reference, hence, *dingo*, 'reconnaissance vehicle', *goonskins* or *giggle suits*, 'working dress', *emu*, 'pick up small pieces of rubbish', *milk run*, 'long aerial reconnaissance', *daisy cutter*, 'anti-personnel bomb', and the *Lady Blamey*, 'bottle with the neck removed to make a drinking vessel'. We probably owe to Australian servicemen many long-lasting colloquialisms, such as *drongo*, 'indolent foolish person, once an RAAF recruit', *troppo*, 'going crazy', *galah*, 'fool', *shoot through*, 'depart quickly', *spine bash*, 'to loaf', *earbash*, *geek*, 'look', *no hoper*, *good guts*, 'information', and well known phrases like *on the nose*, 'no good', *get jack of*, 'fed up', *wouldn't it, pull your head in, come the raw prawn, break it down*. Australians were always ready to adopt terms from elsewhere, such as *half-inch*, 'pinch or steal' from Britain, and *hoojah*, 'person with some self-esteem', *doover*, 'thing, device, concoction of any sort', from India via Britain.

Some of the above may have wider use than Australian, but they illustrate that wartime idiom can be a creative force for colloquial language. It is also true that war often brings to life words and expressions which previously had a more restricted use. This could be tested by surveying the slang of our Vietnam forces to determine the proportion of terms which had earlier currency compared with American-Australian usages like *hoochie*, 'waterproof shelter over a slit trench', *charlie*, 'a Vietcong', *lazy dog*, 'anti-personnel bomb', and *sniffer*, 'a device to detect an unseen nearby enemy'.

In the attempt so far to illustrate the variety of twentieth-century Australian English the meaning of terms has frequently been given. This might appear unnecessary to many people, while others would find the unexplained terms puzzling, and it would indeed be a rare Australian who was familiar with all the expressions used as examples in this article. This makes necessary one or two observations on obsolescence, multiple meaning, and the distribution of Australian vocabulary.

Obsolescence is normal, but is even more noticeable in an idiom like Australian which is not only very colloquial, but also has seen a revolution in its way of life since colonial days. One expected loss is of those terms for things long gone, except in the literature, yet the fact that many are familiar to Australians says something for their tenacity. The special use has gone of *ticket of leave, cabbage tree hat, wide awake* (hat), *prince alberts* or *toe rags, bell topper, pea jacket, free selector, currency lad, emancipist, exclusionist, expiree, transportee, remittance man* (or *prodigal*), many of which would have been 'transported' English. Moving into the twentieth century, we can find a brief currency for a few of the above terms and a simple explanation for loss. Probably social changes explain the way the *squatter* now prefers to be called a *grazier* or *pastoralist,* and the fact that felons have long ceased to be *scragged, stretched, topped,* or *turned off.* The outback drinking place will never again be a *grog shanty,* where *lambing down* of thirsty shearers takes place, and no one wants a revival of the need for *shin plasters,* 'credit slips', *wire faking,* or other terms of depression years. Such food references as *saddle pouch tucker, salt junk, slippery bob,* and *pan jam* are well left to history, as is tea called *Jack the painter* (from its staining) and *post and rail.* The taboo of 'colonial' probably accelerated the loss of this qualifier in *colonial oath, colonial shout, colonial tweed, colonial experience fellows,* which is something of a pity. The *chuffer* became obsolete as soon as this slow stump-burning device was superseded, although I remember the word in World War II for a contraption used to 'boil the billy'. Some terms hang on grimly with the older generation, but I imagine the days are numbered of *dodger*, 'bread', *Johnny cakes, corduroy roads* (American and British also), *the push, slip-rails, wattle and daub* (huts), and *slush lamps.* How long will it be before people familiar with the letters T.A.B. do not know what S.P. stands for, and others begin to ask the meaning of *chip heater, six o'clock swill,* or *dog box carriage*?

Also in the process of obsolescence is a vast number of more slangy terms (many with their origins in eighteenth- and nineteenth-century English) which still have some limited use. Could *bonzer, bosker,* and *cobber* (which *mate* has never replaced) have suffered from overuse by overdone or non-Australians? Other imminent or actual losses which seem regrettable to me are *guiver,* 'talk', *pull foot,* 'hurry', *prad,* 'horse', *chop,* 'criticise', *cronk,* 'unfit', *pelter,* 'a rage', *square,* 'sober', *swallow bobby,* 'make a false statement to avoid customs duty', not forgetting the *quocker-dodger,* 'politician who does as told by his political bosses, but who is still with us as a respectable *party man*'.

The losses above have generally occurred where the needs of slang demanded a number of synonyms each with a possibly very short life. Australians have always been attached to such groupings, whether English, American, or Australian in origin. For example, there always have been plenty of words for policeman (*Charley, crusher, trap, walloper, snaffle man, John, flat, cop, dee, demon,* etc.), and gaol (*chokey, stir, quod, cooler, clink, jug, peter,* etc.), with varying duration and survival. Money in general has a big turnover in naming (*splosh, sugar, boodle, spondulicks, bunch, dough, tin, brass, chips, rhino, shiner, posh, hoot*) and the recent currency adjustment must result in continuing loss of *browns, treys, zacks, deenahs, hogs, bobs, florins, half bulls, quids, rags, smackers, plasters, spins, bricks, monkeys, ponies,* and *boxers,* to saying nothing of the *dollar* which was five shillings not so long ago. We may *chuck, dice, hoik, hoy, hoist,* or *ding* instead of 'throw', and, like most English speakers, we have a number of current and past slang for a girl (*sort, sheila, titter, tabby, cliner, crow, bag, bird*), a fool (*dill, dope, dud, drongo, twit, twerp, droob, nit, nong*), and drunk (*inked, tight, shickered, slewed, squiffy, stung, molo, pissed, spliced*). To suggest complete obsolescence or a certain source for any of these short-lived, often localised terms would be foolish indeed. This raises the more interesting topic of currency of synonymous words in general Australian.

Homogeneity may apply to other aspects of Australian English, but in vocabulary it is not so definite. No scientific work has been done on this, and there is no suggestion of great interference with communication, but it is quite obvious that special naming does exist in different places. Most of us know that a *schooner, middy, pony, glass,* or even *pint* of beer is not the same all over Australia, a *sandwich* is different in Sydney and Brisbane, and, as Turner points out,[24] words like *tissue* and *evening* are different things in different places. A *double* on a bicycle (or is it *grid, pushbike, treadle,* or just plain *bike*?) is a *dink* in Melbourne and a *donkey* in some other places. We should investigate the areas of use of such duplications as *lolly/iceblock, downpipe/spouting, morning sticks/ kindling, gumboots/wellingtons, plant/outfit, shower sandals/thongs, drop scone/pikelet, lumper/wharfie, bingle/prang, shanghai/catapult/ging, topcoat/overcoat, unit/flat, washer/facecloth, port/suitcase, recess/playtime, pavement/footpath/nature strip, waistcoat/vest.*[25] These differences may be geographical or social, or a blend of the two, with a strong influence of fad and fashions, but it is a possible investigation of current vocabulary.[26] Some clear boundaries may be definable, but, as with most colloquial

[24] Turner, op. cit., p. 165.
[25] *Rock melon/cantaloup, pusher/stroller, elastic bands/rubber bands/laquer bands, guernsey/jumper/sweater, dixy/dandy/bucket* (of ice cream), *globe/bulb, lolly/sweet, sweets/pudding/dessert, crackers/fireworks, mackintosh/raincoat, hall/ passage, bathing/swimming* (costume), *jacket/coat, theatre/cinema, mudguard/fender, sitting/lounge/living* (room), *kookaburra/jackass, sealed/bitumen* (road), (laundry) *tubs/sinks, shades/blinds, curtains/drapes, lorry/truck,* (lemon) *butter/cheese,* (peanut) *butter/paste,* (potato) *flakes/chips/crisps, tumbler/glass, vest/singlet, polywogs/ tadpoles, white/silverskin* (onions), *chamferboard/weatherboard, sandshoes/sneakers/ tennis shoes/runners, quilt/eiderdown/coverlet/bedspread, tank/dam, hairpin/bobby pin,* (peanut) *butter/spread.*
[26] In a recent survey (not yet published) of distribution of some terms used by shearers in N.S.W., two conclusions were possible. First, a great deal of slang and colloquialism has extremely limited use, which emphasises the warnings raised early in this article against being too eager to accept slangy attractive expressions as general Australian practice. Second, it would be very difficult to draw firm isoglosses distinguishing areas according to terms used, but there are vocabulary patterns which illustrate some differences between regions, even if these overlap to some extent.

English, there may also be a great deal of synonymy.

One way in which Australian terms (even if once fresh applications of English or American) are kept alive is by further figurative extension. Some of this is slangy and unnecessary; I have heard of a *gibber* of ice, a *prang* in an examination, *percolating* of a car engine, and even a *mob* of sausages. A little more acceptable is the *waddy* for any stick, a *walkabout* for any journey, and the person who drinks little but eats well of the counter-lunch referred to as a *grassy* or *grasshopper*. Just as we reapplied hundreds of English words, like *paddock, creek, dinkum, scrub*, in the nineteenth century, so we are now making good extended use of earlier colloquial Australian. A *concertina*, a slang term for a wrinkly sheep, is now also a side of lamb in some places, a *gun* may be an expert at anything from shearing to T.V. news reading or acting, and *shandigaffs*, 'mixtures' of hay or sheep, join shandy drinks. We now hump other things than the *bluey* and become metaphorically *ropeable*, we *bullock* when working hard at anything, *shepherding* need not refer to sheep, a *cockatoo* is not only a bird, a *ring-in* a horse, or a *boomerang* simply an Aboriginal weapon, and *fossicking* or *petering out* will take place without gold-mining being involved. The nineteenth-century *gee*, 'to urge', has given us *geeman*, 'one whose job it is to encourage patronage, particularly at travelling shows', *peacocking* (once referring to squatters selecting the best land by using dummies) now has the general sense of 'picking the eyes out of'. We have revived *demon*, a nineteenth-century word for trooper, to name a motor cycle policeman, and *retread*, an Americanism for a soldier enlisting a second time, is used in Australia for the retired teacher who returns to his old work. *Dinkum* is no longer a work load but an asseveration, and the *donga*, once a type of depression in sandy country, now sometimes describes the bush in a sense of 'out back'. A *fizz-gig* was a type of fishing spear which transferred to police informer, and to-day survives in the verb *fizz*, to inform on. A *rumper* in the poultry trade is now a domestic fowl with a peculiar feather growth from lack of a tail-bone, but it was earlier a possum or koala whose backside fur had been worn away, thus damaging the pelt. These are just a few examples of extension of meaning, a normal process in any established vocabulary. Sometimes there is a change in status of the word as well; *fair cow*, a common expression in Australia, has lost any connotation of prostitute, the *half-axe*, once a larrikin, is an adolescent where the word does occur, a *lurk* is any profitable activity, and not necessarily criminal, as it once was, and to *shelf* formerly had a sense of ruin rather than its present use of *dob in* or report for some misdemeanour.

Going along with changes like the above is the retention of various senses for informal terms, thus necessitating attention to context before the meaning is clear; for example, *lift* has long had the sense of steal, but it also means to transport or move cattle, goods, etc., from one place to another. The *ringer*, often thought of as the top shearer, is also a stockman who keeps a mob together, and both would be familiar with many of the meanings of *run*, such as a land holding, shift of work, special area of a property, a special group of animals. Our common word *spider* has additional senses of a harness web holding up the trace chains of a team, a spike which holds a candle for an opal gouger, a light racing sulky with very long shafts, and a flavoured soda drink in which a spoonful of ice cream is stirred.

The picture of twentieth-century Australian vocabulary emerging from the study of a large selection of Australianisms such as this tempts one to the general conclusion that our English is not really an unusual linguistic phenomenon and is little different in form from any other type, if we exclude the more slangy usage and the general identifying idiom attached to certain Australian occupations. One fact already noted, and requiring more investigation, is that English speaking people in a new and distant environment will change or re-apply the English words they have in common with the homeland. The sense of many of our 'English' words has shifted, however slightly, to provide a special Australian use. In a brief article on the need for an Australian dictionary, J. R. Bernard has mentioned the different Australian meaning of everyday terms like *house, cottage, yard, football, stove, paddock, cuff*;[27] he points out that many of our fish are not even of the same genus as those of the same name in the *Oxford English Dictionary*, and that some of the birds, plants, and trees in Australia bear English names but are not quite the same.

Thus it must be perfectly clear that Australian vocabulary, along with its other linguistic features, has long since reached a stage where it has an Australian character, and not only in colloquial idiom. It owes a great deal to others but, like them and the mother tongue itself, has used and adapted what is not its own to express its own identity and its own needs. There has been no hesitation about keeping what others have cast aside (*spell* for a rest has long been obsolete in English), changing sense where necessary, and allowing easy transfer from one level of usage to another. The latter has contributed to our reputation for having a colourful, at times vulgar or slangy idiom, when it is often only general Australian and not so slangy in its context. This decision on status is only one of many which face the Australian lexicographer.

It is quite obvious that we are quick to use attractive lively alternatives for existing words and retain them for a very long time; this in turn leads to considerable synonymy at the informal level, and something worth analysing in terms of obsolescence, area of use, and other semantic

[27] Bernard, 'The Need for a Dictionary of Australian English'.

features. There is also a need for general study of the distribution of Australian terms, so that words appearing in any future list can be labelled more accurately, have restricted or obsolescent use recorded, and have proper credit given to the inventiveness[28] of Australians when it comes to naming or using the names of others. With less slangy terms we must have studies on historical principles, beginning with essentially Australian occupations, so that growth, change, and spread, can be properly documented.

A final point worth raising is on attitude to Australian usage. There is plenty to say about the jargon of the 'you beaut, cobber' type of patriot, and some comment on the makeshift nature of our idiom, but there is no need to get our tails between our legs. The best conclusion one can make is to repeat what A. G. Mitchell[29] said some time ago about English in the colonies taking on a national form and colouring. Each national form is shaped by geographical, social, and historical forces, and each within its own environment is good and useful. Australian English is still English but is characteristically Australian; it has shown resource and a feeling for vigorous speech in inventing, borrowing, or adapting words to describe a new environment and its customs, attitudes, and occupations.

---

[28] For testimony of this one has only to recall some of the thousands of suggestions for the name of our new currency. These, in all their colour, wit, triteness, and horror, are discussed in Eagleson, 'Naming a Currency: A Study of Contemporary Methods of Word Creation'.

[29] Mitchell, 'Australian English'.

REFERENCES CITED

Ackroyd, J., 'Lingo-Jingo', *Southerly*, Vol. 7, 1946, pp. 97-103.
Baker, S. J., 'The Influence of American Slang on Australia', *American Speech*, Vol. 18, No. 4, 1943, pp. 253-6.
——, 'Language', in A. L. McLeod (ed.), *The Pattern of Australian Culture*, Ithaca, N.Y., 1963.
Bernard, J. R. L-B., 'The Need for a Dictionary of Australian English', *Southerly*, Vol. 22, 1962, pp. 92-100.
Downing, W. H., *Digger Dialects*, Melbourne, 1919.
Eagleson, R. D., 'Naming a Currency: A Study of Contemporary Methods of Word Creation', *Southerly*, Vol. 23, 1963, pp. 264-70.
Foster, B., *The Changing English Language*, London and New York, 1968.
Maurer, D. W., ' "Australian" Rhyming Argot in the American Underworld', *American Speech*, Vol. 19, No. 3, 1944, pp. 183-95.
Mitchell, A. G., 'Australian English', *Australian Quarterly*, Vol. 23, No. 1, 1951. pp. 9-17.
——, 'Fighting Words', *Salt*, 22 December 1941, pp. 34-6.
——, 'A Glossary of War-Words', *Southerly*, Vol. 3, No. 1, 1942, pp. 11-16.
Morris, E. E., *Austral English, A Dictionary of Australasian Words, Phrases and Usages*, London, 1898.
Ramson, W. S., *Australian English. An Historical Study of the Vocabulary, 1788-1898*, Canberra, 1966.
Schonell, F. J., Meddleton, I. C., Shaw, B. A., et al., *A Study of the Oral Vocabulary of Adults: An Investigation into the Speech Vocabulary of the Australian Worker*, Brisbane, 1956.
Turner, G. W., *The English Language in Australia and New Zealand*, London, 1966.

ENGLISH AS IT IS SPOKEN IN NEW ZEALAND

The white population of the islands of New Zealand consists of about a million and a half people, mostly of English or Scottish descent, if not themselves born in Britain. Systematic settlement began only a century ago; and the ties with 'Home', as 'The Old Country' is still called (it is worth noting that this use of the word is now less common in Australia) are stronger than in any other British Dominion: London is the mecca of most New Zealanders. They believe that they speak the King's English, while they disapprovingly describe their nearest neighbours as speaking 'Australian', or 'with an Australian accent'—a view that Australians themselves sometimes confirm by asserting that New Zealanders, compared with them, speak '100 per cent English'.

Now it is true that there has been a quicker growth of national consciousness in Australia, and that Australian speech and idiom have a quality and character of their own; certain features of 'Austral' English have been recognised for some time, and glossaries of Australian usage have been published.[1] But it has not usually been recognised that the language of the New Zealanders has its own distinctive characteristics, its own blend of idioms and usages. And there has been little attempt to give a picture of English as it is spoken (and written) in New Zealand:[2] partly because any such survey involves a form of self-criticism which it is especially difficult for a native of a small and comparatively isolated community to undertake, lacking as he does adequate standards of comparison; partly because few visitors, even when qualified for such a study, stay long enough to make it. The following account does not pretend to be in any way complete or definitive. For one thing, the influence of Australian

---

[1] E.g. E. E. Morris, *Austral English*.

[2] Partridge, in *A Dictionary of Slang and Unconventional Usage*, gives due attention to Australian and New Zealand slang, though he often fails to indicate points at which they coincide. The *O.E.D.* (especially the Supplement) records a number of New Zealand words and usages.

Since this article was first written, Baker's *New Zealand Slang* has appeared. Its title indicates its limitations, and it contains certain misconceptions, some of them due to the author's failure to recognise adoptions from American speech. It is chiefly valuable for its collection of early usages, now for the most part obsolete.

usage is so considerable that it is probably to be reckoned with even in cases where it is not specifically mentioned. For another, New Zealand is rich in slang, and like most slang it is ephemeral and sometimes esoteric. Rather, the intention is to suggest the general pattern and texture of this language, to separate some of the strands of which it is woven, and to indicate some of the modifications which so-called Standard British English has undergone in the dominion furthest removed from Britain.

PRONUNCIATION

Pronunciation is in some ways the aspect of New Zealand English which can be dealt with most easily, as there are several features which are quite marked, and shared by the majority of speakers. Chief among these are:

(1) The treatment of Standard English [ɑː], as in *art, hard, large, master, task, 'Varsity*. In all such words the vowel is given a much flatter sound than in Standard British English; it closely resembles the vowel found in the same positions in some New England speech, and can best be transcribed as [aː]. What Grandgent says of New England applies to New Zealand: 'Our grass really lies between the *grahs* of a British lawn and the *grass* of the boundless prairies'.[3] Words in which the vowel is followed in the spelling by *r* and a consonant are particularly liable to receive this pronunciation (*r* in such words is generally 'silent', as in Southern England, except where Scottish influence is felt). In many other cases in which Standard (Southern) British English has [ɑː], New Zealand often has a short [æ], as in *dance, path*, etc.; and this value is common in final syllables of such words as *telegraph, contrast*.[4] Fluctuations in the pronunciation of this vowel seem to follow no precise pattern.

(2) The treatment of the Standard English diphthong [aʊ]. One of the ways by which a New Zealander may most easily be recognised is his pronunciation of *cow*. The sound usually heard in such words is often described as nasalised, but it is due to the habit of speaking through the teeth rather than to speaking through the nose (and the conditions producing the sound described in (1) are similar): the first component of the sound is thus closer to [æ] than to [a], and the diphthong can best be represented by [æʊ]. It will be noticed that again there is a parallel with American speech: the same elements have been recognised in the pronunciation of this diphthong in New England dialect and in Southern

---

[3] Quoted in Mencken, *The American Language*, p. 336. Cf. Krapp, *English Language in America*, Vol. II, p. 11; and Hanley, 'Observations on the Broad A'.

[4] In Australia the distinction is apparently between *-ance* words, in which any approach to an [aː] sound would be scorned as 'Oxford English', and other words, in which Standard British English [aː], or an approximation thereto, is usually kept.

American.[5] In some cases—especially in positions of secondary stress—the sound heard is even more obscure, becoming something like [ɛə] in such word groups as *petered out, five thousand pounds*.

(3) The treatment of Standard British English [uː], as in *do, to, move, school, food*. This sound is sometimes diphthongised to [juː], especially in positions of stress. When the diphthong [uə] occurs in such words as *sure, poor*, there is a marked tendency to lengthen the first element, giving [ʃuːə], [puːə]. This feature (which of course is not confined to New Zealand) is not so marked as (1) and (2). But all three developments seem to be results of a similar physical cause. The lips are not fully rounded, but tend to remain flat, and the sounds are partly emitted through the teeth. Various physical or psychological factors may account for this tendency. Perhaps clenched teeth are a concomitant of the pioneering spirit! Or it might be argued that the enunciation has been developed by people accustomed to speak with a pipe or cigarette between their lips. But these explanations are as conjectural as they are incomplete.

(4) A noticeable feature is the pronunciation of final *-y* or *-ey*, in such words as *very, fifty, Godley*, as [iː]. Baker's suggestion[6] that this is 'occasioned very largely by native place-names' ending in *-e, -i*, is not convincing.

(5) The spelling *wh-*, as in *when, wheat, which, while*, usually represents breathed [ʍ]. This speech habit is equally strong in all parts of the country, for both stressed and unstressed positions, in anything that approaches 'careful' pronunciation. The presence of a large Scottish element in the original community, especially in the Otago district of the South Island, may have assisted in its growth. All official radio announcers use it, and are encouraged to do so. The habit is confirmed by the tendency, natural in a country where the tradition of Standard British English is not strong, to pronounce words as they are spelt.

Spelling-pronunciations, in fact, flourish in the dominion—in proper names like *Cowper* or *Trentham* [kæupə], [trɛnθm], as well as in words in which there is variation elsewhere, like *conduit* ([kɔndjuːt], which is general in New Zealand; *been* is always [biːn], never [bɪn]) and *housewifery* [hæuswaɪfəri]. The tendency, illustrated in this last word, to distribute stress as evenly as possible over a series of syllables, is one for which parallels can be found more often in American than in Southern British speech. Several words the New Zealanders have insisted on pronouncing in their own way: *supplejack* is always [suːpl̩dʒæk], and *basic* [bæsɪk] (generalised from the phrase '*basic* [bæsɪk] *slag*'). *Pérsimmon* is a return to, if not a survival of, the usual seventeenth-century pronunciation.

[5] Cf. Krapp, *English Language in America*, p. 192.
[6] *New Zealand Slang*, p. 101.

New Zealanders, like Australians, are often charged with having a cockney accent, but the phrase is not an accurate description of characteristic New Zealand speech: it covers only such cases as the substitution of a sound resembling [aɪ] for [eɪ] in words like *made, major,* and even in these cases the effect is certainly not that of stage cockney. 'Nasalisation' occurs sometimes, but is not very marked. More important, if more intangible, is the difference in intonation that comparison with the speech of Englishmen (and even more, Englishwomen) reveals. One's general impression is that New Zealand speech is more monotonous in its rhythmic pattern than Standard British English, and that the New Zealand voice is generally lower-pitched than the English voice. In short, the resemblance is to *vox Americana* rather than to *vox Anglicana*.[7]

Slight regional differences exist, but have not yet been analysed in detail. A modified form of Scots is widely heard in the province of Otago, originally a Presbyterian settlement; the 'rolled' *r* is most frequent there. Canterbury was originally an Anglican settlement, and it is said that Standard British English can be heard there more easily than elsewhere (some private schools near Christchurch have claimed to teach more 'precise' English than that used in state schools); but typically New Zealand vowels are just as common there as in any other province. In a few other areas immigrants from Europe have left slight traces. Some of the older inhabitants of Dannevirke[8] and the surrounding country—a farming district in the lower half of the North Island, settled by Danes in the last century—could, till recently at least, be detected by a 'foreign' accent. In North Auckland there is a small area between Waiwera and Warkworth which was settled by Austrians, Bavarians, and Bohemians. Here the bilingual stage has already been passed, and the only trace of a foreign influence in the speech of the younger generation is the pronunciation of [dʒ] as [tʃ]; *Jack* and *John* are always [tʃæk] and [tʃɔn]. But such phenomena as these can be observed on a larger scale in other countries, and have only an incidental interest here. The general uniformity of speech from area to area and from class to class reflects the cultural and social homogeneity of the young nation; indeed, it is misleading to talk of classes in a society in which almost all education is in the hands of the state, and in which inequalities of wealth have been steadily reduced. At the same time, isolation from other English speaking countries has doubtless been partly responsible for the development of such phonetic peculiarities as those noted above.

---

[7] It is worth noting that a New Zealand or Australian accent often seems more acceptable to an American audience than a Standard British English accent.

[8] Another place-name of Scandinavian origin, greatly disguised, is *Snufflenose,* a corruption of *Snefjellnes.*

VOCABULARY AND USAGE

New Zealand is primarily a pastoral and agricultural country; hence it is natural that a large part of the New Zealander's vocabulary should be connected with the land. Before there could be crops or pasture the land had to be cleared of *bush*—a word denoting any sizeable growth of trees or fern. The word *bush* was presumably adopted from North America, but it is now used much more widely in New Zealand than in this country. It implies all that was formerly meant by the American 'backwoods'; *to go into the bush* is to go into the wild, uncultivated parts of the country; so to be *bushed* is to be lost—a sense with which the American use ('tired, worn out') is obviously connected. *Bush lawyer* is the name for a troublesome trailing bramble. The *bush hawk, bush warbler,* and *bush wren* are various native birds. *Bush sickness* is a disease afflicting cattle. And *bush fighting* was borrowed from America to describe the skirmishes of the Maori wars.

As the bush was cut down, the timber trade grew up; and it has supplied a wide variety of occupational terms. Thus, a *bush skiddy* is a man who works on the cleared tracks which carry logs to the mill, where it is handled by a *break-down man* (*to break down* in New Zealand means 'to make lighter'). Other terms, more or less self-explanatory, are *breaker-out* (the man who clears a timber-jam; pl. *breaker-outs*), *slip-trucky, scarfer* (see *O.E.D.* under *scarf* sb. 2), *goose man* (*drag* and *goose* are various types of saw; cf. U.S. *drag-saw*).

Gold-mining lured many early travellers to New Zealand from Australia and America, whence they brought the appellative *digger*, which took firm root. It has since become equivalent to 'man, buddy, fellow-countryman', and, since World War I, to 'Anzac'.[9] Its existence was perhaps prolonged by its application to those who followed the hard, semi-nomadic life of digging for kauri gum, and later to the troops who 'shovelled Gallipoli into sandbags'.

Some who came for gold remained to dig for coal. Two words still in use in coal-mining districts—*tom*, an artificial support, and *gad*, a sharp iron instrument—are said to have been introduced by Cornish miners who were among such early immigrants.

The pastoral life of New Zealand also has its own vocabulary. *Share-milker* is explained by its Australian and American parallels *sharefarmer* and *sharecropper. Bobby-calves* are the young calves which become veal. *Paddock* describes any fenced-in territory. The Scottish *byre* is used for a cattlepen in the south of the South Island—a reminder of the origin of

---

[9] Itself a notable contribution to the English vocabulary; made up from the initials of the Australian and New Zealand Army Corps in 1915. *Cobber*, another synonym for *digger*, was originally Australian (Yiddish *chaber*), but is now widely used in N.Z. (see *Notes and Queries*, 28 September 1929, where a derivation from Aboriginal *cubba* is suggested).

the first settlers there. *Billy*—borrowed from Australia, where it was used of the can in which the swagman boiled water and made tea—is now also applied to any can which will contain household milk. *Creek* is used in the American sense of a stream, as well as in the English sense of a small arm of the sea. *Gully*, though it may have been introduced by Californian miners, is used in a wider sense than in America, being applied to any ravine or valley formed by steep hillsides—a common feature of the volcanic landscape.

A few more recent words and adaptations may be cited as indicative of various aspects of life in New Zealand today. The verb *to bach*, to live as a bachelor (which Mencken describes as still on probation in America) has not only extended its meaning—being used to describe the simple life in a cottage—but has also produced a noun *bach*, or *batch*; this is the general term for a small week-end or holiday cottage, often by the sea. *Bungalow* was borrowed from India some forty years ago for the more substantial wooden houses of one storey, with or without verandah. Both the word and the type of building are now somewhat less common. *Morning tea* is an institution characteristic of New Zealand, where housewives and workers habitually make tea in the middle of the morning (in England the phrase usually denotes tea in bed). When this morning break is taken al fresco or in factories it is known as a *smoke-oh*. A *shower* is not now what it once was—a party for the bride-to-be—but a light decorated covering spread over cups and saucers set out on a tray or table. A visitor, reading notices in New Zealand papers, might be puzzled by phrases like 'Rooms with tray' and 'Ladies bring basket'; in both cases the container stands for the thing contained—breakfast and afternoon tea delicacies, respectively. He would also notice that the inhabitants usually say 'last evening' rather than 'last night'—perhaps because the nights are comparatively mild. A common article of furniture is a *stretcher*—a folding camp bed, often used to provide temporary sleeping accommodation in a house; in England the word is practically obsolete in this meaning. A piece of candy is usually called a *lolly*, and the peppermints described in England as *humbugs* become *blackballs* in New Zealand.

In a country richly endowed with golden beaches it is natural that *tennis shoes* or *sneakers* should be known as *sandshoes* (another case of a word staying in circulation in the dominion long after it has gone out of use in England; readers of Patmore will remember that he uses the word in *The Angel in the House*). A plot of land suitable for a building site is in New Zealand a *section*, in Australia a *block*;[10] the *back-blocks*, in both countries, are the rough, sparsely-settled hinterland. 'The King Country' is

[10] *Section* is also used for a fare stage on a street-car route, whilst a probationary student-teacher describes himself as 'on section' when he is paying a periodic visit to the school to which he is assigned.

the district in the North Island which was the home of the Maori King movement of the last century: already its signification has been forgotten by many who use the phrase. In some country districts (the Manawatu, for example) the roads are named *lines*—McDonell's Line, Richardson's Line, Union Line—presumably from early boundary or surveyors' lines. Often the only transport is by large limousines, which are always known as *service-cars*. A pump at a filling-station is a *bowser*—possibly a derivative of the verb *bowse*, to come with a rush, though I cannot find it in current use elsewhere—and petrol is generally known as *benzine*, though it is now coming to be advertised as *gas* at the more modern 'service stations', some of which have been so far Americanised as to describe themselves as 'lubritoriums'. *Radio* has already driven out the English *wireless*, *pack* (of cigarettes, etc.), the English *packet*, *alfalfa*, the English *lucerne*, and *mail*, the English *letters* or *post*. The fruit formerly known as *poor man's orange* has now become *New Zealand grapefruit*.

This infiltration of American words and usages is steadily increasing. It goes on faster than in England, and will doubtless be hastened by the presence of American doughboys and by the improvements in communications with North America which we may expect to follow the war. In recent years the chief American influence has been that of the movies; and, as will be shown later, there has been a generous adoption of American slang and of 'business American'. There is still a strong emotional attachment to England; but strategic, if not economic considerations are likely to bring New Zealand more and more within America's sphere of linguistic influence. Already American novels and magazines, which normally arrive in two weeks, are read as widely as those from Great Britain, which often take two months. The programs of both the government and the commercial broadcasting stations consist largely of recorded material, and much of this, too, comes from America. The exploits of the Lone Ranger are followed as keenly by New Zealand children as by any on this side of the Pacific.

COLLOQUIALISMS AND SLANG

The variations from British usage hitherto noted are not very numerous, or especially surprising. But in the speech of the average New Zealander —particularly, perhaps, in that of the outdoor worker—there is a noticeable element of slang. It leavens the conversation of all grades of society, and is more distinctive, and sometimes more racy, than the English taught in the schools.

There is a wide variety of appellatives. A citizen of New Zealand by birth is, or was (the word is obsolescent) a *pig-islander*: pigs were introduced into the country by Captain Cook (and went wild). An English immigrant is known as a *new chum*, as he has been in Australia for over half a century, or a *Pommy*, probably from the rhyming slang which still flourishes in a certain section of Sydney, and rhymes 'immigrant' with 'pomegranate'; a variant is *Homey* (Great Britain being 'Home'), though in Australia this connotes 'homely'. The phrase *old identity*, to describe an old inhabitant, was popularised by R. Thatcher, of Dunedin,[11] in a song satirising the 'new iniquities'—the Australian mining immigrants of the 1860s. A *cocky* or *cowcocky* (from Australian *cockatoo farmer*) is a small farmer, and a *wharfy* (usually *wharfer*, or *wharf-lumper* in Australia) is a wharf-worker, or longshoreman. The same method of word formation gives, in both countries, *yachty* (yachtsman), *bullocky* (bullock-driver), *bushy* (bushman), *swaggy* (also *swagger*, a tramp carrying a 'swag'). *Joker*, for 'chap', 'guy', goes back to early nineteenth-century English, but still persists strongly in New Zealand. A *toiler* or *battler* is a hard, conscientious worker—both are used with a shade of condescension; *battler* is also found in Glasgow slang, but there it has the signification of a gangster who fights with his fists. A *goer* is either a successful man, or a profligate. A *doer* is a jester, or an eccentric (cf. *O.E.D. Supplement* under *Do*, sb. 2b).

The slang word for girl is *tart*, used, for instance, by schoolboys; it has only lately begun to assume the derogatory sense it now has elsewhere. *Sheila* (whatever its origin, it has doubtless been blended by popular etymology with the Christian name of the same form) denotes girl-friend, as well as girl. *Sister* is also used for a girl as a term of address. It is not, as might be thought, a recent adoption from American films, but a relic of the whaling slang of a century ago.

A Chinese (generally known as 'John') is a *Chow* (a derivative of 'Chow-chow'); a Scotsman is a *Geordie*, and an Irishman, as in vulgar American, a *Mick*. These synonyms are also current in Australia.

Slang terms of praise or social criticism are numerous. A boaster is a *skite*, and there is a verb of the same form; it is obviously the same word as the Scottish noun *skyte* (an opprobrious epithet for an unpleasant or conceited person). A showy appearance is summed up as *flash*, as it was in Victorian England. *Tonky* suggests superior social standing or 'tone'. *Pretty punk* does some of the work performed in America by *lousy*. There is a liking for words in *-er*, and a whole group of them express admiration: *corker, stunner* (both used as adjectives as well as nouns), *snitcher*[12] (cf. U.S. *snitzy*), *bosker*, and *bonzer*; the last was certainly borrowed from Australia. Whether *wowser* (a prohibitionist, an excessively religious

[11] Baker, *New Zealand Slang*, p. 29, disposes of the assumption that Thatcher invented it.

[12] The only quotation given under a noun of this form in the *O.E.D.* is dated 1761: '. . . the Bucks, —Bloods, —Snitchers, —Choice Spirits'.

person, a kill-joy) originated in Australia or New Zealand is uncertain, and so is its etymology.[13] It gained some popularity beyond New Zealand during World War I. The adjective *wowseristic* has been formed from it.

The New Zealander likes his beer—in spite of, or perhaps because of, restrictions on the hours and areas in which it can be sold—and drinking habits have produced, as they always do, a whole crop of slang. One such word has passed into the common speech: *to shout* is, specifically, to 'stand a drink', to shout an order, at the bar; but it now also means to treat another person, no matter what the place or occasion. Beer is dispensed in *handles* (in Australia, *pots*) or *half-handles*. A quart bottle of beer is a *rigger*, and a pint bottle a *marine*: doubtless neither of these terms is peculiar to New Zealand, but they are rarely, if ever, heard in England. *Sly-grog* was originally an Australian term for illicit liquor; the verbal noun, *sly-grogging*, for the traffic in this liquor, is worth recording. The century-old American phrase *to crook the elbow* (to have a drink) and its variant *to bend the elbow* have become naturalised on the other side of the Pacific. A thoroughly drunk man is *stonkered, floored, stunned*, or, as in New York, *shicker*; and this last word, itself of Yiddish origin, has produced *shickered* and *on the shicker. Running the cutter* (i.e. obtaining liquor for people who cannot get it themselves) is used without any appreciation of its original meaning of smuggling. A 'good spree' would be described as a *proper old boozeroo*, this word being of the same pattern as various American words in *-eroo*.[14]

Horse-racing, another popular pastime (including trotting races, or *the trots*) provides two colloquialisms which need explanation. The exclamation *They're off, Mr Cutts!*, announcing that any contest or affair has begun, contains the name of a one-time popular starter at the Auckland races. *That's a stone ginger*, 'a dead certainty', conceals the name of a famous and unbeatable horse, Stone Ginger.

The hardest-worked word in New Zealand is *crook*. It does not carry all the moral implications of *crooked*. A man who is *crook* is ill; a *crook* job is unpleasant or difficult. *To go crook* is to show anger or annoyance, to 'sling off at'; and *to go butcher's hook* is presumably a development of this in rhyming slang. The verbs *to go snaky, to go maggoty* (cf. U.S. *maggoty, whimsical*) have the same implications. Phrases like *mad as a maggot, mad as a meat-axe* are obviously linked with these expressions (some, though not all, of which may be heard in Australia; cf. Australian *snake-headed*, annoyed); whether *mad* in the sense of angry is a survival of an English provincialism, or has been introduced from America, is not clear. Equally meaningless, though of older ante-

---

[13] See Mencken, *The American Language*, p. 265. The word was in use in New Zealand as early as 1895.
[14] See Wentworth, 'The Neo-Pseudo-Suffix "Eroo" '.

cedents, are *mad as one thing, like one thing,* 'with great speed', and the intensives *hanguva, hangershun*—modified forms of *helluva.* To *poke borax at,* 'to tease', comes from Australia, and contains a corruption of an Australian Aboriginal word.

The expressions *too true, too right,* in which *too* has its old intensive value, are in common use; so are *that'll be a picnic, what a picnic* (where *picnic* means 'trouble, bother'). *I'm easy* indicates indifference, willingness to accept whatever is offered or decided—as illustrated in the following quotation from an editorial column: 'The man who affects to be easy whilst secretly and anxiously seeking a way out. . . .' *Don't get off your bike* (from *don't get off your horse,* via a music-hall song?) means 'don't get rattled, excited'. *I'm set* is simply a variant of the widespread *all set*—to be distinguished from the same phrase as used in some Southern English dialects with the very different meaning of 'I'm stuck'. *To have a set on* or *against someone* represents a conflation of the old-established *to have a down on* and the Australian *to have* [a person] *set*; another familiar variant is *to have a derry on, derry* being a substitute for *down,* apparently from the association of the two words in the refrain 'derry down': *to have a derry on blowflies* is to have a strong dislike of them. A person complaining of another's ill-will might also say, 'He's got a proper snitch on me'—obviously a variant of *to snitch upon,* 'to inform against'.

The phrases, *a cow, a fair cow* must have had their origin in paddocks or milking sheds (they are also current in Australia); they are now used to describe anything difficult or unpleasant, from an obstinate engine to a tough problem in mathematics. The Australian asseverations *dinkum, fair dinkum,* 'honest, straight', have produced in New Zealand the meaningless variant *feather dinks.* The Australian *rough as bags* has become *rough as sacks. Bullswool,* the Australian name for the fibre of the stringy-bark tree, expresses scorn or contempt (cf. U.S. *bulldust*; indeed, *bullswool* itself may have originated independently in America). *All done up like a sore toe* describes someone dressed over-elaborately; many New Zealand children go barefoot much of the time, and it is with this circumstance in mind that we must interpret the simile. The exclamation 'good!' has become *goodo!,* on the analogy of *righto!,* and there is even *whacko!,* used to express pleasant anticipation (from such phrases as *whacking good time*). In the mild imperative with *eh*—as in *Give us a pack of cigarettes, eh*—it is tempting to see a reflecion of the egalitarianism that frequently strikes the visitor (who misses the respectful 'sir'). *See you some more* is the common phrase of casual farewell, the alternative being *hooray* (the New Zealand modification of 'hurrah'). The verb *to wait* has acquired an otiose preposition in ordinary use; one is told to *wait on* rather than to *wait,* but if any prepositional sense was ever felt in *on*—as in the American 'wait on me'—it has now been lost. *To get* is regularly used to mean 'to come' or 'to go'—as in *sorry I couldn't get*. The American tag *Let her go, Gallagher*, described by Mencken as 'a short-lived, silly phrase', can still be heard in New Zealand; it presumably goes back to comedians' patter.

A *spell* in New Zealand means a period of rest, rather than of work, and *to have a spell* is to take a rest; in this sense it is probably a remnant of the speech of the New Bedford and Nantucket whalers who once frequented New Zealand waters, *spell oh!* being recorded (in *Moby Dick,* for example) as a call to cease work or strenuous exercise.[15] A *yarn* is simply a talk or a chat, not a sailor's story, nor even a tall story.

In New Zealand slang a penny is a *brown*, a threepenny piece a *thray* (cf. English *tray*), a sixpence a *sax*, presumably from Scottish *saxpence*. *Oxford scholar* is occasionally heard for five shillings; it probably comes from English rhyming slang for 'dollar'.

There are a large number of words and phrases in common use which one could scarcely classify as confined to, or originating in, New Zealand, but which deserve to be recorded in any attempt to convey something of the flavour of the colloquial speech of the country. Amongst these are *tucker*, 'food', *togs*, used of bathing suits rather than of clothes in general, *hippies*, 'bathing trunks', *flopping*, as in *a flopping nuisance*, *to part up*, 'to pay up', *to get hooked*, 'to find a girl friend', *to up sticks*, 'to shift house, move one's belongings', *half-pie*, 'mediocre'. A horse that runs crooked is said to be *stumered*, apparently derived from Glasgow sporting slang. *You've got legs on your belly* would be addressed to a sponger or sycophant. *A clumsy woodser* is clear in its general meaning, though its origin is obscure; *wood* is often, however, used disparagingly. Only a few current phrases can be traced to their creators. One of these is *to give a man his running shoes*, coined by a New Zealand Minister of the Crown as a vivid substitute for the English *sack* or the American *fire*. A glance at Partridge's *Dictionary* will show that the New Zealand Expeditionary Force made their own distinct contribution to soldiers' slang in World War I, typical examples being *typewriter*, 'machine gun', *dangle parade*, 'a "short-arm" inspection', and *mad money*, 'the money which a girl-friend keeps in reserve in case she decides to leave in a hurry'.

No account is taken in the above selection of numerous Americanisms that have by now become almost naturalised in New Zealand speech. However short-lived, they add a distinctive strain; and they remind us

---

[15] It is thus much older than '1.C.19-20', the date given in Partridge, *Dictionary of Slang*, p. 807, and possibly it is many centuries older; cf. *The Owl and the Nightingale*, 1.258, 'lat thine tunge habben spale', where *spale* is more appropriately translated by 'rest' than by Skeat's 'turn of work'.

of an influence which is likely to grow rather than to diminish, especially in a young and small community, which has had few other linguistic wells to draw upon—particularly since emigration from England has dwindled almost to nothing. Many samples of American slang might be cited as having a wider currency in New Zealand than in England. But a certain time-lag must be noted; it may take several years for a popular American expression to reach the Antipodes and be assimilated into current speech there. Indeed, the colloquial speech of both Australia and New Zealand often preserves usages that have elsewhere become archaic or obsolete; and any awareness that such usages are dialectal or argot has usually disappeared. Of the two countries, New Zealand, the more isolated, tends to be the more conservative, sometimes even retaining Australian expressions after they have dropped out of use in Australia itself. Naturally the influence of the Australian vernacular is strong: Australia is the nearest large land mass, its population is five times as great, and the life and culture of the two countries is in many respects similar; and along with the 'Aussie's' nascent nationalism and sense of independence there perhaps goes greater expressiveness and inventiveness in speech than is to be found at present in New Zealand. But sufficient evidence has been adduced above to show that current usage in both countries is by no means identical.

ADOPTIONS FROM MAORI

The natives of New Zealand speak—one need not yet say 'used to speak' —a melodious Polynesian language. But very few *pakehas*, as the Maoris call white men,[16] take the trouble to learn it, with the result that Maori words have hitherto been given very careless, and even corrupt pronunciation. This is especially true of words adopted into English, as the following notes will show.

The number of Maori words in common use is comparatively small and tends to decrease as the Maoris become Europeanised. Amongst such words still in use are: *kai*, 'food', *kit*, 'basket' (from Maori *kete*, 'flax basket'), *kiwi*, 'a flightless bird' (used in the Air Forces of many countries during World War I for men on ground duty only); *kumara*, 'a sweet potato', and sometimes so named; *goory*, 'a mongrel dog', from Maori *kuri*, *pipi*, 'a small mussel', *rakau*, 'wood', *wahine*, 'woman', *whare*, 'hut or dwelling-house', *taipo*, 'devil' (from Maori *taepo*—if indeed this word was originally Maori; it may have been used by Maoris believing it to be English and by Englishmen believing it to be Maori, being originally applied, according to Morris, to the theodolite-

---

[16] For various theories as to the origin of the word, see Baker, *New Zealand Slang*, p. 16.

tripod because it is the 'land-stealing devil'), *hoot*, 'money' (from Maori *utu*, 'revenge', through the intermediate sense of 'compensation'), *puku*, 'stomach', and *pukumu*, 'big stomach' (used jocularly); *tapu*, 'taboo' (being the form of that word in Maori). *Pukkaroo*, adjective and noun, '(to make) worthless, useless'—it could be used, for instance, of an engine that had broken down—is of dubious origin; it is perhaps from the Maori *pakaru*, 'to destroy', or conceivably it is an adaptation of 'buggered', English initial *b-* regularly being unvoiced by the Maori. *Kapai*, 'good, fine', and *tena koe* (a greeting) are less common on New Zealanders' lips than formerly, whilst *e hoa*, an exclamation with the value of 'look here, I say', has become corrupted to the tag *heehaw*, as in 'give us that fork, heehaw'; and *to be pie on*, 'to be very good at', seems to be derived from the Maori *pai ana. Taihoa!*, 'wait a bit', and *kia ora*, 'good luck' (a disguised form of *keora tau*), are well-established adoptions. The word *Maori* itself is occasionally used as a term of contempt—as in *That's a Maori* (of a thing). *Tuatara*, a species of lizard, had a similar but ephemeral use in a limited circle some years ago, when it was applied to anyone toadying to a superior.

Many native names for plants and trees have been supplied with English alternatives. Thus, *kahikatea* has become 'white pine', and *pohutukawa*, since it flowers in December, 'Christmas tree'. But often the Maori name has been kept, as in *kauri, puriri, totara*, and *nikau* (a species of palm). There is one instance of false correctness: Captain Cook called the native *manuka* a 'tea plant'; this became 'tea tree' (the *manuka* grows to tree-height), and then, by an ignorant perversion, 'ti-tree', on the assumption that *ti* was a Maori word. Certain Maori sounds—especially [ɹ], which is pronounced without any discernible vibration—have always given Europeans difficulty. Hence *puriri* has become 'buridi', and *piripiri*, a burr, 'biddybid'. Inaccurate pronunciations were formerly particularly common in the South Island, where the Maoris are fewer and their language less often spoken than in the North. *Kowhai* (a flowering tree) became [goɑɪ], *korari*, 'flax', became [kɪtædi], and words like *mánuka, tótara*, were wrongly accented. But it happens that the worst corruption of all—'portycover' for *pohutukawa* —is reported from the province of Auckland in the North Island.

The Maori treatment of certain English words is conventionally indicated by such spellings as *plurry* and *py korry* for 'bloody' and 'by golly', [b], [d], and [s] causing the greatest difficulty.[17]

[17] Baker, *New Zealand Slang*, pp. 86 ff., gives an interesting list of adoptions, but omits the curious fossil-word *pikopo*, which originated as follows: in the period of rivalry between Protestant and Catholic missionaries a century ago, the Roman Catholic Bishop Pompallier laid stress on the fact that he alone held episcopal rank. The closest that the Maori could come to any form of *episcopos* was *pikopo*; hence the Bishop and his proselytes were known as *pikopo*.

Maori place names inevitably suffer mutilation in spelling[18] or pronunciation—especially in cases where the European does not catch the lightly-sounded final vowel (as in [motətæp] for *Motutapu*, [otəhuː] for *Otahuhu*) or discards all but the opening sounds of a mellifluous polysyllable (as in 'Waimack', a signpost abbreviation for *Waimakariri*). The Maori [ŋ], as in *Whangarei*, is sometimes misinterpreted as [g], and there are a few spelling-pronunciations accepted by the ignorant. But in recent years, as a result of instruction in the schools and on the radio, there has been a noticeable improvement in the treatment of such words. And at the same time, schoolchildren have been encouraged to use the Maori words for indigenous trees and plants.

TRADE WORDS

Nothing shows more clearly the influence of America than the jargon of New Zealand copy-writers, who draw liberally from American fashion magazines. Words like *bobby-pin* (English 'kirby-grip'), *sheer* (dress material), *tubables* (washable frocks), are taken from American, not English, advertisements; so are various portmanteau words, such as *shellubrication* and *gingervating*. The fashion of forming verbs in *-ise* ('personalised gifts') has produced *preservatise* and *bargainised*. The American 'spectator-sports' (of clothes) has been mistranslated in at least one advertisement as 'spectacular-sports'. And in general copy-writers, even when they do not reproduce American trade language, have taken over the habit of inventing 'smart', casual words for the clothes they are advertising. The disease of pseudo-phonetic spelling (*Keen-Kut*, *Tasti*, etc.) is widespread.[19]

A few trade names have caught the public fancy, and become generalised. Thus *Zambuk*, a brand of ointment, is regularly used for a 'first-aid man' (usually a member of the St John Ambulance Corps), or even as an appeal for first-aid; and *Bagwash*, the name of a laundry firm, is now applied to any laundry collected in bags. A system of hire-purchase called the *Lay-by* has resulted in the verb *layby*, pronounced and written as one word.

No analysis of the kind attempted in this article can convey adequately the flavour of the vernacular described. Failing direct observation, this can best be caught in the works of New Zealand writers of fiction who

---

[18] For some early grotesque spellings see Hocken, 'Some Account of the Beginnings of Literature in New Zealand'.

[19] American spellings are becoming increasingly common, at least in *-or* words; e.g. *labor*, *favorite*. Misspellings seem more frequent than in England. In the main street of Auckland I saw several advertisements for 'strawberrys', and a sign 'motor-analiser'. 'Cartoon' is sometimes used for 'carton'!

have allowed their characters to speak in real and not conventional language, and who have described the country and the people out of an intimate knowledge of both. Among such writers Katherine Mansfield is the best known, though it must be remembered that her New Zealand stories, such as *Prelude* or *At the Bay*, describe New Zealand as it was in her childhood over forty years ago; to the same period belongs Jane Mander's *Story of a New Zealand River*. In more recent years, Robin Hyde's *Passport to Hell* offers as realistic a transcript of 'Digger' life and language as could be wished. But more accessible to Americans[20] are the short stories of Frank Sargeson, which have lately been appearing in the American *New Directions* and the English *New Writing*: in these he catches, with remarkable success, 'the manners living as they rise', and colloquialisms as they fall straight from the lips of the average New Zealander.

REFERENCES CITED

Baker, S. J., *New Zealand Slang. A Dictionary of Colloquialisms*, Wellington, n.d.
Hanley, Miles, 'Observations on the Broad A', *Dialect Notes*, Pt 8, 1925, pp. 347-50.
Hocken, T. M., 'Some Account of the Beginnings of Literature in New Zealand', *Trans. and Proc. N.Z. Inst.*, Vol. 33, pp. 472-90.
Hyde, Robin (pseud. for Iris G. Wilkinson), *Passport to Hell*, London, 1936.
Krapp, G. P., *The English Language in America*, 2 vols., New York, 1925.
Mander, Jane, *The Story of a New Zealand River*, Christchurch, 1960.
Mansfield, Katherine, *Collected Stories*, London, 1964.
Mencken, H. L., *The American Language*, 4th ed., New York, 1938.
Morris, E. E., *Austral English, A Dictionary of Australasian Words, Phrases and Usages*, London, 1898.
Partridge, E., *A Dictionary of Slang and Unconventional English*, 4th ed., London, 1951.
Sargeson, F., *Collected Stories*, London, 1965.
Wentworth, Harold, 'The Neo-Pseudo-Suffix "Eroo"', *American Speech*, February 1942, pp. 10-15.

---

[20] This article was originally written for an American audience.

6   G. W. TURNER

NEW ZEALAND ENGLISH TODAY

The recent history of New Zealand has been well described as 'the complex picture of the transfer of working class urban culture-values into an economically successful agrarian landscape, combined with suburban admass'.[1] New Zealanders detect something of their own origins in the recently urbanised English culture described in Richard Hoggart's *The Uses of Literacy*, an origin shared with Australia, though with a respectable emphasis having more in common with South Australia than with the eastern states. This culture, losing any remaining local differences as people from various regions were brought together, devised its own response to new urban settlements in the Antipodes. As these settlements spread into the bush, they developed some new local differences in different settings, but, in an age when transport, particularly by sea, was efficient, they differed from colony to colony less than might have been expected. New Zealand, when the sea was a link rather than a barrier, was part of a total Australasian settlement, even though its unique flora and its Maori population promoted some distinctive vocabulary.

This initially urban culture has become the urbanised farm and suburban culture of New Zealand today. The urban population in New Zealand surpassed the rural in 1911, but this is less important than the strongly urban quality of rural life in New Zealand now. A city uncle cannot buy toys for a country nephew without finding that Santa Claus has visited another branch of the same chain of stores. The backblocks have disappeared. The modern farmer depends on government, science, and manufacturing, on electricity and modern packaging, and is more urbanised than the city-dwellers in many of the countries that border his ocean.

In the days of sealers and whalers, New Zealand was simply part of the Australians' area of operations, so that it is not surprising to find such a dinkum Australianism as *waddy* recorded early in New Zealand to describe a Maori *mere*, or short club; and conversely, for such an undeniable New Zealandism as *karaka* (a laurel-like tree), we can antedate

---

[1] In a book review by Philip Smithells, *Landfall* No. 54, June 1960, p. 206.

the *Oxford English Dictionary* from G. Bennett's *Wanderings in New South Wales* (1834).[2]

When New Zealand had become more settled, Australian sheep and sheep-farmers followed the sealers, whalers, and adventurers of early days. Australians were prominent in the development of Canterbury sheep farms, though in the Wairarapa Scottish shepherds were preferred. (It would be interesting to discover whether any differences in sheep-farming terms in the two areas result from this.) The gold rushes brought a further importation of Australians and their form of English. The prospector was a skilled immigrant bringing a technical vocabulary with him. There were Australians among the mill-hands when the heavy bush of the North Island was cleared for settlement.

At the same time, Australian flora and fauna came to New Zealand, bringing the Australian names. *Bluegum* is a common enough word in New Zealand; a *magpie* is an Australian magpie, introduced last century; and the *silvereye* (or *waxeye*) descends from those unassisted immigrants that appeared from across the Tasman in 1856, earning for themselves a reputation among ornithologists as notable colonisers.

Before the Federation of Australia, which excluded New Zealand, it was perhaps only the influence of Maori in its vocabulary, especially to name local plants and birds, that would have justified distinguishing New Zealand English from the slightly differing and interacting varieties of English used in the mainland colonies of Australia and in Tasmania. Even now the similarities in pronunciation and older vocabulary suggest a single dialect area with two major subdivisions, much as the Anglian dialect of Old English is postulated as a convenient term to include the Northumbrian and Mercian dialects, which share many similarities.

The close early links between Australia and New Zealand make it very difficult to separate the two varieties of English with certainty, unless a word is from Maori, or precisely dated and its origin recorded. One example will illustrate the difficulty. Suppose that a student finds that the expression *to travel at the rate of knots*, 'very fast', is known in New Zealand but appears to be unknown to those Australians he consults. He finds that it is not of recent origin in New Zealand: Wardon's paperback novel, *Macpherson's Gully*, uses it to describe a creek in flood. A check reveals that Sidney Baker cites it as a New Zealandism in *New Zealand Slang*, and omits the phrase from *The Australian Language*. This much information might tempt the student to conclude that the word is probably a New Zealandism—until he discovers that Joseph Furphy uses it in *Rigby's Romance*. Thus documentation and the dating of language are necessary

---

[2] *Waddy* in John Savage, *Some Account of New Zealand. . . ,* London, 1807, p. 66; *Karaka* in Bennett, Vol. 1, p. 336.

G

preliminaries to the adequate description of what is local in a variety of language, though provisional descriptive study, made with proper caution, also guides and stimulates further historical study, and it is, of course, a fact to be recorded that an expression is used in New Zealand, even if it occurs, or has occurred, elsewhere as well. It is also clear from the above illustrations that the documentation of New Zealand English and of Australian English are mutually interdependent.

In the twentieth century, civilisation is so urbanised that the most pervasive new local words are words connected with government and social organisation. Independent government in New Zealand has brought a divergence in political terminology; New Zealanders do not distinguish a Premier and a Prime Minister, such terms as *federal* and *state* have no local meaning, and the New Zealander visiting Australia is intrigued by the grammatically curious word *interstate* in such expressions as *he's gone interstate* or *an interstate honeymoon*.

The words used to name laws, institutions, and governing bodies, however, though differing in the two countries, are formed from the most standardised elements in the existing vocabulary, so that such new names as *National Film Unit* in New Zealand or *Commonwealth Scholarship* in Australia do not have the national flavour of words that were distinctive in the days of bush, gold, and isolated farms. Language is a less immediate source of national awareness than it was, though the passing of a different era, combined in New Zealand with centenaries of successive districts, encourages an interest in local history, including an interest in local language, so that research into the history of words, enshrined in the *Oxford English Dictionary*, its 1930 *Supplement*, and its forthcoming *Second Supplement*, goes on, and some colloquialisms (*dinkum, cobber, fair cow*) become preserved in slightly self-conscious use for a longer life-span than they might naturally have had. Writers drawing on local speech help to preserve it, but also inevitably add to the self-consciousness attaching to the use of local idiom.

If modern urbanisation and administration are a source of some (comparatively unremarked) distinctiveness in life and vocabulary in New Zealand, modern communications also work against distinctiveness. Europe and America, the chief sources of magazines, films, and radio and television programs, have brought New Zealand nearer to Europe than to Australia. *Coronation Street* is felt to be closer to home than *Dad and Dave of Snake Gully*. As general English has changed, in the last generation, enough to supply material for a detailed book, *The Changing English Language*, by Brian Foster, novelties have been disseminated throughout the English-speaking world. A New Zealander reads Foster with a nod of recognition at each new detail. An exception (e.g. *layby* for a roadside parking place) is notable. *Layby* is used differently in New Zealand, as in Australia, for a deposit reserving goods in a shop. This need not preclude the use of the word in the English sense as well, if the density of traffic warranted it, though English migrants have been known to form false hopes of finding a parking place at a shopping centre because of the notice, 'Use our layby'.

Many Americanisms have become current in England this century. New Zealanders are on the same bandwagon, and could not get by without names for a succession of new gimmicks, from radio quiz to babysitters, which have become routine elements of their way of life. Few, in fact, would notice all the eight Americanisms introduced into the foregoing sentence. As I write, I note that the term *panti-hose* is already current in New Zealand.

As is to be expected, a number of the colloquialisms noted by J. A. W. Bennett in 1943 have faded from general use (e.g. *tart, tonky, pretty punk, corker, hippies,* and slang terms for coins used before the change to decimal currency in 1967), as have some terms that might have survived longer but for standardising influences from outside, such as *benzine* (though *penehini* remains the Maori word for petrol), *bowser,* and *service-car.* The colloquial terms have not been replaced by new local words, however, but by the general fashionable colloquialisms, from *After you, Claude* to *zoot-suit,* that have fleetingly flickered in the speech of the whole English-speaking world.

At least part of the difficulty in defining New Zealand English today is that local elements are often hard to distinguish from general Australian English and local innovations hard to distinguish from imports from general world English.

PRONUNCIATION

Since Bennett made his brief comments on New Zealand pronunciation in 1943, no extended survey has been made to check and supplement his observations. The following comments, then, are merely one observer's impressions. The chief advantage the observer of today has over the observer of 1943 is access to accurate and detailed accounts of the pronunciation of Australian English, which help greatly in drawing attention to details in the similar New Zealand pronunciation, but could be misleading in directing attention to pronunciations shared with Australia, and away from those which differ in New Zealand.

Pronunciation, a delicately adjusted system of sounds, is less subject to sporadic change than vocabulary, where elements are added or dropped without noticeably disturbing the total structure of a language. Change does occur; the Maori schoolboy who in 1846 defined a rat as 'cat's wittles' learned his English from men with a pronunciation never heard in New Zealand now. But in general the similarity between Australian and New Zealand English pronunciation noticed by Samuel McBurney last century survives today. When Mitchell and Delbridge surveyed the speech of Australian adolescents and found a number of variations between one speaker and another but no systematic differences of dialect, it is doubtful whether they would have been any nearer to finding a convincing difference of dialect if New Zealand had been included in the survey.

As in Australia, there are differences among speakers in New Zealand conveniently ranged on a scale from 'broad' to 'educated', the educated approaching British English. Range of pitch in all speakers is less than in England, the intonation, stress and speed of speech resembling the Australian. Arnold Wall has drawn attention to the New Zealander's tendency to stress the first syllable in the word *magazine* and even in the phrase *after all*, but Brian Foster notices the same trend in England, seeing it as an American influence.[3] Perhaps in all three countries it is merely an assertion of a natural phonetic tendency in the English language.

There is little that is distinctive about the consonants of New Zealand speech. The distinction between words such as *which* and *witch* is more often preserved in New Zealand than in England, though this distinction is not so universally absent in Southern English as is sometimes thought, as Brian Foster points out.[4] The *l* in words such as *milk* frequently acquires an exaggeratedly dark, almost vocalic, pronunciation with accompanying retraction of the vowel, a pronunciation which seems to link New Zealand with South Australia more than the eastern states.

It is the pronunciation of vowels and diphthongs that distinguishes the speech of Australia and New Zealand together from British English, and, more rarely, distinguishes New Zealand speech from Australian. In both areas the sound corresponding to English /ɑː/ is distinctive. Bennett's *flatter* does not quite locate the distinction; the Australian and New Zealand sound is a more forward sound than the English, nearer to cardinal [a] than to cardinal [ɑ]. The vowel in *mast* is almost a long version of the vowel in *must*, which has the forward pronunciation of recent English as described by A. C. Gimson, not the older retracted pronunciation of the English described by Daniel Jones.

My experience does not confirm Bennett's observation that the vowel of *dance*, *path*, or *contrast* is often /æ/ in New Zealand. On the other hand, in *graph*, and compounds such as *telegraph*, I would think it more widespread. My own pronunciation of *graph* as /græf/ is one of the few things that has made me feel a foreigner in South Australia. (South Australians usually do not pronounce *dance*, *advance*, etc. with /æ/ as speakers in the eastern states do.)

In both Australia and New Zealand, most pure vowels other than the

[3] *The Changing English Language*, p. 236.
[4] Ibid., pp. 251-3.

vowels of *mast* and *must* (the vowels of *pet, pat, pot, port, pert,* and the final syllable of *porter*) are closer, and in the case of *pot, port,* and *pert,* rounder, than their Southern English counterparts. The vowel in *pet* might become very close in New Zealand, particularly among the young, and in the word *yes,* which approaches [jiəs]. When we lived in New Zealand, my six-year-old son asked, 'Dad, what's a hearing?' and I correctly answered, 'A little fish'.

The vowel in *put* has the same phonemic norm in Southern England, Australia, and New Zealand, but the vowel in *pit* is distinctive in each of the three areas. To begin with, the phoneme /ɪ/ occurs more frequently in England than in Australia and New Zealand. In unaccented position it occurs in the final syllables of *wanted, houses,* or *city,* where Australians and New Zealanders would use /ə/ in the first two cases and /iː/ in the last. In New Zealand, /ə/, or a very central variant of /ɪ/ approaching the closer allophones of /ə/, frequently replaces /ɪ/ in stressed syllables as well.[5] This is perhaps the most distinctive mark of a New Zealander's accent to Australians, particularly those in New South Wales and elsewhere who have a markedly forward variant of /ɪ/ in stressed syllables. To these Australians, the New Zealander's *Philip, bit, ship* appear to be pronounced /fələp/, /bət/, /ʃəp/, while conversely a New Zealander might hear the word *ship* as *sheep* in the speech of some Australians.

In spite of all this, there seems to be some tendency in both Australia and New Zealand to raise a final unstressed vowel before /k/, as in the word *paddock*. I used to doubt the existence of any pronunciation justifying the literary use of 'bullick' and 'paddick' to represent Australian speech, but an English friend, a good phonetician, detects an [ɪ] in my own pronunciation of *paddock,* so that this must serve as a reminder of the provisional nature of impressionistic phonetic judgments; though since a New Zealander's /ɪ/ is centralised and his /ə/ close, it is difficult to distinguish the most open allophones of /ɪ/ from the closest allophones of /ə/.

Diphthongs, including the sounds in *beat* and *boot,* which even in England have [ɪi] and [ʊu], distinguish, more than any other segmental sounds, the Australian variety of English. The first element is lowered in *beat* and *boot* to [ə], in *mate* and *moat* to [ʌ]. No lowering is possible in *bite* and *bout,* where British English has [a] as the first element of the diphthong, so that to differentiate *bite* from *bait,* a pronunciation with rounded and retracted first element, in extreme cases to [ɒ], is favoured, and *bout* is kept distinct from *boat* by a raised first element, to [æ] or even [ɛ]. These developments occur in New Zealand as well as Australia,

---

[5] Among speakers with a marked local accent, especially in stressed monosyllables, the two may combine in a short diphthong glide [əɪ]; cf. Kelly, 'The Phonemes of New Zealand English', p. 80.

except that the 'broad' or fully developed accent is thought to be less common in New Zealand. In *beat* and *boot*, the lowering of the first element is generally less marked in New Zealand than in Australia, and accordingly there is greater preservation of the second element, the historical pure vowel sound, [i] or [u]. The pronunciation is perhaps [əi] and [əu] as against Australian [ɑɪ] and [ɑu]. In many cases, the vowel sound of *boot* is fronted rather than diphthongised in New Zealand, and somewhat unrounded. This sound with [ə] added gives the usual New Zealand pronunciation of *sure* as [ʃuə]. The variant [ʃɔː] is less frequent, though *poor* is usually [pɔː]. In *here*, New Zealanders tend to use a high first element, [hiə] rather than [hɪə], and in *there* the first element is again high, almost /ɪ/, but a very forward allophone of it.

VOCABULARY

In vocabulary, as in pronunciation, old and new elements contribute to a new pattern of English, but only some of the novelties can be dealt with here.

Many older local words survive, none older, it seems, than the term *mat* for a Maori garment, which goes back to Tasman's use of the Dutch word *matten* in December 1642, was repeated by Forster, who noted in March 1773 that the Maoris of Dusky Bay 'appeared to be dressed in mats',[6] was used several times by Savage in 1807, and continued to be used by numerous writers thereafter (despite the opposition of some anthropologists) for the kilt or for the shoulder mat worn by Maoris. David P. Ausubel in 1957 thought it worth recording in a short glossary prefacing his book, *The Fern and the Tiki*, the phrase *to go back to the mat* meaning 'to revert to primitive ways'.[7]

The word *mat* in its New Zealand sense thus has over three centuries of recorded history. Other words may have a very short time range. Students in Christchurch about 1950 were using *curly* or *extra-curly* as a general term of approval and *drongo* (obviously of Australian origin, but an import rather than a survival, it seems) to mean 'fool'. These words are not heard now. A full description of a local word must therefore include an indication of the time of its currency, though it is not always easy to date the demise of a word; *Pig Islander*, thought to be obsolescent by Bennett, survives quietly, perhaps because used by Sargeson or because it suits the self-deprecating national consciousness of New Zealanders. *Lucerne* also has outlived its obituary; it seems to have remained the usual term, rather than *alfalfa*.

[6] *A Voyage Round the World* in *George Forsters Werke*, Vol. I, p. 90. Cf. Banks's use, Morrell (ed.), *Sir Joseph Banks in New Zealand*, pp. 131-2.
[7] Ausubel, *The Fern and The Tiki*.

As some words are restricted in time range, so some are restricted geographically. *Marram grass*, growing in sand dunes near the sea, is a local word in New Zealand as in England. A student in Christchurch once wrote in an examination script, 'a *saveloy* in Auckland is called a *baloney*', unwittingly proving the restricted geographical range of the word, which is, of course, *poloney*.

Besides being restricted in time and place, words might be restricted in social range. Often words restricted in this way (slang and colloquialisms) are of short time range or limited geographical distribution, or both, as well. Perhaps it was until recently usual for such popular words to be restricted locally; modern communications have brought slang with a wider geographical distribution but shorter time range.

Local slang of recent origin is not easy to find in New Zealand now. The word *graunch*, 'to grate violently (of machinery, etc.), to break (machinery) through misuse', appears to be recent, though ultimately traceable to English dialect, but it is not very widely used. Two Canterbury students were quoted in *The Dominion*, 11 April 1968, in a report of the *Wahine* disaster: 'They said they could hear the ship "graunching" on the rock'. (The quotation marks were used by the newspaper.)

The phrase *two shows* meaning 'no show', 'no chance', was current for some time. (The two shows are *no show* and *fish-oh*). *No show* itself is American. *Show* in the sense of 'chance' is recorded in America from 1856, and it is tempting to see an origin in the gold-digger's 'show' of gold. Archdeacon Henry Harper encountered the word on New Zealand goldfields in October 1866, and refers to 'We'll . . . give you a show', meaning 'Here's your chance', as 'digger's slang'.[8]

The subdued colour of colloquialisms such as *show*, or the New Zealander's *I don't go much on*, 'I don't much like', allows them to become widely current and survive where more consciously impressive items, such as *bunch of five(s)*, 'fist' (an expression sometimes used informally by the Yorkshire philologist, Joseph Wright, and used in New Zealand in Gordon Slatter's novel, *A Gun in My Hand*),[9] are less frequently used and by fewer people. None of these expressions is the Queen's English, and those such as *to give a man his running shoes* (i.e. 'the sack'), and *snivelling snufflebuster*, which were the English of the Minister of Public Works, the Hon. Robert Semple, thirty years ago, have not survived.

Some widely used Australian colloquialisms are less current in New Zealand. *To be in strife* is more often *to be in the cart* in New Zealand, and *to give it away* might be *to let it go* or *sling it in*, or, with some loss of the Australian's nonchalance, simply *to give up*.

[8] Quoted by May, *The West Coast Gold Rushes*, pp. 305-6.
[9] The context is quoted in Turner, *The English Language in Australia and New Zealand*, p. 121. Cf. Wright, *The Life of Joseph Wright*, Vol. 1, p. 82.

Slang should be distinguished from technical or occupational language. It is true that both entail restrictions in social range, the former more specifically a restriction in social level or tone, the latter a restriction to a particular socially useful occupation. One represents a restriction of manner, the other of subject matter. The two appear to come closest in the less technical and theoretical occupations, where terms are manufactured by popular processes, and such occupations have been prominent in early Australia and New Zealand. The shearer's *ringer of the board* is likely to appear less a technicality than the geologist's *Hokonui deformation*, especially as the word *ringer* has passed into wider currency both in Australia and New Zealand and become a true colloquialism. (*Hokonui* in the sense of 'moonshine, illicit whisky' has no connection with geologists.) The study of local varieties depends, however, on a meticulous separation of varieties and a careful tracing of their interaction, and we must always be aware of the axes of variation in language, in time, place, tone, subject matter, and the spoken or written mode. Failure to do this by Sidney Baker in naming his book *New Zealand Slang* has led to unnecessary neglect of the very useful historical information that his book contains, ranging well beyond the colloquial.[10]

Particular occupations were so dominant at different times in early Australia and New Zealand that many technical terms passed into general use, and even specific sheep-farming, gold-mining, and timber-felling terms are often felt to be general Australian and/or New Zealand English. This is especially true of general farming terms in New Zealand.

No word, perhaps, better illustrates the fusion of suburban and rural life in New Zealand than *section*. It occurs several times in early colonists' letters for a block of land either in town or country. In 1842 Jessie Campbell of Wanganui talks of a purchase of 'cattle for the section', 'visiting country sections', and, in 1845, of 'baking the whole week's bread for the section', suggesting a homestead. Judge Chapman in 1844 had a 'section' of 120 acres at Karori. Sarah Greenwood recorded in 1843 that 'the three boys are living under the tent at the Motueka (our Suburban section) clearing the land for cultivation and preparing for building our house'. The New Zealander still spends weekends clearing a suburban section, and measures it by area, not frontage, as a quarter-acre section, a thirty-

[10] Compare Bennett's footnotes 2 and 17 in this volume, noting that Baker does, in fact, mention *pikopo*, but as a Maori word used in a translation of the Treaty of Waitangi in 1840. The word was used in an English context in a letter dated 17 December 1842 by Sarah Selwyn: 'He asked if she were not a pikopo (Romanist as you would say) many of her party being so'. The old woman addressed replied that her 'glory was to come and smoke her pipe' with the Anglican bishop's family, and that 'she had never smoked any Pikopo Tobacco'. This probably reports a conversation originally in Maori. The letter, as well as other early New Zealand letters cited in the following pages, is reprinted in Drummond, *Married and Gone to New Zealand*, p. 110.

New Zealand English Today 93

perch section, and so on. The New Zealander living in Australia finds it difficult to remember to call his section a 'block' (a word with a similar semantic history).

A remark of Sarah Chapman's in a letter dated 30 November 1844 confirms Bennett's association of the word *line* in its bush sense with surveyors, though not with the normal surveyor's line:

> You can form no idea of the New Zealand bush, it is so thick, and the Supple Jack which is very tough and hard binds it so close as to make it hopeless to attempt to make your way through it without a billhook or compass. We had the Company's Surveyors here to cut lines through our Section, and now have the means of going through with tolerable ease.[11]

It seems that the original *line* was a bush track, which might grow to be a road.

Sheep-farming language and its sublanguage of shearing have been important in New Zealand as in Australia, particularly in Canterbury. The Australian origin of much of this farming has ensured much community of vocabulary. New Zealand has added the name of the *Corriedale* sheep, named after Corriedale sheep station in North Otago, where the sheep were first bred by inbreeding the half-breed progeny of Merino and Romney (later Leicester and Merino) sheep. To avoid the use of gates where a road passes through a sheep station, *cattle stops*, pits covered with spaced horizontal rails or bars allowing vehicles but not cattle to pass, are used. These seem to be called *grids* in Australia.

Shearers have often travelled between Australia and New Zealand, working in both countries, and this would make mutual linguistic influence highly likely, though there are some differences to be noticed between the New Zealand shearing glossary attached to Godfrey Bowen's *Wool Away* and the Australian glossary by J. S. Gunn published by the University of Sydney Language Research Centre as Occasional Papers No. 5 and No. 6. Gold-mining similarly left a common legacy to both countries.[12]

Timber workers used many terms that are now becoming historical, such as *jigger*, a slab or plank inserted at a suitable height into a notch in a tree as a platform, or *drive*, a line of trees on a hillside each partly cut so that the top tree when falling will bring down the others like dominoes. *Bushfire* had a somewhat different connotation in early New Zealand from its Australian one. It was a fire in dry felled timber and rubbish from felled bush. The native bush in New Zealand is denser and less inflammable than Australian scrub. Now that exotic trees, especially *pinus radiata*, dominate New Zealand forestry, true bushfires are a greater

[11] Drummond, *Married and Gone to New Zealand*, p. 69.
[12] For a recently published New Zealand glossary, see May, *The West Coast Gold Rushes*, pp. 526-8.

risk. The language of the new and fast-growing exotic timber industry in New Zealand requires study.

Dairy farmers have been especially important in the development of the North Island. The bush has been cleared (*bush* usually signifies dense forest in New Zealand) and replaced by open paddocks and hedges or shelterbelts of the ubiquitous pine (i.e. Monterey pine or *pinus insignis*, lately usually called *pinus radiata* or *radiata pine*) and macrocarpa (*cupressus macrocarpa*, always called *macrocarpa* in New Zealand, not *cypress* as in Australia. Few think of macrocarpa as a botanical name; the word is sometimes used by poets for its local flavour). The land has been fenced, and where the fence crosses a creek a *floodgate* has been built. This is a floating piece of fence, made with wire and slabs, able to rise in a flood and let at least some of the floating debris through. Usually after a heavy flood in hilly country a farmer has to repair his floodgates.

The technicalities of dairy farming now are often from agricultural chemistry or concern farm machinery (tractors, pick-up-balers, milking machines and the like), though some words considered dialect in England (e.g. a cow *comes in*, 'calves') remain in general use on New Zealand farms.

This brief survey by no means exhausts, even in outline, the topic of technical languages in New Zealand, and interested students might serve linguistic scholarship well by gathering and publishing lists of terms associated with railways, freezing works, waterside workers, paper manufacture, hop-picking, tobacco-growing, woolstores, and other industries in New Zealand.

Special language attaches not only to particular employments but also to particular interests of the general community. As well as occupations there are preoccupations, such as education, sport, transport, cookery, and government, that have special vocabularies but are a specialised part of the language used by everyone in the community.

Since educational terms differ from state to state in Australia, it is not surprising that New Zealand has its own set of names for the stages in a scholar's progress. He passes through primers (usually Primers I to IV, occupying two years in all) and standards (I to VI, a year in each) in the primary school, and Forms III to VI in the secondary school. Where there is an *intermediate school*, the nearby primary schools, or *contributing schools*, are *decapitated* (i.e. lose Standards V and VI), and the intermediate school has Forms I and II. *School Certificate* (often abbreviated *School Cert.*) is the chief written examination for most schoolchildren. At university (colloquially still called *varsity*, not *uni* as in Australia), each year in the study of a subject is called a *stage*; thus English I and Latin I are Stage I subjects. An extra subject studied for one year, such as Early English, might have 'Stage II status'. The staff of a university talk of Stage I, Stage II, Stage III of their own subject, rather than naming the subject, as 'Who's lecturing to Stage I next year?' The term is convenient and New Zealand academics coming to Australia find the habit of using it difficult to lose.

New Zealand secondary schools have an unfortunate reputation as strongholds of authoritarian attitudes. The American sociologist David P. Ausubel seems to have been taken with the word *a growling*, which he defines in the glossary to his book *The Fern and the Tiki* as 'an angry scolding'. He uses it a number of times, not, it seems, quite idiomatically, though it would require a very subtle analysis to say why. Perhaps it is because the tone of the word does not fit in with the formality which characterises American sociological prose even in its more popular manifestations. The phrase *to growl at* (more idiomatic than the noun *growling*) is really a child's word, and might describe what appears to a child to be anger, but if used by an adult it would be more likely to refer to a gruff pretence of anger, not sarcasm or serious reprimand. There is something playful about the word, a suggestion of bears. A playful bear is perhaps not an ideal guardian of the aspirations of the young, outside New Zealand, but a child who gets through a New Zealand school with no worse fate than a 'growling' does well enough.

In the playground, primary-school children talk of the *shelter shed* (where some Australians use *lunch shed* or *weather shed*) and might eat a *playlunch* (as in parts of Australia, but South Australians *eat their recess*) at morning *playtime* (*recess* in South Australia). They name their games variously from school to school; one example must suffice. In Christchurch a game called *barbadore* is played. (It is called *Red Rover* in South Australia, and has a rougher variant called *British Bulldog*.) *Barbadore* is a single unanalysed word to the children who play it, but at the turn of the century the same game was known in my father's Wairarapa school as *bar-the-gate*, so that the etymology 'bar the door' seems certain.

The small child looks forward to the *school picnic* and a *lolly scramble*; his older brother hopes for a *jersey* in the *First XV* (not, as in the Australian Rules zone of Australia, a guernsey in the First XVIII). Older sportsmen follow football (which always means rugby in New Zealand) in Ranfurly Shield (interprovincial) matches, or follow the fortunes of the *All Blacks*, a name which, according to the *Encyclopaedia of New Zealand*, might have originated in a printer's error in a reference to 'all backs' during the 1905 tour of the United Kingdom. The survival of the name would be due to the black jerseys worn by the team. The word *tour* is almost a football term in New Zealand, with political overtones since the popular slogan, 'No Maoris—No Tour', prevented the sending of a racially selected team to South Africa.

Tramping (Australian *bushwalking*) and mountaineering are typically New Zealand sports. Tramping vocabulary merges with the occupational vocabulary of the *deerculler* or *deerstalker*. Barry Crump's popular book about deerstalkers, *A Good Keen Man*, has added a phrase to the local language by the appeal of its title, though quotations and variants of it are not always without irony.

A curiosity among sporting terms is the *maimai*, a shelter used by duck-shooters on Lake Ellesmere. It appears Polynesian, even more so when an origin suggests itself in the word of equally Polynesian appearance, *maemae*, described by Lt.-Col. J. H. H. St John in a footnote in *Pakeha Rambles Through Maori Lands*, as 'a low hut worked up with sticks and interlaced raupo or fern, open in front, with roof reaching the ground on the windward side'.[13] But the architecture of this hut confirms an origin in the Victorian Aboriginal word *mia mia*. Samuel Butler mentioned the huts, calling them *mimis*, ten years earlier.

The modern urbanised adult is much the same wherever he lives, and he needs few local names for his standardised food, clothing, and equipment. The New Zealand housewife thinks her *pavlova cake* unique, but so does the Australian housewife, and the recipe is in *The Penguin Cookery Book* now. Words for a large sausage (the South Australian *fritz*) vary: sometimes it is *German sausage*, sometimes *Belgian sausage*, sometimes *luncheon sausage*. The first is the oldest name, the second a World War I name, the last perhaps an attempt at a neutral, and so permanent, name, but all now occur together. These names, however, are not confined to New Zealand. The name *cheerios* for small cocktail sausages is perhaps more local. Though New Zealand is a cheese-producing country, no names for cheeses proliferate. In the old days cheese was simply 'white' or 'coloured'. The introduction of blue vein and other cheeses has not resulted in purely local names. So with wines: the special associations that attach to place names in France and Germany do not yet cling to Greenmeadows and Te Kauwhata, and even less perhaps to the Department of Agriculture, though time might alter this.

In clothing the *string singlet* is a common but not purely local sign of manhood; the Australian use of *thongs* was new to me in 1965 for what I had known by the trade name *jandals* in New Zealand, but I saw *thongs* advertised in a New Zealand country newspaper in 1967.

In the days of the *native litter*, transport was of a local kind and with local names. In the days of the *jet boat*, it is not. After a jet boat developed by C. W. F. Hamilton, a Christchurch engineer, had successfully negotiated the Colorado rapids in 1960, they were manufactured under licence outside New Zealand, and the name is not merely local.

[13] *Pakeha Rambles Through Maori Lands*, p. 153.

Even the climate in New Zealand is sufficiently similar to the English climate to ensure the survival of standard terms with standard associations. A few local words like the *nor'wester* of Canterbury and the *southerly* (shared with Australia) have their own local associations, but the New Zealand associations of words such as *hot, cold, fine* and even *drought*, and of words indirectly associated with weather, do not vary greatly from English ones. An Adelaide schoolboy, when asked why pipes sometimes burst in winter, suggested, 'Well, I suppose there's the cold air on the outside of the pipe, and then, I suppose, the warm tobacco. . . .' A boy growing up among New Zealand's sharp frosts would have immediately understood the term 'burst pipes'. Such connotations of words become important in discussing literature, but are a little outside the usual description of language.

When established names are changed in a modern standardised community, they are more likely to be changed by advertisers and public relations men than by traditional linguistic processes. In 1967, the New Zealand growers of tree tomatoes thought that they would be better able to market their fruit under the name *tamarillo*. Interviewed by *The New Zealand Woman's Weekly*,[14] the growers said that they needed an appealing, musical name, easy to spell and pronounce, and with exotic overtones. Influenced by a Latin American name for a small tomato, *tomatillo*, they worked in (how could they not?) the name of the commander of one of the first Maori canoes, Tama, and then, deciding that *tamatillo* was not yet sufficiently easy to say, changed this to *tamarillo*. A curious bit of etymological engineering, and one which overlooked the uncertainty about plurals of words in *-o* (*The Women's Weekly* chooses *tamarillos*), but perhaps it is not atypical of the processes which are beginning to mould language in a highly urbanised age.

New Zealand, with nothing to correspond to the competing state parliaments of Australia, has developed an efficient and pervasive government. This directly affects New Zealand English in the names of government agencies and acts, and indirectly in the effects these agencies and acts have on social life. Thus the introduction of the *forty-hour week* in 1936 not only brought this term into currency but changed the meaning of *weekend* (a two-day holiday, or, in *Labour weekend*, more). As the forty-hour week extended to shops in 1944, *half holiday* disappeared and a new emphasis was given to *late shopping night* or *Friday night shopping* and all the local associations of 'Friday night', a time in country towns to be in the streets and talk to friends.

Even gambling is principally an area of government activity in New Zealand. Perhaps two-up was never so common in New Zealand as in

[14] 20 March 1967, p. 85.

Australia; certainly one Dan Maloney, who wrote *The History of the Addison's Flat Gold Fields*, included a chapter on two-up in his book, but the chapter, quoted in its entirety, runs

Two up
was never played at Addison's. Forty-fives was the favourite card game.

In any case gambling, apart from racing, was likely after 1931 to be a ticket in an art union, subject to a lottery tax of 10 per cent on the nominal value of tickets sold. This measure of government participation and the larger scale of the lottery distinguished the New Zealand *art union* from the less official Australian ones. It was something of a state lottery, and has since 1961 been replaced by the *Golden Kiwi* lottery, which is entirely a state lottery. Off-course betting on racing is likewise brought within the orbit of government control by the *Totalisator Agency Board* or *TAB*, which has been imitated in Australia and elsewhere.

The government has long engaged in transport in New Zealand. The New Zealand Railways are government-owned. The initials NZR must be among the most familiar of initials to all New Zealanders, and when a man charged with stealing a tarpaulin marked NZR pleaded that he did not realise that the letters indicated ownership, and was acquitted, all must have felt something of Mr Bumble's astonishment at the law's occasional unawareness of what is everywhere else well known.

The social reforms of the late thirties, bringing what was then an advanced system of social security, have led to changes in the names of pensions. Universal superannuation, to which everyone contributes during a working life, is clearly something to which all are entitled, and the term *pension*, which had gathered connotations of charity, except in the case of war pensions, has given way to *superannuation benefit*. Even those in need of a more generous *age benefit* need not call it a pension. Child allowance is called a *family benefit* in New Zealand, and what was once the dole is an *unemployment benefit*. There are also *invalids' benefits*, *sickness benefits*, and others.

In other ways government activities have been extended and brought up to date. In 1943 a *Department of External Affairs* was established. A relic of the old order, a *country quota*, which allowed a smaller number of electors in rural constituencies by adding 28 per cent to the rural population, was abolished by the Electoral Amendment Act of 1945. Culture is aided by the *National Library Service*, the *National Orchestra*, and the *New Zealand Broadcasting Corporation* or *NZBC*, while children at school receive excellent *Bulletins* and a *School Journal* from the *School Publications Branch* of the Department of Education. These *School Bulletins* ought to follow the *TAB* across the Tasman.

There are safeguards against the abuse of power in the detailed work of government agencies. One is the *remit*, a resolution from below sent to conferences of any organisation and ultimately to the government. It is a peaceful means of making public opinion known to a government. Another safeguard is the *ombudsman*, who will investigate complaints by citizens against government agencies. Though New Zealand was the first Commonwealth country to appoint an ombudsman, the name was used in New Zealand and elsewhere before the appointment was made in 1962.

A less benign aspect of government is remembered in the *Emergency Regulations* of 1951, and in New Zealand, as elsewhere, *security* is not only social and comforting but also associated with secret police. The frequent use of the phrase *dependent economy*, from the title of the book, *The Instability of a Dependent Economy*, by C. F. G. Simkin, indicates an anxiety of another kind.

Examples of the impingement of politics on New Zealand English could be multiplied, but the interest is more often sociological and political than linguistic. This is because the words, from the administrative Latin component of language, come to the people from above. The government is *they*. Latin origin does not preclude the full popularisation of a word (e.g. *remit* or *macrocarpa*), but, until Latin is more universally taught, much of the language of administration will remain as something known from outside and a little alien to most New Zealanders.

The Maori language no longer contributes greatly to the general English vocabulary in New Zealand. Such recent influence as there has been is in the political sphere. *Maoritanga*, which is gaining wider currency, was devised by the Young Maori Party, and shows European influence in its formation. The word *maaori* originally meant 'clear, intelligible, ordinary', so that, in older Maori, *maaoritanga* might have been an abstract noun meaning 'explanation'. But the word for 'ordinary' (people) was given to Europeans wanting a general name for all the native tribes of New Zealand, and this European sense of *maaori* enters into *Maoritanga*, 'Maori ways and culture'. The preservation of Maori identity, *Maoritanga*, as the Maori is Europeanised, is a political problem discussed in both languages.

Another word recently more prominent in English contexts is *marae*. It refers to the open courtyard in front of a Maori meeting house, but it has come to be used for the oratory and community organisation conducted there. Its overtones recall those of the Latin *forum*.

The word *Pakeha* (European New Zealander) is of long standing, but is perhaps undergoing subtle changes in use as it becomes especially associated with political contexts. 'Maori and Pakeha' (always in that order) rings in many a Pakeha politician's speech. (As a further sign of humility, he frequently writes *pakeha* with a lower case *p*.) The Maori sometimes uses *Pakeha* in a different way. My mother observed two Maori children walking down the street ahead of her, the younger crying, to the embarrassment of the elder, who muttered fiercely, 'I'll give you to the Pakeha'.

It is well to remember when writing of New Zealand English that English is used not only as a first language but also as a second language in New Zealand, and that those who use it as a first language are not all of European descent. Eric Schwimmer[15] gives an illustration of the relevance of this to the Maori's use of English. In Maori, *iwi* means 'bone' and also 'tribe'. (The usual English term *tribe*, which also translates *hapuu*, is an approximate translation, but English lacks exact kinship terms for Maori social organisation; *iwi* means the totality of one's kinsmen.) A Maori adopting English might use 'my bones' to mean his relatives. If this is found laughable by Pakehas (who might forget our strange uses of *blood*), he learns to say 'my relations'; but he still thinks of *iwi*, so that *relations* will have a special meaning for him.

The same is true when English expressions pass into Maori. A *komiti* (committee) on the marae, with its *tiamana* (chairman), *hekeretari* (secretary), and *kai-tiaki i nga moni* ('money-keeper', treasurer) may seem English enough, but the *tiamana* expects a proper speech.

There is much politico-linguistic controversy about the pronunciation of Maori place names in New Zealand. From a linguistic point of view it might seem that the names must be anglicised, as it is difficult to change to a different system of phonetic sounds in mid-sentence. But the linguist merely demonstrates a difficulty, not an impossibility. Many people use French words with near-French pronunciation in English contexts. It can be argued that it is precisely the effort required that makes continuous courteous acknowledgment of the respect due to another group of citizens. It is an ambitious system of linguistic etiquette. In 1964 the ambition seemed to me unlikely to succeed, but during a visit to New Zealand in early 1969 I was surprised to find how much the introduction of correct Maori pronunciation of Maori place names in television weather reports was taken for granted, and when I prided myself among friends on remembering how to pronounce such familiar names as *Kohimaramara*, I felt that my pronunciation was thought a little rough and old-fashioned.

The recent extension of Teachers' Training College courses should permit the teaching of enough Maori to ensure correct pronunciation by teachers. The interest so awakened could do something to bring Pakeha and Maori (in *that* order) closer together, so that future linguists may be able to record a richer infusion of Polynesian elements in the English spoken in New Zealand.

---

[15] *The World of the Maori*, p. 128.

REFERENCES CITED

Ausubel, D. P., *The Fern and the Tiki*, New York, 1965.
Baker, S. J., *The Australian Language*, Sydney, 1945.
———, *New Zealand Slang. A Dictionary of Colloquialisms*, Wellington, n.d.
Bennett, George, *Wanderings in New South Wales*, London, 1834.
Bowen, Godfrey, *Wool Away*, 3rd ed., Christchurch, 1963.
Butler, Samuel, *A First Year in Canterbury Settlement*, ed. A. C. Brassington and P. B. Maling, Auckland, 1964, reprint of first ed., London, 1863.
Crump, Barry, *A Good Keen Man*, Wellington, 1960.
Drummond, Alison, *Married and Gone to New Zealand*, Hamilton, 1960.
Forster, George, *A Voyage Round the World*, in *Georg Forsters Werke*, ed. Robert L. Kahn, Berlin, 1968.
Foster, B., *The Changing English Language*, London and New York, 1968.
Furphy, Joseph, *Rigby's Romance*, ed. R. G. Howarth, Sydney, 1946.
Gunn, J. S., 'The Terminology of the Shearing Industry', University of Sydney, Australian Language Research Centre, *Occasional Papers* Nos. 5 and 6.
Hoggart, Richard, *The Uses of Literacy*, London, 1958.
Kelly, L. G., 'The Phonemes of New Zealand English', *Canadian Journal of Linguistics*, Vol. 2, No. 2, 1966, pp. 79-82.
Maloney, Dan, *The History of Addison's Flat Gold Fields*, Westport, 1923.
May, P. R., *The West Coast Gold Rushes*, 2nd rev. ed., Christchurch, 1967.
Morrell, W. P. (ed.), *Sir Joseph Banks in New Zealand, From his Journal*, Wellington, 1958.
St John, Lt-Col. J. H. H., *Pakeha Rambles Through Maori Lands*, London, 1873.
Schwimmer, Eric, *The World of the Maori*, Wellington, 1966.
Simkin, C. F. G., *The Instability of a Dependent Economy: Economic Fluctuations in New Zealand 1840-1914*, London, 1951.
Slatter, Gordon, *A Gun in my Hand*, Christchurch, 1959.
Turner, G. W., *The English Language in Australia and New Zealand*, London, 1966.
Wardon, R., *Macpherson's Gully*, Christchurch, 1892.
Wright, E. M., *The Life of Joseph Wright*, Oxford, 1932.

7 DON LAYCOCK

PIDGIN ENGLISH IN NEW GUINEA

The history of New Guinea Pidgin English, Melanesian Pidgin, Neo-Melanesian, or Talk Boy, to give it only some of its many names,[1] can be traced back with certainty only about one hundred years. With such a short time span, at such a late stage of human history, when modern technology has facilitated the making, keeping, and multiplying of historical records, one might expect that the documentation of the history of Pidgin would be a simple matter; but such is not the case. The reason it is not so probably lies in the attitudes of the white colonisers of the Pacific, many of whom considered the 'rude barbaric jargon' they used in their daily intercourse with native peoples to be, like the native peoples themselves, unworthy of serious consideration, or even of any more notice than would suffice for daily needs. Nor were the illiterate indigenes in a better position to record the language which many thought to be the true language of the white man. Perhaps some of the answers about the early days of Pidgin lie waiting to be discovered in old correspondence and mission records, and will become available when a full history of the Pacific comes to be written. Until that time, the history of New Guinea Pidgin can be given only in outline, with some *a priori* assistance from the knowledge gained from other areas of the world as to how pidgin languages originate, grow, and spread.

The origin of pidgin languages and creoles[2] has been extensively

---

[1] Throughout this article, 'Pidgin' (capitalised), without further specification, refers to New Guinea Pidgin, and 'pidgin' to pidgin languages in general. No attempt is made to cover the closely related pidgins spoken in the British Solomon Islands, or in the New Hebrides (Beach-la-Mar), although the latter is taken into account in the history of New Guinea Pidgin.

The etymology of the word 'pidgin' is in doubt, although the explanation that it is a Chinese corruption of 'business' ('business English') is usually accepted. However, a plausible case has been made for deriving it from 'Pidian', an old word for Indians on the boundary between Brazil and French Guiana (Kleinecke, 'An Etymology for "Pidgin" ', pp. 271-2).

[2] A pidgin language is said to have become 'creolised' when it becomes the first language of some of its speakers, and the resulting language is called a 'creole'. Pidgin English is creolised to an unknown extent in New Guinea, among perhaps 10,000 or more speakers, mainly on Manus and New Britain.

Pidgin English in New Guinea

debated in recent years,[3] after more than a quarter of a century's general acceptance of Bloomfield's statement that pidgin languages arise from the mutual imitation, by speakers of different languages, of each other's errors in speaking the other's language, or a simplified form of a common language:

> a jargon or a lingua franca is nobody's native language but only a compromise between a foreign speaker's version of a language and a native speaker's version of the foreign speaker's version, and so on, in which each party imperfectly reproduces the other's reproduction.[4]

However, the general agreements in structure between pidgin languages from quite diverse areas and times has led linguists to believe that either the mental processes leading to the forging of a pidgin are the same in all cases, or pidgin languages grow to resemble one another by a process of 'convergent development'.[5] The arguments are much too complex to summarise here,[6] but much of the discussion turns on the 'genetic' relationships of pidgin languages—that is, to what extent pidgins, or mixed languages in general, can be said to be the direct 'descendants' of their main contributing languages. Whinnom[7] provides useful biological models, and a theory of 'tertiary hybridisation', which have yet to be generally assimilated. For Hall,[8] Pidgin English is a descendant of English, and Haitian Creole a descendant of French, without further refinement. However, the question of 'mixed languages' in general has recently been re-argued by Pawley;[9] and certainly many of the linguists[10] who have looked closely at pidgin languages and native languages in the Pacific area tend to have reservations about regarding any pidgin as a direct offshoot of any of its contributing languages. It seems to me that, in spite of the name, it is not realistic to regard Pidgin English as a form of English, certainly not in the same sense as American English is regarded as being a form of English. Nor can Melanesian Pidgin English be regarded as a form of any Melanesian language, in spite of the considerable structural and

---

[3] See especially Hall, 'Creolized Languages and "Genetic Relationships" '; further, articles by Cassidy, Knowlton, Rossetti, Stewart, and Whinnom (in bibliography to this chapter).

[4] *Language*, p. 473.

[5] Weinreich, 'On the Compatability of Genetic Relationship and Convergent Development'.

[6] A brief account is given in Wurm, 'Pidgins, Creoles, and Lingue Franche'.

[7] 'Linguistic Hybridization and the "Special Case" of Pidgins and Creoles'.

[8] 'Creolized Languages'.

[9] 'On the Internal Relationships of Eastern Oceanic Languages', Port Moresby, 1969 (mimeo.).

[10] See especially articles by Capell, Laycock, and Wurm (in bibliography to this chapter).

lexical contributions made by many, in parts unidentified, Melanesian languages.[11]

A pidgin language, on the usual view, can develop anywhere speakers of two or more different languages meet—though hardly 'in the space of a few hours', as claimed by Hall[12]—and, except in the case of creolisation, is native to none of its speakers. The languages involved may be of any type, and there is at least one well-authenticated case—that of Police Motu in Papua—where the essential contributing languages were all indigenous languages of Papua-New Guinea. The more usual instances of pidginisation, however, involve a language of the Indo-European family on the one hand, and, on the other, languages totally different in structure, such as Chinese, African languages, American Indian languages, or native languages of the Pacific. Almost all recorded pidgins are of this type. It has even been suggested[13] as a possible hypothesis, that all European-based pidgins have a common origin in the pidginised form of Italian and Spanish known as Sabir, and widely spoken in the Mediterranean during the Middle Ages; subsequent pidgins based on European languages are 'relexifications' and 'restructurings' of earlier pidgins. On this view, a Portuguese version of Sabir was brought to the Malay archipelago and to Macao; in Macao and Hong Kong, this Portugese pidgin became adapted by the nineteenth-century English settlers of China, the Portuguese vocabulary being replaced by English vocabulary, yielding Chinese Pidgin English, which ultimately stands at the base of the English-based pidgins of the Pacific.

However, Hall[14] provides a diagram of the evolution of various English-based pidgins which separates Chinese Pidgin English off sharply from 'South Seas Pidgin English', deriving them all ultimately from seventeenth-century English, but the eighteenth-century Pacific trade with China, especially in sandalwood and trepang, cannot have been wholly without influence on Pacific pidgins.

[11] Most linguists would nowadays reject, along with Whinnom ('Linguistic Hybridization'), the 'now despised formula of "primitive" creolistics that a pidgin is made up of the vocabulary of one language and the grammar of another', while agreeing with him that 'the observation may be faulty but it reflects a basic reality'.

[12] 'A pidgin can arise—on occasion, even in the space of only a few hours—whenever an emergency situation calls for communication on a minimal level of comprehension' (*Introductory Linguistics*, p. 378). By 1966 Hall has revised this to read: 'only a few hours' trading is necessary for the establishment of a rudimentary pidgin, and a few months or years suffice for the pidgin to assume settled form' (*Pidgin and Creole Languages*, p. xiv). To the author, even the revised time scale appears far too short.

[13] By Whinnom, in 'The origin of European-based Pidgins and Creoles'. This view has been opposed by Vintila-Radulescu, in 'Remarques sur les idiomes créoles'.

[14] 'How Pidgin English Has Evolved'.

ORIGINS OF NEW GUINEA PIDGIN ENGLISH

Whether or not there was influence from Chinese Pidgin English, there grew up, in the eighteenth century in the Pacific, a pidgin language known as Beach-la-Mar (from *bêche-de-mer*, a French name for the trepang), which is still spoken to some extent in the New Hebrides and Fiji. This language, which is described, amusingly if unsatisfactorily, by Churchill, and for which a brief vocabulary is provided by Schmidt,[15] is the direct ancestor of Solomon Islands Pidgin and New Guinea Pidgin, though it shows many differences from both.

By about the middle of the nineteenth century two new motifs in the development of New Guinea Pidgin make their appearance: the development of the Queensland sugar industry, and the appearance of German trading (later, colonial) interests in the Pacific. The relative importance of these two streams has been debated,[16] but it is certain that both played an important part in the development of Melanesian pidgins in general. The Queensland sugar industry required large numbers of labourers who could stand tropical conditions and hard work. In the opinion of the time, it was felt that the first condition excluded white Australians, and that the second excluded Australian Aborigines, so, in 1847, the iniquitous system of 'blackbirding' was introduced, although it was not till later that it became a major industry. Natives of coastal regions of Melanesia—principally the Solomon Islands, Fiji, the New Hebrides, the Louisiade archipelago, New Britain, and New Ireland—were cajoled, kidnapped, or coerced by 'blackbirders' into working for two years on the Queensland canefields. Perhaps in some cases they already spoke Beach-la-Mar or some other form of pidgin; in any case, a pidginised language grew up very quickly in this artificial Queensland community, though records of it are scanty.[17] Here, too, the present-day pattern of the spread of Pidgin was first established, in that the new language tended to be used more as a means of communication between natives of quite diverse linguistic backgrounds, rather than as the vehicle of commands of white overseers.[18]

---

[15] Churchill, *Beach-la-Mar*; Schmidt, 'Le Bichelamar'.

[16] By, for example, Salisbury, in 'Pidgin's Respectable Past'.

[17] A Pidgin English was already current in Australia among the Australian Aborigines, and this may have had some effect on the pidgin of the island labourers. However, no elements in modern New Guinea Pidgin, whether in lexicon or structure, are attributable to the influence of Australian Pidgin English.

[18] This is even more the case today, and, as Wurm remarks (p. 36), 'the number of Europeans in the Territory who can lay claim to full native mastery of the language is astonishingly small' ('English, Pidgin, and What Else?'). In the opinion of the present writer, the number of good European speakers of Pidgin in the Territory is perhaps no more than a few hundred. Much of Hall's analyses of Pidgin suffer from being based on the Pidgin spoken by Europeans rather than natives—an approach justified by him (in *Melanesian Pidgin English*) on the grounds that, as Pidgin is native to neither Europeans nor Melanesians, it is just as valid to use

During the course of the Melanesian labour system in Queensland, and at the end of it in 1902, natives were repatriated when their time had expired. If they were lucky, they were taken to their home islands; others were dropped at the ship's captain's nearest guess as to where they had come from.[19] But, wherever they ended up, they took Pidgin with them, and spread it through countless villages throughout Island Melanesia and New Guinea.

At the same time—the second half of the nineteenth century—Germany was becoming interested in the Pacific, and German traders were operating out of Samoa as far as New Guinea. Their contact with other Pacific islanders, and the fact that their ships' crews were for the most part from Island Melanesia, and already familiar with Beach-la-Mar, helped spread Pidgin throughout New Guinea, and, by the time Rabaul was fully functioning as the German administrative capital in the 1880s, Pidgin had become thoroughly established in the New Britain area—a fact which accounts for the large Tolai (Kuanua) element in the vocabulary of New Guinea Pidgin.

The Rabaul pidgin became, in the course of time, blended with the pidgin of the returning Queensland labourers, and the new language spread rapidly through German New Guinea, in spite of German efforts to replace it with German. In Papua, the opposition of Sir Hubert Murray to Pidgin, and his efforts at establishing Police Motu as the lingua franca, delayed the spread of Pidgin in Papua for some time, but the extensive population movements during World War II brought many Pidgin speakers into Papua, and the opening up of new Highlands areas in Papua has relied on Pidgin as a lingua franca, rather than on Motu. In recent years Pidgin has been spreading throughout all parts of Papua and New Guinea. It is now spoken by well over half a million people in the Territory—for the most part indigenes—and is thus far and away the majority language of Papua-New Guinea, with over twice as many speakers as English, over

---

European informants. This ignores the fact that the non-European speakers of Pidgin are numerically preponderant, and that the amount of Pidgin commonly spoken by Melanesians is far greater than can be observed among Europeans. In the same work (p. 10), anthropologist Gregory Bateson is quoted as supporting a view identical with that of the present author: 'I took the position that Pidgin English is primarily a lingua franca used on plantations, etc., between natives of different linguistic groups, and I regarded this language as the orthodox Pidgin, which the whites try to learn, with varying degrees of success'.

[19] An additional reason for natives being landed at other than their home 'passages' is given by W. G. Ivens, (in an appendix, 'The Queensland Labor Trade', to *Dictionary and Grammar of the Language of Sa'a and Ulawa, Solomon Islands*, 1918, p. 227): 'One used to hear of cases where men were landed elsewhere than at their own homes, owing to a fear of reprisals for some act of wrong-doing which they had committed and which had led to their recruiting'.

Pidgin English in New Guinea 107

four times as many speakers as Police Motu or the largest regional language (Population Census 1966).[20]

CHANGING ATTITUDES TO NEW GUINEA PIDGIN

In the first part of the second half of the nineteenth century, when Pidgin was establishing itself in the New Guinea area, one reads of neither praise nor blame; the existence of Pidgin was simply taken as a fact of life in the islands. But after the establishment of Australian and German control in New Guinea and Papua, two main voices of opposition made themselves heard: that of Sir Hubert Murray in Papua, and that of Baron von Hesse-Wartegg in New Guinea. The latter wrote:

> At the present time it is still possible to eradicate pidgin English. However, if another century passes, this will have to be recognised as impossible, due to the growing population which will by then have become utterly used to it, and in another fifty years the German Reich will here possess a protectorate in which the Mission population will speak only English. This would surely be sad and shameful for the world-position and esteem of Germany.[21]

As has been mentioned, Sir Hubert Murray's unyielding disapprobation of Pidgin resulted in the temporary establishment in Papua of Police Motu, a pidgin language based on an indigenous language (Motu) of the Port Moresby area. In the German-administered areas, however, the more complex linguistic situation negated attempts to establish a native language over a large area. Attempts to establish German as the language of the colony had no better success, although the history of German rule in the area was too short for us now to be able to assess what might have been achieved.[22] Accordingly, the German administrators accepted the use of Pidgin, and the first scientific descriptions of New Guinea Pidgin English

---

[20] The actual figures and percentages of the population of Papua-New Guinea, over the age of ten years, speaking one of the three major languages of the area, as calculated from the 1966 census, are given in the following table:

Language	INDIGENOUS		NON-INDIGENOUS	
	Persons	*Proportion**	*Persons*	*Proportion**
English	193,337	13·26	25,694	97·18
Pidgin	531,690	36·46	17,665	66·81
Police Motu	118,575	8·13	2,196	8·31

* Of total population ten years of age and over, percentage. (From *Population Census 1966: Preliminary Bulletin No. 20: Summary of Population*, Bureau of Statistics, Konedobu, 1969). The number of non-indigenous speakers of Pidgin (based on interviewees' own claims) is greatly exaggerated.

[21] Cited (and translated?) by Baker, in *The Australian Language*, p. 327.

[22] It is still possible to find natives on the north coast, and in New Britain, who have some knowledge of German, from early schooling in that language; but most of these learnt their German at missions *after* the cessation of German administrative control.

were made by Germans.[23] For linguistic reasons excellently outlined by Höltker,[24] Pidgin became the language of Catholic missions in New Guinea (based mainly at Alexishafen and Vunapope), and many scriptural works were written in it; later, dictionaries and grammars appeared from the same sources.[25] In general, speakers of languages other than English have been at least tolerant of Pidgin, having none of the emotional attitudes that English speakers tended to have towards any 'corruption' of their language.[26]

After the mandation of German New Guinea to Australia after World War I, little is heard of Pidgin from Australian sources, except perhaps the comment of the government anthropologist, F. E. Williams, that 'at present the means of communication (in Papua and New Guinea) are pidgin Motu, pidgin English, telepathy, and swearing'.[27] In fact, as Smith[28] points out, the Australian administration never had a consistent or clearly-enunciated language policy. In practice, Pidgin English and Police Motu tended to be used by administrators for all communication with natives, and for schooling, while lip-service was paid to the fostering of English. World War II brought a new practical interest in Pidgin, and the first of Robert A. Hall's publications on New Guinea Pidgin dates from this time, as do also a number of army manuals, of which those by Helton[29] and Murphy[30] are typical, though some of the Pidgin—and the advice[31] —of the former are suspect.

[23] See especially works by Friederici, Nevermann, Schurchardt, and Thurnwald (in bibliography to this chapter).

[24] 'Das Pidgin-English als sprachliches Missionsmittel in Neuguinea'.

[25] Notably those by Fathers Schebesta, Schebesta and Meiser, and Mihalic (see bibliography to this chapter).

[26] This applies equally to non-European migrants to the Territory. The Chinese traders who entered New Guinea under the German administration dealt mainly with the natives and, perforce, learned Pidgin; many never acquired English, and even today it is not uncommon to meet old Chinese with whom one can converse only in Pidgin. This accounts for the remark on the title page of an odd manual entitled *Pidgin English as Used in the Mandated Territory of New Guinea*, by Helton: 'This language is used in conversation with Natives, Asiatics, and German White Missionaries'.

[27] Quoted in Reinecke, 'Marginal Languages'.

[28] 'An Educational Balance Sheet'.

[29] *Pidgin English as Used in the Mandated Territory of New Guinea*.

[30] *The Book of Pidgin English*.

[31] Notably the 'howler'-like quality of the following instructions (p. 9), under the heading, 'Don't Do These Things':

Interfere With Native Women. They might be found willing parties but will spread the news of the affair so as to arouse the jealousy of their husbands. This would mean death or hindrance to the next white man passing that way.

Interfere With Village Pigs. This would be nearly as bad as interfering with the women.

After the war debates for and against Pidgin continue, the main supporter being Robert A. Hall, jun. The United Nations' oft-quoted 1953 —and ill-advised—resolution that Pidgin English be immediately 'abolished' in the Trust Territory provoked a great deal of comment, largely again by Hall, but also by others, in the pages, principally, of such periodicals as *South Pacific* and the *Pacific Islands Monthly*. Most writers appear to support Pidgin, in varying degrees; the main opponent of this period is A. French, who objects to Pidgin on well-known and rational-sounding grounds, but who is unfamiliar with the general linguistic situation on an area where it is inevitable that Pidgin and English must be complementary, not competing, languages:

> What appears to be shocking is the official encouragement of pidgin by the printing of newspapers, books and *school primers* in it. Now it should be obvious that if a native is literate, he is educationally far removed from the stage when it is (theoretically) necessary to speak to him in words of one syllable. To send children to school and encourage them to read pidgin instead of normal English seems odd in the extreme. If natives wish to read in English, it is surely desirable to teach them the English with which they will be able to do so. There is something fantastic about teaching children pidgin English so that they will grow up to read pidgin newspapers and pidgin books and government directives in pidgin. The sensitive native may find it very sinister, because of the gulf that is thereby driven between him and the literate white.[32]

The debate has recently been revived, and similar views are expressed by Gunther.[33] A more balanced case against Pidgin on educational grounds has been expressed by Smith.[34] Against these views are ranged those of the linguists, Laycock[35] and Wurm.[36] Arguments now turn, however, on the possibility of Pidgin becoming a genuine national language of an independent Papua-New Guinea, and for the first time the voices of the indigenous people of the Territory are being heard. As Wurm has pointed out, however, any decisions on the future use of Pidgin in the Territory are not likely to be taken on rational linguistic grounds, but for emotional reasons, either emotional identification with a language that is regarded as being genuinely something that has grown up in New Guinea, on the part of the natives, or emotional opposition to a 'bastard language' on the part of expatriate Europeans.

---

[32] 'Pidgin English in New Guinea', p. 59. See also the same author's 'A Linguistic Problem in Trust Territory'.

[33] 'More English, More Teachers!'

[34] 'An Educational Balance Sheet'.

[35] 'Pidgin's Progress'; also 'Merits of Pidgin'.

[36] 'English, Pidgin, and What Else?'; see also 'Pidgin—A National Language', and 'Papua-New Guinea Nationhood; The Problem of a National Language'.

THE NATURE OF NEW GUINEA PIDGIN ENGLISH TODAY

In spite of the large number of publications on Pidgin English, few people, other than those who speak it well, have much knowledge of what the language is like.[37] Many 'examples' of Pidgin are, as Hall has pointed out,[38] imaginary examples concocted by journalists and amateur philologists, though perhaps none more barbarically than this contribution (quoted in its entirety) by a soldier ('VX20954') on active service in New Guinea:

ALL ABOUT COCONUTS

No—this isn't going to be a dissertation on the origin, botanical peculiarities, or commercial values of the coconut. It's a transcription of a Milne Bay fuzzy-wuzzy's idea of a 'heap silly dam' nut'.

'One time, longa go', says Jimmy, 'we all live much happy. No work. Jes' catchem fish, findem plenty munga in jungle. Now all that no more. Him white mans come, makem poor Jimmy work all day long times, givem strange talks 'bout planetations and fackiterries. Me sweat plenty much—achem in back. All time plant dam' coconuts—one, two, three, millions ob 'em. Big white fella say all for good of black mans. Me no see. Makem all dese trees grow. Now dam' nuts fall aplonka all over. So silly it is. Nuts come bang down on poor Jimmy's head one time. All same give one big 'ead ache. An' what they do wid all dese nuts? Makem all time small bits in choppity injin. Plenty heap work more. Coconuts now all ober dam' Papua. Much trouble bring. Jimmy no laik. All same makem sick like hell. Pah!'

Yes—well, we Diggers think he's got something there![39]

Aside from the fact that coconuts antedate Europeans in the Milne Bay area, and that a falling coconut is usually fatal to anyone it strikes,

---

[37] Even Hall's texts, especially those published in *Melanesian Pidgin English*, show a number of Europeanisms, and occasional mistranslations, as where *mankimasta* (a native servant in the personal service of a European) is translated as 'presumably the white man in charge of the new recruits'! (p. 72). Another text, provided by the anthropologist John Whiting, is somewhat suspicious, and for that reason is worth citing in full, with the translation given:

klostu lɔŋ ars bɪlɔŋ kokonus tri,
wənfɛla meri kəməp lɔŋ mi,
sɪdawn lɔŋ gras—
i-gat bɪgfɛlə ars—
i-tɔk i-lajk pušpuš lɔŋ mi.

By the base of a coconut tree/ a woman came up to me,/ sat down on the grass/ (she had a broad arse)/ and said she would like intercourse with me. (p. 83)

The 'limerick' form of this song, and its thematic resemblance to a bawdy parody of 'Under the Shade of the Old Apple Tree', as well as the occurrence of Pidgin words in unusual forms or meanings (*kokonus* for *kokonas*, 'coconut'; *tri* for *diwai*, 'tree'; and *gras* for *kunai*, 'grass'), all suggest that this text is not a native-produced Pidgin song, but a song invented by the European informant, and that Hall in including it has either been fooled by this, or else is indulging in a mild form of academic joke.

[38] In *Hands Off Pidgin English!*, p. 15.

[39] In *Jungle Warfare: With the Australian Army in the South West Pacific*, Australian War Memorial, Canberra, 1944, p. 14.

phrases such as 'Heap silly dam' nut' (from cowboy films), 'munga' (army slang from North Africa), as well as the whole construction and vocabulary (reminiscent of Dixie and the cotton fields), betray the fact that this cannot possibly represent any form of Pidgin, or English for that matter, ever spoken in the Milne Bay area.

Almost equally fanciful in its idea of what Pidgin is like, but differing from the former extract in that it may well be a genuine piece of Pidgin *as spoken by Europeans*, is the following proclamation, supposedly made to the natives of Rabaul after the Australian capture of the former German town in 1914:

> All boys belong one place, you savvy big master he come now, he new feller master, he strong feller too much, you look him all ships stop place; he small feller ship belonga him. Plenty more big feller he stop place belonga him; now he come here he take all place . . . You look him new feller plag; you savvy him? He belonga British; he more better than other feller; suppose you been makem paper before this new feller master come, you finish time belonga him first; finish time belong him, you like makem new feller paper longa man belonga new feller master, he look out good alonga you; he give good feller kai-kai. Suppose you no look out along him, he cross too much. English new feller master he like him black feller man too much . . . You look out place along him, he look out place alonga you. You no fight other feller black man other feller place, you no kai-kai man. You no steal mary belonga other fella black man . . . Me been talk along you now, now you give three goodfeller cheers belonga new feller master. No more 'um Kaiser . . . God Save Um King.[40]

It is easier to show the general reader, by such examples, what Pidgin is not, than to provide examples of what it is. A number of texts have been published, mainly by Hall,[41] but these have the disadvantage of being transcribed in a scientific orthography unreadable to the layman, and of being dictated by European speakers of Pidgin—albeit excellent speakers. More modern texts have been published by Laycock[42] and Wurm[43] transcribed from tape-recordings of stories told by indigenous speakers. Another example of good modern Pidgin can be found in a play by Leo Hannet, an indigenous student at the University of Papua-New Guinea; the following extract and translation of a spirited dialogue between husband and wife are given here to offset the impression made by the pseudo-Pidgin cited above:

[40] Quoted in Biskup, Jinks, and Nelson, *A Short History of New Guinea*, p. 87. A suspiciously similar passage is quoted by Sayer (*Pidgin English*, p. 19) as being a government notice 'issued to the West African natives after the British obtained victory over the German forces in Togoland and the Cameroons in the great World War'. This notice may have been copied from the New Guinea proclamation, or both may be equally spurious.
[41] See bibliography, various dates.
[42] 'Course in New Guinea (Sepik) Pidgin'.
[43] 'Course in New Guinea Highlands Pidgin'.

RAMRAM: Tande, bringim hap paia i kam; mi laitim simok bilong mi . . . Tande, kam sikirapim baksait bilong mi.
TANDE: Oloman! Yu no save sikirapim baksait bilong yu yet. Yufela ol man i olosem wanem?
RAMRAM: Kam sikirapim baksait bilong mi—Hariap, yu tink mi baim yu nating a? Yu tink $2,000 i samting nating? Wan handred beg rais na suga na ol kain samting—yu inap kandim a?
TANDE: Na husat i tokim yu long maritim mi? Mi bin laik go skul nurs long P.M.C. na yu kam kolim mi.
RAMRAM: Turu a? Na husat i seksek long lukim mi taim mi pinis wok long Rabaul?
TANDE: Husat i bin seksek long yu? A! mi les long pasin bilong yufela ol man i les oltaim. Liklik wan siling i kam i go tasol long spak, spak na spak oltaim. Sapos i nogat ai raun yufela i katim kona nabaut.
RAMRAM: Na yufela ol meri i no gat nans long yu. Yufela pauda, pauda oltaim—ologeta mani i go tasol long pauda na ol samting i smel. Tasol maski long ol. Kam tasol na sikirapim baksait long mi.
TANDE: Oloman, yufela olosem wanem.[44]

Translation:

R: Tande, bring me a light, I want to light my cigarette . . . Tande, come and scratch my back.
T: What, can't you scratch your own back? Who do you men think you are?
R: Come and scratch my back! Hurry up! Do you think I bought you for nothing, eh? You think $2000 is nothing? A hundred bags of rice, and sugar, and everything—could you count it, eh?
T: Well, who asked you to marry me? I was going to go to nursing school when you came for me.
R: Is that so? And who was all a-quiver for me when I finished work in Rabaul?
T: Who was all a-quiver for you? Ah, I'm tired of the way you men go on. Every last shilling we get goes on drinking, drink, drink all the time. If you're not always rotten you all mope all the time.
R: And you women have got no sense. You powder yourselves up all the time—all the money goes on powder and perfume. But forget about that. Just come and scratch my back.
T: Well, you men are the limit.

No full-scale structural account has been provided for Pidgin to date; the best sources are still the cited works by Hall, though the general reader may get more from the introduction to Mihalic's Dictionary. The basis for a transformational analysis of Pidgin is provided by Hooley.[45] A fuller description will be given in a forthcoming handbook by Wurm.

---

[44] 'Em Rod Bilong Kago', in *Kovave* (A Journal of New Guinea Literature), pilot edition, Port Moresby. Typographical errors and some orthographical inconsistencies have been corrected. The rapidly changing nature of Pidgin is evidenced by the fact that two phrases (*katim kona nabaut* and *ol meri i no gat nans*) are unfamiliar to the present author and to European Pidgin speakers of his acquaintance; however, the word *nans* may be a misprint for *sens*, 'sense'.

[45] 'Transformations in Neomelanesian'.

Pidgin English in New Guinea

The following brief account is based on the present author's own acquaintance with Pidgin.

Phonology

The orthography used by Mihalic,[46] and now undergoing revision, recognises the following orthographic symbols, which correspond fairly closely to the phonemes of the language: *a b d e f g h i j k l m n o p r s t u v w y*. The only digraph used is *ng* for [ŋ]. For many Pidgin speakers, however, *f* does not contrast with *p*, nor *v* with *b* (or *w*); and *j* is not often heard, being normally replaced by *s*. On the other hand, the vowel symbols each conceal at least two phonemes in many varieties of Pidgin, as evidenced by the contrast in vowel quality heard in such groups as *hat*, 'hot' / *hat*, 'hard'; *wet*, 'wait' / *bet*, 'bed'; *nil*, 'nail' / *pis*, 'fish'; *kol*, 'cold'/ *dok*, 'dog' / *bol*, 'testicle'; *pul*, 'paddle' / *pul* (or *ful*), 'fool'. In some regional dialects of Pidgin, native linguistic habits may give rise to phonological shifts that sometimes preserve intact the basic phonemic pattern, and at other times obscure it by ignoring the distinctions between some phonemes. Voiceless stops are frequently fricativised in medial position, and unreleased finally; voiced stops are frequently prenasalised in medial position, and devoiced finally.[47] Phonemes *r* and *l*, or *t* and *s*, or *t* and *r*, do not contrast in all dialects of Pidgin, resulting in confusion between such minimal pairs as *lait*, 'light' / *rait*, 'right, writing'; *tait*, 'current' / *tais*, 'swamp'; and *katim*, 'cut' / *karim*, 'carry'.

The restricted phonology and dialect variants of Pidgin have given rise to a number of homophonous and near-homophonous forms, a short list of which follows,[48] with the English words from which they are derived:

banis—bandage, fence	*kol*—coal, cold, call
bek—bag, back	*kot*—court, coat
bikhet—bighead, pig-headed	*lain*—line, learn
gol—goal, gold	*leta*—ladder, letter
hat—heart, hard, hot, hat	*mas*—mast, March, must
het—hat, head	*pait*—bite, fight
is—east, yeast	*pas*—pass, past, fast[49]
kat—cut, card	*plaua*—flour, flower

[46] *Grammar and Dictionary of Neo-Melanesian.*
[47] According to the analysis of Hall in *Melanesian Pidgin English*; however, it seems better to say, as does Mihalic, that voiced stops never occur finally, and to write *pik*, *dok*, rather than *pig*, *dog*.
[48] From processed data sheet for talk, 'The Potential of Pidgin', given by Laycock to the Anthropological Society of New South Wales, 6 September 1966.
[49] According to Lyle Steadman (A.N.U., personal communication) these homophones cause great difficulty on the football field. In normal Pidgin, *pasim* means 'to stop, to fasten', but this has been influenced by English 'pass' (as in 'pass the ball'), and one hears soccer players saying *Pasim bol! Nogat, mi no tok long pasim, pasim tasol!* ('Pass the ball! No, I don't mean stop it, pass it!') Such a semantic ambiguity will of necessity be quickly resolved, probably by the development of another term for 'pass'.

ples—place, village
pris—preach, priest
rait—right, write, ride
sel—sail, shell
siot—shirt, short
sip—ship, jeep, cheap, sheep [50]

sol—shoulder, soul, salt
sok—chalk, sock
spet—split, spade
tait—tight, tide
tret—trade, thread
win—wind, win[51]

Such words are often reinterpreted by native speakers of Pidgin as having the meaning of any possible shared semantic component of the different meanings; thus, *banis* strictly means 'to enclose', a meaning which fits equally well with 'bandage' and 'fence'—and, should the English words 'punish' and 'banish' be taken over into Pidgin, it is likely that they would be given the form *banisim*, with the extended meaning of 'to punish by putting inside (or outside) an enclosure, to ostracise'. In this way English words are semantically restructured in Pidgin.

An anomaly is caused in Pidgin by the fact that in Australian English, the dialect of English which has had the greatest influence on it in recent years, final post-vocalic r does not occur; this results in such pairs as *resa*, 'razor' / *resarim*, 'shave'; *hama*, 'hammer' / *hamarim*, 'to hammer'; *ona*, 'honour' / *onarim*, 'to honour'; *ova*, 'over' / *ovarim*, 'to put over'[52]—but note also *sela*/*selaim*, 'to catch'.

Some such anomalies stem from the inconsistent spelling of Pidgin. The orthography of Pidgin has been a vexed question for many years, and is not yet solved. Initially, the debate turned on whether Pidgin should be spelt so as to approximate English orthography and sound-values, or whether it should be spelt in an approximately phonetic/phonemic way.[53] The latter view has won out, but the regional differences in pronunciation, and varying degrees of competence in English, have meant that no standard

[50] The more usual term for 'sheep' is reduplicated: *sipsip*.
[51] Typical of Pidgin reinterpretation of the semantic range of English words is the use of *windua* for 'window' (*win*, 'wind', plus *dua*, 'door').
[52] Hall (in *Melanesian Pidgin English* and *Pidgin and Creole Languages*) writes the base forms of such words with final *-r*, on the grounds that the final vocalic element of words like *spia*, 'spear', is, in some dialects of Pidgin, really an allophone of the *-r* phoneme, as evidenced by the reappearance of the *-r* in the verb forms (*spirim*, 'to spear'). This analysis is not justified for either Australian English or Pidgin, however, and reflects Hall's use of speakers of American English as informants for his Pidgin descriptions, without reflecting that Pidgin speakers whose first language was American English are a tiny minority of Pidgin speakers, and that their usage is to be taken as non-standard.
Even less justifiable is the use of postvocalic *-r* to indicate the 'long' *a* of *hart*, 'heart'; *ars*, 'arse'. The fact that English orthographic conventions and American speech habits have at least subconsciously influenced Hall is demonstrated by the fact that in the song quoted in note 37, *ars* rhymes with *gras* (not *grars).
[53] For discussion and examples of competing orthographies, see Hall, *A Standard Orthography and List of Suggested Spellings for Neo-Melanesian*, and 'L'ortografia delle lingue pidgin e créole'; also Mihalic, *Grammar and Dictionary*; and Turner, 'Written Pidgin English'.

Pidgin English in New Guinea 115

orthography has yet been accepted, although the spellings of Mihalic's dictionary (currently undergoing revision) and of the recent New Testament translation (*Nupela Testamen*) can be expected to have a lot of influence; these two orthographies differ only slightly from each other. But the spelling of Pidgin used by both natives and Europeans is still very much in a state of flux, rather like the situation with regard to English spelling up to about the seventeenth century, and it is likely to be some time before the question is resolved to everyone's satisfaction.

Lexicon

Though Pidgin is a 'mixed' language, it is in fact somewhat less hybrid in its vocabulary than is English. A realistic count of the vocabulary[54] gives the following figures (which differ only slightly from the count made by Salisbury):[55] English 77 per cent, Tolai 11 per cent, other New Guinea languages (principally Austronesian languages of New Britain and New Ireland) 6 per cent, Malay 1 per cent, German 4 per cent, Latin 3 per cent. No counts have been made for running text, but impressionistically one can say that the proportion of English vocabulary may drop as low as 60 per cent, or rise above 90 per cent, depending on the subject of discourse.

Even this does not give a true picture. Less than half the German words, for example, are in common use, and many of these are gradually being replaced by English equivalents. All of the Latin terms are ecclesiastical, and are used only in mission contexts. The total number of Malay words is only about twenty. And claims that Pidgin has a significant proportion of Portuguese, Spanish, and Polynesian words are wildly exaggerated. The only Portuguese words in Pidgin appear to be *bilinat*, 'areca nut', *pikinini*, 'child', and *save*, 'know'; while from Spanish there are only the words *pato*, 'duck', and *kalabus*, 'prison'. From Polynesian languages there are only about seven words, of which *kanaka*, 'native', *kaikai*, 'food', *lotu*, 'church', and *taro*, 'taro' are typical. The vocabulary of Pidgin is thus no more 'mixed' than any modern European language.

In recent times, however, the influx of new English words has increased considerably; this fact was also noted by Hall,[56] and a warning sounded against indiscriminate borrowing from English by Laycock,[57] lest this lead to the proliferation of homophonous forms and an ultimate break-down of Pidgin structure. It remains to be seen whether Pidgin can survive the continuous influence from English without altogether losing its own identity

[54] From Mihalic, *Grammar and Dictionary*.
[55] 'Pidgin's Respectable Past'.
[56] 'Innovations in Melanesian Pidgin (Neo-Melanesian)'.
[57] 'Pidgin's Progress'.

and becoming a form of 'broken English', such as that spoken by Australian Aborigines.

Grammar

Pidgin shares with English the same major word classes—noun, verb, pronoun, adjective, and adverb—but it uses them with greater flexibility, so that the same 'base' may be used as many different 'parts of speech'; thus we have *strongpela man*, 'strong man', *man i strong*, 'the man is strong', *rop i no gat strong*, 'the rope has no strength', *strongim pos*, 'strengthen the post', and *tok strong*, 'speak loudly' (attributive adjective, predicative adjective, noun, transitive verb, adverb). Not all bases can undergo the same changes, however; thus, *muruk*, 'cassowary', is noun only, *gat*, 'have', is verb only, and *tru*, 'truly', is adverb only.

The pronouns are *mi*, 'I', *yu*, 'thou', *em*, 'he, she', *mipela*, 'we (exclusive)', *yumi*, 'we (inclusive)', *yupela*, 'you', *ol*, 'they'. The form *yumi* is used when the person addressed is included in the action, as when a missionary says *Jisas i dai long yumi*, 'Jesus died for us'; *Jisas i dai long mipela* would mean 'Jesus died for us (missionaries) (and not for you, the congregation)'. Basically, there are only two numbers, singular and plural, but Pidgin is much freer than English in optionally specifying the number of people in a situation: *mi tripela*, 'the three of us (exclusive)'; *yumi tupela*, 'the two of us (inclusive)'; and so on.

Characteristic of Pidgin is the predicate marker *i*, which occurs with all predicates when the subject is third person singular, or plural, all persons; thus, *tispela man i blak*, 'this man is black'; *mipela i go nau*, 'we go now'; *ol meri i stap sikirapim kokonas*, 'the women are grating coconut'. After certain auxiliary verbs such as *ken*, 'be permitted', and *inap*, 'be able', its use is optional: *yupela ken (i) go*, 'you all can go'; *em i inap (i) karim diwai i hevi*, 'he is able to carry a tree which is heavy'.

The only other suffix occurring with verbs is *-im*, which yields active/ transitive/causative verbs: *bruk*, 'broken', *brukim*, 'to break', *pairap*, 'explode', *pairapim*, 'cause to explode'. In some cases the meaning is slightly altered: *kaikai*, 'to eat', *kaikaiim*, 'to bite'.

Tense with verbs is shown by time adverbs (*bai*, 'future tense', *pinis*, 'past tense'), or by auxiliary verbs (*ken*, 'future auxiliary', *bin*, 'past auxiliary'): *tumara bai mi go/ tumara mi ken i go*, 'I shall go tomorrow', *aste mi go pinis/ aste mi bin go*, 'I went yesterday'. The difference between the two usages is largely regional. Where the context makes the tense clear, the tense indication is often omitted: *long naintin-piptinain mi stap Rabaul*, 'in 1959 I was living in Rabaul'.

Most adjectives precede the noun they qualify, and take the suffix *-pela* in attributive position: *olpela haus*, 'an old haus', *strongpela ston*, 'a hard stone' (but note: *haus i ol*, 'the house is old', *ston i strong*, 'the stone is strong'). A number of other adjectives, usually polysyllabic, and often derived from Melanesian languages rather than English, do not follow these rules: *liklik haus*, 'small house', *banana mau*, 'ripe banana', *man marit*, 'married man'. Nouns may also function as attributive adjectives, and in this usage always follow the noun they qualify, and take the main stress: *bokis ain*, 'a metal box', *pik man*, 'a male pig'. These are to be distinguished from noun-noun compounds, which are written as one word, with the attributive noun first, and which, in common with most Pidgin words, take the main stress on the first syllable: *blakbokis*, 'flying fox', *singgelmeri*, 'unmarried woman', *sithaus*, 'latrine'. Both attributive noun-phrases and noun-noun compounds can have the same meaning: *nilpis / pis nil*, 'fish species (with spines)'.

Other types of compound in Pidgin involve a verb and its object, like English 'picklock': *optin*, 'tin-opener', *wetkot*, 'a man awaiting trial', *tanimtok*, 'interpreter'.

On the syntactic level, conjoining of clauses in Pidgin is characterised by co-ordination rather than subordination, though some subordinating conjunctions occur, and their use is on the increase. In most varieties of Pidgin now heard, constructions such as *Mi stap Rabaul; orait, mi stap, na tispela meri i kam sikirapim mi*, 'I was in Rabaul; there I was, and this woman came to make up to me', are frequently replaced by constructions involving subordinating conjunctions: *Taim mi stap Rabaul, tispela meri i kam sikirapim mi*, 'when I was in Rabaul, this woman came to make up to me'; *taim* here is abbreviated from *long taim*, 'at the time (when)'. Similarly, *long wonem*, 'for what', is used for 'because', although *bikos* is also heard.

Literature in Pidgin

Almost all available written material in Pidgin, apart from the collections of anthropologists and linguists, comes from either the missions or the administration. Among the former, the most prolific producers of Bible translations, hymn books, prayer books, and Bible stories have been the Catholic missons based at Alexishafen and Vunapope, though in recent years Protestant missions in Lae, Madang, and Wewak have also been producing similar material in Pidgin. The administration sponsors a newspaper in Pidgin, and produces manuals dealing with such subjects as forestry, hygiene, and politics. However, there is to date little creative literature in Pidgin, a fact which was deplored by Hall over fifteen years ago.[58] Some Europeans, largely as a *tour-de-force*, have translated into

[58] 'The Provision of Literature in Neo-Melanesian'.

Pidgin extracts from European literature,[59] but, whatever the merits of these translations—and all suffer from Europeanisms and a lack of feeling for creativity within Pidgin itself—they have not been accessible to the indigenous people of Papua-New Guinea. Since the establishment of the University of Papua-New Guinea, however, students are being encouraged to write, in English or Pidgin, and a number of Pidgin plays have been written as well as many poems and songs. An extract from one of these plays has been cited above; the same issue of *Kovave* contains some Pidgin songs, and future editions will continue this policy. In this way a medium is provided for an indigenous Pidgin literature; it remains to be seen whether this will in fact develop, but the prognosis seems good.

THE FUTURE OF PIDGIN

The future of Pidgin in Papua and New Guinea is inextricably bound up with two other factors; the linguistic situation in the Territory as a whole, and the question of developing nationalism and future independence. The linguistic situation has been surveyed by Wurm;[60] briefly, the position is that there are some 700 distinct languages in Australian-administered Papua-New Guinea, none of which has a sufficient number of speakers to have any hope at all of being used to any extent beyond their present boundaries. If the Territory is ever to achieve any kind of political cohesion, a unifying language is essential, and the only candidates for election are English and Pidgin. At present Pidgin seems in the stronger position, as being the language best known to residents of all races in the Territory; but increasing education in English, and the prestige value of English as a language for communication with the outside world, may tip the scales the other way. The final decision may well depend on what New Guinea's leaders think of Australia's administration; if they choose Pidgin, it will be because they regard English as the language of the foreign colonialists, and wish to use a language with which they can emotionally identify. If they choose English, however, it will be a vindication of administration policy. If this is to be the case, then Pidgin could be regarded even now as obsolescent, even though it may take a century to disappear, and join such other Pidgins as Chinese Pidgin as a historical curiosity. But the current strength and rapid development of Pidgin makes such an outcome not necessarily a historical inevitability, and Pidgin may yet come to take a place among the fully-recognised languages of the world.

[59] Murphy, *The Book of Pidgin English*, translation of passages from Shakespeare; Gaywood, 'The Use of Pidgin English', translation of a passage from Sophocles; Hall, 'Pidgin languages', translation of the myth of Theseus and Ariadne.

[60] See, especially, 'Language in Papua-New Guinea', 'The Papuan Linguistic Situation'.

REFERENCES CITED

Baker, S. J., *The Australian Language*, 2nd ed., Sydney, 1966.
——, 'The Literature of Pidgin English', *American Speech*, Vol. 19, 1944.
——, 'Pidgin: Birth of a New Language', *Sydney Morning Herald*, 18 July 1953, p. 7.
——, 'Pidgin English', *Australian Encyclopedia*, 1965.
——, 'Pidgin English', *Encyclopedia Brittanica*, 1950 ed.
Bateson, Gregory, 'Pidgin English and Cross-Cultural Communication', *Transactions of the New York Academy of Sciences*, Vol. 2, 1943, pp. 137-41.
Biskup, P., Jinks, B., and Nelson, H., *A Short History of New Guinea*, Sydney, 1968.
Bloomfield, L., *Language*, New York, 1933.
Brown, E. T., Reply to French, *Australian Quarterly*, Vol. 26, No. 1, 1954, pp. 94-5.
'Buk bilong Askim', South Sea Evangelical Mission, n.p., n.d. (mimeo.).
Buk bilong beten end singsing bilong ol katolik, Westmead, 1960.
Buk raring na singsing, Vunapope, 1951.
Buk Song Bilong Lotu long Tok Pisin, Palmerston North, n.d.
Capell, Arthur, 'Oceanic Linguistics Today', *Current Anthropology*, Vol. 3, 1962, pp. 371-428.
Cassidy, F. G., 'Toward the Recovery of an Early English-African Pidgin'. In *Colloque sur le multilinguisme*, Deuxième Réunion du Comité Interafricain de Linguistique, Brazzaville, 16-21 July 1962, Bureau des Publications CCTA, London, 1964, pp. 267-77.
Churchill, William, *Beach-la-Mar*, Carnegie Institute of Washington Publication No. 154, Washington, 1911.
Clerk, D. H., 'Pidgin English: South Pacific Polyglot', *Pacific Discovery*, Vol. 8, No. 5, 1955, pp. 8-12.
Dawkins, Harry, 'The Possibilities of Pidgin', *Pacific Islands Monthly*, Vol. 24, No. 2, 1953, pp. 55-9.
——, 'Pidgin English in New Guinea', *Australian Quarterly*, Vol. 23, No. 4, 1951, pp. 57-60.
French, A., 'A Linguistic Problem in Trust Territory', *Eastern World*, Vol. 9, No. 1, 1955, pp. 21-3.
Friederici, Georg, 'Pidgin-Englisch in Deutsch-Neu-Guinea', *Koloniale Rundschau*, 1911, pp. 92-106.
Gaywood, H. C., 'The Use of Pidgin English', *South Pacific*, Vol. 5, 1951, pp. 101-3.
Gunther, J. T., 'More English, More Teachers!' *New Guinea*, Vol. 4, No. 2, 1969, pp. 43-53.
Hall, Robert A., jun., 'Can Pidgin be Used for Instruction in New Guinea?', *Pacific Islands Monthly*, Vol. 25, No. 1, 1954, pp. 17-98.
——, 'Colonial Policy and Neo-Melanesian', *Anthropological Linguistics*, Vol. 1, No. 3, 1959, pp. 22-7.
——, 'Creolized Languages and Genetic Relationships', *Word*, Vol. 14, 1958, pp. 367-73.
——, 'Expert Urges Extended Use of Pidgin English', *Pacific Islands Monthly*, Vol. 24, No. 10, 1954, pp. 47, 49-50.
——, *Hands off Pidgin English!*, Sydney, 1955.
——, 'How Pidgin English has Evolved', *New Scientist*, Vol. 9, 1961, pp. 413-15.
——, 'Innovations in Melanesian Pidgin (Neo-Melanesian)', *Oceania*, Vol. 26, 1956, pp. 91-109.
——, *Introductory Linguistics*, Philadelphia, 1964.
——, 'The Life-cycle of Pidgin Languages', *Lingua*, Vol. 11, 1962, pp. 151-6.
——, *Melanesian Pidgin English: Grammar, Texts, Vocabulary*, Baltimore, 1943.
——, *Melanesian Pidgin Phrase-Book and Vocabulary*, Baltimore, 1943 (identical with the edition published for the United States Armed Forces Institute (1942?)).
——, 'Neo-Melanesian and Glottochronology', *International Journal of American Linguistics*, Vol. 25, 1959, pp. 265-7.

———, ' "Neo-Melanesian" Instead of "Pidgin English" ', *Modern Language Notes*, Vol. 30, 1955, p. 76.
———, 'L'ortografia delle lingue pidgin e créole', *Ioanni Dominici Serra ex munere laeto infereae—Raccolta di studî in onore di G. D. Serra*, Naples, 1959, pp. 205-13.
———, 'Pidgin', *Encyclopedia Brittanica*, 1961 ed.
———, *Pidgin and Creole Languages*, Ithaca, 1966.
———, 'Pidgin English', *Current Affairs Bulletin*, Vol. 14, No. 12, 1954 (unsigned).
———, 'Pidgin English and Linguistic Change', *Lingua*, Vol. 3, 1952, pp. 138-46.
———, 'Pidgin Languages', *Scientific American*, Vol. 200, 1959, pp. 124-34.
———, 'The Provision of Literature in Neo-Melanesian', *South Pacific*, Vol. 7, 1954, pp. 942-4.
———, Review of Sayer, *Pidgin English, Language*, Vol. 20, 1944, pp. 171-4.
———, 'A Scientific Approach to Pidgin', *Papua and New Guinea Scientific Society Annual Report and Proceedings*, 1954, pp. 21-5.
———, 'Sostrato e lingue créole', *Archivio glottologico italiano*, Vol. 40, 1955, pp. 1-9.
———, 'A Standard Orthography and List of Suggested Spellings for Neo-Melanesian', Port Moresby, 1955 (mimeo.).
———, 'The Status of Melanesian Pidgin', *Australian Quarterly*, Vol. 26, No. 2, 1954, pp. 85-92 (also *South Pacific*, Vol. 7, 1954, pp. 916-20).
———, 'Two Melanesian Pidgin Texts (with commentary)', *Studies in Linguistics*, Vol. 1, No. 6, 1942, pp. 1-4.
———, 'The Vocabulary of Melanesian Pidgin English', *American Speech*, Vol. 18, 1943, pp. 192-9.
———, ' "Yes" and "No" in Neo-Melanesian', *Modern Language Notes*, Vol. 71, 1956, pp. 502-3.
——— and Bateson, G., 'A Melanesian Culture-contact Myth in Pidgin English', *Journal of American Folklore*, Vol. 57, 1944, pp. 255-62.
Hannet, Leo, 'Em Rod Bilong Kago', *Kovave*, 1969, pp. 47-51.
Helton, E. C. H., *Pidgin English as Used in the Mandated Territory of New Guinea*, Brisbane, n.d.
Holahi-haho! Buk bilong Singsing, Westmead, 1960.
Höltker, Georg, 'Das Pidgin-Englisch als sprachliches Missionsmittel in Neuguinea', *Neue Zeitschrift für Missionswissenschaft*, Vol. 1, 1945, pp. 44-63.
Hooley, Bruce A., 'Transformations in Neomelanesian', *Oceania*, Vol. 33, 1963, pp. 116-27.
Hull, Brian, 'The Use of Pidgin in the House of Assembly', *Journal of the Papua and New Guinea Society*, Vol. 2, 1968, pp. 22-5.
Jespersen, Otto, *Language, Its Nature, Development, and Origin*, London, 1922.
Kleinecke, David, 'An Etymology for "Pidgin" ', *International Journal of American Linguistics*, Vol. 25, 1959, pp. 271-2.
Knowlton, E. C., jun., 'Pidgin English and Portuguese'. In *Proceedings of the Symposium on Historical, Archaeological and Linguistic Studies on Southern China, South-East Asia and the Hong Kong Region*, ed. F. S. Drake, Hong Kong, 1967, pp. 228-37.
Landtman, Gunnar, *The Kiwai Papuans of British New Guinea*, London, 1927 (esp. Chapter 33, 'The Pidgin-English of the Kiwais').
———, 'The Pidgin English of British New Guinea', *Neuphilologische Mitteilungen*, Vol. 19, 1918, pp. 62-74.
Laycock, Donald C., 'Course in New Guinea (Sepik) Pidgin' (with tape recordings). Department of Anthropology (Linguistics), Canberra, 1965 (mimeo.).
———, 'Merits of Pidgin', *The Australian*, 17 January 1966.
———, 'Papuans and Pidgin: Aspects of Bilingualism in New Guinea', *Te Reo*, Vol. 9, 1966, pp. 44-51.
———, 'Pidgin's Progress', *New Guinea*, Vol. 4, No. 2, 1969, pp. 8-15.

———, 'The Potential of Pidgin', [data sheet for] paper read to the Anthropological Society of New South Wales, 6 September 1966 (mimeo.).
Levi, Laurel, *Pidgin English Kuk Buk*, Rabaul, 1964.
Liklik Katolik Baibel, Alexishafen, 1934, and later editions.
Lokol Gavman long Territory bilong Papua and New Guinea, Department of Information and Extension Services, Port Moresby, 1967.
McDavid, Raven, Review of Hall, *Melanesian Pidgin English* and *Melanesian Pidgin Phrase-Book*, *Language*, Vol. 20, 1944, pp. 168-71.
Marshall, A. J., 'Pidgin English of the South Seas', *Geographical Magazine*, Vol. 22, 1949, pp. 292-305.
Mead, Margaret, 'Discussion of the Symposium Papers', *Anthropological Linguistics*, Vol. 1, No. 3, 1959, pp. 32-33.
———, 'Talk Boy', *Asia*, Vol. 31, 1931, pp. 141-51, 191.
Mihalic, Francis, *Grammar and Dictionary of Neo-Melanesian*, Techny, Illinois, 1957.
Morgan, Raleigh, Review of Hall, *Hands off Pidgin English!*, *Language*, Vol. 32, 1956, pp. 368-74.
Murphy, John J., *The Book of Pidgin English*, Brisbane, 1943.
Nevermann, H., 'Das melanesische Pidgin-Englisch', *Englische Studien*, Vol. 63, 1929, pp. 252-68.
Nupela Testamen bilong Jisas Kraist, British and Foreign Bible Society, Port Moresby, 1968.
Pieris, W. V. D., *Gutpela Samting long Kokonas*, Sydney, 1955.
Pionnier, Fr, 'Pidgin English ou Biche-la-Mar', *Revue de linguistique et de philologie comparée*, Vol. 46, 1913, pp. 100-17, 184-98.
Population Census 1966. Preliminary Bulletin No. 20: Summary of Population, Bureau of Statistics, Konedobu, 1969.
Prick van Wely, F. P. E., 'Das Alter des Pidgin English', *Englische Studien*, Vol. 44, 1912, pp. 295-6.
Reed, Stephen Winsor, 'The Making of Modern New Guinea, with Special Reference to Culture Contact in the Mandated Territory', *American Philosophical Society Memoir* No. 18, 1942, Philadelphia, 1943.
Reinecke, John E., Marginal Languages: A Sociological Study of the Creole Languages and Trade Jargons, Yale University Ph.D. dissertation, 1937.
Roberts, Edmund, 'Pidgin English: A True Lingua Franca', *Eastern World*, Vol. 6, No. 10, 1952, p. 29.
Rossetti, A., 'Langue mixte et mélange des langues', *Acta linguistica*, Vol. 5, 1945-9, pp. 73-9.
Salisbury, R., 'Pidgin's Respectable Past', *New Guinea*, Vol. 2, No. 2, 1967, pp. 44-8.
'Sampela Tok bilong Baibel', South Sea Evangelical Mission, n.p., n.d. (mimeo.).
Sayer, Edgar Sheppard, 'Pidgin English', Toronto, 1939 (mimeo.).
Schebesta, J., *Pijin-Grammatik*, Alexishafen, n.d.
——— and Meiser, Leo, *Dictionary of Bisnis-English (Pidgin English)*, Alexishafen, 1945.
Schmidt, H., 'Le Bichelamar', *Études mélanesiennes*, NS Vols. 10-11, 1956-7, pp. 119-36.
Schuchardt, Hugo, 'Beiträge zur Kenntnis des englischen Kreolisch. II. Melaneso-Englisches', *Englische Studien*, Vol. 13, 1889, pp. 158-62.
———, 'Kreolische Studien. V. Über das Melaneso-Englische', *Sitzungsberichte der k.k. Akademie der Wissenschaften zu Wien (Philosophisch-historische Klasse)*, Vol. 105, 1883, pp. 131-61.
Smith, Geoffrey, 'An Educational Balance Sheet', *New Guinea*, Vol. 4, No. 2, 1969, pp. 16-29.
Stewart, W. A., 'Creole Languages in the Caribbean'. In *Study of the Role of Second Languages in Asia, Africa, and Latin America*, ed. Frank A. Rice, Washington, 1962, pp. 34-53.
Thurnwald, Richard, *Ethno-psychologische Studien an Südseevölkern auf dem Bismarck-Archipel und den Salomo-Inseln*, Leipzig, 1913.

Tudor, Judy, 'Pidgin—"Illegitimate" but here to stay', *Pacific Islands Monthly*, Vol. 24, No. 1, 1953, pp. 135-6.
Turner, G. W., 'Written Pidgin English', *Te Reo*, Vol. 3, 1960, pp. 54-64.
Vintila-Radulescu, Ioana, 'Remarques sur les idiomes créoles', *Revue roumaine de linguistique*, Vol. 12, 1967, pp. 229-43.
Wedgwood, Camilla, 'The Problem of "Pidgin" in the Trust Territory of New Guinea'. In *The Use of Vernacular Languages in Education*, UNESCO, Paris, 1953, pp. 103-15 (also *South Pacific*, Vol. 7, 1954, pp. 782-9).
Weinreich, Uriel, 'On the Compatibility of Genetic Relationship and Convergent Development', *Word*, Vol. 14, 1958, pp. 374-9.
Whinnom, K., 'Linguistic Hybridization and the "Special Case" of Pidgins and Creoles', n.p., 1967 (mimeo.).
———, 'The Origin of European-based Pidgins and Creoles', *Orbis*, Vol. 14, 1965, pp. 509-27.
Wurm, Stephen, 'Course in New Guinea Highlands Pidgin' (with tape recordings), Department of Anthropology (Linguistics), Canberra, 1965 (mimeo.).
———, 'English, Pidgin, and What Else?', *New Guinea*, Vol. 4, No. 2, 1969, pp. 30-42.
———, *Handbook of New Guinea Pidgin*. Pacific Linguistics C2, Canberra, (in press).
———, 'Language in Papua-New Guinea', *Current Affairs Bulletin*, Vol. 43, No. 7, 1969 (unsigned).
———, 'Papua-New Guinea Nationhood: The Problem of a National Language', *Journal of the Papua and New Guinea Society*, Vol. 1, 1966, pp. 7-19.
———, 'The Papuan Linguistic Situation'. In *Current Trends in Linguistics, Vol. 8: Linguistics in Oceania*, The Hague, (in press).
———, 'Pidgin—A National Language', *New Guinea*, Vol. 7, No. 1, 1966, pp. 49-54.
———, 'Pidgins, Creoles, and Lingue Franche'. In *Current Trends in Linguistics, Vol. 8: Linguistics in Oceania*, The Hague, (in press).

MICHAEL G. CLYNE

MIGRANT ENGLISH IN AUSTRALIA

Successive waves of individual, group, and chain migration from non-English-speaking countries have made Australia a potentially ideal laboratory for the study of languages in contact. Unfortunately, very little advantage has so far been taken of the opportunities available for on-the-spot research in this field, though the conclusions of such investigations could be applied in migration planning and in the teaching of English as a second language. They could also throw light on possible linguistic and sociolinguistic universals of language contact.

Three main complexes of research topics will be considered in this paper: firstly, bilingualism, second language learning, language shift, contrastive structure, interference phenomena in migrant English; secondly, speech-communication patterns; and thirdly, stabilised interference, substrata, and the influence of migrant English on Australian English.

BILINGUALISM

The term 'migrant English' is something of a misnomer. There are as many types of migrant English as there are migrants to speak it. Variations will be produced by such factors as the migrant's mother tongue and any other language(s) he may speak; the age at which he migrated; his previous contact with English and the nature of this contact; his educational background and literacy; his social contacts in Australia; and his communication habits and environment.

That language and social assimilation are closely connected is shown in the results of sociological and psychological surveys.[1]

Language assimilation is a dual process affecting not only English but also the mother tongue, and any material collected on migrant English is of additional value if supplemented by a sample of the informant's first language. A full investigation of English marked by interference from another language must be made with reference to the language which is

[1] See Zubrzycki, 'Immigrants and Cultural Conflict', *Settlers of the Latrobe Valley*; Taft, *From Stranger to Citizen*.

causing the interference. Comparative data in English and the mother tongue are being gathered in surveys being conducted in the Wollongong-Port Kembla district and in Queensland. The new way of life and environment confronting the migrant in Australia may not be covered by his vocabulary in his mother tongue, resulting in the transference of English lexemes and/or sememes into the first language. Such transference is also promoted by morphemic correspondence between the items of the two languages, and by an inclination to choose the item requiring the least articulatory, semantic, or syntactic effort (i.e. fewer syllables, reduction in the numbers of a given field, and the construction least taxing on the temporary memory, respectively).[2] A modest start has been made at collecting material of this kind.[3] It would be worthwhile to countercheck to what extent these and other linguistic and extra-linguistic factors function as interference catalysts in the English of migrants of different language backgrounds.[4]

Brief recordings of the informants' English made in conjunction with the migrant German project[5] suggest that lexical and syntactic transference in both directions is promoted by these causes. The use of actual German lexemes in English is usually indicative of little contact with monolingual Australians and/or much contact with bilinguals, who converse in both languages and are able to decode the 'mixture'. But the majority of informants often transfer the meaning of a German word to the nearest English equivalent. One of the most acute problems of German and Dutch-speaking migrants in both their first and second languages appears to be the use of prepositions. The relation of this to the structural similarity of the bilingual's languages, and the amount of morphemic overlap, could be shown through investigations into the bilingualism of other groups of migrants.

Generally there is, among adults and older children, a high correlation between proficiency in the mother tongue and proficiency in the new language. Some migrants find themselves in a state of 'linguistic homelessness'[6] in which they are no longer able to fully express themselves in their first language, while their English is very broken and inadequate. It would be possible, by considering four pairs of contact situations in Australia, to observe and contrast interference phenomena between similarly structured

[2] See Clyne, *Transference and Triggering*, pp. 71-83.

[3] For German: Clyne, 'Some Instances of Limitations on Speech Capacity as Exhibited in German-English Bilinguals'; also *Transference and Triggering*. For Dutch: Nijenhuis, *Het Nederlands in Australië*. For Italian: Rando, 'Influenze dell' inglese sull' italiano di Sydney'; Andreoni, 'Australitalian'.

[4] See the table in Weinreich, *Languages in Contact*, pp. 64-5.

[5] A research project supported by the Australian Research Grants Committee. Part of this is reported on in Clyne, *Transference and Triggering*.

[6] See Schischkoff, 'Heimatlose in der Sprache'.

languages with similar sociological conditions[7] prevailing in the migrant group (compare English-German with English-Dutch); very differently structured languages with fairly similar sociological conditions (compare English-German with English-Hungarian); similarly structured languages with different sociological conditions (compare English-Italian with English-French); and differently structured languages with different sociological conditions (compare English-Dutch with English-Turkish).

Tarnawski's pilot study on migrant English deals with the aural-oral command of the Australian English of sixty-four post-war German-speaking migrants in Brisbane.[8] The informants were tested in discriminatory perception of Australian English phones that contrast with German ones, ability to reproduce Australian English phones heard on tape, and facility at selecting from pairs of sentences those sentences which contain syntactic or semantic features transferred from German. The tests were also administered on a control group of native Australian English speakers, and listener tests with native speaker informants were employed to assess the proficiency of the migrant subjects. In addition free speech was recorded and analysed by auditory and acoustic methods, and intonation tests were given. The subjects were classified according to a social rating scale, educational background, and the extent of their formal tuition in English. The latter variable functioned only in the phonological recognition and grammar and idiom recognition tests, while education was a factor in the conversation.

A project now under way at Wollongong University College is aimed at examining the English phonology, lexicon, and grammar of German, Greek, and Spanish migrants in the Wollongong-Port Kembla industrial area by means of periodic tape recordings, in relation to sociological factors and to English influence on their mother tongue.

Thorough investigations into migrant English, culminating in contrastive analyses between Australian English and the mother tongues of migrants, are an essential prerequisite for the drawing up of effective teaching programs in English for New Australians.[9]

Apart from phonemic gaps in the migrant's base language (e.g. the absence of phonemes /θ/ and /ð/ in some languages, which promotes the non-differentiation of /sɪŋk/ and /θɪŋk/, and /boʊt/ and /boʊθ/ in the

---

[7] E.g. distribution and attitudes of migrants, choice of language used, education and literacy, relationship to Anglo-Saxon civilisation.

[8] Tarnawski, The Aural and Oral Command of English of a Group of German-speaking Migrants in the Brisbane Area.

[9] See Platt, 'A Comparative Study of the Phonetics of Australian English and German'. Some contrastive analysis work has already been done by the Commonwealth Office of Education for its teachers' booklets, *English—A New Language*.

speech of German and other migrants[10]), the social stratification of Australian English should be taken into account in descriptions of the phonology of migrants' English. A migrant who, in his mother tongue, does not use [ɛɪ], [ʌɪ], or [ʌ·ɪ] (Cultivated, General, and Broad Australian respectively for the diphthong in *make*), will substitute a near equivalent from his first language. Whether [eː] or [aɪ] is chosen will frequently depend on which variety of Australian English the speaker is most often confronted with, or which social group he wishes to identify himself with. He may, in fact, be less able to discriminate between [ʌɪ] and [aɪ] than between [eː] (the monophthong separating [ɛ] from [ɪ]) and the diphthong [ɛɪ], and thus choose [aɪ],[11] which an Australian hearer might interpret as 'very broad'. Similar hypotheses can be framed for [oː] versus [au] (Australian English [ou]-[ʌu]). Previous knowledge of English tends to favour a British or American pronunciation sometimes modified towards Cultivated or General Australian.

The migrant's first working environment in Australia may often be of decisive importance. Some new arrivals (especially displaced persons) with a good educational background have 'picked up' Broad Australian phonology, vocabulary, and grammar from workmates while working in temporary menial jobs in order to establish themselves. Such a discrepancy between a higher sociolect of the mother tongue and a lower sociolect of English has not always helped the marginal intellectual back to his original social status.[12] On the other hand, some migrants (especially young people) have, through social contact in Australia, acquired a 'higher' sociolect of English than that of their native language. Sometimes a phoneme from the migrant's dialect overlaps, or nearly overlaps, with either the Cultivated, General, or Broad Australian sound and is therefore employed, irrespective of which Australian English sociolect is generally spoken by the person concerned. These phenomena could profitably be traced in the English of migrants of different language and social backgrounds. The results of the Mitchell and Delbridge survey suggest that the children of immigrants are a little more likely to speak Cultivated Australian and a little less likely to speak Broad Australian than children of Australian-born parents.[13]

Items from the overlapping area between English and the other languages—consisting of proper nouns, lexemes identical or nearly identical in the two languages, and unintegrated and partially integrated

[10] Tarnawski's German-speaking informants realise /ð/ as [t] in final position, but the majority realise it as [s] in initial position.
[11] See Koch-Emmery, 'Die Rolle der Zweisprachigen im heutigen Australien'.
[12] For discussion of the term 'sociolect' see Hammarström, *Linguistische Einheiten im Rahmen der modernen Sprachwissenschaft*, p. 11.
[13] Mitchell and Delbridge, *The Speech of Australian Adolescents*, pp. 44-5.

'loanwords'—can act as trigger words.¹⁴ The ambiguous affiliations of the trigger words cause many speakers to lose their linguistic bearings, and they switch into the other language for the rest of the sentence, for several sentences, or until the next trigger word. Such switches will also occur at the beginning of a phrase in anticipation of a trigger word. Among trilinguals, an English loanword used in both the other languages may cause switching between the two other languages. Such switching occurs mainly—though not exclusively, since the speaker tends to speak his first language to bilinguals and English to monolinguals—from the mother tongue into English. Switching can also be externally conditioned, by setting, topic, or interlocutor.

If a person of an age at which his speech habits are already fixed begins to learn a new language, it is very likely that his speech in this new language will be marked by phonic interference (i.e. he will have a 'foreign accent', especially when talking under stress conditions). Haugen asserts that speech habits are usually fixed by the fourteenth year, but our observations among German-speaking migrant children in Australia suggest that the crucial age is probably twelve.¹⁵ There will, of course, always be individuals who do not master certain sounds (e.g. the Australian English [ɹ]) even if they have spoken English since an early age, and others who, though they learn the language in the later years of adolescence, cannot be detected as 'foreigners'. There is a need for a large-scale research project on the speech of people of different language and social backgrounds who have migrated at different ages, to throw light on the fixing of phonological habits. This could be verified by listener tests with monolingual Australians as informants.

At the lexical and grammatical levels of language it would be very much more difficult to establish at what age the handicaps of interference become insuperable. Zabrocki's experimental courses lead to his postulation of the acquisition of structural matrices, which is usually completed by the age of fifteen: from that age it becomes increasingly difficult to build up the matrices, which are the speaker's means of 'transforming reality' into a particular language.¹⁶ Tests similar to those designed in Canada by Lambert and his associates¹⁷ could be used to correlate age at arrival in Australia and language dominance of migrants of different bilingual backgrounds. This could show under what conditions true (balanced) bilingualism is feasible. Diachronic material collected over a period of some years could

---

¹⁴ See Clyne, *Transference and Triggering*, pp. 84-99.
¹⁵ Haugen, *The Norwegian Language in America*, Vol. 2, p. 334; also Clyne, *Transference and Triggering*, p. 26.
¹⁶ See Zabrocki, 'Kodematische Grundlagen'.
¹⁷ See Lambert, 'Measurement of the Linguistic Dominance of Bilinguals'; also Lambert, Havelka, and Crosby, 'The Influence of Language Acquisition Contexts on Bilingualism'.

indicate the extent to which a knowledge of English may deteriorate again in the later years of a migrant's life. (We have observed this phenomenon occasionally among German-speaking pre-war migrants.)

The language assimilation of British and North American migrants is also worth investigating to establish the extent and speed of phonetic, lexical, and grammatical adjustment; though this is, of course, largely idiolectal and could best be described in terms of case studies.

We have mentioned the importance of setting and interlocutor in determining which language an item (or items) is (are) chosen from. It is largely a question of 'Who speaks what language to whom and when?'[18] Many bilinguals use mainly one language for some domains and the other for different domains, for example the mother tongue for home and church, English for neighbourhood and work.[19] Some pre-school children (especially only children) of German parents do not know the English for objects around the house or the German for most concepts not relating directly to home life. Many German-speaking post-war immigrants employ English to talk about life in Australia and German to describe their past experiences in Europe. A phenomenon recurring in families of different nationalities is that children speak English with their parents' pronunciation and intonation in conversation with them, but otherwise employ an English indistinguishable from other Australian children.

Mitchell's enumeration of 'absorption, dispersal, interaction, generalisation, and levelling' as 'ruling tendencies'[20] still holds true today. Migrant children of the same ethnic group will usually chatter in English while playing on the streets of outer Melbourne suburbs. A limited survey[21] appears to indicate that German-speaking post-war migrants address their children in German while the latter answer chiefly in English (most especially after the age of ten, or where there is more than one child). This pattern is also widespread among Dutch migrants and perhaps in other ethnic groups too. Second generation children who answer their German-speaking parents in English will occasionally slip into their English a German item used by their parents in the previous sentence (e.g. 'Wenn du allein gehst.' 'But I'm not going *allein*'). R. Johnston[22] proves her hypothesis that, in Polish migrant families, more boys than girls prefer to speak English at home. Most of the boys in her sample would rather talk English, while nearly half the girls wish to speak both languages. The absence of a common active linguistic medium in the bilingual pattern of communi-

[18] Cf. Fishman, 'Who Speaks What Language to Whom and When'.
[19] See Fishman *et al.*, *Language Loyalty in the United States*; also Fishman's *Bilingualism in the Barrio*.
[20] See p. 10.
[21] Clyne, 'The Maintenance of Bilingualism'.
[22] Johnston, 'Language Usage in the Homes of Polish Immigrants in Western Australia'.

cation can lead to a breakdown in parental control.[23] This is especially so where the parents speak poor English and are regarded by their children as 'foreigners'.

SPEECH COMMUNICATION PATTERNS

Hymes and Neustupný,[24] among others, have stressed the need to consider the problems of speech as well as those of language in the broad context of communication problems. Not only *how* something is said, but also *what* is said, should be described. Different ethnic groups behave differently under the same circumstances. *What* a migrant says in a given situation or in response to a certain stimulus may be just as indicative of his assimilation or non-assimilation as the phonology, lexicon, or syntax of his English. A useful and fascinating study could be made by drawing up comparisons of communication patterns between Australian English and other speech communities. It may well be that most misunderstandings between 'New' and 'Old' Australians are due to dissimilarity of communication patterns.

In both speech analysis and descriptions of communication patterns, speaker-hearer relations are obviously of paramount importance. Not only do we need to know how migrants communicate with Australians, but also how Australians communicate with migrants, and migrants of different language backgrounds with each other. Is there, for instance, developing among Australian foremen and unskilled workers of different nationalities a Pidgin English similar to the 'auxiliary code' which has become the medium between guest workers and locals in Germany, a code of the type which Bloomfield describes as 'a compromise between a foreign speaker's version of a language and a native speaker's version of the foreign speaker's version, and so on, in which each party imperfectly reproduces the other's reproductions'.[25] To what extent is English being adopted as a lingua franca among immigrants of different nationalities in place of, say, German, Yiddish, or 'Pan-Slavic'? Or to what degree is the lingua franca among multilinguals a mixture of English and one of these Old World linguae francae? Do Australians in Fitzroy, Carlton, and St Kilda (or the corresponding suburbs in Sydney) need a smattering of a foreign language to get by? If so, does this affect their English in any way? (We have evidence that, in an extreme case, the English vowel and consonantal systems and intonation patterns of a monolingual Australian will be adapted

[23] See Zubrzycki, 'Immigrants and Cultural Conflict'.
[24] See Hymes, 'Models of the Interaction of Language and Social Setting'; Neustupný, 'Some General Aspects of "Language" Problems and "Language" Policy in Developing Societies'.
[25] Bloomfield, *Language*, p. 473; also Clyne, 'Zum Pidgin-Deutsch der Gastarbeiter'.

to that of a New Australian spouse, and that this form of English is then employed even in conversation with other monolingual Australians.) All these questions are yet to be investigated and would make good topics for theses and research projects.

STABILISED INTERFERENCE

While stressing the importance of 'absorption, dispersal, interaction, generalisation, and levelling' in the development of Australian English, Mitchell refers, in his chapter, 'The Australian Accent', to the possibility of 'pockets of distinctive usage', a question which he chooses to leave open 'until more detailed evidence is available'.[26]

While the 'melting pot situation', where individuals and families of different language backgrounds are rapidly assimilated into an English-speaking community, has generally predominated here at least since the turn of the century, Australia has also had her share of rural ethnic group settlements. These included the old German *Sprachinseln* (enclaves) of Hahndorf (settled as early as 1839), Lobethal (1842), and the Barossa Valley (1842) in South Australia, the Tarrington-Tabor district near Hamilton, Western Victoria (1853), parts of the Wimmera and the New South Wales Riverina (second half of the nineteenth century, settled largely through remigration), and some districts of Southern Queensland. In addition, closed settlements of Russians were later founded in the Gladstone district of Queensland, and the areas of concentrated Italian settlement and chain migration in the Innisfail and Ingham areas originated in the early twentieth century. In such areas there was little or no need for assimilation and language shift,[27] as *the community as a whole* (or a closed section within it) maintained the first language. In most of the German settlements, German (often a local blending of various East Central German or other dialects with stabilised phonic, lexical, and syntactic interference from Australian English) was, for two or three generations, the dominant language of community, church, and school, and it was principally World War I (and finally World War II) that led to language shift. Consequently nearly all bilinguals from the former German *Sprachinseln* are now in the over-55 age group, and the more fluent German speakers are to be found in the 75-plus group. In the Barossa Valley, especially, many of those 55 and over still regularly speak the language at home and with friends and relatives.[28]

[26] See p. 7.
[27] The opposite of 'language maintenance', change from the use of the mother tongue to that of the language of the host community.
[28] Clyne, 'Deutscher Idiolekt und deutscher Dialekt in einer zweisprachigen Siedlung in Australien'; also 'Decay, Preservation and Renewal: Notes on some Southern Australian German Settlements'.

The English phonology of (second, third, and fourth generation) Australians in the 75-plus age group, and less strongly in the 55-and-over group, in old German *Sprachinseln* deviates in some ways from most other forms of Australian English. In the Barossa Valley, for instance, the following tendencies are prevalent in the English of our informants in this age group:

1. Monophthong [oː] instead of, or in free variation with, the more usual Australian English diphthong, e.g. [goː], go (cf. German [oː]).

2. Close [eː] instead of [ɛɪ] (or [eɪ]), [ʌɪ], or [ʌˑɪ], e.g. [leːtɐ], later (cf. German [eː] which is closer than the first part of the Australian English diphthong).

3. [ɛ] as in German, slightly more open than in normal Australian English, e.g. [brɛkfəst], breakfast.

4. [ɔ] closer than Australian English, e.g. [gʔt], got; [oklʔk], o'clock (cf. German [gʔt]).

5. A certain amount of nasalisation (far more than usual in General or Cultivated Australian similar to that of our informants), e.g. [tãˑɪm], time; [nãˑɪt], night; [dãːnsəs], dances.

6. [ʊ] for [uː] in [lʊθəɹɐn] Lutheran (cf. German [lʊtəɹaːnɐ]).

7. [d] for initial [ð], e.g. [diː], the; [dæt] or [dɛt], that; [dɛn], then. (There is no /ð/ in German. However, we have not observed any substitutions of /θ/, another phonemic gap in German.)

8. Voiceless consonants [t], [s], and [k] for voiced consonants [d], [z], and [g] in final position (as in German), e.g. [bæːt], bad; [bɹʌθahʊds], brotherhoods; [wɔs], was; [θɪŋk], thing. (This last substitution is not unusual in broader forms of Australian English.)

Of these tendencies, the last three are particularly widespread. All the above-mentioned peculiarities can be attributed to the influence of some form of German. The speech of some of our subjects also appears to be marked by distinctive intonation. This, too, would be a rewarding topic of research, though it would be facilitated by more basic studies on the intonation of Standard German and of German dialects.[29]

Jernudd[30] included a tape of one elderly Barossa Valley informant among material in listener tests for his investigations on regional and social variations in Australian English. Although some listeners did recognise the

---

[29] For a study of the English of the bilingual generation of two Queensland German settlements, see Tarnawski's two theses cited in the bibliography to this chapter.

[30] Jernudd, 'A Listener Experiment: Variations of Australian English'.

regional background of the Barossa Valley informant, others distributed her quite freely across the Victorian map. This could be due to a process of elimination or, as Jernudd has suggested to me, to her being mistaken for a migrant and placed in a rural locality where the listener knew that there were migrants. Perhaps many of the listeners had never heard an elderly Barossa Valley speaker before.

In the Tarrington-Tabor area of the Victorian Western District—an area even now inhabited almost exclusively by Australians whose ancestors came from Germany in the nineteenth century—many of the elderly people devoice final consonants (e.g. [kʌntɹiːs], countries; [faɪf], five) and articulate [d] in free variation with [ð] in words starting with /ð/ (e.g. [dɛn]-[ðɛn]-[di]-[ði]).³¹ The sounds [w] and [v], and [r] and [ɹ] stand in free variation in the English as well as the German of our bilingual informants. Some of them realise Australian English vowel phonemes, more consistently than German ones, as monophthongs.³² Perhaps this is because English was used more as a formal than a colloquial language in the area, and 'pure' vowels were considered more 'refined'. Or perhaps the English of the elderly generation is still based on that of the nineteenth century Scottish squatters who settled the areas surrounding the old German *Sprachinseln*. The pronunciation [lvθəɹən], with short /ʊ/ for [luːθəɹən] or [ləʊðəɹən] or [luːðəɹən], is widespread in the Tarrington area among people aged 55 and over. There seem also to be intonation patterns characteristic of speakers from the old German settlements in Victoria and South Australia.

Also characteristic of the English of many elderly Tarrington and district residents is the generalisation (or near-generalisation) of the accented form of the English definite article, for example 'he sponsored the [ði] German migrants; you ask me the [ði] questions; in the [ði] history'.

This may explain the assignment of most English 'stabilised loans' in Tarrington-Tabor German to the feminine.³³

Apart from occasional deviations from English grammatical norms in the speech of individuals (e.g. the children*s was* small), there seem to be no grammatical peculiarities in Barossa Valley English. Some of the bilinguals experience prepositional interference from German; for example, We went down *with* car; Pastor Renner is like the Chaplain *from* the home (cf. German, *mit, von*). The use of the definite article with names of languages in Tarrington (in *the* English, (in) *the* German) suggests 'stabilised interference' from German, as does the absence of the preposition after *plenty* and a *little bit* (e.g. *plenty* trees; *a little bit* English).

---

³¹ This substitution is recorded in Barossa Valley English, but not in Marburg or Guluguba-Downfall Creek (Tarnawski, The English of German-speaking Bilinguals, p. 56).
³² Clyne, 'Deutscher Idiolekt', p. 92.
³³ Ibid., p. 89.

In both the Barossa Valley and the Tarrington area, the use of 'bring with', 'come with', and 'take with', (cf. German *mitbringen, mitkommen, mitnehmen*) is common among the bilingual generations, as is the loan-extension of the English 'yet' and the exaggerated use of 'already', according to the model of *noch* and *schon* respectively, for example 'I have a German Bible *yet*'; 'this has happened different[34] times *already*'.

The extension of the use of *already* is found also in the speech of monolingual speakers of Australian English of German descent in Western Victoria and the Barossa Valley. Widespread in the speech of people of all age groups from the Western District area under consideration is the use of *to* for family relationship, where Australian English would usually employ *of*, for example 'He's an uncle *to* David Nagorcka' (colloquial German, *Er ist* dem *David Nagorcka sein Onkel*).

A detailed investigation of the English of the various former *Sprachinseln* in Australia (covering people of all age groups) could bring to light small areas of regional distinctiveness due to non-English substrata. In those areas where population movement has been considerable in recent years, the above-mentioned features will probably disappear completely. In some districts they are regarded as *denominational* characteristics (e.g. peculiar to Lutherans). Where (as in the Tarrington-Tabor area and some other rural settlements) the holdings remain in the hands of the pioneer families, substratum peculiarities may well be preserved as *dialectal* features.

Research in the Innisfail and Ingham areas of North Queensland[35] suggests that the Italian influence on the phonology of local Australian English is almost entirely restricted to the speech of first generation migrants. The broken grammatical forms employed by the first generation informants are attributed by Sharwood to the fact that in the district the migrants feel no need 'to become at all proficient in English'.[36]

What influence are the first languages of migrants exerting on Australian English? There is no evidence that there is any substantial influence of this kind, except in some idiolects. Apart from the few enclaves mentioned above, no areas absorbed a sufficiently large group of linguistically homogeneous migrants, so that the already existent Australian English dominated throughout. However, just as some German features have survived in the English of rural areas of German settlement, there may be peculiarities in the English of third generation inhabitants of Melbourne's 'Chinatown', Little Bourke Street. This might well warrant investigation. Similar to the odd Germanisms in the English of a third or fourth generation

---

[34] Loan extension of German *verschieden*.

[35] See Sharwood, Spoken English in two areas of Italian Settlement in North Queensland; also Sharwood and Horton, 'Phoneme Frequencies in Australian English: A Regional Study'.

[36] Sharwood, Spoken English, p. 271.

Australian, which may now be termed 'Lutheranisms', are the Yiddish words occasionally employed in the English of non-Yiddish-speaking Australian Jews, for example 'the whole place has gone *meshugge* (or *mishigge*)' (mad);[37] 'we've been *shlepping* around all day' (pushing, dragging). Members of the Reformed Churches of Australia, whether themselves Dutch-speaking or not, call their minister *dominee* ['doumɪneɪ] or ['doːmɪneː] (Dutch 'minister').

Certainly the 'Europeanisation' of Australia's eating and drinking habits promoted by large-scale post-war non-British migration, and to a lesser extent by the advent of the German, Austrian, and Czech refugees of 1938-9, has been accompanied by a popularisation of the names of the foreign foods. Words such as the following, which in 1939 were relatively unknown among monolingual Australians, are now well and truly part of Australian English: *capuccino, espresso, gelato, mocca, pizza, spaghetti bolognese, goulash, paprika, sauerkraut, weiner (wiener) schnitzel, yogh(o)urt,* and the 'loanblends' *liverwurst* and *apple strudel*. The origin of *fritz*, the South Australian name for the pork German sausage, at present remains obscure. Perhaps South Australians of British descent were responsible for the transfer of a Christian name common among South Australian Germans to one of the sausages they made and ate. Early migration from the German-speaking countries has enriched Australian English vocabulary with several of the distinctive words recorded by Baker, for example *spieler*, 'gambler', *shicer* or *shyster* (German *Scheisser*), 'swindler, crook or racecourse welsher' (earlier, 'an unproductive goldmine'), and *swatser* (German *Schwarzer*), 'blackfellow, native'. *Sane* [sɛin] or [sʌin], an alternative name for the old shilling note, is presumably derived not directly from Standard German [tseːn], ten, but from the [sɛin] [sʌin] of the East Central German-based dialects of many German-speaking settlements in Australia. According to Baker again, *bonzer* is derived from Spanish *bonzana*. Yiddish has given Australian English at least two words—*shicker*, 'drunken', and *cush* (synonym for 'bonzer'), both of Hebrew origin, and probably also *cronk* (Yiddish, *kronk*, cf. German *krank*), 'horse running crookedly', and *clinah*, 'girl', which could, however, have come from German.[38]

Throughout this short paper we have referred to numerous openings for investigation. The enormous field of language contact studies in Australia is still comparatively untapped, and it is hoped that before long linguists working on both English and foreign languages, psychologists, sociologists, educationalists, and others will co-operate in this area. There is a need for

[37] These words occur also in American English.
[38] See Baker, *The Australian Language*, pp. 96, 126, 289; but see also Ramson, *Australian English*, pp. 160-2.

adequate archives (tapes, newspapers, letters, diaries) of the various migrant communities and descendants of non-English migrants in various parts of Australia. This would provide the research material required as a starting point to solve many of the open questions in the field.

REFERENCES CITED

Andreoni, G., 'Australitalian', *University Studies in History*, Vol. 5, 1967, pp. 114-19.
Baker, S. J., *The Australian Language*, Sydney, 1945.
Bloomfield, L., *Language*, rev. ed., London, 1935.
Clyne, M. G., 'Decay, Preservation and Renewal: Notes on some Southern Australian German Settlements', *AUMLA*, Vol. 29, 1968, pp. 33-43.
―――, 'Deutscher Idiolekt und deutscher Dialekt in einer zweisprachigen Siedlung in Australien', *Wirkendes Wort*, Vol. 18, 1968, pp. 84-95.
―――, 'The Maintenance of Bilingualism', *Australian Journal of Education*, Vol. 12, 1968, pp. 125-30.
―――, 'Some Instances of Limitations on Speech Capacity as Exhibited in German-English Bilinguals', *Papers and Proceedings of the Tenth Congress of the Australasian Languages and Literature Association*, Auckland, 1966, pp. 251-9.
―――, *Transference and Triggering*, The Hague, 1967.
―――, 'Zum Pidgin-Deutsch der Gastarbeiter', *Zeitschrift für Mundartforschung*, Vol. 25, 1968, pp. 130-9.
Fishman, J. A., *Bilingualism in the Barrio*, Report to U.S. Office of Education, 1968.
―――, 'Who Speaks What Language to Whom and When?', *La Linguistique*, Vol. 2, 1965, pp. 67-88.
―――, et al., *Language Loyalty in the United States*, The Hague, 1966.
Hammarström, U. G. E., *Linguistische Einheiten im Rahmen der modernen Sprachwissenschaft*, Heidelberg, 1966.
Haugen, E., *The Norwegian Language in America*, 2 vols., Philadelphia, 1953.
Hymes, D., 'Models of the Interaction of Language and Social Setting', *Journal of Social Issues*, Vol. 23, 1967, pp. 8-28.
Jernudd, B. H., 'A Listener Experiment: Variations of Australian English', *Kivung*, Vol. 2, 1969, pp. 19-29.
Johnston, R., 'Language Usage in the Homes of Polish Immigrants in Western Australia', *Lingua*, Vol. 18, 1967, pp. 271-89.
Koch-Emmery, E., 'Die Rolle der Zweisprachigen im heutigen Australien', *Moderne Sprachen*, Vol. 7, 1963, pp. 52-60.
Lambert, W. E., 'Measurement of the Linguistic Dominance of Bilinguals', *Journal of Abnormal and Social Psychology*, Vol. 50, 1955, pp. 197-200.
―――, Havelka, J. and Crosby, C., 'The Influence of Language Acquisition Contexts on Bilingualism'. In S. Saporta (ed.), *Psycholinguistics: A Book of Readings*, New York, 1961, pp. 401-14.
Mitchell, A. G. and Delbridge, A., *The Speech of Australian Adolescents*, Sydney, 1965.
Neustupný, J., 'Some General Aspects of "Language" Problems and "Language" Policy in Developing Societies'. In J. A. Fishman, C. A. Ferguson, and G. Das Gupta (eds.), *Language Problems of Developing Nations*, New York, 1968, pp. 285-94.
Nijenhuis, J. G. J., *Het Nederlands in Australië*, Sydney, 1967.
Platt, H., 'A Comparative Study of the Phonetics of Australian English and German', *Phonetica*, 1970, in press.

Ramson, W. S., *Australian English: An Historical Study of the Vocabulary, 1788-1898*, Canberra, 1966.
Rando, G., 'Influenze dell' inglese sull' italiano di Sydney', *Lingua Nostra*, Vol. 29, 1968, pp. 17-22.
Schischkoff, G., 'Heimatlose in der Sprache'. In *Wirkendes Wort. Sammelband I: Sprachwissenschaft*, Düsseldorf, 1962, pp. 28-30.
Sharwood, J., Spoken English in Two Areas of Italian Settlement in North Queensland, 2 vols., M.A. thesis, University of Queensland, 1964.
―――― and Horton, J., 'Phoneme Frequencies in Australian English: A Regional Study', *AUMLA*, Vol. 26, 1966, pp. 272-302.
Taft, R., *From Stranger to Citizen*, Perth, 1965.
Tarnawski, L. L. K., The Aural and Oral Command of English of a Group of German-speaking Migrants in the Brisbane Area, M.A. thesis, University of Queensland, 1965.
――――, The English of German-speaking Bilinguals, B.A. (Hons.) thesis, University of Queensland, 1961.
Weinreich, U., *Languages in Contact*, New York, 1953.
Zabrocki, L., 'Kodematische Grundlagen', *Glottadidactica* I, 1966, pp. 4-42.
Zubrzycki, J., 'Immigrants and Cultural Conflict', *Research Group for European Migration Problems Bulletin*, The Hague, 1957, pp. 71-7.
――――, *Settlers of the Latrobe Valley*, Canberra, 1964.

9   T. E. DUTTON

INFORMAL ENGLISH IN THE TORRES STRAITS

There are several good reasons for writing about informal English[1] in the Torres Straits.[2] One is that, with the increasing interest being shown in the speech of minority groups in the Australian community, linguists are interested in knowing what sort of English is spoken there—an area of Australia which has different linguistic and social backgrounds from other parts previously studied in some detail—and whether this English is similar to or different from other varieties which have been labelled Aboriginal English,[3] Neo-Nyungar,[4] and Northern Territory Pidgin.[5] But another and

[1] In this paper informal English refers to the variety of English used in free, group conversation between familiar persons discussing familiar topics.

[2] The Torres Straits is that stretch of water separating the mainland of Australia from that of New Guinea (see map).

[3] In this paper Aboriginal English and other similar terms will be used linguistically (not ethnically) to denote distinctive varieties of Australian English. For descriptions of various aspects of Aboriginal English spoken in Queensland see E. H. Flint's 'Aboriginal English', and Dutton's 'The Informal English Speech of Palm Island Aboriginal Children'. For accounts of early, colonial Aboriginal English and the effects of Aboriginal languages on the development of Australian English see Baker, *Australia Speaks*, esp. pp. 189-93; *The Australian Language*, esp. pp. 309-26; Ramson, 'The Currency of Aboriginal Words in Australian English'; *Australian English*, esp. pp. 105-12; and Turner, *The English Language in Australia and New Zealand*, esp. pp. 199-213.

[4] Neo-Nyungar is a term Douglas invented to denote 'the present everyday speech' of Aborigines in the southwest corner of Western Australia. This speech is a mixture of English and Nyungar, the Aboriginal vernacular formerly used in this part of Australia which is now only imperfectly known by the older people. Nyungar and Neo-Nyungar are different from two other varieties of speech used by the same Aborigines, viz. Wetjala and Yeraka. The former is the best English these Aborigines use when talking to white people. The latter is a play language (based on English) which is mainly used by women. See Douglas, *The Aboriginal Languages of the South-West of Australia*.

[5] Northern Territory Pidgin is, as the name suggests, a variety of English spoken in the Northern Territory of Australia. The first account of this language was published by Sayer in *Pidgin English*. This account consists mainly of vocabulary and has been severely criticised by Hall in his review of it in *Language*, 1944. Hall has himself referred to Northern Territory Pidgin on pp. 10, 80, and 100 of his own book, *Pidgin and Creole Languages*, supplemented by some second-hand text material on pp. 151-2. Recently Jernudd has given a socio-linguistic description of the present-day use of various forms of English in the Northern Territory in his 'Social Change and Aboriginal Speech Variation in Australia'. This is a tentative and preliminary version of a paper to be published in the first issue of the Journal

137

most important reason is that the Torres Straits occupies a particular place in the study of varieties of informal English speech in Australia, since it was here that linguists made the first systematic observations on any such variety in Australia. This was at the close of the nineteenth century when the historic Cambridge Anthropological Expedition came to the Torres Straits.[6] This expedition was led by A. C. Haddon, marine zoologist-turned-anthropologist, and included among its team of seven members the linguist S. H. Ray. It is to Ray that we are indebted for a description of 'the jargon English of the Torres Straits'.[7] This account (though defective in certain respects to be discussed later) is a valuable contribution to Oceanic linguistics generally since the history of 'jargon English' is of particular relevance to the history and development of pidgin languages in the Pacific. It is especially relevant to that of the nearest Pacific pidgin, Neo-Melanesian,[8] about the history of which there has been some recent controversy.[9] Apart from these purely linguistic reasons, however, a knowledge of the structure and use of Torres Straits Islands informal English is of practical importance to education in English for Islanders, and perhaps not inconceivably to politics in this area.

Thus the purpose of this paper will be to describe the principal linguistic features of the present-day informal English speech of Torres Straits Islands children; and to discuss this speech in relation to that of Ray's 'jargon English', and, to a lesser extent, to other varieties already mentioned. During this discussion some mention will also be made of the speech of the Northern Peninsula Reserve, Cape York.[10]

This description (considered to be introductory only) is based on linguistic material collected by the author during field work in the Torres

---

of the Linguistics Society of Australia. Although Dr Jernudd's article does not contain illustrative material of Northern Territory Pidgin, the author has informed me (personal communication) that he expects to be publishing some statement of the structure of Aboriginal English varieties in the Northern Territory at some later date. I should also like to thank Dr Jernudd for his comments on an earlier draft of this paper.

[6] This expedition visited the Torres Straits for six months in 1898. Its results were published in six volumes in 1907 as *Reports of the Cambridge Anthropological Expedition to the Torres Straits*, Cambridge.

[7] Ray was primarily responsible for Volume III (Linguistics) of the *Reports*. Unless otherwise stated all references to Ray's work will hereafter be to this volume, so that only page numbers will be given. 'The Jargon English of the Torres Straits' is described by Ray between pages 251 and 255.

[8] See Mihalic's *Grammar and Dictionary of Neo-Melanesian*, for example.

[9] See discussion by Wurm in 'Pidgin—A National Language'; by Salisbury in 'Pidgin's Respectable Past'; and by Laycock in 'Pidgin's Progress'.

[10] The Northern Peninsula Reserve was established in 1948 on Cape York Peninsula for the settlement of indigenous people from Saibai Island, Torres Straits, following the inundation of their island. Since then Aboriginal communities from Mapoon River and Lockhart River Missions have also been resettled there from 1962 to 1964. The 'towns' of Bamaga, New Mapoon, Umagico, and Cowal Creek

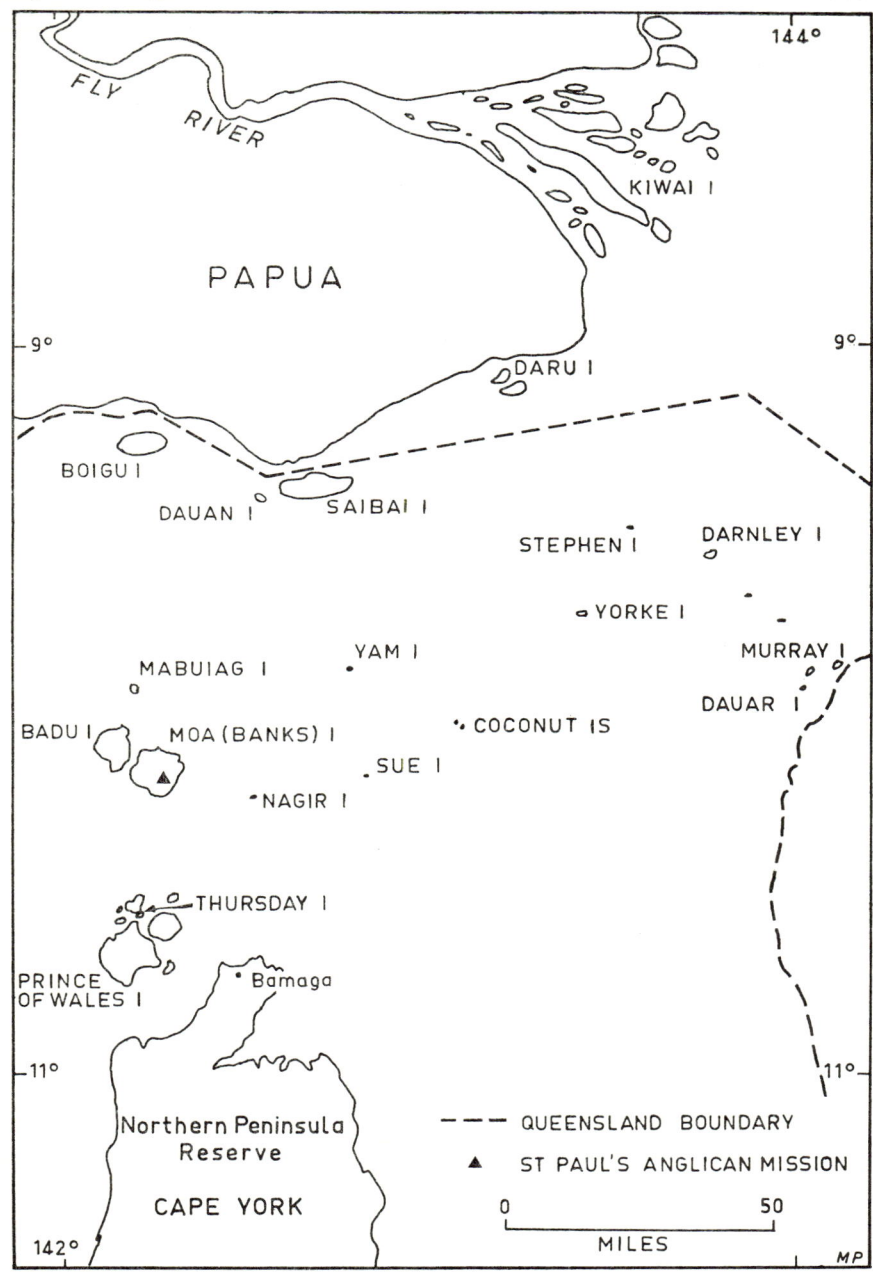

Map of the Torres Straits

Straits in 1965. Historical and anthropological notes are based mainly on work done by Jeremy R. Beckett.[11]

LINGUISTIC AND SOCIAL BACKGROUND OF TORRES STRAITS ISLANDERS

In pre-European contact times the Torres Straits was inhabited by a small indigenous population scattered over the more habitable islands of the archipelago encompassed by the Straits.[12] These inhabitants spoke two distinct languages—Miriam in the east, and Mabuiag in the west.[13] According to Ray, Miriam is a Papuan language related to Kiwai on the New Guinea mainland and spoken on and around the islands Murray, Stephen, Darnley, and Duar. It is unrelated to Mabuiag, which is an Australian language spoken in various dialects (e.g. Saibai, Mabuiag, Muralug, Tutu) across the remaining islands.

Physically the Islanders were similar to the dark-skinned, frizzy-haired Papuans of the New Guinea mainland to their immediate north, though culturally they were somewhere between these and the Australian Aborigines to the south. Most of their time was spent in subsistence activities of fishing, hunting turtle and dugong, and/or gardening—depending on the nature of the islands they inhabited; the remainder was devoted to religious and ceremonial activities, into which head-hunting was integrally interwoven. Social life was organised on the clan system with little intermarriage (but some intercommunication for ceremonial purposes) between groups.

Documentary evidence has it that the Islanders were first contacted by Europeans when the Spanish navigator Torres (whose name the Straits now bear) passed through the area in 1606.[14] Albeit it was not until the mid-nineteenth century that the Islanders were really subjected to intensive contact. Then came a great influx of peoples from all parts of the Pacific (especially Loyalty Islanders, Samoans, and Rotumans). Some came as

---

are included in this reserve. In 1964 the total population of the Northern Peninsula Reserve consisted of 584 Torres Straits Islanders, 258 full-blood and 163 mixed-blood Aborigines. Thus this paper provides evidence for Flint's distinction of areas (c) and (d) of Aboriginal English in Queensland. See p. 6 of Flint's 1968 paper, 'Aboriginal English'.

[11] Dutton, The Informal English Speech of Palm Island Aboriginal Children, North Queensland, 1965, and also the thesis abstract in *Journal of English Linguistics*; Beckett, Politics in the Torres Straits Islands; letter to Dutton from Beckett, 9 July 1969. I should like to express my thanks to Dr Beckett both for comments on an earlier draft of this chapter and for permission to quote from his thesis.

[12] Beckett (Politics in the Torres Straits Islands, p. 6) suggests that the population in 1860 was probably somewhere between three and four thousand.

[13] Mabuiag and Miriam are often referred to as the western and eastern languages of the Straits respectively. Grammar and vocabularies of each with sundry other notes (including a discussion of the relationship between these two languages and neighbouring ones) are provided by Ray in Part I of his report.

[14] It is probable, however, as Beckett suggests, that other adventurers from the Near East and India preceded Torres.

missionaries with the London Missionary Society; the majority were brought (often against their will) to assist their European masters as workers in the rich shell and bêche-de-mer marine industry. Islanders worked with these, and a considerable number of the immigrants married Island women and settled down in the Straits. Their impact on the culture was immense, affecting not only the language of the Islanders but also their music, dancing, cuisine, and architecture. They presumably brought with them from their homelands a ready-made and useful contact language in the form of a variant of what Reinecke calls 'Beach-la-mar',[15] a pidgin language which had grown up in the sandalwood trade in the Pacific, and which the Islanders also adopted as they were drawn into closer association with these foreigners and their European masters.

In 1897 the Torres Straits was declared a reserve and the government tried to separate the Pacific Islanders from the native population, forcing them on to several of the islands, notably Badu, Darnley, Hammond, and Moa (at St Paul's Anglican Mission). Later some of these were joined by a few unrepatriated kanaka labourers from the Queensland canefields who married Mabuiag women and remained.[16] In these mixed settlements a kind of pidgin based on the earlier beach-la-mar was presumably the common everyday language. Elsewhere Islanders continued to speak their individual vernaculars, using a similar pidgin as a means of communicating with strangers and Europeans. When Haddon and Ray visited the area in 1898 as members of the Cambridge Anthropological Expedition, Ray wrote up a short description of this pidgin. Following Haddon's usage,[17] Ray called this speech 'jargon English', and noted that it was the usual medium of communication between Europeans, including Australians, and the Islanders (generally the older men) of the Straits and 'by the people of Mowata[18] and Kiwai on the opposite coast of New Guinea'.[19] Ray also noted at the same time that this language was 'more generally used in the Western Islands than in the Eastern', and that in the latter group it

---

[15] See Reinecke, Marginal Languages, esp. pp. 734-6. In these pages Reinecke referred to the speech situation in North Queensland and the Torres Straits. Reinecke maintained that the form of English used there was a pidgin which originated on the canefields of Queensland during the kanaka days of the late nineteenth century, whence it was 'probably carried along the coast by men who had been in contact with the Queensland centres and the Melanesian trade'. From the historical picture just presented Reinecke's order of preference for the introduction of this speech into the Torres Straits probably needs to be reversed so as to give due emphasis to the importance of the hundreds of Pacific Islanders ('Melanesians' in Reinecke's terms) who were introduced into the area before and during the establishment of the sugar industry. 'Beach-la-mar' is derived from the French word 'bêche-de-mer' for trepang, or sea slug.

[16] C. Turner, a retired Department of Native Affairs officer-cum-schoolteacher of long and varied experience in the Torres Straits, personal communication, 1965.

[17] See, for example, Haddon's *Head-Hunters Black, White, and Brown*, pp. 10, 33.

[18] 'Mowata' is also spelled 'Mawata' by Ray in his report, p. 510.

[19] Ray, p. 251.

appeared 'to be going out of use among the younger generation, more correct English taking its place'. Ray's description is based mainly on information collected by A. C. Haddon,[20] and is therefore both restricted and unreliable in certain respects. For example, Ray did not give any indication of the phonetic features of the jargon he described, merely giving examples in equivalent English spelling. The description is, nevertheless, extremely valuable as the only record of English spoken in the Torres Straits in former times.

Today there are some fifteen communities scattered throughout the Torres Straits. All are small (populations of fewer than 500) and generally isolated by distance and irregular contact with the outside world. English is still the official medium of communication, and is taught by European teachers in the most populous centres and by native teachers in others. In most areas the vernacular has declined in use, and in some (notably Moa Island) is now almost extinct. The total population of the Straits is probably well in excess of 7,000 Islanders.[21]

MATERIAL AND TECHNIQUES

In 1965 I visited the Torres Straits to collect tape recordings of the informal English speech of Torres Straits Islands children as part of my investigation of the nature of such speech used by different Aboriginal groups throughout Queensland.[22]

Short recordings of from five to ten minutes' duration were made of groups of children (mostly males) aged between twelve and fourteen years from widely separated areas of the Torres Straits, viz. Bamaga (on the Northern Peninsula Reserve, Cape York), St Paul's Anglican Mission (on Moa (Banks) Island, Saibai and Murray Islands.[23] Most of the resulting

---

[20] Other examples of this pidgin are given in the Reports of the Cambridge Anthropological Expedition, Vols. 1, 2, and 6, and in Haddon's *Head-Hunters Black, White, and Brown*. No attempt will be made in this chapter, however, to give a listing of all previously recorded vocabulary of Torres Straits jargon English.

[21] In 1963 Beckett estimated the population to be 7,250. See his Politics in the Torres Straits Islands, pp. 396-7, for a discussion of population trends in the Straits between 1913 and 1963.

[22] This field work was sponsored by the Queensland Speech Survey, which is studying the varieties of English spoken in Queensland. The aims and methods of this survey have been outlined and discussed in various papers by Flint. See, for example, those by Flint listed in the bibliography of this chapter.

[23] See map. The approximate distances in miles between the surveyed areas are as follows (Thursday Island (T.I.) is the administrative centre of the Torres Straits):

From	To	Distance
Saibai I.	Murray I.	90
Saibai I.	T.I.	80
Murray I.	T.I.	120
Moa (Banks) I.	T.I.	35
Bamaga	T.I.	24

texts were transcribed in the field with the aid of the actual informants, and background information about the informants and about the nature and use of their speech was also gathered. Samples of these texts are reproduced in the appendix to this chapter.

PRESENTATION

For present purposes the informal English of the Torres Straits Islands will be treated as structurally uniform, although it may be, as Dr Beckett suggests (personal communication), that the informal speech of the Moa Islanders (at St Paul's mission) is probably more extreme[24] than that of the other areas surveyed, for the historical reasons already outlined. To some extent the recordings support this impression, particularly in the vocabulary used by the informants and in their rhythmic tempo of articulation, and intonational features. But no significant statements can be made from the small samples of speech obtained, since none of the speech communities has been studied in depth, and vocabulary varies from speaker to speaker and for different topics of conversation. For example, in the material collected vocabulary variation is most noticeable in those texts dealing with such traditional activities as hunting and fishing.[25] In these texts informants use many words which are apparently based on former vernacular words used for describing particular aspects of these activities, and, since they reflect different linguistic backgrounds, can be expected to be different. Vocabulary differences, then, will not be treated as significant, although, as will be seen later, this vocabulary is not without linguistic interest. Grammatical and phonological differences are not as marked throughout the region, and will be ignored here. This will not only simplify descriptive statements but will also facilitate comparison between present-day English and that recorded by Ray, which, incidentally, he treated as uniform. In this way similarities and differences between the two historical varieties can be brought into focus, except that no present-day equivalents can be given of Ray's vocabulary. This is because the material collected was for a different purpose and insufficient time was spent in the area to check these features of Ray's account. Nor can any comparison be made with the sound system of jargon English used at the beginning of the century, since, as has already been pointed out, Ray did not give any indication of the phonetic features of the English he described.

In the following description of the linguistic characteristics of the informal English of the Torres Straits Islands, phonology will be treated first,

[24] I.e. observationally least like Australian English.

[25] This kind of observation has already been made of the informal English speech of Palm Island Aboriginal children in similar conversations. See Dutton, 'The Informal English Speech of Palm Island Aboriginal Children', pp. 25, 33n.

followed by grammar and lexis. All illustrative material will be in bold and cited in an orthography based on broad IPA phonetic script.[26] Phonetic values of the orthographic symbols will be presented in the section on phonology. Stress and intonation have not been studied, and are not included in the illustrative material. Examples are written with spaces between 'words'. English glosses are given in single quotes and individual words (and parts thereof) are glossed below the relevant Torres Straits material. The following symbols are used in addition to orthographic ones:

Symbol	Meaning
/	tentative pause (as at commas in written English)
//	long pause (as at the end of a sentence)
/–/	hesitation pause
:	(following a letter) length
( )	optional features enclosed
<	derives from

Capital letters are used to indicate personal and proper names.

Finally, the grammar of this English will be described in general terms in which the traditional notions of sentence, clause, word etc. will be used. This is dictated partly by the nature of the material collected, and partly by a consideration of the aims of this chapter. It is hoped, however, that this description will be sufficient to excite interest in this fascinating field, leading to more detailed studies later.

THE PRINCIPAL LINGUISTIC CHARACTERISTICS OF TORRES STRAITS ISLANDS INFORMAL ENGLISH

Phonology

The phonology of Torres Straits Islands English has not been studied in detail but it is apparent that this is similar to General Queensland English[27] in most respects, except that:

1. English ə: (as in 'turtle') is usually said as o: (as in 'torch');

2. r is generally trilled;

3. the sounds f and p, s and ʃ ('sh'), d and ð ('th' as in 'there') are not consistently distinguished;

4. some English consonant clusters are rendered differently in Torres Straits Islands English, e.g., **aksi**, 'ask'.

These characteristic features are undoubtedly the result of interference

---

[26] See *The Principles of the International Phonetic Association*, London, 1949.

[27] Flint distinguishes between General and Educated Queensland English (see 'Aboriginal English', p. 20n.).

Informal English in the Torres Straits

between former vernaculars and English as it was being learned in one form or another.

Charts 1 and 2 show the approximate phonetic values of the orthographic symbols used to represent vowels:

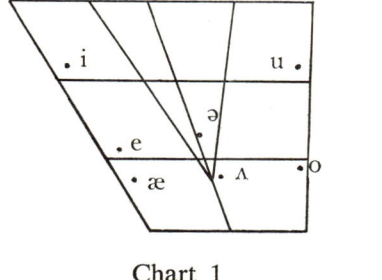

Chart 1

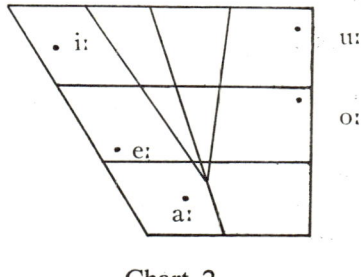

Chart 2

Glides are written as sequences of two vowels. Consonants have approximately the same phonetic value as in English except for the cases noted above.

Grammar

The most striking grammatical aspect of Torres Straits Islands English is that the speech consists of a large number of short sentences paratactically arranged (i.e. placed side by side without conjunctions). Take, for example:

mipelʌ	gou daun //	teik spi	mituː tʌdʌrʌl //
me fellow	go down	take spear	me two go fishing

gou ðat wei //	mituː	gou nau //	kʌm frʌnt
go that way	me two	go now	come front

pain	ən	lukt	ðæt //	oləseim	treit	wʌd //
point	and	looked	that	all the same	thread	there

yalaiwʌp   //
yalai-fish

'We went down and took a spear to go along the beach looking for fish. We went that way. We went until we came in front of the point and I saw that fish with a mark like a thread along its back. It was a **yalai** (= garfish?) fish.'

Conjunctions are rarely used, except for the occasional 'and' or 'but'. For example:

em slu: raun	n	ai draivem tru:
it slew around	and	I drove it through

'it turned sharply and I drove it (the spear) through'

and:

bʌt em nou won dem bʌt i bi givii loː sekən
but he no want them but he be give it long second
'but he didn't want it so he gave it to the second one'.

Note that in this last example the second bʌt is equivalent to 'so' in General Queensland English.

No relative clauses were observed, although a variety of adverbial clauses were. Two of these, viz. concessional and purpose, are markedly different from General Queensland English. Thus, for example, concessional clauses are marked by the repetition of the same verb (the number of repetitions indicating the relative time elapsed), as in:

mituː   gou gou gou
me two go go go
'we(2) went until . . .'

or again in:

spirim spirim spirim // wen oːl kʌm tumaːs miplʌ seili //
spear it spear it spear it   when all come too much me fellow sail it
'we kept spearing (fish) until we had a lot. Then we sailed (the canoe home).'

Purpose is expressed by the juxtaposition of different verbs, as in:

em luk gou on top
he look go on top
'he went up on the beach to look around'.

Time and conditional clauses are usually marked by wen, 'when', and if, 'if', respectively, as in English. For example:

wen oːl kʌm tumaːs
when all come too much
'when we had a lot . . .'

if ai lai yuː aksi Nako
if I lie you ask Nako
'if you don't believe me ask Nako'.

Sometimes wen, 'when', is not used for time clauses, as, for example, in:

kʌm from preː   ai teik of
come from prayer I take off
'when I came from Church I took (the other clothes) off'.

Informal English in the Torres Straits

Equative clauses, which in English involve some copula (e.g., 'is, was') are of two kinds. In sentences expressing a relation between things or attributes of things no copula is used in Torres Straits Islands English. For example:

i wet
he wet
'it is/was wet'.

ðis wʌn di:p wotʌ
this one deep water
'this/that is/was deep'.

These are different from those involving a person. Here the copula bi, 'be', is used. Take, for example:

ai bi fored
I be forward
'I was in the bows'.

Phrase structure is also different from English. Thus locative phrases and time phrases are either unmarked, or marked by loŋ, 'long', where in English they would be marked by some preposition such as 'at', 'to', etc. Often also these phrases will have wʌd, 'there', occurring after the noun as some kind of intensifying demonstrative. The following are illustrative examples of locative and time phrases:

(wi bi gou)   Tiai wʌd
we be go   T.I. there
'we went to Thursday Island'.

ʌndʌnið   loŋ   wʌnem
underneath long what
'underneath what'.

(plei) loŋ   sanbis
play   long sand beach
'(play) on the beach'.

loŋ I:stʌ
'at Easter'.

Comparative phrases are quite varied—some contain laik, 'like', as in English; others are built around kain, 'kind, sort' or oləseim, 'just like'. The following examples illustrate:

ðis kain wʌn hiʌ
this kind one here
'this sort'.

'(speak) like this'
'(speak like this'
oləseim treit wʌd
all the same thread there
'just like a thread'
(nou swim) laik ðat
no swim   like that
'(don't swim) like that'.

Another noticeable feature of these kinds of phrases is that definite and indefinite articles are used differently from in English. Compare, for example:

(kʌm) in ʌ tu: diŋi
come in a two dinghies
'came in two dinghies'

wʌn big waitpis
one big whitefish
'a big white-fish'

ðə las Sʌndei
the last Sunday
'last Sunday'.

In these phrases wʌn is regularly used for the indefinite article. Finally, in possessive phrases the possessor follows the possessed item and is 'linked' with it by bəloŋ, 'belong', as in:

beli bəloŋ miplʌ
belly belong me fellow
'our bellies'

neim bəloŋ kenu
name belong canoe
'the name of the canoe';

except for the first person when the equivalent of the English form 'my' is used as in English. For example, mai dedi, 'my father'.

Other salient grammatical features of Torres Straits Islands English are:

Verbs. Generally the simplest indicative form of the English verb is used, for example, mi gou, 'I went'. Transitive verbs are usually distinguished from intransitive ones by -em, -im, -i suffixed to the verb, as, for example, in kes-em, 'get'; split-im, 'split'; and shʌt-i, 'shut'. Intransitive verbs are not marked in this way, for example, gou, 'go'; kʌm, 'come'.

Another noticeable feature of verb structure is that past tense may be unmarked, as in mipelʌ gou daun, 'we went down', or marked in one of two ways: by -z, as in we-z te:n bak, 'we turned back'; or by bi, as in

Informal English in the Torres Straits

wi bi gou, 'we went'; ai bi got (36),[28] 'I got (36)'. Present and future tense were not observed. Nor were verbal expressions expressing 'let' or 'ought'.

Finally, verbs are negated by nou, 'not', for example, nou swim, 'don't swim'.

Nouns. As in Aboriginal English no distinction is made between singular and plural number of nouns in the form of the noun, for example, to:tl eg, 'turtle egg(s)'; plei ma:bl de: 'play marbles there'. When required, number will be indicated by some numeral adjective such as wʌn, 'one'; plenti, 'plenty'.

Pronouns. The following subject pronouns were observed: ai, mi, 'I'; yə, yu:, 'you' (sing. or pl.); i, em, 'he, it'; mitu:, 'we(2)'; mitu: Nako, 'Nako and I'; yutu: 'you(2)'; ðemtu:, 'those(2)'; wi, mipelʌ, yumi:, 'we'; ðemplʌ, 'they'. The same forms seem to be used for object pronouns, except that mi (not ai) is always used of 'me'. These observations are similar to those of Ray except that the following pronouns were not observed:

1. 'he' for the female pronoun 'she';
2. 'me' used preceding 'I', as, for example, in 'me I go';
3. 'fellow' suffixed to 'we' for the pronoun 'we'.

Interrogative Pronouns. Hu ðat, 'who', and wʌnem, 'what' (and the associated form wʌnem kain, 'what kind of') are used for person and things respectively.

Exclamations. None of those listed by Ray were observed. The following were, however, o, 'oh'; e, 'heh'; dzi:wi, 'gee whiz'; and sa:, 'look out!' These are to be distinguished from introducers such as oukei, 'okay', and orait, 'all right', which are used to mark a change in action or state during story telling.

Lexis

As has already been pointed out, one of the salient features of the vocabulary of Torres Straits Islands children is the large numbers of apparently vernacular-based words which are used in topics of conversation about traditional activities. It is necessary to say 'apparently vernacular-based', since of those vocabulary items which informants assured the author were vernacular items, many are only uncertainly related to words listed in the vocabularies of the Mabuiag and Miriam languages by Ray. If they were only vernacular words they have undergone phonetic and/or semantic change over the last half-century.[29] Take, for example, the following:

[28] For some reason this is not said as *ai bi get* (36).
[29] Provided, of course, that Ray's entries can be regarded as reasonably accurate —which may not always be the case.

Word	Meaning given by informants	Comments
wʌd	'there'	Probably related to wad (adj.) 'another' (Ray, p. 127).
puri:	'baby shark'	Probably related to puwi (noun), 'the flying-fish' (Ray, p. 120).
yalaiwʌp	'a kind of fish with a black thread-like line down its back'	Apparently this is a combination of two words yalai and wʌp. At least wʌp seems to be related to wapi (noun), 'fish' (as, for example, in pokam-wapi (noun), 'the flying-fish'), as listed by Ray (p. 129).[30] Yalai may be the present-day equivalent of zaber (noun), 'garfish', since the kind of fish the informants were talking about was long and thin and swimming near the surface of the water, and these are characteristics of garfish.
mʌtʌ[31]	1. 'easily' (as an adverb in such expressions as mʌtʌ gou daun, 'went down easily'); 2. 'plenty, a lot' (as an adjective in such expressions as mʌtʌ to:tl, 'plenty of turtles'; and mʌtʌ dʌs, 'a lot of dust').	Probably related to mata (adv.), 'only, constantly, still, alone', as, for example, in mata-kurdar (adv.), 'quickly', listed by Ray (p. 111).

[30] Dr Beckett (personal communication) reports that in a lot of Mabuiag words ending with vowels the vowels are scarcely voiced, so that one tends to hear wʌp for wʌpi.

[31] Dr Beckett (personal communication) also reports that mʌtʌ is one word which has expanded its meaning considerably, even to meaning 'nice'. Badu Islanders innovate in this way quite consciously, as a kind of word play.

Informal English in the Torres Straits 151

Word	Meaning given by informants	Comments
baiwʌltʌman	'method of fishing using canoe or dinghy in which fisherman stands on bows and is pushed along the shallows by another'	Part of this (viz. bai-) is probably related to buai (noun), 'bows of canoe' (as, for example, in buai-garka (noun), 'the "forward" man of a canoe') listed by Ray (p. 93).

The remainder are words which do not have any apparently related form in Ray. Either Ray has not recorded them or the present-day forms represent neologisms or some vernacular-based word which has undergone considerable phonetic changes. Two such words will be found in Sample 1 (see appendix) viz. bureʌ and tʌdʌrʌl. Informants gave the meanings of these as 'white-haired' and 'to walk along the beach looking for fish' respectively.

There are, of course, other words which are still in use in the vernacular today. Thus waː or wa is used for 'yes', and yaː for 'there' in the text material. So is ati for 'grandfather', although Ray (p. 91) records it as atei. It is not known if this difference represents a phonetic change. If it does it is important as distinguishing the present generation from that of their fathers.[32] Similarly with tiʌm, which informants said meant 'person'. This is probably the same word, tiom, as Ray (p. 124) records for 'boy'. In the text the informants are referring to someone similar to the schoolteacher Miss St George in height and hair colour. It is possible they could have been referring to the author, in which case 'person' would not represent much of a semantic shift from 'boy', although he is not 'white-haired'. No final decision on this was obtained from the informants, and therefore it is not known how inclusive tiʌm is.

Apart from the apparently vernacular-based vocabulary which has just been discussed, the remainder of the vocabulary in these texts is mostly of English origin. Three types can be conveniently distinguished.

Firstly, there are lexical items whose form and/or usage and meaning appear to be distinctive of Torres Straits Islands English. Some of these differences are probably to be related to nineteenth-century English and beach-la-mar origins. For example, **spot** (verb) has the apparent meaning 'to thrust head/snout out of water'. In Torres Straits Islands English this is applied to turtles when they surface to breathe, and represents an exten-

---

[32] My thanks are due to Dr Beckett for the sociolinguistic observation.

sion of meaning, 'to spout' (which is normally only applied to whales and perhaps other large sea mammals), in present-day General Queensland English. Other examples whose differences from General Queensland English are more or less self-evident are: wiŋ (noun), 'flipper (of a turtle)'; gou autsaid (verb phrase), 'go beyond protected waters of a lagoon, or go beyond a fringing reef'; spiːk foː[33] (verb phrase), 'tell to' (as in Deba spiːk foː miː pul, 'Deba told me to pull'); swim glaːs (noun), 'diving goggles'; prəp(ʌ) or prʌpʌ (adverb), 'really, very' (as in prʌpʌ pul, 'very full'); nou teik loŋ (phrase), 'close by' (apparently from English 'it won't take long to get there'); Tiai (noun), 'Thursday Island';[34] plenti (adjective), 'very many' (and less often 'plenty'); nʌðʌ (adjective), 'other' (less often 'another'); nau (adverb), 'then, now' (depending on context); aiən (noun), 'spear with iron point'.

Secondly, there are words which appear to have meanings similar to those in the slang or colloquial language of other varieties of Australian English. For example, kræk (verb), 'crack, hit, strike'; meit (noun), 'mate'; yaːn (verb), 'yarn'; holʌ (verb), 'holler, call out loudly'; hoːl (verb), 'pull in, haul in'; and sluː raun, 'slew round, turn sharply' (probably originally from nautical English).

Finally, there are those English-based words whose origins may not be transparent to those unfamiliar with this kind of speech. Many of these are common to Neo-Melanesian of New Guinea. Examples are: sakim (net) [< English 'chuck-him (net)'], 'cast (a net)'; wʌntaim [< English 'one time'], 'together, simultaneously'; pas or pastaim [< English 'first time'], 'first(ly)'; baimbai [< English 'by and by'], 'later, afterwards'; wʌnem [< English 'what name'], 'what'; oləseim [< English 'all the same as'], 'just like'; kesem or kest [< English 'catch'], 'catch, get'; mai smol dedi [< English 'my small daddy'], 'my uncle'; pasim loŋ [< English 'fasten long'], 'fasten to, with'; olgeðʌ (mæn) [< English 'altogether man'], 'everyone'; oːli [< English 'all he'], 'everyone'; loː ai wotʌ [< English 'long high water'], 'at high tide'.

There are a few words (also common to Neo-Melanesian) whose origins are other than English. For example, lavalava [< Austronesian], 'loin cloth'; kaikai [< Austronesian], 'food (when used as a noun), eat (when used as a verb)'; sævi [< Portuguese], 'know, remember'.

THE STATUS OF TORRES STRAITS ISLANDS INFORMAL ENGLISH

Three points are worth making.

[33] Some variation is noticeable in this form. For example, one informant consistently used *spiːk mi:* for 'tell me'.

[34] *Tiai* ('T.I.') for 'Thursday Island' is as popular an abbreviation amongst the local European population as amongst the Islanders.

First, Torres Straits Islands informal English is a pidgin language, for two reasons.[35] The first is that from a social point of view this variety of English is the normal method of communication between most Europeans and Islanders, and between Islanders from different (mutually unintelligible) vernacular areas (e.g., Saibai and Murray Islands). In some areas (notably Moa and Darnley Islands) where, for historical reasons, there is no common vernacular or the vernacular has disappeared, this variety of English has become the common primary language, or mother tongue of the community. Here, as has already been pointed out, the most extreme forms of the language are likely to be found. Elsewhere the speech is closer to standard Australian English, particularly in vocabulary. It ought to be emphasised, however, that Islanders, like Aborigines in other parts of Queensland, can adapt their speech to changing social situations, so that when talking to a strange European, for example, they adjust their speech as best they can to Standard Australian English. In conversations with familiar persons they use a variety of English similar to that described in this paper.[36]

The second reason why Torres Straits Islands English is to be regarded as a pidgin language is that linguistically it is characterised by a 'reduced' grammatical structure (as compared with Australian English), and by a mixed vocabulary. Indeed, in many ways it is similar to Neo-Melanesian, one of the best known pidgins of the Pacific, in structure and vocabulary, although it is distinct from it. The similarities are undoubtedly to be explained by their connections with beach-la-mar and the differences to different social and linguistic backgrounds of the early participants.

Second, Torres Straits Islands informal English is somewhat different from Queensland Aboriginal English, although there are some obvious similarities between them. Examples are bin and bi as past tense markers; 'eh' as a regularly occurring question tag; the same morpheme is used for singular and plural number; and simple sentence structure.

Torres Straits Islands informal English is not easily understood by Aborigines in Queensland, except by those on the Northern Peninsula Reserve, Cape York, where many Islanders, and some Aborigines who have worked in the marine industry, are now living. Here the younger generation of Aboriginal children who have recently (1962-4) moved to this reserve are acquiring the speech habits of the Islands children living on the same reserve. These habits are more obvious when Aboriginal children are speak-

[35] The criteria used for making this decision are those suggested by Hall in *Hands Off Pidgin English*, esp. p. 20.
[36] Thus Dr Beckett (personal communication) found that when he first went to the Torres Straits on field work the Islanders initially spoke to him in 'a limited, somewhat halting standard English'. Later on as both parties became more familiar to each other the Islanders 'tended to revert to a form of English' similar to that just described.

ing in mixed Aboriginal-Islands company. Amongst themselves the same Aboriginal children speak in a similar way to that of Aboriginal children of the same age from other settlements in Queensland (except for minor differences).

Third, from the linguistic evidence presented in this paper it is clear that Torres Straits Islands English is very similar to Ray's 'jargon English', and undoubtedly represents an extension of it. However, it is not quite clear from present evidence how relevant Ray's social observations are today, except that, at least as far as children are concerned, Torres Straits Islands informal English is very much alive and not 'going out of use' as Ray suggested. This is to the detriment of the vernaculars which seem to be falling into disuse amongst them. On the other hand the general standard of English which these same children use in classroom situations is improving. Yet the facts seem to suggest that the variety of informal English which they use outside of these contexts is likely to continue for some time to come. What is most likely to happen is that over the generations this speech will approximate more closely to General Queensland English as education in English is developed in the Straits,[37] until a situation something similar to that already noted for Aboriginal children is arrived at.[38] Some variation in this regard is already apparent in the areas surveyed. This variation tends towards English rather than towards some other language. In fact, it may well be that a situation of variation which approximates that of the Aboriginal English one (of a continuum of idiolectal variation rather than a single fairly uniform variety of pidgin) already exists. We cannot tell without more extensive research in this area.

---

[37] At least this is what educationists would like to see.
[38] See Dutton, 'The Informal English Speech of Palm Island Aboriginal Children'.

Informal English in the Torres Straits 155

APPENDIX

This appendix contains four text examples of the informal English speech of Torres Straits Islands children from the four sampled areas:

Sample 1: St Paul's Anglican Mission, Moa (Banks) Island;
Sample 2: Saibai Island;
Sample 3: Murray Island;
Sample 4: Bamaga (Northern Peninsula Reserve).

Different speakers are indicated by different numbers on the left-hand side preceding the text material but separated from it by a colon.

Sample 1: St Paul's Anglican Mission, Moa (Banks) Island

This is an extract from a conversation about fishing.

4: ðæt taim wi   bi gou Tiai wʌd //   'That time we went
   that time we been go T.I. there   to Thursday Island.'

?: (Whispering in background)

4: oː dis tiʌm   prəp Misiːn Dzoːdz³⁹   'Oh, this person was
   oh this person proper Miss St George   tall just like Miss
   toːl // bureʌ //   St George—
   tall   white-hair   white-haired.'

2: e nou laːp! //   'Heh, don't laugh!'
   heh no laugh

4: Bogo yʌndei   kræk yuː? //   'Boko, do you want
   Boko you want I crack you   me to hit you?'

3: (Indistinct) mipelʌ gou spiri pis // Sigʌn⁴⁰// 'We'll go to spear fish
                we   go spear fish   Sigun   at Sigun.'

1: ye / wen yəbi gou Boigu⁴¹ ʌ? //   'Yes, when you go to
   yes when you be go Boigu eh?   Boigu eh?'

4: laːs /—/ laːs wiːk wʌd mipelʌ bi   'Last—last week we
   last   last week there we been   went to what's-the-
   wʌnem   hiʌ // spiri pis // ai spir ʌ   name-of that place to
   what name here spear fish   I spear a   spear fish. I speared
   wʌn big mʌlet ðis kain wʌn hiʌ //   a big mullet, you
   one big mullet this kind one here   know the sort.'

?: (laugh)

4: yuː sævi ðæt aː /—/ nʌðʌ Sʌndi   'You know that ah—
   you know that ah — other Sunday   other Sunday Nako
   mituː   Nako / plei maːbl deː   and I played marbles
   we two   Nako play marble there   at Grandfather

³⁹ Miss St George: a European teacher at St Paul's Anglican Mission School, Moa (Banks) Island.
⁴⁰ Name of coastal point.
⁴¹ Name of island in northwestern Torres Straits.

/ aːti Zʌwaihausʷʌd // mipelʌ Zawai's house. We
grandfather Zawai house we went down and took
gou daun // teik spi mituː tʌdʌrʌl⁴² a spear to go along
go down take spear we two tadaral the beach looking for
// gou ðæt wei // mituː gou nau / fish. We went that
go that way we two go now way. We walked until
kʌm frʌnt pain ən ai lukt ðæt // we came in front of
come in front point and I looked that the point and I saw
oləseim treit wʌd / yalaiwʌp⁴³ // that fish with a line
all the same thread there yalaiwap like a thread along its
 back. It was a
 Yalaiwap.'

1: big wʌn ? // 'Was it a big one?'
big one

4: big wʌn meit // if ai /—/ if ai lai yuː 'It was a big one,
big one mate if I if I lie you mate. Ask Nako if
ʌksi Nʌko // em kʌm // ai got foː niu you don't believe me.
ask Nako it came I got four new It came. I had four
spiʌ // new spears.'
spear

1: huː ðæt meik ðəm foː yuː // 'Who made them for
who that make them for you you?'

4: mai dedi // ai meik /—/ meikem // 'My father. I took
my father I make make it up the spear and
ai kesem⁴⁴ // meikem streit // em sluː straightened the
I catch it make it straight it slew prong. The fish turned
raun n ai draivem ðruː // dziːwi sharply in the water
round and I drive it through gee whiz and I speared it. Gee
hedz got splitim // ai put mai hæn whiz its head was split
head was got split it I put my hand open. I put my hand
gou insaid / gou rait insaid // wəz inside its head. It
go inside go right inside we was went right in. We
təːn bæk // laːs Sʌndi kʌm from turned back. Last
turn back last Sunday came from Sunday after church
preːʌ / mituː gou teik ʌ diɲi gou spire we(2) took a dinghy
prayer we two go take a dinghy go spear and went fishing. First
wʌn puriː paːs // of all we speared a
one baby shark first baby shark.'

1: yuː rəmembə ðə laːs Sʌndei yutuː 'Remember last
you remember the last Sunday you two Sunday when you(2)
painde toːtl eg deː // found turtle eggs
find turtle egg there there.'

⁴² 'To walk along the beach looking for fish'. See discussion, p. 151.
⁴³ 'Kind of fish with a black thread down its back'. See discussion, p. 150.
⁴⁴ *Kesem*, 'catch it (up)', i.e. 'take it up'. It may also mean 'to arrive at a place'.

Informal English in the Torres Straits

4: wʌ yai⁴⁵ gou yaːn // yuː lisen //
   yes here I go yarn you listen
   ai spirid ðʌ puriː ʌ // oukei mituː
   I speared the puri eh okay we two
   baiwʌltʌmʌn⁴⁶ nau gou // ai bi fored //
   fished now go I be forward
   mituː gou gou gou aː /—/ mituː kæri
   we two go go go ah we two carry
   /—/ em luk gou on top // ai stæn
      he look go on top I stand
   ʌwei ət ʃoːt trauzis // kʌm from preː
   away with short trousers come from prayer
   ai teik oːf // em luk gou on top deː
   I take off he look go on top there
   luk toːtl θreik deː // mituː gou ən
   look turtle track the e we two go and
   dzis bin gou on top / i stil wet /
   just been go on top it still wet
   mituː diginim // mituː spirim paːs
   we two dug it we two spear it first
   // spiri wʌd // mituː wʌnde gou nau
      spear there we two wanted go now
   liːvi ðʌ toːtl eg // ai kest ðə wʌn
   leave the turtle egg I catch the one
   aiən / ai draivim // mʌtʌ gou daun
   iron I drive it easily go down
   spiri / ai luk // wai i wet // ai spirim
   spear I look why it wet I spear it
   gen ai luk aː i wet // mituː diginim
   again I look ah it wet we two dig it
   got ðəm big griːn toːtl eg // oːl ði eg
   got them big green turtle egg all the egg
   i lei on top wʌn ə ðouz big wʌn //
   it lay on top one of those big one

'Yes, I'm talking now. You listen. I speared the baby shark eh? Okay we(2) went in the dinghy, one pushing and the other standing on the bows. I was up front on the bows. We kept going. We carried—he (my friend) went up on the beach to look around. I stood back in my short pants. When I came from church I took the others off. He went up the beach and looked. He saw turtle tracks there. We went and saw that the turtle had just been up the beach because the tracks were still wet. We dug. We speared into the sand first. We wanted to go and leave the turtle eggs. I took up the iron spear and drove it in. It went down easily. It was wet. I speared again. I looked. It was wet again. We dug and got those big green turtle eggs. A big egg lay on top.'

1: yutuː diginim teik im kʌm haus
   you two dig them take them come house
   ʌ //
   eh

'You (2) dug them out and brought them home eh?'

4: teik em kʌm haus // mituː teik
   take them come house we two take
   ðem kʌm // ai bi got θəːtisiks / em
   them come I be got thirty-six he
   got θəːti //
   got thirty

'Brought them home. We took them home. I got 36. He got 30.'

---

⁴⁵ *Yai* < *ya*, 'there', and *ai*, 'I'.

⁴⁶ Baiwʌltʌmʌn, 'method of fishing (using canoe or dinghy in which fisherman stands on bows and is pushed along the shallows by another)'. See discussion, p. 151.

Sample 2: Saibai Island

This is an extract from a conversation about toy canoe racing.

11: loŋ I:stʌ //   'At Easter.'
    long Easter

12: loŋ I:stʌ // Kʌŋ // Kʌŋ bin kʌm   'At Easter. *Kang* came
    long Easter   Kang   Kang been come   first. *Kang* won.
    fə:st // Kʌŋ bin kʌm fə:st // ʌnʌðʌ   Another time we
    first   Kang been come first   another   handicapped *Kang*.
    reis mi puti Kʌŋ biain // mplʌ gou   They started first and
    race I put Kang behind   we go   *Kang* followed. It won
    pa:s // Kʌŋ i sta:tiŋ biain // em win   the race. Afterwards
    first   Kang he starting behind   he won the captain of *Kang*
    ðə reis // (whispering) ʌptə /—/ i bi   received some money.
    the race   after   he be   But he didn't want it
    givi mʌni fo: kʌptən bloŋ Kʌŋ bʌt   so they gave it to the
    give money for captain belong Kang but   second canoe's captain
    em nou won dem bʌt i bi givi lo: named—who is it?—
    he no want them but he be give long   Mebai. The second
    sekən // neim bəloŋ ðʌtʌ mʌn / u   one belonged to
    second   name belong that man   who   Enosa, and the third
    dat ia   / Mebai // kenu bəloŋ em /   one to Kala. The
    that here Mebai   canoe belong them   minor placings
    sekən wʌn kenu bəloŋ Enosʌ // ðə:d   received sugar-cane.'
    second one canoe belong Enosa   third
    wʌn kenu bəloŋ Kʌlʌ // a: /—/ bʌt
    one canoe belong Kala   ah   but
    ðem sekən wʌn i bi givi ðəm ðemplʌ
    them second one he be give them them
    // sugə kein //
      sugar-cane

Sample 3: Murray Island

This is an extract from a story about turtle hunting.

15: mi: / ʌnə mai frend miplʌ gou fo: kese   'My friend and I went
    me   and my friend we   go for catch   to catch turtles on the
    tot /—/ tə:tl lo: ri:f // mplʌ gou kese   reef. We caught a
    turt — turtle long reef   we go catch   small one. We brought
    wʌn / smo:l wʌn / mplʌ teikem kʌm   it back. My friend
    one   small one   we take them come   said to me, "You go
    // mai pren i spi:k mi: / yu gou   and cut it up and
       my friend he speak me   you go   we'll eat it". (cough)
    kʌtem ən yumi gou kaikai // (cough)   And we took it, cut it
    cut them and you me go eat   up, and ate it. In the
    ən mplʌ teik əm nʌ kʌtem en   morning we got up
    and we take them and cut them and   and went to Dauar
    mplʌ kaikai // moniŋ taim mplʌ get ʌp /   Island, and caught
    we eat   morning time we get up   small—caught many
    miplʌ gou fo: Dauar ailn / enə kese   turtles. We brought
    we   go for Dauar Island   and catch   them back and made

smo:l /—/ kese o:l to:tol // teikem	a big feast. We cut
small catch all turtle take them	them up, prepared
kʌm n meikem big fi:st // mplʌ kʌtem	them, and boiled
come and make it big feast we cut them	them. Then they took
//meikem gud // boilem pinis ən mplʌ	it and put it in a tin
make them good boil them finish and we	and we boiled it and
teikem / putim insaid / lo: tin ʌn	put it on tables. Make
take them put them inside long tin and	—put it on the tables.
mi /—/ ən miplʌ boilem // ən teikem	Make—we made a
me and we boil them and take them	big feast. When we
gou putim lo: teibl // meik /—/	got up our stomachs
go put them long table make	were full. . . .
putim loŋ teibl // miplʌ meik ʌ big	
put them long table we make a big	
fi:st (whispering) wen miplʌ get ʌp beli	
feast when we get up belly	
bəloŋ miplʌ prʌpʌ pul //	
belong us proper full	

Sample 4: Bamaga

This is an extract from a rambling conversation.

10: ai gou ya:n yupələ wʌn sto:ri bəloŋ /—/	'I'm going to tell you
I go yarn you one story belong	a story about a
bloŋ mʌmigoust // wa: / hi gou wʌn /	mummyghost. Yes,
belong mummyghost yes he go one	he went one—he got
hi got / ðæt taun wʌd hi stop daun ðis	—that town, you
he got that town there he stop down this	know the kind, where
kain ʌ taun a: /—/ ai got haus de: //	he stopped. I got a
kind a town ah I got house there	house there. He had
hi got lo: /—/ wʌn haus / hi got ʌ	a lo(ng) . . . There
he got long one house he got a	were two small girls
tu: smo:l gə:l u: bin stop ðə: // ðem	in there. They slept
two small girl who been stop there them	up on top of the hill.
tu: sli:p ən top loŋ i:l // wen naitaim	When night-time
two sleep on top long hill when night time	came, you know the
ðis kain ðæt ðiŋ i meiki noiz ausaid	kind, that thing made
this kind that thing he made noise outside	a noise outside near
loŋ /—/ do: // o:rait / bin gou //	the door. All right it
long door all right been go	went (?). It saw a
em i luk wʌn mæn i stæn ʌp kʌm //	man coming. The
he he look one man he stand up come	man took it away.
ðə mæn bin teikim gou // gə ðə: rait	They went for a very
the man been take it go get the right	long way away.'
əloŋ wei // propʌ lo:ŋ wei //	
a long way proper long way	

REFERENCES CITED

Baker, S. J., *Australia Speaks: A Supplement to 'The Australian Language'*, Sydney, 1953.
——, *The Australian Language*, Sydney, 1966.
Beckett, Jeremy R., Politics in the Torres Straits Islands, Ph.D. dissertation, Australian National University, Canberra, 1963.
Douglas, Wilfred, *The Aboriginal Languages of the South-West of Australia*, Australian Institute of Aboriginal Studies Monograph No. 14, Linguistic Series No. 4, Canberra, 1968.
Dutton, T. E., 'The Informal English Speech of Palm Island Aboriginal Children, North Queensland', *Journal of English Linguistics*, Vol. 3, 1969, pp. 18-36.
Flint, E. H., 'Aboriginal English: Linguistic Description as an Aid to Teaching', *English in Australia* No. 6, 1968, pp. 3-21.
——, 'The Question of Language, Dialect, Idiolect, and Style in Queensland English', Linguistic Circle of Canberra, *Bulletin* No. 2, 1965, pp. 1-21.
——, 'The Survey of Queensland Speech', Linguistic Circle of Canberra, *Bulletin* No. 1, 1964.
——, 'Theoretical and Descriptive Problems of Linguistic Variation: A Report on Research in Progress under the Queensland Speech Survey', paper delivered to AULLA Congress, Melbourne, August 1964 (mimeo.).
Haddon, A. C., *Head-Hunters Black, White and Brown*, London, 1901.
Hall, Robert A., jun., *Hands Off Pidgin English!*, Sydney, 1955.
——, *Pidgin and Creole Languages*, Ithaca, 1966.
——, Review of E. P. Sayer's *Pidgin English*, *Language*, Vol. 20, 1944, pp. 171-4.
Jernudd, Björn H., 'Social Change and Aboriginal Speech Variation in Australia', *Working Papers in Linguistics* No. 4, University of Hawaii, 1969, pp. 145-68.
Laycock, D. C., 'Pidgin's Progress', *New Guinea*, Vol. 4, No. 2, 1969, pp. 8-15.
Mihalic, Francis, *Grammar and Dictionary of Neo-Melanesian*, Techny, Illinois, 1957.
Ramson, W. S., *Australian English: An Historical Study of the Vocabulary 1788-1898*, Canberra, 1966.
——, 'The Currency of Aboriginal Words in Australian English', *Occasional Paper* No. 3, Australian Language Research Centre, Sydney, 1964.
Ray, S. H., Volume III (Linguistics) of *Reports of the Cambridge Anthropological Expedition to Torres Straits*, Cambridge, 1907.
Reinecke, John E., Marginal Languages: A Sociological Survey of Creole Languages and Trade Languages, Ph.D. dissertation, Yale University, 1937.
Salisbury, Richard F., 'Pidgin's Respectable Past: A Matter of New Guinean Pride', *New Guinea*, Vol. 2, No. 2, 1967, pp. 44-8.
Sayer, E. P., *Pidgin English*, 2nd ed., Toronto, 1943.
Turner, G. W., *The English Language in Australia and New Zealand*, London, 1966.
Wurm, S. A., 'Pidgin—A National Language: 300,000 New Guineans Can't be Wrong', *New Guinea*, Vol. 1, No. 3, 1966, pp. 49-54.

A COMPARISON OF SPOKEN AND WRITTEN ENGLISH: TOWARDS AN INTEGRATED METHOD OF LINGUISTIC DESCRIPTION

There are wide linguistic differences between the educated spoken English of Australian matriculation students and the written English they may have to study at a university. This paper will use an integrated method of linguistic description to compare the grammatical, lexical, and semantic characteristics of spoken and written English.

The search for an integrated method of linguistic description is one of the main activities of current linguistic research. Katz and Postal assert that the linguistic description of a natural language must consist of three components—a syntactic, a semantic, and a phonological.[1] Of these the syntactic component is the generative source in the linguistic description. It specifies the abstract set of formal structures which underlie the sentences of a language. The semantic component of the description assigns to each particular structure a semantic interpretation, describing the meaning of the sentence which possesses that underlying structure, and the phonological component assigns to it a phonetic representation. The whole description must show the basis of the relation between sounds and meaning in actual language communication. From this statement of the authors it may be deduced that to describe the grammar, vocabulary, and phonology of a language separately is useless, without an attempt to show how these are interrelated and function together as a communicative system.

The semantic component of the linguistic description must provide a meaning for each of the lexical items of the language, and also show how the semantic interpretation of a sentence possessing a particular underlying structure is related to the meaning of its lexical items. The semantic description must consequently specify, firstly, relevant syntactic information (e.g. form-class, noun), and then the general semantic properties of the lexical items—their 'semantic markers' (e.g. whether animate or inanimate). These general semantic properties are really a conceptual generalisation

---

[1] *An Integrated Theory of Linguistic Descriptions*, pp. 1, 12-13. The principles expounded here are developed later by Katz in *The Philosophy of Language*. An earlier statement of them is in Katz and Fodor, 'The Structure of a Semantic Theory'.

from their perceived attributes; but the generalisation is such as is relevant to language.[2] Thus *plant* linguistically belongs to class inanimate of lexical items, although a plant, in objective reality, is 'living'. The indefinite pronoun *nothing* could, in a suitable context, substitute for *plant*; *nobody* could not.

The semantic description also specifies for each lexical item a 'distinguisher' (representing what is idiosyncratic about its meaning) and a selection restriction, which states the necessary condition for it to combine with other lexical items in sentence relationships. Thus the generalised semantic features of a verb are related to the semantic features, not only of noun object, but also of noun subject.[3] The sentence, *The table drank a glass of water*, is not acceptable because the verb semantically cannot co-occur with a noun/inanimate subject.

Very recent research on the generalised semantic features of lexical items has suggested that some of them may be termed binary, being distinguished by contrast of one essential feature (e.g. animate/inanimate), some are hierarchically ordered, and others are cross-classifying.[4]

The above principles concerning generalised semantic features and their relationship to grammatical structure have proved useful in the present study. Experience in this and in previous research has tended to suggest that a hierarchy of binary features can be distinguished. The highest, most inclusive binary classification would appear to be into lexical items denoting observable/measurables ('concrete nouns') and those denoting non-observable/measurables ('abstract nouns'), other binary classes being ordered below. This classification proved very relevant to the comparison of spoken and written English. Abstract nouns were of very high frequency in the written discourse examined; and, because of selection restrictions in sentence structure, this meant also that verbs and adjectives at least had the same abstract semantic feature.

Katz and Postal acknowledged that they worked within the framework of generative grammar, but sought to incorporate within it recent developments in semantics. It easily escapes notice, however, that Chomsky, as early as 1957, had foreseen the need for a later correlation of syntax and semantics.[5] Even after asserting then that 'grammar is best formulated as a self-contained study independent of semantics', he concluded by saying:

> Nevertheless, we do find many important correlations, quite naturally, between syntactic structure and meaning . . . These correlations could form

[2] Langendoen, *The Study of Syntax*, p. 37, pertinently observes that such general semantic features are conceptually and perceptually based, and are not to be identified with classes of objects and properties of the physical world.

[3] This point is discussed in Langendoen, *The Study of Syntax*, p. 42; cf. Chomsky, *Aspects of the Theory of Syntax*, pp. 95, 114.

[4] Langendoen, *The Study of Syntax*, pp. 35-7.

[5] Chomsky, *Syntactic Structures*, pp. 106-8.

part of the subject matter for a more general theory of language concerned with syntax and semantics and their points of connection.

The development of this fuller theory was realised in *Aspects of the Theory of Syntax*.[6] The useful principle of deep and surface structure stated here is further developed in later work.[7] Deep structure is defined as

> the abstract underlying form which determines the meaning of the sentence; it is present in the mind, but not necessarily represented directly in the physical signal. The surface structure of sentence is the actual organization of the physical signal into phrases of varying size, into words of various categories, with certain particles, inflections, arrangements, and so on.[8]

Exploration of the relationship between the deep structure (as thus defined) and the surface structure of English spoken and written discourse is one aspect of the following study.

In a very recent publication, Chomsky expresses a belief that immediate current developments in linguistics point towards 'a kind of synthesis of philosophical grammar and structural linguistics'.[9] Mere description of linguistic structure will not elucidate the problems of language, unless it is related to the way in which meaning is communicated. This also has been a principle of the following study.[10]

The grammatical relevance of the prosodic (or 'suprasegmental') patterns of intonation, stress, and length in relation to pause is less emphasised by the transformational-generative grammarians than the relationship between grammar and semantics. P. Lieberman makes some interesting correlations, sometimes supported by acoustic data, between suprasegmental phonological features and syntactic structure, and also surveys earlier studies in intonation. *The Sound Pattern of English* deals mainly with stress

---

[6] Especially pp. 148-92. The changes made by Chomsky in his expanded theory are well explained in Zatorski, 'Early and Later Versions of the Theory of Transformational Grammar'. Account is also taken of them in Cattell, *The Design of English*, e.g. pp. 97-102. Jacobson exhaustively reviews *Aspects of the Theory of Syntax* in *Linguistics* No. 28, December 1966, pp. 111-26.

[7] E.g. in *Cartesian Linguistics*, pp. 31-51.

[8] Chomsky, 'The Current Scene in Linguistics', p. 2.

[9] *Language and Mind*, p. 58.

[10] Criticism of Chomsky's views is not lacking, e.g. that in Hockett, *The State of the Art*. Chomsky himself is very open-minded concerning current linguistic developments: 'Any theory of grammar which can be formulated today must be highly tentative. . . . Linguistics is a living subject' (*Topics in the Theory of Generative Grammar*, p. 92). Another theory which aims at integrated linguistic description is that of Lamb, *Outline of Stratificational Grammar*. Lamb recognises an interrelated six-strata structure in language, with three main components—semology, grammar, and phonology. The phonetic (or hypophonemic) stratum is regarded as the lowest, and the semantic (or hypersememic) as the highest. Semantics is thus incorporated into grammar and the interrelationship of linguistic systems is recognised: pp. 1-2, 18-21. Lamb acknowledges a debt to Hjelmslev and Hockett for points of his theory.

patterns.[11] Moreover, comparatively little attention is given in transformational-generative grammar to the levels of linguistic structure above the sentence.

Teachers of English, whether to mother-tongue or to foreign learners, find the need to consider the way in which English sentences may be linked to form more inclusive units of language, and this also involves, in the spoken medium, reference to intonation.

Thus F. C. Johnson finds the need for a systematic description of both the 'positional' and semantic behaviour of suprasententials—'words and constructions which function in a grammar of "larger than sentence" units of language', such as *moreover, at that time*.[12] These signals vary in spoken English from ordinary co-ordinating conjunctions in having different intonational characteristics.

Similarly, Scott and Bowley, in their normative grammar of English based upon linguistic principles, include a brief chapter on grammar 'beyond the sentence'.[13] Linguistic theory should therefore provide for the adequate description of English grammar above the sentence, and should also describe the relationship of intonation to this in the spoken medium.

A theory which provides for this, and also allows for the integration of grammar and semantics, is that of M. A. K. Halliday.[14] It is one which

> requires an analysis of at least sentence, clause, and group structures and systems, with extension where possible above the rank of sentence . . . The analysis . . . needs to provide a basis for semantic statements, and to handle with the minimum complexity grammatical contrasts such as those in English expounded by intonation and rhythm.[15]

These are the requirements of the theory which enable it to be usefully applied in linguistic and literary study, in language teaching, and in sociological research.

Halliday postulates for the description of language three general levels of substance, form, and context. The substance is the material of language, phonic or graphic; the form is the structuring of substance so that it becomes a meaningful communicative medium; and context is the relation of the form to linguistically relevant features of the situations in which language operates, and to linguistic features other than those of the item under attention.

To the general level of substance corresponds the specific level of

---

[11] Lieberman, *Intonation, Perception, and Language*, pp. 120-1, 171-95. Chomsky and Halle, *The Sound Pattern of English*.
[12] Johnson, 'English Suprasententials', p. 4.
[13] Scott, Bowley, *et al.*, *English Grammar*, pp. 203-11.
[14] 'Categories of the Theory of Grammar'. The theory is slightly modified and developed in Halliday, McIntosh, and Strevens, *The Linguistic Sciences and Language Teaching*, pp. 15-40.
[15] Halliday, 'Syntax and the Consumer', p. 16.

phonetics; to that of form correspond the specific levels of grammar and lexis (vocabulary), which are interrelated; and to that of context corresponds the specific level of semantics. Phonology and graphology are 'interlevels' relating spoken or written substance to formal patterning.

Context is also an interlevel of linguistic description. It includes all statements of the relationship of the formally patterned grammatical and lexical units to the relevant features of the language situation between which they signal meaningful relationships.

Language has both formal and contextual meaning.[16] The formal meaning of a linguistic item or category, either grammatical or lexical, derives from its relation to other formal units or categories within the larger structural pattern. A formal item, however, whether grammatical or lexical, may also have contextual meaning, deriving from its relationship, through the formal linguistic network, to relevant features or items of the language situation. The latter term may apply of course to subjective, purely conceptual situations as well as to those of objective reality.

Halliday recognises four categories of the theory of grammar—unit, structure, class, and system. Grammatical structure is conceived in terms of a hierarchy of grammatical units ordered by rank, where a sentence consists of clauses, a clause of groups or phrases, a group or phrase of words, and a word of morphemes. Starting from the top (structurally most inclusive) unit of the hierarchy, each unit consists of one, or more than one, unit of the rank next below (next less inclusive).[17] Thus a word may consist of one, or more than one, morpheme, e.g. *tear/tearful*.[18]

Units do not necessarily occur in communicative discourse in this hierarchical order. Thus a clause may form part of a group structure (e.g. *The documentary program which I was watching last night* was 'Four Corners').

Grammatical classes of units (e.g. nominal, verbal, adjectival, and adverbial) are defined consistently by operation in the structure of the unit next above.[19] The category of system applies to formal patterns where there is a restrictive set of contrastive possibilities (e.g. *this/that* are terms in a demonstrative system).

Halliday, for the purposes of theoretical discussion, took the sentence as the highest rank of the grammatical hierarchy. He recognised, however, that other units above the rank of sentence might be distinguished.[20]

Pickett distinguished in the structure of spoken conversation in that

---

[16] Contextual meaning is extensively discussed in J. Ellis's chapter, 'On Contextual Meaning', in Bazell, Catford, *et al.* (eds.), *In Memory of Firth*, pp. 79-95; and in Dixon, 'On Formal and Contextual Meaning'.
[17] Halliday, 'Categories of the Theory of Grammar', p. 251.
[18] In the following description, a unit consisting of one unit of the rank next below is termed 'simple'; a unit consisting of more than one is termed 'complex'.
[19] 'Categories of the Theory of Grammar', p. 260.
[20] Ibid., p. 253n.

language at least six structural levels (i.e. ranks): below discourse—the highest, most inclusive unit—an utterance unit was distinguished, in addition to the usual units below sentence.[21] The following study, pursuing these suggestions in Pickett and Halliday, recognises ranks of units above sentence: for written English, discourse, paragraph unit, paragraph, and sentence group; for spoken English, discourse, utterance, and sentence group.[22] This permits a complete description of each type of material, when Halliday's five ranks of sentence and below are added.

The description of function words is possible within the framework of Halliday's grammatical theory.[23] This is because they are structurally definable, since they operate in elements of structure of all syntactical units from utterance to group/phrase rank. All have formal, and some also have contextual, meaning (e.g. prepositions).

Among function words are the sequence signals called by Johnson 'suprasententials', and also the class called in the following description 'sentence group operators', which are very frequent in spoken discourse. Sentence group operators are sometimes dismissed as meaningless, but they have various communicative functions in the chain of discourse.[24] Some of them are important intonation bearers and are on the border of paralanguage.

The systematic study of function words, as in White's description of prepositions within the framework of Lamb's theory, is comparatively rare.[25] Scott and Bowley treat function words where necessary in their linguistically-based grammar (e.g. p. 71). Hill has compiled a dictionary of prepositions and adverbial particles describing many of the contextual meanings of these, but its structural description is not on modern linguistic lines.[26] This study, however, shows the need which teachers of English feel for the systematic description of function words.

Halliday's linguistic theory not only provides for a detailed description of all grammatical units of the hierarchy, thus enabling deep and surface structure relations to be discerned. It also offers, in its interlevel of context, opportunity for complete contextual description and for the correlation of grammar and semantics. The linguistic description which is the basis of the following study joins a contextual description to the formal description of units at the various ranks of the hierarchy. Semantic correlations are clear at word rank. The selection restrictions which operate upon word

[21] 'The Grammatical Hierarchy of Isthmus Zapotec'.
[22] Criteria for the delimitation of the utterance unit are stated in Söderlind, 'Utterance, Sentence and Clause as English Speech-Units', p. 53.
[23] Function words (Fries's term) are otherwise called 'grammatical' or 'structural' words.
[24] Some of these are described in Klatte, 'Sentence Morphemes in English'.
[25] White, 'The Methodology of Sememic Analysis with Special Application to the English Preposition'.
[26] Hill, *Prepositions and Adverbial Particles*.

units when they enter into higher-ranking structure are revealed in this joint formal and contextual description. To this is added a statement of intonation patterns, to form a complete integrated linguistic description. The conclusions presented below are based on relevant data abstracted from this.

Comparison of the written and the spoken medium of English must take account of several levels of linguistic variation. Within the one language, English, variations of dialect, both regional and social, style and register, and idiolect may occur. Both the written and the spoken medium may be subject to any of these. The selection of material for the following study took account of these considerations.

Two English discourses, a written and a spoken (henceforward called W and S), were chosen for detailed analysis and comparison. They were of comparable length (W had 1,524 running words, S had 1,526). S consisted of a recorded unrehearsed conversation, mainly about television and other entertainment, between four speakers aged 17-18 years chosen at random from a senior form of a leading secondary school. The speakers exhibited no distinctive dialectal or idiolectal characteristics. Their competence as speakers appeared approximately equal. Together they represented the average competence of speakers belonging to other groups in the same recorded corpus.

Their average rate of articulation (including pauses in the time span) was relatively fast (5·1 syllables per second); the whole conversation lasted 5 minutes 40 seconds. Pauses were few and not long: the longest pause within utterances was 0·6 seconds, and only one pause (1·5 seconds) occurred between utterances. As often in informal conversation, pauses did not always occur at syntactic boundaries. Deviant utterances, where a break in syntactic structure or intonation contours caused communicative confusion, constituted only 2·8 per cent of the material. However, interrupted and incomplete clauses, due to mutual interruption, overlapping, and interpolation of utterances in the fast exchange of speech, constituted 7·9 per cent and 3·9 per cent of the material respectively.

The written discourse (W) consisted of part of an article on linguistics, written in Standard British English, but employing the specialised vocabulary of that science.

Differences of dialect and idiolect were not apparent in these discourses. However, linguistic comparison had to take account of differences of style (governed by communication content and purpose); of register (governed by the social relationship of the participants and social aspects of the language situation); and of medium.

Discourses differing sharply in style were chosen for two reasons. The first was to characterise the extreme ends of the written-spoken continuum. In between, many grades of difference will lie: for example, obviously the dialogue of a realistic play or novel approaches that of spoken conversation in style. It is more useful first to discover the maximum rather than the minimum difference between the two media, and then to characterise intermediate variations.

The second reason concerns possible applications of the comparative study. S can be taken as representative of the normal conversational speech of students entering an Australian university; W is representative of written material which they may soon have to study if they enrol in any subject such as linguistics, philosophy, or the social sciences. A comparison of the two could possibly reveal facts of educational or social interest.

Some points of the descriptive procedure which was followed call for comment.

First, the scope of the following study does not permit a full statement of the intonation patterns. Only salient points of the results of this description are incidentally included. These patterns were found to be extremely important in the grammatical analysis, as well as in the contextual description of the spoken sample, however. As Halliday says, they have two kinds of function, one being contextual, the other formal—'to show the structure of the discourse, how it is broken up into message units, where the new information resides, what special contrasts are intended and so forth'.[27] Intonation was found to have these functions in the spoken discourse.

Second, Goldman Eisler, in psycholinguistic experiments concerned with spontaneous English speech, used, as a measure to indicate relative complexity of sentence structure, the proportion of subordinate clauses in the total number of clauses of the language material. This was termed a Subordination Index.[28] In the following study, one of the measures used to indicate relative structural complexity was the proportion of complex to simple and co-ordinate sentences. However, it was felt that a more effective measure of such complexity would be, as Goldman Eisler realised, the depth of structural subordination.

Accordingly, the proportion of clauses embedded (or 'nested') in the first and in successive layers of structure was observed and calculated, and this provided a clause-embedding index. Similarly, a group and phrase-embedding index was prepared. These measures, together with that provided by the proportion of sentence types, provided an effective means of comparing the degree of structural complexity in the two discourses.

Third, contextual description was found to be possible with most grammatical units. To some few it was found not to apply—particularly to

---

[27] Halliday, 'Language and Experience', p. 98. Halliday deals formally with the relationship between intonation and grammar in 'Notes on Transitivity and Theme in English' and in *Intonation and Grammar in British English*. R. Quirk and D. Crystal, in their chapter 'On Scales of Contrast in Connected English Speech' in Bazell *et al.*, *In Memory of Firth*, also furnished suggestions for the present study.

[28] Eisler, *Psycholinguistics*, p. 70.

certain function words. The preposition *of*, for example, belongs to a structurally defined class of prepositional function word units. It has various contextual meanings (e.g. possession) in different grammatical and situational contexts, but sometimes it has none, and serves the purely formal function of adjectival subordinator (e.g. in *the scale of rank*, expressible also as *the rank scale*). The borderline between formal and contextual meaning is sometimes extremely difficult to define, as Jespersen pointed out, though not in those terms, long ago.[29] The two possibly constitute a semantic continuum.[30] The following description will note where such borderlines occur.

Fourth, the lexical description took account of lexical compounds as well as of simple and complex words. Lexical compounds—'any group of morphemes or words whose meaning cannot be deduced from the meanings of its parts'[31]—have various quasi-grammatical structures. For the purposes of this study, lexical items such as *break into* (interrupt), similar to that exemplified by Halliday, *made . . . up*,[32] will be treated in the grammatical statistics as compound words, in addition to such combinations as *standpoint*. Other lexical compounds with phrasal or clausal structure (e.g. *as a matter of fact*; *I mean* as an interpolation) will be treated separately.

Fifth, the relative frequency of occurrence in W and S of the various structural patterns and classes of formal units and of the types of contextual meaning associated with them was calculated. These data, presented in the following section, were made the basis for a comparison of the linguistic characteristics of the two discourses. An attempt was made to judge the total communicative effect of each discourse by considering its formal and semantic characteristics together.

The formal and contextual description of W and S shows striking differences as well as similarities between them.

Non-principal sentences occur frequently in S, but not at all in W.[33] The

---

[29] Jespersen, *The Philosophy of Grammar*, p. 33. Jespersen used 'empty' to denote 'lacking in contextual meaning'.

[30] The problem is discussed in my 'Item and Relationship Signals in Grammar-Lexis Patterning'.

[31] Healey, 'English Idioms', p. 71, thus defines 'idiom', his term for what is here called 'lexical compound'.

[32] 'Categories of the Theory of Grammar', p. 267n. Halliday realised the difficulty that subjecting such items to grammatical analysis left their lexical relations unaccounted for.

[33] 'Non-principal sentence' denotes a grammatical unit which is the exponent of an element of sentence group structure, but which in itself is other than a non-subordinate clause, in its internal structure. With lexical exponents, it has the essential characteristic of a sentence specified by Halliday ('Categories', p. 252) as a 'unit which more than any other offers itself as an item for contextual statement, because it does the language work in situations' (e.g. in 'Where are you going tonight? *To the football match*', the answer, though formally a phrase, fulfils the sentence function in the language situation). The term 'non-principal' is that early used by Nida in *Syntax: a Descriptive Analysis*, p. 26.

formal patterns of non-subordinate clauses are broadly similar in both discourses, but those of subordinate clauses are more varied in W. The distribution of grammatical clause classes and the relative distribution of group and phrase units are similar in both.

The written discourse has, however, more complex sentence group, sentence, group, and word structure; more transitive and fewer intransitive clauses; a greater frequency of the passive voice, with consequent greater complexity of clause structure; a greater depth of clause, group, and phrase structure; more class nominal and fewer class verbal, adjectival, and adverbial group units; more class adjectival and fewer class adverbial phrase units; more complex and fewer simple and compound word units; more class nominal and adjectival, and fewer class verbal and adverbial word units; more lexical words and fewer function words; and, among the function word classes, fewer pronouns and sentence group operators and more prepositions.

Both W and S have very few prefixing words; but derivational (word-forming) suffixes predominate in W, whereas grammatical relationship suffixes (e.g. that of the third person singular present tense of verbs) predominate in S.

W differs from S also in contextual clause types. It has more cognitive (statement-type), but fewer interrogative, non-subordinate clauses than the spoken. On the other hand, S has more cognitive subordinate clauses ('indirect statements') and fewer interrogative subordinate clauses ('indirect questions') than W.

The striking difference in generalised semantic features between the two discourses is that W has far more class nominal words denoting non-observable/measurables ('abstract nouns'), whereas S has more denoting observable/measurables ('concrete nouns').

Another notable fact is that in W words of Latin and Greek origin predominate, whereas the reverse is true in S. The details of these formal and contextual differences and similarities between W and S now follow.

FROM DISCOURSE TO SENTENCE

W has two main structural divisions or elements. The exponents of these are the main units of the discourse corresponding contextually to a theoretical introduction and a linguistic description.

The first main unit has two elements of structure, each expounded by a complex paragraph group unit. Each paragraph group has three elements of structure, each expounded by a paragraph unit.

The second main unit of discourse has also two elements of structure, each expounded by a simple paragraph group unit. Each simple paragraph group unit consists of one paragraph unit only.

Formal signals which distinguish the constituent units of the discourse, and also the paragraph group units, are parataxis, various sequence signals (e.g. *in the first place* . . .; *in this view, then,* . . .), and a conventional graphological device of technical writing, decimal numbering (the introduction being numbered 0·1, 0·2, the description 1·1, 1·2 . . .).

S does not have clearly defined higher-ranking units corresponding to those of W just described. It does, however, fall into three phases: an initial phase of conventional conversational exchange (utterance 1-48); a vigorous spontaneous discussion when a topic of mutual interest arises (49-120); and a concluding phase (121-32), when the speakers appear to tire physically and interest slackens.

The utterances of the second phase differ from those of the other two in having a faster rate of utterance; a wider range of pitch, loudness, and length contrasts; and more complex grammatical structure. The detailed description of these differences is not possible here.

The paragraph units of W and the utterance units of S have elements of structure expounded by sentence group units. The formal signals distinguishing sentence groups in W are parataxis and lexical sequence signals; in S, they are parataxis and sequence signals in correlation with phonological signals of stress and intonation patterns related to pauses. Intonation terminals (falling, level, or rising) are particularly important criteria for delimiting structural groupings.

S has many simple sentence groups consisting of one sentence only. W has none, all its sentence groups being complex. Sentence groups in S may consist of a combination of principal and non-principal sentences, whereas in W they consist of the former only. Sentence groups have elements of structure expounded by sentence units.

SENTENCE RANK

W has a higher percentage of complex, and also of simple and co-ordinate sentences than S, but has no non-principal sentences at all. In S non-principal and simple principal sentences together constitute 75·2 per cent of sentence occurrences. The effect of these combined factors means that S has a generally uncomplicated sentence structure:

	% of total sentence occurrences			
	principal			non-principal
	simple	complex	co-ordinate	
W	50·0	27·6	22·4	—
S	38·8	17·7	7·1	36·4

Non-principal sentences in S are of various contextual types. Intonation signals often help to mark these (e.g. *Back to the subject of television!* is marked intonationally as a command, not a statement).

	% of total non-principal sentence occurrences					
	declarative	stative	interrogative	imperative	greeting	attention call
S only	70·4	9·8	4·3	4·3	2·8	8·4

CLAUSE RANK

Transitive clauses, whether non-subordinate or subordinate, are more frequent in W than in S:

	non-subordinate clauses % of total occurrences		subordinate clauses % of total occurrences	
	transitive	intransitive	transitive	intransitive
W	59·3	40·7	56·2	43·8
S	39·2	60·8	50·0	50·0

The structural patterns of non-subordinate clauses are broadly similar in both W and S. Those of subordinate clauses in S have fewer realisations and variants, however.

In both discourses the SPC, not the SPCA, pattern is realised most frequently.[34] The passive voice is more frequent in W than in S, in both non-subordinate and subordinate clauses.

	Non-subordinate clauses: structural patterns	
	generalised type	main realisations, with variants in brackets
W	SP(CA)	*SPCA* (FSPCA); *SPC* (S_1PCS_2, S_1PCFS_2, FSPC); *SPA* (SP_1AP_2, SPFA, $FSP_1A_1P_2A_2$, $S_1P_1FS_2P_2A$)
	SAP(C)	*SAPC* (SA_1PCA_2); *SAP* (SA_1PA_2)
	SPAC	*SPAC* (SP_1AP_2C, FSPAC, $FSP_1A_1P_2CA_2$)
	PS(CA)	*PSCA* (P_1SP_2CA)
	P(CA)	*PCA, PA*

[34] The symbols S, P, C, A represent the main elements of clause structure: subject, predicator, complement, and adverbial. The symbol F indicates a structural element expounded by a function word (usually a conjunction, e.g. *that*, or a sequence signal) which is not part of the internal structure of the clause unit, but helps to signal external relationships to other units. Such notation as $P_1 \ldots P_2$ indicates structural places expounded by units with discontinuous constituents.

Comparison of Spoken and Written English 173

Non-subordinate clauses: structural patterns—*continued*

	generalised type	main realisations, with variants in brackets
	PAC	*PAC*
	ASP(C)	*ASPC* (A_1SPCA_2, A_1SPA_2C, AS_1PS_2C); *ASP* (A_1FSPA_2, FASP)
	APS(C)	*APSC* (AP_1SP_2C, $A_1P_1SP_2CA_2$, FAPSC); *APS*
S	SP(CA)	*SPCA* (S_1PCS_2A, SP_1CFP_2A, FSPCA); *SPC* (S_1PCS_2, FSPC, $FSPCF_1F_2$); *SPA* (SP_1AP_2, FSPAF); *SP* (FSP)
	SAPC	*SAPC*; *SAP* (SA_1PA_2)
	SPAC	*SPAC* (SP_1AP_2C)
	PSC(A)	*PSC*, *PS*
	P(CA)	*PC*, *PA*
	ASP(C)	ASPC (ASP_1CP_2, $A_1SP_1A_2P_2C$); *ASP* (FASP)
	APS(C)	*APSC*, APS (A_1PSA_2)
	CPS(A)	*CPSA* (CP_1SP_2A, CP_1SP_2AF); *CP*

Subordinate clauses: structural patterns

	generalised type	main realisations, with variants in brackets
W	SP(CA)	*SPCA* (FSPCA, $FS_1PCA_1S_2A_2$); *SPC* (FSPC); *SPA* (FSPA); *SP* (FSP, FS_1PS_2, FSPF)
	SPAC	(FSPAC, $FSPA_1CA_2$)
	ASP(C)	*ASPC*; *ASP* (A_1SPA_2, $AS_1P_1S_2P_2$, AS_1PFS_2)
	APS(C)	*APSC*, *APS* ($AP_1S_1P_2S_2$)
	CSP(A)	*CSPA*, *CSP* (C_1SPC_2)
S	SP(CA)	*SPCA*, *SPC* (FSPC), *SPA*, *SP*
	ASP(C)	*ASPC* (A_1SPCA_2, FASPC); ASP
	CSP(A)	*CSPA*, *CSP*
	P(CA)	PC

Most frequently occurring patterns: non-subordinate clauses

W % of total occurrences	S % of total occurrences
SPC: 30·8	SPC: 36·4
ASPC: 18·2	SPCA: 17·2
SPCA: 11·4	SP: 15·2
SPA: 11·4	SPA: 9·9
ASP: 5·7	ASPC: 3·9

Percentage of non-subordinate clauses with the passive voice:
W, 16·5 per cent; S, 7 per cent of total clause occurrences.

Most frequently occurring patterns: subordinate clauses

W % of total occurrences	S % of total occurrences
SPC: 26	SPC: 35·0
ASP: 18	ASPC: 28·3
SPCA: 16	SPCA: 11·7
ASPC: 12	ASP: 10·0
	SPA: 6·7

Percentage of clauses with the passive voice:
W, 12 per cent; S, 1·7 per cent of total clause occurrences.

Percentage of statement-type noun clauses with the conjunction 'that':
W: with *that*, 85 per cent; without *that*, 15 per cent.
S: with *that*, 20 per cent; without *that*, 80 per cent.

The structural patterns alone are not always definitive in signalling contextual differences. Some of the above patterns (e.g. SPCA/PSCA, statement/question) may signal different contextual clause types. However, function words (e.g. *how? what?*), punctuation, or intonation patterns may also help to signal such differences. Punctuation or intonation may also neutralise structural contrasts (e.g. *You are going to watch the television program tonight?*).

A description of the integrated system whereby structural, lexical, and intonational or graphological signals differentiate contextual clause types is too lengthy to undertake here.

The high frequency in W of the conjunction *that* in the statement type of noun clause, and its low frequency there in S, does not involve any communicative difference. Clause relationships in S are often signalled as much by stress-intonation-length patterns as by function word connectives. Indeed, in fast speech, *that*, where it occurs, is phonemically so much reduced that it is scarcely heard. Its total omission therefore involves no serious communicative loss. In W, however, *that* is an easily perceived visual signal of clause division and relationship; hence perhaps its more frequent occurrence.

The distribution of grammatical classes of subordinate class nominal, adjectival, and adverbial clauses is broadly similar in W and S. However, W has a clause-embedding index as high as 13, whereas the highest in S is 5:

	distribution of grammatical classes			% of total clause occurrences clause-embedding index												
	nom.	adj.	adv.	1	2	3	4	5	6	7	8	9	10	11	12	13
W	47·8	19·6	32·6	36·9	34·8	13·0	6·5		2·2	2·2		2·2				2·2
S	46·6	18·9	34·5	51·8	34·5	8·6	1·7	3·4								

W differs from S in its distribution of contextual types of non-subordinate clauses. It has more cognitive (statement-type) and fewer interrogative clauses. In both W and S, however, cognitive clauses occur more frequently than all other types. The relative distribution of the declarative, stative, and equative sub-types of cognitive clauses is also broadly similar in W and S:[35]

	cognitive			% of total clause occurrences				
				imper.	inter.	cond.	comparative	greeting
W	decl. 60·7	stat. 28·7	eq. 3·2					
		92·6		3·2	2·1	2·1		
S	decl. 52·3	stat. 24·5	eq. 5·3					
		82·1		1·3	11·9	3·3	0·7	0·7

S differs from W in its distribution of contextual types of class nominal and class adverbial subordinate clauses. It has more cognitive, fewer interrogative, and no imperative type class nominal clauses. It differs also in the contextual types of class adverbial clauses: it has more temporal clauses (W has actually none) and more conditional clauses; fewer reason and manner clauses; and no result and concessive clauses at all.

[35] Equative: as defined and illustrated in Halliday, 'Notes on Transitivity and Theme in English', pp. 67-8, 223-4. Two sub-types of equative clause are illustrated in *the leader is John* and *what John saw was the play*.

These differences appear to be related to stylistic factors or to syntactical-semantic features. Time is not usually relevant to an abstract discussion on grammatical theory, but relevant to a discussion of entertainment programs. Result is often signalled closely enough in spoken discourse by co-ordinate clauses with *and*; and concession closely enough by co-ordinate clauses with *but*, with supporting intonation patterns.

	clause nominal % of occurrences				clause adverbial % of occurrences					
	cognitive		imper.	inter.	temp.	reas.	man.	res.	cond.	conc.
W	decl. stat. eq. 64·5 16·1									
	80·6		3·3	16·1	40·0	6·6	20·0	13·4	20·0	
S	decl. stat. eq. 61·5 34·7 1·9									
	98·1			1·9	25·0	30·0	5·0		40·0	

GROUP PHRASE RANK

Both W and S have more group than phrase units, but the percentage of group units is greater in S than in W:

	% of total occurrences of group and phrase units	
	group	phrase
W	60·1	39·9
S	72·7	27·3

W has more fully-structured group units of the pattern premodifier-head-postmodifier (MHQ) than S:

	% of total group structure occurrences		
	MHQ	MH	HQ
W	28·5	58·2	13·3
S	13·7	77·0	9·3

Class nominal group units occur much more frequently than class verbal, adjectival, and adverbial group units in W. S has relatively more class verbal, adjectival, and adverbial units than W:

Comparison of Spoken and Written English

	% of total occurrences of group units			
	$G^{nom.}$	$G^{v.}$	$G^{adj.}$	$G^{adv.}$
W	78·1	16·9	4·1	0·9
S	54·0	24·6	11·9	9·5

Embedding of group units is much deeper in W than in S. Some group structures have an embedding index as high as 14 in W, whereas the highest in S is 8. Embedding in the first and second layers of structure occurs much more frequently in S than in W:

	% of total occurrences of group units													
	1	2	3	4	5	6	7	8	9	10	11	12	13	14
W	26·7	26·1	17·0	12·3	5·9	5·6	1·5	1·7	1·7	0·3		0·6		0·6
S	45·6	32·5	11·9	5·5	1·2	2·9		0·4						

The following is the distribution of the structural patterns of prepositional, infinitive, and participial phrase units in W and S:[36]

	% of total phrase structure occurrences					
	prepositional				infinitive	participial
W	FG 53·5	FW 25·8	FP 3·0	F-CL 1·0	(F)V(CA)	V(CA)
	83·3				7·1	9·6
S	FG 32·4	FW 4·0	FP 23·0	F-CL		
	59·4				17·6	23·0

W has a higher frequency of class adjectival and a lower frequency of class adverbial phrase units than S:

	% of total occurrences of phrase units		
	$P^{nom.}$	$P^{adj.}$	$P^{adv.}$
W	6·1	47·8	46·1
S	6·5	30·9	62·6

[36] F, G, P, W, and CL represent structural elements at which operate function word, group, phrase, word, and clause units respectively. In infinitive phrases optional F is expounded by *to*. V indicates a structural element expounded by a verb participle, and C and A complement and adverbial elements respectively.

Embedding of phrase units is much deeper in W than in S. Some phrase units have an embedding index as high as 13, whereas the highest in S is 7:

	% of total occurrences of phrase units												
	1	2	3	4	5	6	7	8	9	10	11	12	13
W	20·5	29·8	17·9	9·8	9·8	4·7	3·8	1·7	0·4	0·4	0·4		0·8
S	37·5	26·9	21·2	4·8	7·7		1·9						

W has a wider range of contextual types of class adjectival and class adverbial phrase units than S:[37]

	% of total occurrences of class adjectival phrase units							
	poss.	part.	ag./inan.	ben.	compar.	ag./an.	adj./gen.	goal
W	10·1	17·4	0·9	0·9	3·7	0·9	57·8	8·3
S	3·1	12·5			6·3		78·1	

	% of total occurrences of class adverbial phrase units											
	temp.	loc.	dir.	man.	reas.	pur.	ref.	conc.	ag./an.	ag./inan.	ben.	comp.	neg.	acc.
W	1·0	33·8	18·0	17·1	1·0	8·6	4·2	1·0	3·8	1·9	1·0	7·6	1·0	
S	3·1	30·9	20·0	4·6	1·5	9·2	13·8				6·2	9·2		1·5

WORD RANK

S has a greater frequency of simple lexical words and lexical word compounds than W:

	% of total occurrences		
	simple	complex	compound
W	50·3	45·5	4·2
S	56·0	29·5	14·5

Complex words with prefixes are rare in W, but almost absent in S.[38] In both W and S complex words with suffixes predominate:

[37] The class adjectival types are possessive, partitive, agent/inanimate (instrument), benefactive, comparative, agent/animate, general adjectival qualifier, and goal. These last two are on the borders of formal meaning (see above, p. 169). The class adverbial types are temporal, locative, directional, manner, reason, purpose, referential, concessive, agent/animate, agent/inanimate, benefactive, comparative, negative (e.g. *without* the book), and accompaniment.

[38] Complex words are here defined as those which, in the present state of the language, have active word-forming prefixes and suffixes. The linguist with a knowledge of Latin and historical English grammar will of course recognise internal structure in many more words than these.

	% of total complex lexical word occurrences		
	Rs	pRs	pR
W	91·9	6·6	1·5
S	99·0	1·0	—

W has a greater percentage of class nominal and adjectival, and a smaller percentage of class verbal and adverbial lexical word units than S:

	% of total grammatical class occurrences			
	nominal	verbal	adjectival	adverbial
W	52·2	20·3 (v./cop. 3·3)	24·2	3·3
S	33·9	40·9 (v./cop. 10·2)	17·6	7·6

Lexical words are more frequent than function words in W, but in S function words are notably more frequent than lexical words:

	% of total word unit occurrences	
	lexical words	function words
W	54·2	45·8
S	40·7	59·3

The relative distribution of structurally defined function word classes in W differs notably from that in S in two points: W has a greater percentage of class prepositional, and a smaller percentage of class pronominal and sentence group operator function words than S:[39]

[39] The classes are pronominal, verb/auxiliary, prepositional, conjunctional, adjunctive, adjectival, adverbial, sentence group operator, syntactical, nominal, and negator. Sequence signals are, of course, structurally differentiated in the linguistic description upon which these statistics are based, but their occurrences are here shown, together with those of co-ordinating conjunctions, as a greater degree of detail is not necessary here. 'Adjunctive' here denotes a class of function words, structurally distinguished from adverbs, which operate as premodifiers in adjectival and adverbial groups (e.g. *very* bad, *quite* brilliantly). Class 'syntactical' includes function words which have no contextual meaning, but are purely syntactical signals (e.g. *it* as subject element exponent anticipating a following clause). Class adjectival includes deictics and many other types operating in the M element of group structure. Class adverbial includes such words as *why?* Class nominal includes measure words like *a pint* of....

	Pn.	v./aux.	prep.	% of total grammatical class occurrences		adjunc.	adj.	adv.	sent. operator	gp. syntac.	nom.	neg.
				conj.								
				sub.	co-ord. and seq. sig.							
W	9.8	7.8	23.8	5.1	6.1	2.6	32.2	2.2	3.1	5.0		2.3
					11.2							
S	29.3	13.5	10.5	2.9	5.9	6.5	13.2	0.4	12.1	4.6	0.1	1.0
					8.8							

The relative distribution of contextual types of class pronominal function words in W and in S is broadly similar:

	% of total occurrences of class pronominal function words						
	pers.	indef.	inter.	dem.	rel.	intensif.	recip.
W	43.1	24.6		13.9	15.4	1.5	1.5
S	55.7	22.9	3.0	12.4	4.5	1.0	0.5

The relative distribution of contextual types of class prepositional function words in W does not differ significantly from that in S. Prepositions relating to time are absent in W and those relating to manner are absent in S; but the relative frequency of both is low. Locationals and directionals in W co-occur most frequently in phrases with nouns denoting non-observable/measurables. Therefore the 'location' and 'direction' signalled by these prepositions is conceptual (e.g. this unit is assigned *to* this class; structural statements have a different function *in* this model).

	% of total occurrences of class prepositional function words																
	loc.	dir.	temp.	man.	pur.	part.	acc.	rel.*	ref.	ben.	comp.	poss.	ag./inan.	ag./an.	neg.	goal	adj./sub.†
W	31.0	11.4		4.4	2.5	11.4		0.6	2.5	1.9	8.3	10.8	3.2	1.3	0.6	4.4	5.7
S	25.8	22.9	2.9		1.4	7.1	1.4		11.4	8.6	7.1	1.4	1.4				8.6

* Relational.
† This includes some prepositions with which the presence of contextual meaning is doubtful.

MORPHEME RANK

The observations here concern bound morphemes only. Derivational suffixes are relatively more frequent than grammatical relationship suffixes in W, whereas in S grammatical suffixes predominate. Some words have both types (e.g. *users*). Verbalising derivational suffixes do not occur in S. Derivational prefixes are rare in W, but in S hardly occur at all.

In S the negative occurs as a function word, *not*, only where it is emphatic and bears a stress and intonation peak (e.g. *not too badly*). Elsewhere it occurs as a suffix, *-nt*, /ṇt/ (e.g. in *didn't*). In W *not* occurs as a suffix in *cannot* (weak form), but most frequently it occurs as a function word:

	prefixes	% of total bound morpheme occurrences									
		derivational suffixes				grammatical relationship suffixes					
		nom.-g.	verb-g.	adj.-g.	adv.-g.	-s -es pl.	vb., 3 sing. pres.	partic. -ing	partic. -ed -en	comp. -er -est	neg.
W		10·9	1·4	31·2	5·8	19·7	9·3	4·9	9·3	2·3	0·6
	4·6	49·3				46·1					
		nom.-g.	verb-g.	adj.-g.	adv.-g.	-s -es pl.	vb., 3 sing. pres.	partic. -ing	partic. -en -ed	comp. -er -est	neg.
S		14·6		18·9	7·3	14·0	6·1	20·1	1·9	0·6	15·9
	0·6	40·8				58·6					

SEMANTIC AND LEXICAL FEATURES

W differs from S in a notable predominance of class nominal words denoting non-observable/measurables over those denoting observable/measurables. In S, however, the latter are more frequent than the former:

	% of total occurrences of class nominal lexical words	
	$W^{nom.}$ denoting O/M	$W^{nom.}$ denoting non-O/M
W	13·9	86·1
S	65·8	34·2

Lexical words of Latin and Greek origin occur more frequently than words of English and other origin in W, whereas in S the reverse is true:

	% of total lexical word occurrences	
	words of Latin and Greek origin	words of English and other origin
W	56·3	43·7
S	48·0	52·0

Lexical compounds with a quasi-grammatical clause or phrase structure (as distinct from the other compounds already described) constitute 5·4 per cent of the S material, but only 1·5 per cent of the W material.

In S, compounds such as *I mean, I think, as a matter of fact*, which are marked by stress and intonation as interpolations in the structure of the utterance, serve as a delay mechanism allowing the speaker, who is conversing spontaneously, time to think what he wants to say next. W, however, is the result of prior planning and revision, and so such delay devices, if ever they occurred, have been eliminated. Lexical compounds are therefore confined to sequence signals and connectives such as *in the first place*. . . .

The differences between W and S revealed by the foregoing description outweigh the similarities. What is the linguistic significance of these differences, in relation to differing style, register, and medium? Have these differences any educational or social significance?

The formal and contextual differences between W and S could scarcely be assigned each to a single cause, since the grammatical, lexical, and phonological signals of both constitute an interrelated system.

Thus the greater frequency in W of nominal group units, especially of the fully structured MHQ type, is clearly related to the greater frequency in it of class nominal and adjectival words and of class adjectival phrases: full group units consist of noun heads, premodifier adjectival words, and postmodifier adjectival phrases or clauses. The greater frequency in W of class prepositional function words is obviously related to the more frequent occurrence in it of prepositional phrase units and the less frequent occurrence of infinitive and participial phrases.

The more frequent occurrence in S, and the less frequent occurrence in W, of class verbal and adverbial word, class verbal and adverbial group, and class adverbial phrase units is related to the lexical and semantic, and in turn to the stylistic differences between the two discourses. The main purpose of W is to define linguistic concepts and to state theoretical principles. The means most appropriate for this are nominal words denoting non-observable/measurables, with adjectival word and phrase modification (i.e. nominal group units, linked in clause structure). Appropriate also is the greater range in W of contextual types of class adverbial and class adjectival phrase units, since more types of contextual relationship are perceived by the author and expressed in this kind of writing.

The communicative interchange in S, however, concerns observable/measurables for the most part—people, things, action-relationships between them, and the observable ways in which these action-relationships are established. The linguistic means most appropriate to this are verb/adverb modification in clause structure and suitable lexical words.

The more frequent occurrence of the passive voice in W is probably determined by a register feature of the writer-reader situation. The author is unwilling to over-use the personal pronoun lest this should create an unfavourable impression of egotism upon his reader; and so he says 'these structures were assigned to this system', in preference to 'I assigned these structures to this system'.

The greater frequency of premodifier adjectival groups in S is also determined by a register feature of the language situation. Most of the premodifiers are intensifiers like *very* and *quite*. The feature of emphasis is natural and common in a speech situation where social equals informally discuss a subject of mutual interest.

Differences between W and S which are characteristic of the spoken medium are the frequency of non-principal sentences, and of sentence group operators. Non-principal sentences are structurally and semantically part of the chain of spoken discourse. They are linked to it by syntactical and lexical sequence signals, and especially by phonological intonation and stress patterns. It is this last fact which probably explains their presence in S and their absence in W. Though not usually possessing clause structure, they do not interrupt the communicative continuity of the discourse, because their structural integration in it is mainly through the suprasegmental phonological pattern. Occasionally these non-principal sentences are grammatically independent of the chain of discourse, when they are evoked by some extralinguistic feature of the situation—as, for example, when one speaker interrupts the conversation of a group to speak to an intruder who has entered the room.

Sentence group operators are important bearers of modal and other intonation signals. This, together with their time-delay function described above, helps to explain their frequency in spoken discourse.[40]

The greater frequency of interrogative clauses and of pronouns in S than in W obviously results from the different language situation, which here determines the form of the language medium. It is interesting to note that many pronouns which have the lexical form of personal pronouns in S are contextually indefinite pronouns: *you, they, them* sometimes do not refer to participants in the language situation, but could easily be replaced by *one, people*. This is a common register feature of familiar spoken conversation.

The more frequent occurrence of function words than lexical words in S is related to the greater frequency in it of pronouns and sentence group operators. However, this predominance of function words has an important influence on the semantic content of S. If lexical words are fewer, then fewer meaning relationships are likely to be signalled, since lexical items have situational reference. In W, the greater number of lexical words has the potential of signalling more numerous and complex meaning relationships.

The depth of structure in S is sometimes less even than grammatical statistics show. In the following sentence from S, the second noun clause is embedded within the first: *I think you'll find later on you'll get better*

[40] The contextual functions of some of these is described, though not in modern linguistic terms, in West, 'Conversational Tags'.

programs. However, the intonation-stress-length pattern virtually neutralises this second embedding. The words *I think* are short, unstressed, and low pitched. The complex sentence effectively begins at *you'll find*. . . . Sentences of this type occur frequently in spoken discourse. Once again the need for an integrated description of syntactical, lexical, and phonological signals is apparent.

The more frequent occurrence in S of lexical compounds such as *break into* (interrupt) perhaps helps to compensate for the less frequent occurrence in it of complex words. In the utterance from which this example is taken, *into* is phonologically bound to *break* and virtually constitutes a suffix. However, the two elements of this compound are separable in other contexts, and this constitutes the main difference of such compounds from complex words with bound morphemes. Even without such considerations, however, the examination of the two discourses would suggest an hypothesis of interest to typologists, that modern English is predominantly a suffixing language.

In conclusion, it is worth noting that neither W nor S exploits the whole grammatical repertory of written and spoken English.[41] Each exploits only a part of this. Their respective repertories sometimes coincide, sometimes do not.

It now remains to discuss the possible educational and social significance of the linguistic differences between W and S. The foregoing comparative analysis has demonstrated that the grammatical structure of W is generally more complicated than that of S. It has also demonstrated that the two discourses have notable lexical and semantic differences. The notable predominance of abstract nouns in W indicates the conceptual nature of the discourse content. Many of these words are complex in structure, and their lexical form is derived from Latin or Greek. A university student who knew Latin at least would easily recognise the lexical root, prefixes, and suffixes of words such as *exponence* and *recursive*. A student who did not know Latin would not, however, easily see either structure or meaningful lexical form in many such words which occur in W. He would have to learn them as entities, without aid from the perception of their structure.

When the greater grammatical complexity of W is considered together with its notable lexical and semantic differences from S, the total communicative difference between W and S comes to appear very great. When this communicative difference is related to the present comparatively infrequent study of Latin in Australian schools and universities, the difficulties of comprehension which speakers such as those of S would face when beginning study at a university of reading material such as W may be under-

[41] The basis of this statement is a comparison of the two discourses with the information contained in a total tentative repertory of English structure compiled during a long period of research.

stood. S is typical enough of the conversational spoken English of students about to enter a university, and W is typical enough of what they may have to study in linguistics and similar subjects. Difficulties which students are said to encounter in written English are attributed to various causes, but rarely to a simple linguistic fact. Present educational circumstances are tending to widen the gap between spoken and written English; and the two, though necessarily they must always differ, have less in common than they had formerly. When Latin is not studied, the tendency will be to avoid words of Latin origin in ordinary conversation as well as in writing.

The mere realisation of the communicative problem illustrated in the differences between W and S could point to immediate practical solutions. The first would be a more concentrated attempt to teach the structure and vocabulary of written English, against a background of knowledge of the structure and vocabulary of spoken; and a clearer realisation by students of the need to study the written form of their own language systematically. The second would be a more systematic attempt by textbook authors to follow the well-recognised principles of technical writing: above all, to maintain structural simplicity in sentence, group, and phrase structure, avoiding undue embedding of the sentence sub-units one within another. This, and the use of simple and co-ordinate rather than complex sentences, would help to keep the structure of written English closer to that of the spoken English used daily by young students.

Vocabulary differences between written and spoken English will always exist. Every university subject requires processes of conceptual thinking and every discipline needs specialised vocabulary and technical terms. Many of these are already conventionally established and are of Latin and Greek origin. However, a recognition and understanding of word structure undoubtedly facilitates acquisition of this necessary technical vocabulary, since much of it consists of complex words.

Linguistic science can describe the differences between written and spoken English precisely, and thus provide the textbook writer, the teacher, and the student with the means of solving problems of communication in English. It can also similarly assist the teacher of English as a second language by helping to define teaching objectives. However, linguistic research can assist in these ways only if it aims at examining the whole structure of the language and employs an integrated method of description for this purpose. Such research is time-consuming and requires for its highest success the efforts of a highly trained team—linguists, psychologists, educationists, teachers, and textbook writers. The first step towards the initiation of such research is the realisation of the need for it. The foregoing discussion has endeavoured to point to this.

REFERENCES CITED

Bazell, C. E., Catford, J. C., et al. (eds.), *In Memory of Firth*, London, 1966.
Cattell, N. R., *The Design of English*, Melbourne, 1966.
Chomsky, N., *Aspects of the Theory of Syntax*, Cambridge, Mass., 1965.
——, *Cartesian Linguistics*, New York and London, 1966.
——, 'The Current Scene in Linguistics', *Praxis des Neusprachlichen Unterrichts*, Vol. 15, No. 1, 1968.
——, *Language and Mind*, New York, 1968.
——, *Syntactic Structures*, The Hague, 1957.
——, *Topics in the Theory of Generative Grammar*, The Hague, 1966.
—— and Halle, M., *The Sound Pattern of English*, New York and London, 1968.
Dixon, R. M. W., 'On Formal and Contextual Meaning', *Acta Linguistica Academiae Scientiarum Hungaricae*, Vol. 14, 1964, pp. 23-45.
Eisler, F. Goldman, *Psycholinguistics*, London and New York, 1968.
Flint, E. H., 'Item and Relationship Signals in Grammar-Lexis Patterning', *Proceedings of the Tenth International Congress of Linguists*, 1967, in press.
Halliday, M. A. K., 'Categories of the Theory of Grammar', *Word*, Vol. 17, 1961, pp. 241-92.
——, *Intonation and Grammar in British English*, The Hague, 1967.
——, 'Language and Experience', *Educational Review*, Vol. 20, No. 2, February 1968, pp. 11-24.
——, 'Notes on Transitivity and Theme in English', *Journal of Linguistics*, Vol. 3, No. 2, 1967, pp. 203-21.
——, 'Syntax and the Consumer', *Monograph Series on Languages and Linguistics* No. 17, Georgetown University, 1964.
——, McIntosh, A., and Strevens, P., *The Linguistic Sciences and Language Teaching*, London, 1964.
Healey, A., 'English Idioms', *Kivung*, Vol. 1, No. 2, August 1968, pp. 71-108.
Hill, L. A., *Prepositions and Adverbial Particles*, London, 1968.
Hockett, C. F., *The State of the Art*, The Hague, 1968.
Jacobson, S., Review of N. Chomsky, *Aspects of the Theory of Syntax*, *Linguistics* No. 28, December 1966, pp. 111-26.
Jespersen, V., *The Philosophy of Grammar*, London, 1924.
Johnson, F. C., 'English Suprasententials', *Kivung*, Vol. 1, No. 1, April 1968, pp. 3-7.
Katz, J. J., *The Philosophy of Language*, New York and London, 1966.
—— and Fodor, J. A., 'The Structure of a Semantic Theory', *Language*, Vol. 39, April-June 1963, pp. 170-210.
—— and Postal, P. M., *An Integrated Theory of Linguistic Descriptions*, Cambridge, Mass., 1964.
Klatte, W. F., 'Sentence Morphemes in English', *Canadian Journal of Linguistics*, Vol. 12, No. 2, 1967, pp. 90-6.
Lamb, S. M., *Outline of Stratificational Grammar*, Washington, 1966.
Langendoen, D. T., *The Study of Syntax*, New York, 1969.
Lieberman, P., *Intonation, Perception and Language*, Cambridge, Mass., 1967.
Nida, E. A., *Syntax: A Descriptive Analysis*, Summer Institute of Linguistics, Glendale, California, 1946.
Pickett, V. P., 'The Grammatical Hierarchy of Isthmus Zapotec', *Language*, Vol. 36, No. 1, Pt 2, January-March 1960, Supplement, pp. 11-17.
Scott, F. S., Bowley, C. C., et al., *English Grammar: a Linguistic Study of its Classes and Structures*, Auckland, 1968.
Söderlind, J., 'Utterance, Sentence and Clause as English Speech-Units', *English Studies*, Vol. 45, 1964, Supplement, pp. 50-6.

West, M., 'Conversational Tags', *English Language Teaching*, Vol. 17, No. 4, July 1963, pp. 164-7.

White, J. H., 'The Methodology of Sememic Analysis with Special Application to the English Preposition', *Mechanical Translation*, Vol. 8, 1964, pp. 15-31.

Zatorski, R., 'Early and Later Versions of the Theory of Transformational Grammar', *Zeitschrift für Phonetik, Sprachwissenschaft und Kommunikationsforschung*, Vol. 20, No. 3, 1967, pp. 259-70.

G. K. W. JOHNSTON

THE LANGUAGE OF AUSTRALIAN LITERATURE

In his introduction to *The Literature of Australia*, the editor, Geoffrey Dutton, notes the omission from it of 'any discussion of Australian language and idiom'. This omission, he says, is 'due partly to lack of space and partly to lack of sufficient research at this stage of Australian history . . . Despite pioneering work by Sidney J. Baker and Ralph [sic] Partridge, we still await some definitive study. . . .'[1]

The omission from a book largely concerned with the criticism of Australian literature of a study of its language is, indeed, unfortunate. In the past, critics have often tended to neglect the verbal level of Australian writing, and to focus attention rather on its ideas and attitudes; in consequence they have often failed to detect uncertainty of tone, roughness of texture, and falsity of emotion. And it is deficiencies on the verbal level, more than any other, that have prevented many Australian writers from the highest achievements. However grand their conceptions, as with Brennan; interesting their material, as with the realist novelists; or ambitious their intentions, as with Patrick White, all too often they have been let down by their language—inappropriate, dull, or pretentious.

An increased attention to the language of Australian literature is, then, clearly needed. But it is a different kind of attention from that which we usually associate with the names of Baker and Partridge: while informed by linguistic knowledge, it must be an essentially critical attention. The proper understanding and assessment of Australian literature is not likely to be greatly illuminated by advances in the study of Australian English, although in fact, the 'definitive study' awaited by Dutton is now much nearer than when he wrote, as the result of recent research by a number of scholars. But their work can at best illuminate only that small area of Australian speech which is distinctive.

To the linguist, Australian English is a dialect: that is, a regional variety of English with its own peculiarities of pronunciation, vocabulary, idiom, and syntax. These peculiarities make Australian English distinctive from Standard English and from the other regional dialects (e.g. Canadian,

---

[1] Dutton (ed.), *The Literature of Australia*, p. 8.

American, and New Zealand English). But they constitute a very small proportion of Australian speech, and even less of its written language.

This situation is clearest where vocabulary is concerned: even in its colloquial form, Australian English consists overwhelmingly of words and phrases which it shares with Standard English. The words which make it distinctive, chiefly terms for features of the natural environment, are a very small percentage of the total. Linguists, naturally, give much more attention to them because they are distinctive; as Ramson has said: 'No one in his right mind would want to rewrite the *Oxford English Dictionary*, duplicating as much of its material as has a history of usage in . . . Australian'.[2]

And in its written form, the vocabulary of Australian English is even less distinctive, even more overwhelmingly dependent on the common stock of English words. Realistic fiction, reflecting the colloquial form, may be studded with *cobbers*, *battlers*, and *gullies*; but most general prose and nearly all verse has probably less than one per cent of dialect words.

Where sounds are concerned, the situation is more complex. Certainly, in its colloquial form, Australian English has a distinctive phonetic character, which linguists have described and explained. But in its written form, which is to say in literature, this character disappears, it seems, almost entirely. This is certainly true as far as the quality and quantity of the sounds—the vowels, consonants, and diphthongs—are concerned. One may be able to find some rhymes in Australian poets which only hold good if the words are pronounced as in Australian English, but they will be few, and hardly of any more significance than the few Cockney rhymes in Keats.

Intonation may well be a different matter: it is related to the other aspects, idiom and syntax. The syntax of Australian English does have a few peculiarities of its own, which have not been much studied. They rarely appear in writing; in speech they are usually accompanied by an unusual inflection of the voice, by varieties of intonation. It may be that there is an affinity between the intonations of Australian conversation and the rhythms of its prose, for instance, but this is hard to demonstrate. Behind the written words of Australian literature one can sometimes hear a speaking voice, but it is not clear that the intonation of that voice is distinctively Australian.

Technical investigations into the distinctive features of Australian English, then, are not likely to yield much in the way of enlightenment to the critic of Australian literature. This is not surprising, because the critic's concern with language, though it needs to be informed by sensible notions of linguistics, or at least free from erroneous ones, deals with other questions. The critic is primarily concerned with style, 'which has nothing to

[2] Ramson, *Australian English*, p. 7.

do with pronunciation or grammar. It has something to do with ease and freedom in the use of language.'

These are the words, significantly, of a fine critic. They occur in Lionel Trilling's seminal essay on *Huckleberry Finn*, where he notes that the basis of this novel's greatness is Twain's linguistic triumph: 'the style of the book . . . is not less than definitive in American literature. The prose of *Huckleberry Finn* established for written prose the virtues of American colloquial speech.'[3]

In explaining the meaning of this statement, Trilling discusses the language of nineteenth-century American literature in terms which apply no less forcibly to Australian literature. In fact, his discussion is a model, not only because the problems it treats are essentially the same as we encounter in reading Australian literature but also because Trilling exemplifies the critical, as distinct from the linguistic, attention to language which I am desiderating. This passage explains the basic issues:

> In the matter of language, American literature had a special problem. The young nation was inclined to think that the mark of the truly literary product was a grandiosity and elegance not to be found in the common speech. It therefore encouraged a greater breach between its vernacular and its literary language than, say, English literature of the same period ever allowed. This accounts for the hollow ring one now and then hears even in the work of our best writers in the first half of the last century.[4]

And Trilling goes on to suggest that English writers of equal stature would never have lapsed into rhetorical excess in the way that Cooper and Poe often, and Melville and Hawthorne sometimes, do. This analysis holds true for Australian writers as well, especially for poets: Bernard O'Dowd most obviously, of course, but also Brennan and Baylebridge; and in prose, Patrick White, for the tendency did not die out with the nineteenth century.

The reason, I suggest, that any colonial literature—I use the term descriptively, not pejoratively—has a 'special problem' with language lies in the undeveloped state of colonial societies. Language is essentially social, and the style, the linguistic quality, of great writers—Chaucer, Shakespeare, Pope, Yeats, for instance—reflects in its fineness the quality of the society they lived in. The colonial writer, on the other hand, is faced by a persistent problem: the disparity between the inherited medium and the local audience.

The language, the inherited medium of colonial literature, is the heritage of centuries of thought and feeling, of civilisation in short; the colonial audience is small, uncultivated, uncertain in its civilisation. In the literature of a developed society—medieval London, Elizabethan or Augustan Eng-

---

[3] Trilling, reprinted in Clemens, *Adventures of Huckleberry Finn*, p. 319. Trilling's essay is also reprinted in his book, *The Liberal Imagination*.

[4] Trilling, loc. cit.

land, Yeats's Ireland—there exists a series of relations between the spoken and the written tongue which the writer can manipulate to achieve his effects. This applies equally to sounds and words: the rhythm and diction of fine poetry can be colloquial or highly literary, existing at several points along the scale between Chaucer's urbane conversation:

> That ye han seyd is right ynough, ywis,
> And muchel moore; for litel hevynesse
> Is right ynough to much folk, I gesse . . .

and Pope's wit:

> Three things another's modest wishes bound,
> My Friendship, and a Prologue, and ten Pound . . .

between Shakespeare's Germanic plainness:

> No longer mourn for me when I am dead
> Than you shall hear the surly sullen bell . . .

and Milton's hieratic Latinity:

> Each perturbation smooth'd with outward calme
> Artificer of fraud. . . .

To read an extended passage of any major English poet is to see how immensely varied are the resources available to him in vocabulary and speech patterns, and how delicate is the question of what constitutes a proper, a vital relation between the written language and the spoken language. No one who dismisses Milton as not writing English can be fully aware of the infinite subtlety of his language, drawing on the rich resources of an immense vocabulary; varying skilfully the emphasis between the native, concrete, colloquial element and the imported, abstract, literary element; and counterpointing the metrical ictus with the stresses of speech.

It is hardly surprising that colonial writers who inherited this sophisticated medium, developed by the pressures of varied social and intellectual experience, were often uncertain in their use of it, especially in the achievement of the correct tone, for tone is largely a matter of linguistic awareness, of estimating exactly the effect words will have; and their effect depends largely on their associations, colloquial or literary.

In the early decades of the nineteenth century in America, in writers with pretensions—Cooper and Irving, for instance—the language is the bookish variety of English, somewhat more old-fashioned, and studded of course with outlandish place and personal names. Hawthorne's speech is similar, but more vital and classical. In Melville we see the beginnings of the vernacular tradition which flowers in the work of Twain, but we also find, in his verse as well as his prose, much confused and ambitious rhetoric.

In Twain, American writing ceased to be colonial because it at last asserted the strength, honesty, and vigour of the vernacular. A workable relation between the spoken language and the written language was established, particularly in the structure of the sentence, 'which is simple, direct, and fluent, maintaining the rhythm of the word-groups of speech and the intonations of the speaking voice'. On this a 'classic prose' was based, and it is in this sense, as Trilling points out, that Hemingway's famous declaration that 'all modern American literature comes from one book by Mark Twain called *Huckleberry Finn*' must be understood.

Hemingway's remark comes from his disquisition on literature in *Green Hills of Africa*, but his own best exemplification of the strength and purity of vernacular prose is to be found in his early short stories, as Ford Madox Ford and Edmund Wilson have shown.[5] There, as in much of Faulkner when he is at his best, the influence of Mark Twain is clear, encouraging 'written prose [with] the virtues of American colloquial speech', to use Trilling's formulation. American prose, then, achieved a workable relation with speech; in poetry and drama, as the persistent influence of Whitman witnesses, a vernacular tradition has been established but without comparable artistic success.

In Australia, where the differences between literary and colloquial language have been at least as marked as in the United States, the attainment of a flexible, expressive literary language has been a long, slow process. Until recently, only a few writers in prose or verse managed to do equal justice to the vigour and liveliness of speech, on the one hand, and to the range and subtlety of formal discourse on the other. In general, what we find is either bookishness or slang, either lack of vitality or lack of discipline. The duller parts of Henry Handel Richardson exemplify the bookish fault, a failure to infuse the heavy diction of ambitious literature with the liveliness of speech; conversely, the triviality of ordinary speech, unshaped by formal considerations, can be seen in the realist novelists, who faithfully reproduce the inarticulateness of uneducated people, or in Miles Franklin, publishing the garrulity of adolescence.

Of course, it can be said that in one kind of Australian writing the vernacular is triumphant: the old bush songs and ballads. While this is true, it does not affect my main point—the need for an adequate language for Australian literature—because the bush songs and ballads are in origin essentially *oral*, not literary, and their history, modes of transmission, and merits are alike those of spoken composition. At later stages these merits find their way into some kinds of written poetry, but the song and ballad proper get their liveliness and point at the cost of dealing with a severely restricted range of experience. This can be clearly seen if one compares Section VIII (Contemporary Poetry) of Russel Ward's *Penguin Book of*

[5] See Wilson, *The Wound and the Bow*, pp. 192-3, quoting Ford.

The Language of Australian Literature

Australian Ballads with the preceding sections: the later, more sophisticated poems are not ballads in form at all, as Ward recognises.

In Australian verse fully within the literary tradition, as distinct from the oral, the search for a satisfying language has been a long and difficult one, only recently successful. The object of the search can be best described —and this is, of course, not accidental—in the words of a poet who has achieved it: in his 'William Butler Yeats', A. D. Hope speaks of

> . . . that noble, candid speech
> In which all things worth saying may be said,
> Which, whether the mind asks, or the heart bids, to each
> Affords its daily bread . . . .[6]

Note the precise adjectives: 'noble' and 'candid'. These are essential qualities of the language of good poetry: neither is fully effective without the other, and together they characterise an idiom which is capable of expressing both emotional and intellectual experience, what 'the heart bids' and 'the mind asks'. Candour saves a noble idiom from pomposity and artificiality; nobility confers on the vitality of speech a necessary formality. In the great poems of Yeats—'Among School Children', for example—the poet's own characteristic idiom displays both qualities at their finest.

In one sense, the history of Australian poetry is the history of the search for such a speech. We begin too late to enjoy to the full the Augustan balance of formality and vitality, for in Michael Massey Robinson's Odes (1810-21) and in W. C. Wentworth's much better poem, 'Australasia' (1823), the eighteenth-century idiom is at its last gasp. Wentworth is not as derivative as Robinson, and no doubt we should make large allowance for the fact that 'Australasia' was a prize poem at Cambridge—the genre can be seen still frozen in its neo-classical mould a hundred years later in Michael Thwaites's 'Milton Blind', which won the Newdigate in 1938—but the style of the following passage, for example, does not match its prophetic accuracy:

> And, O Britannia! shouldst thou cease to ride
> Despotic Empress of old Ocean's tide;
> Should thy tamed Lion—spent his former might—
> No longer roar the terror of the fight;
> Should e'er arrive that dark disastrous hour
> When bow'd by luxury, thou yield'st to pow'r;
> When thou, no longer freest of the free,
> To some proud victor bend'st the vanquish'd knee—
> May all thy glories in another sphere
> Relume, and shine more brightly still than here. . . .[7]

[6] *Collected Poems*, p. 72.
[7] Wentworth, from 'Australasia', *Poetry in Australia*, Vol. 1, p. 48.

Later in the century we see other kinds of imitativeness, which are invariably an index of the poet's failure to bridge the gap between literary and colloquial language, or (changing the metaphor) to find an idiom successfully blending them. In Henry Kendall, for example, there is a clear division between poems which are vernacular and lively, like 'Jim the Splitter', and those which are literary and soporific. The opening stanzas of 'Jim the Splitter' show that Kendall was to some extent aware of the dichotomy:

> The bard who is singing of Wollombi Jim
> Is hardly just now in the requisite trim
>   To sit on his Pegasus fairly;
> Besides, he is bluntly informed by the Muse
> That Jim is a subject no singer should choose;
>   For Jim is poetical rarely . . .
> You mustn't, however, adjudge him in haste,
> Because a red robber is more to his taste
>   Than Ruskin, Rossetti or Dante![8]

His notion of the 'poetical' means that when Kendall writes a serious poem —'Orara', for example—he is rarely fresh and lively, more often solemn and vague, and his language constantly echoes his Romantic predecessors. Where it is original—and Kendall was much given to coining words, nearly always compound expressions like 'hill-heads', 'far-folded'—it departs further from common speech even than they did. This is not to say that in the great bulk of Kendall's verse there are not passages and sometimes whole poems of considerable beauty, but these are nearly all Poe-esque in their 'indefiniteness'.

The language of the poets at the end of the nineteenth century and in the early part of the twentieth, until the 1920s, mostly continues the older modes of neo-Classicism and Romanticism, but some modulate into the Symbolist derivative of Romanticism. Bernard O'Dowd's inflated rhetoric draws on the devices of classicism, but its disciplined logic is replaced by rant and hand-me-down Miltonics:

> She is the scroll on which we are to write
> Mythologies our own and epics new:
> She is the port of our propitious flight
> From Ur idolatrous and Pharaoh's crew.
> She is our own, unstained, if worthy we,
> By dream, or god, or star we would not see:
> Her crystal beams all but the eagle dazzle. . . .[9]

Victor Daley's allegiance, in a poem like 'Dreams', is to Poe and his evocations of reverie:

---

[8] Kendall, from 'Jim the Splitter', ibid., p. 80.
[9] O'Dowd, from 'The Bush', ibid., p. 186.

> I have been dreaming all a summer day:
> Shall I go dreaming so until Life's light
> Fades in Death's dusk, and all my days are spent?
> Ah, what am I the dreamer but a dream!
> The day is fading and the dusk is cold.[10]

Remoteness from 'dull Reality' (Poe's phrase) is essential to this kind of Romantic poetry, and it goes hand in hand, as one might expect, with remoteness from ordinary speech and its sometimes blunt vigour. In Daley, as in Kendall, we see a separation between a literary style for 'poetical' topics and a colloquial style for the features of ordinary life, including such a phenomenon as the editor of the Red Page of the *Bulletin*, whose

> daring hand
> Explores the entrails of the land,
> And finds, beneath a greasy hat,
> An Austral Homer at Cow Flat.[11]

And in Brennan the divorce between the realities of Australian life—mirrored in the spoken language—and the material of poetry is complete: the fact that he was a Triton among the minnows of Edwardian Sydney nowhere declares itself more obviously than in the unreality of his language.

Reading Brennan, one is conscious all the time that this is the poetry of a man unused to communication, of a learned scholar between whose speech and verse there is no vital relation because literature for him meant a world apart, whether across the seas in France or across the ages in Eden. It is true, as G. A. Wilkes has shown, that in one sense he was not 'isolated': his wide reading gave him a nobility of vision which he attempted to incarnate in noble poetry.[12] But his own remark to D. J. Quinn retains its poignant meaning: 'As far as "national" traits go, I might have made my verse in China'.[13] Substitute 'social' for 'national' and you see the reason for the unreality of Brennan's diction: this is the language of a poet unaccustomed to the vigour, let alone the candour, of the speech of intellectual equals.

My contention, then, is that Australian poetry before the 1920s suffered even more than English poetry from false notions of the 'poetical' which led to the use of vigorous colloquial language only in light verse, serious verse being expressed in a special poetic diction, whether neo-Classical or Romantic. If this is correct, the impact of 'modernism' (as it used to be called) takes on an even greater value in the development of Australian poetry. We are accustomed to think of the early Eliot, the poet of the metropolitan desert, as the exemplar of Slessor in subject-matter, turning

---

[10] Daley, from 'Dreams', ibid., p. 169.
[11] Daley, from 'Narcissus and Some Tadpoles', ibid., p. 174.
[12] Wilkes, 'Brennan and his Literary Affinities'.
[13] Quoted by Wilkes, p. 72.

away from the Victorian palaces of art to the realities of modern city life, but perhaps more important still is Eliot's impact on the language of poetry. Drawing equally on Spenser and the music hall, on the exotic and the local, Eliot's wide-ranging and yet astringent idiom reunited literary and colloquial. In purifying the dialect of the tribe, he showed the poets of the 1920s the way to write with nobility and candour.

Furnley Maurice, in his book of essays, *Romance* (1922), shows some consciousness of the possibility that 'modernism' in poetry might lead Australian verse away from its besetting triviality, gaucherie, and staleness, but the first poet really to exemplify the benefits of the new approach to poetry, and the poetic language, is Kenneth Slessor. A passage from a later work, 'Five Bells', shows Slessor's habitual verbal skill at its most effective:

> In Melbourne, your appetite had gone,
> Your angers, too; they had been leeched away
> By the soft archery of summer rains
> And the sponge-paws of wetness, the slow damp
> That stuck the leaves of living, snailed the mind,
> And showed your bones, that had been sharp with rage,
> The sodden ecstasies of rectitude.[14]

Everywhere in Slessor's verse—even in the poems where he succumbs to the Lindsayite urge to visit various ancient, medieval, and Augustan never-never lands—his sharp and yet delicate sense of English idiom is manifest; I doubt if ever before was an Australian poet so skilled with the language, and few have been since, as Chris Wallace-Crabbe stresses in his perceptive article on Slessor in the volume edited by Geoffrey Dutton mentioned above, significantly entitled 'Kenneth Slessor and the Powers of Language'.

In Slessor's generation and the subsequent one, Australian poetry at last found a 'noble, candid speech in which all things worth saying may be said'. In the poetry of A. D. Hope, Judith Wright, and James McAuley a new subtlety of expression accompanies a wider range of experience; the diction is mature and varied, neither grandiose with false nobility nor formless with excessive colloquialism; of it we can say, in Eliot's memorable words:

> And every phrase
> And sentence that is right (where every word is at home,
> Taking its place to support the others,
> The word neither diffident nor ostentatious,
> An easy commerce of the old and the new,
> The common word exact without vulgarity,
> The formal word precise but not pedantic,
> The complete consort dancing together)
> Every phrase and every sentence is an end and a beginning,
> Every poem an epitaph.[15]

[14] Slessor, *Poems*, p. 104.   [15] Eliot, *Four Quartets*, pp. 42-3.

Of Judith Wright's diction I shall have something to say later; concerning Hope's and McAuley's, perhaps one should first decry the label 'Classicist' which some commentators have attempted to pin on them. When one reads these two poets, one is conscious not of any sterile imitation of the eighteenth century, but rather of the comprehensive literary and philosophical experience which lies behind the work of both and reveals itself in their wide range of vocabulary and idiom.

Hope received his early academic training in philology, and remains a highly gifted linguist, at home in a number of languages and able to find his way about in several more. This sometimes comes out in his poetry in a jocular way, as in the virtuoso poem, 'A Blason', but more often in the impeccable sense he has of the nuances and pressures that words exert. Consider the bird in 'The Death of the Bird':

> A vanishing speck in those inane dominions,
> Single and frail, uncertain of her place,
> Alone in the bright host of her companions,
> Lost in the blue unfriendliness of space . . .[16]

where the sense of bewildering vacancy in 'inane dominions' is fostered by the use of 'inane' in both its etymological and current senses, and the blank abstractness of 'unfriendliness' seems all the greater beside the specific vividness of 'blue'. Effects of contrast are common in Hope's poetry, and often underlying them is his sense of the tactile differences between the common Germanic gristle of English and the colourful variety of the words it has imported from a score of languages. McAuley's poetic idiom appears to me as sensitive as Hope's, but not as varied. The lucidity which he takes as his aim, and counsels another poet to practise:

> Let your speech be ordered wholly
> By an intellectual love;
> Elucidate the carnal maze
> With clear light from above[17]

has of recent years made his verse increasingly sparer and plainer in its diction. His poems, when they succeed, then have an almost Biblical austerity:

> Take salt upon your tongue
> And do not feed the heart
> With sorrow, darkness or lies:
> These are the death of art.[18]

But if anyone doubts McAuley's sense of language, he has only to set his poem 'Autumn', a translation of a poem by Rilke, alongside any other rendering, even Leishman's, and he will be convinced.

[16] *Collected Poems*, p. 70.
[17] From 'An Art of Poetry', *Selected Poems*, p. 31.
[18] From 'To Any Poet', ibid., p. 37.

I doubt if the importance of the linguistic achievement in the poetry of Slessor, Judith Wright, Hope, and McAuley is fully realised. In the following generation, a number of poets—Vincent Buckley, Evan Jones, Chris Wallace-Crabbe, and R. A. Simpson, for example—show that they understand it, but they have been characterised as 'academic' and 'suburban' by no less a critic than Miss Wright herself, who prefers the verse of Francis Webb or John Blight. Perhaps the poetry of Buckley and the others lacks the pioneer vigour of an earlier, provincial Australia, but it has a control, a sense of language and form, which point to a superior civility.

The poetry of the latest generation is perhaps too close to us for us to get it into perspective, but on the whole it seems to me not to reach the standard of Slessor, Judith Wright, Hope, and McAuley. One reason is that in Australia, as in England and America, there is a fashion for despising formal regularity and linguistic decorum. One had hoped that the achievement of the poets named would be recognised as exemplary, and Australian poetry would persist in an idiom which would serve as the medium of expanding experience in our increasingly sophisticated society. But in many young Australian poets overseas literary fashions have reinforced their natural insensitivity to language.

The influence of the general poetic climate is not to be underrated. In Slessor and the others named, Australian poetry attained a literary idiom effectively related to the life of speech. But it is noteworthy that while the basis of this idiom is colloquial—there is little literary artificiality about the lines of Slessor quoted above, for instance—the colloquial speech involved is not markedly Australian, in the sense of being heavily vernacular. The diction of modern poetry in English is international, so that it would be hard to tell an unsigned lyric by an Australian or American poet from one by an Englishman or a New Zealander. In more recent years this fact has led some Australians to imitate—more or less consciously—the reaction in America against the 'formalist' conception of poetry, and to make in effect little distinction between verse and vernacular expression. The consequences, as I see them, are formlessness and vulgarity; the 'Australian language' in Sidney J. Baker's sense of the term has very little to do with the true language of Australian poetry.

In Australian prose, to turn now to this genre, the relation between formal speech and the vernacular has always been absent or uneasy. In the nineteenth century we have, in ordinary workaday prose, nothing specifically Australian in the style: its plain and unpretentious quality echoes rather the practicality and good sense of the eighteenth century in England. The Royal Society, Defoe, the *Spectator*—these are its antecedents. The style of *Ralph Rashleigh* belongs to this tradition. In the prose of literature, which attempts to be something more than a means of recording and transmitting information, there is the same bookishness as is observable in

America in the work of Irving and Cooper. Mrs Campbell Praed, for instance, often gives more vigour to this kind of idiom, but when she is being sententious, as in the preface to *Policy and Passion,* one is inevitably reminded of Cooper:

> It has been my wish to depict in these pages certain phases of Australian life, in which the main interests and dominant passions of the personages concerned are identical with those which might readily present themselves upon an European stage, but which, directly and indirectly, are influenced by striking natural surroundings, and by conditions inseparable from the youth of a vigorous and impulsive nation.[19]

In the prose of Joseph Furphy an uneasy co-habitation of the colloquial and literary is clearly to be seen:

> Just at sunset I struck the partly-plain patch of sixty or eighty acres, where the gilgie ought to be. I unyoked with despatch, then left the bullocks, and rode round, looking for a clump of mallee, which would indicate the immediate neighbourhood of the water. No use. I could find no mallee anywhere. Night came on—richest starlight, though, of course, dark in the scrub—and still I objurgated round, and purposely scattered the bullocks to search for themselves, and anathematised in all directions, and consigned the whole vicinity to the Evil One, for lack of that clump of mallee.[20]

Even in a short passage like this the uncertainty of tone is evident: it is a peculiar idiom that swings from colloquial plainness to recondite Latinity ('objurgated') and back so easily. I do not think one's doubts about Furphy's sense of language—about its sensitivity, not its range—can be disposed of simply by regarding Tom Collins as a *persona,* because, while it is clear that Furphy is satirising Collins, the standpoint from which the satire is conducted is not. There was, I think, enough of Collins in Furphy himself to make him unaware of the tedium Collins often induces by his prolixity and heavy-handed jocosity.

Lawson was, like Furphy, extremely self-conscious in his use of the vernacular. (Indeed, most of the Australian writers in prose and verse with whom one associates a heavy dependence on the vernacular—C. J. Dennis and John O'Grady, for example—have been very self-conscious about it.) Lawson's prose has vernacular elements, but it has quite a different effect from the language of Twain, where the vernacular becomes the very tissue of the prose. Lawson consistently uses the vernacular to record conversation, but the voice of the narrator in most of his stories is not always colloquial in tone or vocabulary and is sometimes, on the contrary, quite formal. And in some of the stories the effect depends upon the *difference* between the quoted language of the characters and the connecting prose of the narrator; consider, for instance, the conclusion of 'The Bush Undertaker':

[19] Praed, *Policy and Passion.*   [20] *Such is Life,* p. 67.

'Theer oughter be somethin' sed,' muttered the old man; 'taint right to put 'im under like a dog. Theer oughter be some sort o' sarmin.'

He sighed heavily in the listening silence that followed this remark and proceeded with his work. He filled the grave to the brim this time, and fashioned the mound carefully with his spade. Once or twice he muttered the words, 'I am the rassaraction.' As he laid the tools quietly aside, and stood at the head of the grave, he was evidently trying to remember the something that ought to be said. He removed his hat, placed it carefully on the grass, held his hand out from his sides and a little to the front, drew a long deep breath, and said with a solemnity that greatly disturbed Five Bob: 'Hashes ter hashes, dus ter dus, Brummy—an'—an' in hopes of a great an' gerlorious rassaraction!'

He sat down on a log near by, rested his elbows on his knees and passed his hand wearily over his forehead—but only as one who was tired and felt the heat; and presently he rose, took up the tools, and walked back to the hut.

And the sun sank again on the grand Australian bush—the nurse and tutor of eccentric minds, the home of the weird.[21]

The difference here is similar to a number of effects in *Such is Life* which H. J. Oliver has pointed out in his contribution to the volume edited by Geoffrey Dutton ('. . . some of the comedy of the novel comes from the very contrast between Collins's diction, on the one hand, and the simplicity of Thompson or the sanguinary conversation of the bullock-drivers, on the other').[22]

Neither Lawson nor Furphy, then, did for Australian prose what Twain did for American prose. In Huck, Twain found the perfect speaking voice to record his vision of a developing America, of the loss of freedom as 'sivilisation' advanced inexorably westward. The vernacular as Twain uses it embodies a whole way of life, with its own wry wisdom and sense of values. Evidently the same could not be said of the vernacular in colonial Australia, because Lawson and Furphy did not adopt it as a mode of narrative or exposition. And in the years since they wrote, at the level of literature as distinct from that of commercial fiction, no tradition has developed of written prose embodying the flavour and vividness of the vernacular. Most of the best prose written by Australians nowadays has as little dependence on the vernacular as does the best poetry: the prose of Alan Moorehead or Geoffrey Blainey, for example, is accomplished, but it is hard to see that there is anything specifically Australian about its idiom or style.

To the point here is the work of a writer who has contributed greatly to both Australian verse and prose. In Judith Wright's *The Generations of Men*, in which we see the same qualities as we find in her poetry, the inerrancy of her prose style depends on a highly skilled use of the common stock of the English language, not upon a special local idiom. In one of

[21] *Henry Lawson, Best Stories,* ed. C. Mann, pp. 31-2.
[22] Dutton, *The Literature of Australia,* p. 302.

The Language of Australian Literature

her poems, there is a conscious contrasting of the language of literature with the vernacular: the third and fourth stanzas of 'South of My Days', uttered by Dan, the old drover, have the syntax and vocabulary of the vernacular:

> Droving that year, Charleville to the Hunter,
> nineteen-one it was, and the drought beginning;
> sixty head left at the McIntyre, the mud round them
> hardened like iron; and the yellow boy died
> in the sulky ahead with the gear, but the horse went on,
> stopped at the Sandy Camp and waited in the evening.
> It was the flies we seen first, swarming like bees.
> Came to the Hunter, three hundred head of a thousand—
> cruel to keep them alive—and the river was dust.
>
> Or mustering up in the Bogongs in the autumn
> When the blizzards came early. Brought them down;
>   we brought them
> down, what aren't there yet. Or driving for
>   Cobb's on the run
> up from Tamworth—Thunderbolt at the top of
>   Hungry Hill
> and I give him a wink. I wouldn't wait long, Fred,
> not if I was you; the troopers are just behind,
> coming for that job at the Hillgrove. He went
>   like a luny,
> him on his big black horse.[23]

But the stanzas which frame old Dan's talk are in the standard speech of Miss Wright's verse—not vernacular, but not artificial either—that 'noble, candid speech' which Hope wrote of as Yeats's habitual idiom. The effect of 'framing' that Miss Wright uses in this poem in some ways resembles the abovementioned effects of contrast in Lawson and Furphy; and in the minds of all three writers, it is clear, the vernacular is a possible instrument of conversation but not the normal vehicle of literary expression. The direct relevance, then, of studies in Australian English to the creation and assessment of a language for Australian literature is limited: the work of the linguist may help us to appreciate and understand the language of old Dan, the drover; only the critic can help us with the language of the poet.

---

[23] From 'South of My Days', *Selected Poems*, p. 6.

REFERENCES CITED

Clemens, S. L., *Adventures of Huckleberry Finn*, ed. S. Bradley, R. C. Beatty, and E. H. Long, New York, 1962.
Dutton, G. (ed.), *The Literature of Australia*, Ringwood, 1964.
Eliot, T. S., *Four Quartets*, London, 1944.
Furphy, Joseph, *Such is Life*, Sydney, 1962.
Hope, A. D., *Collected Poems*, Sydney, 1966.
McAuley, James, *Selected Poems*, Sydney, 1963.
Mann, C. (ed.), *Henry Lawson, Best Stories*, Sydney, 1966.
Maurice, Furnley (pseud. for Frank Wilmot), *Romance*, Melbourne, 1922.
Moore, T. Inglis (ed.), *Poetry in Australia*, Vol. 1, Sydney, 1964.
Praed, C., *Policy and Passion*, London, 1881.
Ramson, W. S., *Australian English: An Historical Study of the Vocabulary, 1788-1898*, Canberra, 1966.
Slessor, K., *Poems*, Sydney, 1962.
Trilling, Lionel, *The Liberal Imagination*, New York, 1950.
Ward, Russel, *Penguin Book of Australian Ballads*, Melbourne, 1964.
Wilkes, G. A., 'Brennan and his Literary Affinities', *Australian Quarterly*, Vol. 31, No. 2, 1959, pp. 72-84.
Wilson, Edmund, *The Wound and the Bow*, London, 1961.
Wright, Judith, *The Generations of Men*, Melbourne, 1959.
———, *Selected Poems*, Sydney, 1963.

12   SUSAN KALDOR

ASIAN STUDENTS AND AUSTRALIAN ENGLISH

Australia's universities and other institutions of higher education have, for the past two decades or so, been host to an increasing number of students from Southeast Asian countries.[1] Gaining one's higher education in a foreign country and providing higher education to students from a foreign country are processes which require adjustments of all kinds on the part of all those who are, centrally or marginally, involved in them. The problems inherent in such a situation have received a great deal of attention in the literature of cross-cultural education.[2] It is generally recognised that problems of communication play a very important role, and need to be examined in detail. This article represents some findings of a study of communication problems between Asian[3] students and speakers of Australian English at the University of Western Australia.[4]

The use of English between Asian students and speakers of Australian English is a complex instance of language contact. The Asian student is a bilingual or multilingual who, typically, learnt one Asian language as his mother tongue, subsequently learnt English, and, in many cases, other Asian languages as 'other tongues', who may have gained his primary and secondary education in any one or several of these languages, and who is now gaining his tertiary education in English.[5] The typical speaker of Australian English is a monolingual[6] who gained his entire education in his mother

[1] For a background history and contemporary survey see Hodgkin, *Australian Training and Asian Living*.
[2] See Hodgkin, 'Cross-Cultural Education in an Anthropological Perspective'.
[3] The term 'Asian' will be used for the sake of simplicity, but reference will be made mainly to students from Southeast Asia.
[4] The material is made up of replies to questionnaires, formal and informal written matter, recorded conversations, and notes collected since 1960. The study has been aided by a University of Western Australia Research Grant since 1967. I am indebted to Michael Robinson, Pamela Minchin, and Ruth Snell, who have, at various times, assisted with laborious transcription and analysis, and who have contributed many ideas and insights.
[5] Those who come to Australian residential private schools for secondary education will not be considered here.
[6] I do not intend to go into the problem of the definition of bilingualism for the purposes of a general theory. From the point of view of this article, a monolingual is a person who has never used habitually a language other than his mother tongue.

tongue apart from having possibly taken one or two other languages as high school subjects.

What are the problems that are likely to arise when the two types of speakers attempt to communicate in the medium of English in an Australian speech community?

The Asian student may experience difficulties while striving to attain the following communicative skills: first, speaking (writing) fluently and in keeping with the phonological (orthographic), syntactic, and semantic rules of 'English';[7] second, speaking (writing) in accordance with the sociolinguistic rules[8] that govern speech (writing) behaviour in Australian society in general and in a student sub-culture in particular; third, understanding English spoken rapidly and naturally by monolingual speakers of different varieties of Australian English (understanding written English texts of different types including those containing vocabulary and idiom specific to Australian English); and fourth, interpreting the speech (writing) behaviour of Australians.

The problems of the speaker of Australian English mostly[9] stem from the fact that the bilingual/multilingual Asian speaker often fails in one or more of the communicative skills as outlined above. The Australian's problems, then, are first, speaking (to a much lesser extent, writing) with the expectation that he will be only partially understood, a situation which may pose some strain on the otherwise automatic use of his mother tongue; second, maintaining 'natural' speech behaviour without some of the reinforcements to which he is accustomed in purely monolingual conversation; third, understanding speech (writing) that is deviant from the point of view of his internalised knowledge of Australian English phonological (orthographic),[10] syntactic, and semantic rules; and fourth, interpreting speech (writing) behaviour that is deviant from the point of view of his internalised knowledge of the rules that govern speech (writing) behaviour in Australian society.

In each case, the first two are problems in 'encoding', and the last two are problems in 'decoding'. Encoding problems are, of course, much more serious for the Asian student than they are for the speaker of Australian English, whose largely automatic encoding processes are only slightly disturbed in the manner described above.

The Asian student's difficulties may be traced to several factors in his

[7] The question of the particular variety of English will be discussed below.

[8] In the sense developed in Hymes, 'The Ethnography of Speaking'.

[9] But not exclusively, of course. A speaker of Australian English may have initial difficulties in communicating with a native speaker of another English dialect.

[10] Orthographic deviations are included here only for the sake of a complete list of possibilities. They are common among monolingual speakers of English, and it is not easy to find criteria to separate foreign spelling errors from native ones.

socio-cultural-linguistic background. The most important of these will be discussed here briefly.

MOTHER TONGUE AND 'OTHER TONGUES'

In the linguistic (psycholinguistic) literature of recent years, great emphasis has been placed on the essential differences between the processes of mother tongue acquisition and the learning of subsequent languages later in life. Since Weinreich developed the concept of 'interference',[11] there has been, among students of bilingualism, widespread acceptance of the fact that the structure of the language first acquired builds powerful interference in the path of learning the structure of other languages.[12] The Asian student's mother tongue thus sets the scene for his first encounter with English.

To be sure, there are many properties of the English language which are old acquaintances of every teacher of English as a foreign language all over the world as being predictable areas of difficulty to his pupils. One need only mention the ubiquitous 'anomalous finites', the 'count noun/mass noun' distinction, the tense-aspect relationships, or the question tags, as indispensable components of textbooks of English for foreign learners.

Some aspects of the structure of English present particular hardship to speakers of a restricted number of languages only. Generalisations can often be made for all languages belonging to the same language family, as, for example, it is fair to assume a difficulty with English intonation, stress, and rhythm patterns in speakers of any of the Sino-Tibetan languages. Sometimes 'genetically' unrelated languages share certain properties which constitute problem areas in English. In this regard it is of interest to note the common feature of difficulty with English word-final consonant clusters among speakers of a number of Southeast Asian languages, some of them genetically unrelated to each other (e.g. Chinese, Bahasa Indonesia, Thai).

Ultimately, however, it is necessary to take into account not only the specific language, but the particular dialect of a language that the student has learnt as his mother tongue. A speaker of a Chinese dialect which has no syllable-final stops (e.g. Foochow, Mandarin dialects) may tend to omit all syllable-final stops in English, while a speaker of a dialect with a limited number of syllable-final stops (e.g. Cantonese, Hakka, Hokkien)[13]

[11] *Languages in Contact.*
[12] Some writers suggest new terminology to replace Weinreich's. See Clyne, *Transference and Triggering*. It has also been pointed out that not all the properties of bilingual speech can be described in terms of interference from another language. See Kaldor, 'The Study of Bilingualism', and Mackey, *Language Teaching Analysis*, p. 111. However, the significance of mother tongue influences on second language learning has not been questioned.
[13] For comparative phonological sketches of the Chinese dialects see Voegelin, 'Languages of the World'.

may have less trouble in producing such sounds, but may fail to distinguish between voiced and unvoiced pairs such as /bæt/ and /bæd/.

Of the 136 Asian students enrolled in various years of study who answered questionnaires or were interviewed in 1960, 102 were speakers of a Southern Chinese dialect, 9 of Malay, 9 of Tamil, 4 of Vietnamese, 3 of Hindi, and one each of Urdu, Batak, Gorontalo, Konkani, Pidgin Portuguese, Siyin, Thai, Sundanese, and Punjabi. Of the 69 first-year students who acted as linguistic informants in the 1967 follow-up study, 63 were speakers of a Southern Chinese dialect, 3 of Tamil, and 1 each of Hindi, Thai, and Malay.

Mother-tongue interference may be modified by a great many factors in individual cases. An important modifying influence is exercised by other languages used habitually by the speaker. A child growing up in Southeast Asia may need to use several languages or dialects in addition to his mother tongue for everyday communication or in his studies. To take some specific examples from amongst Asian students at the University of Western Australia: a speaker of Gorontalo and a speaker of Batak, both from Indonesia, used Bahasa Indonesia as their language of education. A speaker of Hakka from Malaysia used Cantonese as a regional lingua franca with other Chinese speakers, gained his education in Mandarin Chinese, and used Malay in inter-ethnic communication. Another Hakka speaker from Singapore used Hokkien as a regional lingua franca and otherwise shared the languages of the former speaker. An Indian student learnt Bhojpuri as his mother tongue, spoke it later only to his grandmother, used Hindi with his mother and father, Punjabi, Bengali, Gujarati, and Urdu to friends, and English in the classroom. A Vietnamese used French, and a Laotian French and Thai, habitually at various times.

Of the 63 Chinese students in the 1967 sample, 42 spoke habitually a second language or dialect in addition to English. Of these, 32 learnt Mandarin Chinese as a medium of primary education, 6 also as a medium of secondary education, 33 spoke Malay, 16 used regularly a Southern Chinese dialect other than their own, and 9 mentioned the frequent use of all of the following: Mandarin Chinese, Malay, and several Southern Chinese dialects.

Any of the languages or dialects with which a student has had close contact is likely to provide further patterns of interference with English and modify the original interference patterns of the mother tongue.

MODELS OF ENGLISH

We have so far considered the linguistic forces that impede the process of acquiring English. It is equally important to look at the problem of what kind of English has been acquired under what circumstances.

From the point of view of experience with English, Asian students may be divided into two main categories: those who come from countries or territories where English has been or was, until recently, one of the main languages of instruction in the schools, where it is or used to be an official language, and where it has been functioning as a lingua franca among speakers of different languages (e.g. Malaysia, Singapore, Hong Kong); and students from countries where English has never been either a medium of instruction in the schools or an official language (e.g. Indonesia, Thailand).

Within the first category a further division has to be made, between students who gained their education wholly or partly in English and those who went to schools where the language of instruction was a language other than English.

Those who attended an English school had the maximal exposure to models of English that is possible anywhere outside a monolingual English-speaking community. Nevertheless, these models differ markedly in nature and scope from models available to native speakers of English in their own linguistically homogeneous[14] environment.

In the English schools attended by students of the first category, a form of the educated Southern dialect of England was regarded as the ideal model. However, such a model was, in fact, not supplied in the speech of many of the teachers, who, themselves bilingual or multilingual speakers of Asian languages, were subject to the same linguistic interference phenomena as were their pupils. The function of English rarely extended beyond situations involving formal study. The words of a Chinese student from Malaysia illustrate this type of situation vividly:

> I learnt English ever since I was seven . . . While at school, I did not have many chances to do much for myself where English was concerned. Firstly, it can be attributed to the fact that the student population was a multi-racial one. We come from different homes, some from Chinese families, others from Malay families and the rest from Indian, Eurasian or Sikh families. We converse with one another in our mother tongue or a common language (for example, Malay was usually spoken when a Chinese or an Indian came together) except during lessons or in communication with the teaching staff, when we have to use English. In short English was generally spoken during the appropriate lesson hours . . . one of the most unique things that was left out in our English lessons then was conversational English. . . .
> [written sample]

Those who received their schooling in an Asian language had even more limited exposure to models of English. These students did not acquire English in the context of other school subjects, and had little opportunity to develop areas of specialised vocabulary, even for formal study purposes.

---

[14] For a discussion of linguistic homogeneity see Fishman, 'Some Contrasts between Linguistically Homogeneous and Linguistically Heterogeneous Polities'.

Both the English-educated and the non-English-educated of the first category are likely to have used English as an inter-ethnic lingua franca. Such use of English usually goes with free mixing of words from several languages, and results in the interchange of different patterns of interference. An example is the following conversation, observed during preparations by students from several mother-tongue groups for the celebration in Perth of the anniversary of Malaya's Independence:

> 'Play louder.'
> 'Very loud already, man.'
> 'Turn down, lah.'
> 'Get money, lah, twenty pounds.'
> 'Twenty pounds lot money lah.'
> 'Too much, give back, lah.'
> 'If don't get enough money, how can, man?'
> 'Baik lah, tonight get money, lah.'

The same students spoke in grammatically and lexically much more 'controlled' English in the company of Australian English interlocutors. However, the levelling influence of local (Southeast Asian) forms of English can be observed even in controlled speech. Saunders reports in 'The Teaching of English Pronunciation to Speakers of Hokkien' that the English of Hokkien speakers at the Nanyang University in Singapore differs considerably from the English of Hokkien speakers in Taiwan. While the latter exhibits features which are predictable from the comparison of Hokkien and English phonology, the former resembles more closely the English used by other mother-tongue groups in Singapore and Malaya.

Students in the second category learnt English as a secondary school subject only, and did not use English for inter-ethnic communication. The model of English that this group received varied according to the teaching methods employed and to the teachers' own competence in English, but was, at any rate, usually restricted to the single context of a foreign language class.

ETHNIC AFFILIATION AND THE INFLUENCE OF THE FAMILY

Formal education represents but a portion of a person's linguistic experiences during the period of primary and secondary education. Linguistic socialisation continues in the home throughout a speaker's childhood and adolescence. Students from different ethnic categories in the same country (e.g. Chinese, Malay, and Indian students from Malaysia) learnt, in the informal environment of home and surroundings, not only different languages but also different cultural values and norms relating to speech behaviour. When to speak (or not to speak), how to speak to various persons, what to say (or not to say) in a given situation, are all part and parcel of what Hymes has termed a speaker's 'communicative competence'. Traditional Chinese attitudes to speech between older and younger persons, men and women, paternal grandmother and father, are all reflected in the following description by a Hokkien student from Kuala Lumpur of a family meal:

> When all the foods are ready, we have to wash our hands before sitting on our usual seats. The position of the seat is significant to our Chinese people. Those who are eldest should face the door and then we sit according to our own age. Because we, the sons, are afraid of our father and have a great respect for our grandmother, we talk little in front of the meal. Always, my grandmother, who is eighty-two years old, starts the ball rolling. She is the one that we all love her very much though her appearance appears quite stern and strict. She concerns my father very much. In the earth, we think that my father is everything for her. She asks how the work is going on? Is the boss happy? and so forth . . . The dialogue is continuing until the meal finishes. My mother seldom talk, she just sit silent or sometimes she likes to ask us few questions about our school life. We sit like dumb. Our eyes are on the foods and our ears are listening of what the conversation is going on. . . . [written sample]

Malay attitudes relating to speech between older and younger siblings was expressed in the following remark made by a Malay student from Malaysia: 'I had a nice letter from [name]. He is my younger brother who respects me most.' [oral sample]

Westernisation often leads to the loss of traditional attitudes towards speech and acts as a levelling force. The next excerpt, from a Hokkien girl from Singapore, illustrates an interpretation of a speech event that could come from a Westernised member of any ethnic category:

> Dinner at home is a rather informal occasion where everyone turns up at the dining-room most unpunctually, grabs a plate of rice, shoves food on it and dashes off with food and all recline before the television set . . . forks and spoons are used all the time as we seem to have lost our knack of eating rice from a bowl with a pair of chopsticks. . . . Conversation at the table runs mainly on the topic of the day's events. Dad would have some grumble, Mum would insist again and again that one shouldn't watch television so much, and I would sit in front of the television set with a glazed look in my eyes. Conversation topics change remarkably quickly during meals. [written sample]

FIRST CONTACT WITH AUSTRALIAN ENGLISH

We have seen the interplay of linguistic and extralinguistic experiences prior to arrival in Australia. A prognosis for successful or unsuccessful initial communication in Australia on the part of the individual student must be based on the particular configuration of these experiences and of other variables inherent in the student's own personality. There are, at the same time, certain features in the situation arising on arrival in Australia which are shared by students of different backgrounds. These can be summed up in the following three points:

First, in Australia the Asian student is for the first time in a predominantly monolingual, linguistically homogeneous speech community, where a full and unique model of English becomes suddenly available and where his speech and verbal behaviour is assessed in terms of this full model. Australian English differs in phonology, idiom, and structure of discourse (even if not so much in syntax) from all previously encountered models of English, even the 'ideal' norm of Educated Southern English.

Second, he is separated from members of his original environment, other than those who may be in Australia as fellow students. New social relationships have to be established, and sociolinguistic rules have to be acquired for establishing them.

Third, attitudes to Australian English are affected by the temporary nature of the students' contact with it. Asian students come to Australia for the specific purpose of gaining higher education, to return to their home countries on completion of their courses. For long-term goals, Australian English may not be the most suitable model for imitation. Students may be more strongly motivated to acquire some 'general form of English with international prestige', and may resist becoming 'too Australian' in accent or speech behaviour. In this respect Asian students' communication problems differ from those of non-English migrants in Australia whose adjustment to Australian English is a long-range goal.

The impact of the new linguistic environment has been expressed by Asian students in many a vivid comment given in speech and writing.

To some, the flow of Australian English speech seems, at least for a while, an unanalysable mass of sound:

> I seldom catch what they say especially when they are conversing among themselves. [Hokkien from Malaysia, oral sample]

> It is hard to understand why they don't open their mouths. [Indonesian, oral sample]

> Maybe it [the difficulty] is due to the Australian accent. I sometimes find it hard to listen to what they are saying and at one time or another I just cannot figure out what they want to say. I find them murmuring in their words and their low masculine tones are too hard to be clearly heard. [Cantonese from Hong Kong, written sample]

Others isolate early some of the popularly recognised characteristics of Australian English phonology:

One has sometimes to pronounce 'male' as 'mile' before one can be understood. [Hokkien from Malaysia, oral sample]

Colloquial idiom specific to Australian English presents a problem:

I have yet to get use to Australian phrases such as 'drinkum'.[15] [Tamil from Malaysia, written sample]

More frequently, it is simply colloquial idiom—not necessarily Australianisms—that the new arrival cannot decode or use:

A lot of slang is used by students . . . I think that is actually a barrier to new boys. . . . [Malay from Malaysia, oral sample]

Frequently words are omitted in speech and one wonders whether it was the accepted style of the place or whether it was the speaker's bad breathing technique which drowned the words unintentionally. I had the opportunity to experience one such encounter with a fellow Australian collegian who passed my room and seeing me engaged with reading queried casually: 'You studying here?' It was rather trying, having to figure out whether he meant to ask: 'Have you been studying here (all this while)?' or 'Are you studying (in this room)?' In any case a positive answer was the solution and no embarrassment was caused. . . . [Chinese from Malaysia,[16] written sample]

If I use some of the language . . . I . . . usually use at home . . . [I will not be understood] . . . the other day I was . . . in the petrol station and I said . . . where can I throw this piece of paper . . . he wouldn't understand me and then . . . a friend next to me . . . said . . . What he means is where to chuck this piece of paper. [Cantonese from Malaysia, oral sample]

Australian behaviour seems more informal and casual than the patterns to which the student was accustomed in his home country:

the first step into the Australian life . . . [is] one of casualness . . . you see a child speaking to a parent so casually. . . . [Hokkien from Malaysia, oral sample]

the life here will be very different from Malayan life . . . here is more equal . . . if I see a lecturer I won't be embarrassed at all, back home, in Malaya, I am . . . My professor of department . . . he'll say good morning to you even before you say good morning to him, but at home even an ordinary teacher . . . he insists that you should say good morning to him first. . . . [Teochew from Malaysia, oral sample]

Within such apparent informality, there are subtle rules signalling speaker-hearer relations which are difficult to detect:

I do not know when I am polite in Australia, when I am not . . . . [Japanese, oral sample]

[When I talk to people] I have to say something not to annoy or insult . . . I do not always know how. . . . [Hokkien from Malaysia, oral sample]

[15] Presumably 'dinkum'.
[16] No dialect information available.

Difficulties arise out of lack of experience in specific speech settings:

> [It is] sometimes hard to carry on a dinner conversation because at home we don't talk so much when we have our dinner. . . . [Hokkien from Malaysia, oral sample]

The new arrival is unfamiliar with many a handy topic for casual conversation:

> the first difference that I found is that the Australians are interested in the football, back home we just play soccer and . . . discuss things on that point . . . When I first came here those boys they used to talk about the weather and the places and so on which we haven't seen yet . . . and in no position to discuss. . . . [Hokkien from Malaysia, oral sample]

A new type of interlocutor may present an early problem in communication:

> He [the new arrival] feels funny to see white skinned porters . . . walking about carrying his luggage . . . he is not used to such a sight . . . In his country, all white men seemed to be 'big shots'. He does not know whether to pay the porter or not. Only later he will learn that he might have been sworn at if he had handed the porter some change. . . . [Hakka from Malaysia, written sample]

BILINGUAL SPEECH AND THE MONOLINGUAL DECODER

We have looked at some of the ways in which the new linguistic environment affects the Asian student. We may now take a sample stretch of speech recorded with an Asian student shortly after his arrival in Australia and subject it to detailed analysis from the point of view of the Australian English decoder.

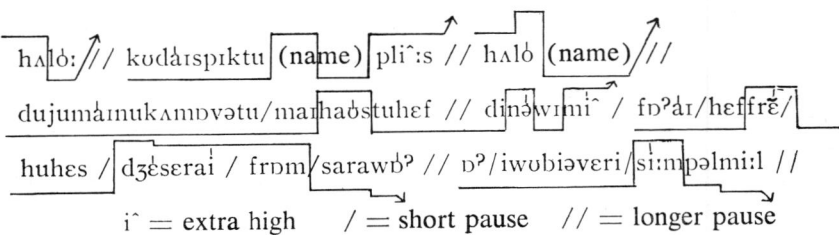

[Foochow from Malaysia, oral sample]

The following table shows the phonological deviations from Australian English found in the above utterance:

Asian Students and Australian English

Chinese speaker's 'over to my house' with the Australian English speaker's 'over', 'round to my place', 'round'; the Chinese speaker's 'dinner' with the Australian English speaker's 'tea'.

Such a comparison highlights features which may, following Kachru,[20] be termed 'contextual deviations' from the sociolinguistic norms of a homogeneous monolingual speech community in the sense that 'this would not be said in this style by this type of speaker to this type of hearer in this type of situation'.[21] 'Do you mind' is a deviation in terms of the topic (invitation), 'to my house', and, in certain situations, 'dinner', a deviation in terms of student-to-student (young person to friend) relationship. 'For' (for I have a friend) would be used by Australian students only in creative or formal writing, if at all, but hardly ever in conversation.

The foregoing was given as an illustration of the way in which deviations at all levels intermingle with non-deviant items to form a single utterance. The effect on the hearer can only be gauged if all simultaneous and dynamically interacting features of a communicative act are taken into account.

It is, however, necessary for the investigator to isolate single types of deviation for various purposes—to be able to characterise the communication problems of one linguistic or ethnic group as compared with those of another, and to be able to investigate the relative importance of various types of deviation in a variety of communicative events, for example.

DEVIATIONS FROM AUSTRALIAN ENGLISH IN CHINESE STUDENTS' SPEECH

In the remainder of this article, a brief review of deviations characteristic of Chinese speakers—the largest single linguistic-ethnic category in the sample—will be given. In conclusion, some consequences of deviations will be considered. It is important to note that many Chinese students among the informants speak English with hardly any or only a few of the deviations listed, and the frequency of occurrence of any of the types shows a great deal of variation in individual cases.

Phonology

The following were the main types of phonological deviations found in the speech of Chinese students of five dialect categories (Hakka, Teochew, Cantonese, Foochow, Hokkien):

1. Devoicing or dropping of voiced stops (mainly alveolar and velar) or their replacement by a glottal stop in medial or final positions. Examples recorded: meːri (married), suːsaɪ (suicide), faɪn (find), wiʔkɛːn (weekend), aiwuʔlaɪ (I would like), boːt (board), bɛt (bed).

[20] B. B. Kachru, 'The Indianness in Indian English', *Word*, Vol. 21, No. 3, 1965, pp. 391-410.
[21] Cf. Hymes, 'The Ethnography of Speaking'.

2. Dropping of voiceless stops (mainly alveolar or velar) or their replacement by [ʔ] in medial or final positions.²² Examples: flaɪ (flight), tunaɪ (tonight), əpɒinmən (appointment), lasbuʔ (last book), saɪkiætriːs (psychiatrist), səspɛʔk (suspect), dipaʔmən (department), ɛːpoː (airport), ɛsplein (explain), kwaiʔ (quite), lɛtʃrə (lecturer), laɪʔlihud (likelihood), mɛʔæmistɛʔ (make a mistake).

3. Replacement of interdental voiced and voiceless fricatives by alveolar stops initially, medially, and finally; their omission finally. Examples: dɪs (this), wɪd (with), wɪ (with), wɛdə (weather), tɪŋk (think), tɛŋk (thank), triː (three), sʌmtɪŋ (something), futpaː (footpath).

4. Devoicing or dropping of voiced labiodental and alveolar fricatives finally. Examples: wɒs (was), tʃaɪniːs (Chinese), pliːs (please), əraɪvs (arrives), ɒlweɪ (always), hɛf (have), gif (give), ailideə (I live there).

5. Omission of voiceless labiodental and alveolar fricatives finally. Examples: sɛl (self), waɪ (wife), saɪən (science).

6. Omission of /l/, finally, interchange of /l/ and /r/ initially and medially. Examples: staɪ (style), fɒwaɪ (for a while), prɒbrəmz (problems), saikərɒdʒɪkəri (psychologically), dʒɛnɛleɪʃn (generation), lizən (reason).

7. Devoicing of voiced affricates in all positions. Examples: tʃuvənaɪl (juvenile), vilætʃ (village), kɛbetʃ (cabbage).

8. Partial or full omission of consonant clusters, mainly medially and finally, or their replacement by [ʔ]. Examples: jusɛʔ (yourself), maɪsɛʔ (myself), dɛlɪkwɛnsɪ (delinquency). The omission of clusters of which the first member is a nasal is often accompanied by the nasalisation of the preceding vowel: əpɔɪʔmə̃ (appointment), paũɒf (pound of), kɔ̃sənæn (consonant).

9. Insertion of [ʔ] before a final voiceless stop, when the latter not omitted. Examples: laiʔk (like), dɪskraɪʔp (describe), eːpɒʔt (airport).

10. Replacement of rising glides, Australian English /ɛɪ/ and /oʊ/,

²² It is interesting to note here that the omission of /t/ and other consonants has been recorded in Mitchell and Delbridge, *The Speech of Australian Adolescents* (p. 51) as elisions characteristic of Australian speech. Further data, at present unavailable, would be necessary to separate Australian English omissions fully and systematically from those of foreign speakers. It seems that the elision of /t/, for example, occurs in Australian English in such positions as in 'most of', 'next day', 'last September', but does not occur in 'fligh*t* eighteen', 'tonigh*t* I will', 'airpor*t* at eight'. As noted by Mitchell and Delbridge, much of the 'acceptability' of elided forms depends on such factors as speed—elision is not acceptable in careful, slow speech. In the case of Asian students, elision has to be looked at also from the point of view of its combination with other features, e.g. the quality of the neighbouring vowel sound. A very fronted and short [a] in 'last' (last book), preceding the elision of /t/, gives a different effect from that of elision following the more central /a/ of Australian English speakers.

Asian Students and Australian English

by short or long vowels. Examples: lof (loaf), roːt (road), kop (cope), smokt (smoked), etin (eighteen), leːdi (lady), greʔ (great), mekliv (make leave), trɒt (throat). It is interesting to note that a glide is often maintained when an *i* or *y* occurs in the spelling: trein (train), weɪs (ways).

11. Raising of tongue height in front vowels. Examples: liˆv (live), diˆnə (dinner), siːˆmpəl (simple), mɛn (man), hɛf (have).

12. Lowering of tongue height and reducing of length of mid back vowel, Australian English /ɔ/ [ɔː]. Examples: pɒk (pork), fɒti (forty), tɒk (talk), fɒʔ (for).

13. Replacement of central vowel in unstressed positions by a variety of other vowels. Examples: áɪkɛndúdæt (I can do that), déɪʃuʔgó (they should go).

14. Deviant intonation patterns in the speech of Chinese students display the following features: lack of smooth transition, lack of gradual long rise or fall on single stressed syllable, 'silent' jumps between two level syllables. Stress contrasts are weak or absent and the relatively stronger stresses are often misplaced. Stress usually, but not always, goes with high or extra high pitch, and hardly ever occurs on low or extra low syllables. The rhythm is characterised by a succession of staccato short syllables, interspersed with longer syllables before pauses. Length itself is often deviant from Australian English patterns due to the general lack of glides and the incomplete or absent consonant clusters. There seems to be virtually no limitation on the number of fast staccato syllables, as may be seen in the following example:

Hallo, Qantas airway can you tell me what time the flight four two three arrives from Singapore . . . mmm thank you . . . ah . . . can you check for me whether the person is called mister [name] is on the board. . . .

ᴗ = short   — = long

Grammatical

Grammatical deviations in Chinese students' English were concentrated in the following problem areas:

1. In forming noun phrases: lack of count noun / mass noun distinction, for example 'I have to obtain quite a few informations', '. . . sending some of moneys home to parents', 'five pounds of potato'; the omission, inappropriate insertion or wrong choice of determiners, for example 'and dozen oranges', 'give me a pound of the beetroot'; omission of possessive suffix, for example 'I used my guardian, I borrowed it from him', 'who

is doing Honour course', 'I attend a young people bible study', 'having an affair with the psychiatrist wife'; omission of plural suffix, for example 'was kidnapped by bandit', 'I got a lot of book out of the library'.

2. In forming verb phrases: wrongly formed tenses, tenses fluctuating within the same narrative, for example:

> he stopped and pick her up . . . and on the way she reckoned she was cold . . . so he took off his leather jacket and give to her . . . so he went to the same place again . . . the next day . . . and knock at the door . . . and an old lady open the door and he asked her about . . . you know this girl . . . and give a description of it . . . and anyway the old lady tell her that that's her daughter;

incomplete phrasal verbs, for example 'shall I come and pick you', 'I came to pick you'; lack of number concord, for example 'there has been some circumstances', 'and the husband know everything then'; incomplete transitive verb phrases, for example 'you want me to put in dialogue form', 'he gave to her'; wrongly used modal auxiliaries, for example 'I will like to if I could'.

3. In forming prepositional phrases: prepositions omitted, wrongly inserted or confused, for example 'a couple other', 'when will flight eighteen be arriving Perth', 'taking a good look what is going on', 'I am planning to go down Kojonup', 'not in the mood of reading'.

4. Inadequate transformational rules to form: negative constructions, for example 'I not fully understand', 'I think I not have any'; question tags, for example 'you want me to put in a formal way, is it?'; relative clauses, for example 'the officer that was told about the recent changes', 'this widow it was Italian, went to . . .', 'I read some books which is the textbook of first year commerce'; *tell whether/tell if* and *tell when/tell who* type constructions, for example 'can you tell me will that plane arrive on time', 'may I know the aeroplane arrives', 'I ring up to ask whether you be free enough'; various combinations which should result in *verb + ing* forms, for example 'did you have any difficulty to understand me'. The difficulty with transformational rules often results in a succession of separate independent clauses, where a speaker of Australian English would probably use dependent clause constructions, for example 'then I start cooking my lunch for group of my friends . . . for we are staying together . . . so I have to do the cooking for them'.

Vocabulary and Idiom

The analysis of deviations in Chinese students' speech in the use of vocabulary and idiom has not yet been completed in this study. The following examples may give some indication of the nature of these: 'If you are a degree man, you can be sure you get a place', 'he suddenly struck lottery prize', 'he got in love with her', 'it is hard to cope up with', 'I have to make my mind later on', 'if you contact with ordinary people', 'are you sure you are not pulling off my leg or something?', 'my mother accent is Hakka', 'what makes you so interesting about our language?'. Examples of wrongly used Australian English idiom were 'I was crooked' (in place of 'I felt crook') and 'fair dinkum' (when intending to say 'fair enough').

Contextual

Contextual deviations in the elicited or observed free speech of Chinese students occurred mainly in the following forms: inadequately developed 'linguistic routines'[23] for initiating conversations, for example 'I was looking for some informations and I think you can help me', 'hello, this is Mr C. Who is speaking over there, please?'; and for responding to routine questions, for example 'yes, I agree with you' in response to the important Australian English routine, 'lovely day isn't it?', 'I don't mind, thank you very much' in reply to 'would you like to come to tea on Sunday?', 'exactly' as an answer to 'would Monday 10 a.m. be all right for you?'; the use of formal, written or business-letter style when casual conversational style is called for, for example 'I will not be interested in that angle just now because of urgency of hard work', 'can I see you to get some invaluable help from you', 'one should draw attention of forthcoming students to the problems', 'yesterday being Sunday and I am a Christian I spend a whole day in church'; the mixing of deferential and familiar styles, for example 'oh, hello, Sir [to professor], when will you be free?'; in classifying a speech event differently from the Australian English interlocutor, for example the utterance, 'I knew if I followed you I'd find a couple of nice girls' spoken by an Australian student in addressing a Chinese student at a dance—and probably intended as 'friendly rubbishing'—was interpreted by the Chinese speaker as 'Australian flattering talk which is unnecessary and embarrassing'; being silent when idle talk is the norm, for example over the dinner table; in using vague intonation patterns where definite statement is required, for example saying 'yes' ↘ when intending 'yes' ↘.

CONSEQUENCES OF INADEQUATE COMMUNICATION

The immediate communicational consequences of deviations such as the ones listed above depend on many factors, some related to redundancies in linguistic or extralinguistic context, others to the monolingual Australian English hearer's ability to guess, restructure, and adapt himself to the foreign speaker's patterns. The following list represents the range of possibilities:

[23] Cf. Hymes, 'Linguistic Aspects', p. 338.

1. The utterance may be decoded as intended or almost as intended with the aid of anticipation and through the perception of redundant signals.

2. It may be misunderstood as regards referential meaning. This can happen when the deviation offers the hearer an alternative, equally likely interpretation in the given situation.

3. It can be misinterpreted as regards the speaker's intentions and attitudes. This happens only when no redundant behavioural clues are present in the situation. A friendly smile, for example, prevents over-formal speech style from being interpreted as an expression of distance or disdain.

4. It may go partially or wholly uncomprehended as regards referential meaning, and the hearer may wait for the next utterance, where he can pick up the thread of conversation again.

5. The speaker's intentions and attitudes may remain incomprehensible to the hearer during part of an exchange.

It would go beyond the purpose of this article to attempt an evaluation of the long-range consequences of inadequate communication. A great deal of future work is needed before such long-term effects can be fully understood. What individuals can do on a practical level to overcome the adverse effects of faulty communication across languages and cultures can well be summed up by giving this final quote from a Chinese student: 'Language difficulties can be overcome quite easily if you have a common topic, common ground to talk about, real interest . . . so you get beyond superficial conversations'. The many Asian students who have become successful communicators in Australia will undoubtedly agree with him.

REFERENCES CITED

Catford, J. C., *A Linguistic Theory of Translation*, London, 1965.
Clyne, M. G., *Transference and Triggering*, The Hague, 1967.
Fishman, J. A., 'Some Contrasts between Linguistically Homogeneous and Linguistically Heterogeneous Polities'. In J. A. Fishman, C. A. Ferguson, and J. Das Gupta (eds.), *Language Problems of Developing Nations*, New York, 1968.
Hodgkin, M., *Australian Training and Asian Living*, Perth, 1966.
———, 'Cross Cultural Education in an Anthropological Perspective', *Anthropological Forum*, Vol. 1, No. 2, 1964, pp. 232-47.
Hymes, D. H., 'The Ethnography of Speaking'. In T. Gladwin and W. Sturtevant (eds.), *Anthropology and Human Behavior*, Washington, D.C., 1962.
———, 'Linguistic Aspects of Cross-Cultural Personality Study'. In B. Kaplan (ed.), *Studying Personality Cross-Culturally*, Evanston, 1961, pp. 313-59.
———, 'On Communicative Competence'. In S. Diamond (ed.), *Anthropological Perspectives on Education*, New York (in press).
Kaldor, Susan, 'The Study of Bilingualism as an Approach to Language Problems of Asian Students at the University of Western Australia', *Anthropological Forum*, Vol. I, No. 1, 1963, pp. 112-21.
Mackey, W. F., *Language Teaching Analysis*, Bloomington, 1967.
Mitchell, A. G., *The Pronunciation of English in Australia*, Sydney, 1946.
——— and Delbridge, Arthur, *The Speech of Australian Adolescents*, Sydney, 1965.
Saunders, W. A., 'The Teaching of English Pronunciation to Speakers of Hokkien', *Language Learning*, Vol. 12, No. 2, 1962, pp. 151-7.
Voegelin, C. F. and Voegelin, F. M., 'Languages of the World: Sino-Tibetan Fascicle Three', *Anthropological Linguistics*, Vol. 7, No. 4, 1965.
Weinreich, U., *Languages in Contact: Findings and Problems*, New York, 1953.

DAVID BLAIR

A BIBLIOGRAPHY OF AUSTRALIAN ENGLISH

Bibliographies, by their very nature, must reflect something of the progress of their selected discipline. A bibliography of writings on Australian English shows that, as a scientific study, linguistics in Australia is still very much in its infancy. Even today, the bulk of such a bibliography concerns 'popular answers to popular questions'—material written mostly for, and often by, non-specialists. The tradition begun by Samuel McBurney (*202*) in 1889 was not really carried forward for another fifty years, apart from the lexicography of Morris (*115*).

It is clear, too, that the lexicon of Australian English has received more attention than the sound structure—there are almost half as many entries again in the lexicon section as there are for phonology. It may be noted that, of the Occasional Papers of the Australian Language Research Centre (*002*), only two deal with phonology, while ten are concerned with matters of vocabulary. Studies of syntax are few and far between indeed.

In several respects, the Australian situation appears comparable to that of Canada. W. S. Avis (*A Bibliography of Writings on Canadian English*, Toronto, W. J. Gage, 1965) notes that of his 168 entries, 124 were published since the end of World War II, and that only 25 items appeared before 1930. Avis takes this to be 'an indication of greatly increased interest in the kind of English spoken in Canada'; and we would, I think, be justified in seeing a similar situation reflected in the entries given below. A rise in interest during the 1940s can be seen in popular material and, to a lesser extent, in work of a more academic nature; one hopes that the trend will keep bibliographers busy in the future.

In a bibliography of this size, a rigorous subject division does not seem necessary. Five sections follow: one contains entries whose primary concern is with Australian vocabulary and idiom; another is concerned with prosodic and phonological aspects of Australian English—the pronunciation or 'accent'. These two are preceded by a general section containing entries which could not easily be allocated to 'lexicon' or 'phonology'—works which give equal prominence to both, general introductory works, studies of syntax and usage, and some teaching materials.

Section IV deals with migrant varieties of English in Australia while

Section V contains a few selected entries on the study of place names. For further works in the latter field of study, reference must be made to Eagleson (*014*), and to the valuable bibliographies in J. S. Ryan (*262*).

Ephemeral materials (newspapers, magazines) are not comprehensively included in this bibliography, largely because of the difficulty of verifying references. There is a comprehensive listing of theses in Australian universities up to 1965, and a selection for later years. School texts are excluded, as are articles on English not specifically Australian (with occasional exceptions in the case of well-known Australian scholars).

Reviews are listed after the work in question. Unless they are substantial or of particular interest, they are not given separate entries. All, however, are indexed. Cross references are kept to a minimum by use of the index, which lists all authors mentioned in the bibliography.

I GENERAL

001   ALEXANDER, D. H. Yarrabah Aboriginal English. B.A. dissertation, University of Queensland, 1965.

002   AUSTRALIAN LANGUAGE RESEARCH CENTRE. *Occasional Papers.*
    1. The University of Sydney ALRC: An Introduction. *G. H. Russell, 035.*
    2. Australianisms in Early Migrant Handbooks, 1788-1826. *R. D. Eagleson, 073.*
    3. The Currency of Aboriginal Words in Australian English. *W. S. Ramson, 132.*
    4. Australianisms in Early Migrant Handbooks, 1827-1830. *R. D. Eagleson, 074.*
    5, 6. The Terminology of the Shearing Industry. *J. S. Gunn, 089-90.*
    7. Rates of Utterance in Australian Dialect Groups. *J. R. Bernard, 162.*
    8. An Outline Word Phonology of Australian English. *A. I. Jones, 197.*
    9. Fresh Evidence from Early Goldmining Publications, 1851-1860. *E. A. Cooke, S. E. MacCallum and R. D. Eagleson, 066.*
    10. Early Goldmining Terms and Popular Collocations. *E. A. Cooke, S. E. MacCallum and R. D. Eagleson, 065.*
    11. Bibliography of Writings on Australian English. *R. D. Eagleson, 014.*
    12, 13, 14. The Terminology of Australian National Football. *R. D. Eagleson and I. McKie, 081-2.*

003   BAUGH, Albert Croll. *A History of the English Language.* London, Routledge and Kegan Paul, 1951, xiii 509 pp. //Ramson, *130*, p. 26: 'Brief notes on the character and affiliations of Australian English, (pp. 394-5)'.

004   BROOK, George Leslie. *English Dialects.* London, Andre Deutsch, 1963, 224 pp. //Australian English, pp. 129-33.

005   CATTELL, Norman Raymond. 'The Meaning of "The Doctrine of Usage" '. *AUMLA*, Vol. 24, 1965, pp. 264-71.

006   ———. Procedures in the Syntactic Analysis of Spoken English: A Critical Examination of the Main Procedures; Proposals for a Procedure and Method Derived from an Examination of Australian Material. M.A. thesis, University of Sydney, 1961.

007 CHURCHILL, William. *Beach-la-Mar, the Jargon or Trade-speech of the Western Pacific.* Carnegie Institution of Washington Publication No. 154. Washington, Carnegie Institution, 1911, 54 pp. //The influence of Australian English, itself a 'brutal maltreatment' of the mother tongue, p. 14.

008 CUNNINGHAM, Peter Miller. *Two Years in New South Wales. A Series of Letters . . .* London, Henry Colburn, 1827, 2 vols., xii 352, viii 346 pp. //English slang in N.S.W., Vol. II, p. 59; London mode of pronunciation, Vol. II, p. 60.

009 DELBRIDGE, Arthur. 'The Use of English in Australian Literature'. *Harvard Educational Review*, Vol. 34, 1964, pp. 306-11. //Reprinted in EMIG, J. A., FLEMING, H. T., and POPP, H. M. (eds.), *Language and Learning*, New York, 1966, pp. 275-81.

010 DIXON, James. *Narrative of a Voyage to New South Wales and Van Diemen's Land in the Ship 'Skelton' during the Year 1820.* Edinburgh, John Anderson, 1822, viii 13-148 pp. //Casual comment, 'better language', p. 46.

011 DOUGLAS, Wilfred H. 'The Aboriginal Languages of South-west Australia. Speech Forms in Current Use and a Technical Description of Njungar'. *Australian Aboriginal Studies* No. 14 (Linguistic Series No. 4). Canberra, Australian Institute of Aboriginal Studies, 1968, vii 105 iii pp. //Varieties of Aboriginal English in the southwest, pp. 8-27.

012 DUTTON, T. E. Some Phonological Aspects of Palm Island Aboriginal English: A Study of the Free Conversational Speech of Four Aboriginal Children on Palm Island Aboriginal Settlement in North Queensland. M.A. thesis, University of Queensland, 1964.

013 EAGLESON, Robert Donn. 'Australian English Under Investigation: The University of Sydney Australian Language Research Centre'. *Vestes*, Vol. 9, 1966, pp. 17-21.

014 ——. 'Bibliography of Writings on Australian English [and] Word and Phrase Index to Occasional Papers 1-10'. *Occasional Paper* No. 11, Sydney University ALRC, October 1967, 19 pp.

015 ——. 'The Domain of the Doctrine of Usage'. *AUMLA*, Vol. 25, 1966, pp. 254-9.

016 ——. 'Premeditated and Unpremeditated Speech: The Nature of the Difference'. *English Studies*, Vol. 39, 1958, pp. 145-54.

017 ELKIN, Adolphus Peter. 'Aboriginal Languages and Assimilation'. *Oceania*, Vol. 34, 1963-4, pp. 147-54.

018 ELLIOTT, Ralph Warren Victor. Reviews of:
Ramson, *Australian English, 130.*
Gunn, 'Terminology of Shearing Industry', *089-90.*
Jones, 'Outline Word Phonology', *197.*
AUMLA, Vol. 28, 1967, pp 303-5.

019 FLINT, Elwyn Henry. 'Aboriginal English: Linguistic Description as an Aid to Teaching'. *English in Australia* No. 6, 1968, pp. 3-21.

020 ——. 'The Influence of Prosodic Patterns upon the Mutual Intelligibility of Aboriginal and General Australian English'. In WURM, S. A. (ed.), *Festschrift Capell*. Linguistic Circle of Canberra Publications, Series C, Pacific Linguistics, in press.

021 ——. 'Item and Relationship Signals in Grammar-lexis Patterning'. *Proceedings of the Tenth International Congress of Linguists*, Bucharest, (in press).

022 ——. 'The Question of Language, Dialect, Idiolect and Style in Queensland English'. Linguistic Circle of Canberra Publications, *Bulletin* No. 2, 1965, pp. 1-21.

023 HARRIS, J. K. 'Linguistics and Aboriginal Education: A Practical Use of Linguistic Research in Aboriginal Education in the Northern Territory'. *Australian Territories*, Vol. 8, No. 10, 1968, pp. 24-34.

024   JERNUDD, Björn H. 'Social Change and Aboriginal Speech Variation in Australia'. *Working Papers in Linguistics* (University of Hawaii, Department of Linguistics), Issue No. 4, May 1969, pp. 145-68. //Preliminary publication only. To appear in journal of the Linguistic Society of Australia.

025   MEREDITH, Louisa Anne. *Notes and Sketches of New South Wales, during a Residence in that Colony from 1838 to 1844*. London, John Murray, 1844, xii 164 pp. //Snuffle, nasal twang, p. 50; semantic change, p. 60.

026   MITCHELL, Alexander George. 'The English Language in Australia'. *Literary Criterion* (Mysore), Vol. 6, 1964, pp. 126-40.

027   NATIONAL IDENTITY CONFERENCE. *National Identity: Literature and Language in the Commonwealth*. Brisbane, 1968. //Papers from a conference, University of Queensland, August 1968, under the auspices of Association for Commonwealth Literature and Language Studies.

028   O'GRADY, John Patrick (Nino Culotta, pseud.). *Aussie English; An Explanation of the Australian Idiom*. Sydney, Ure Smith, 1965; London, Vane, 1966, 104 pp.
       Review: Anthony BURGESS, 'Stryne Agyne', *The Listener*, 31 March 1966, p. 480.

029   PARTRIDGE, Eric Honeywood and CLARK, John W. *British and American English since 1900. With Contributions on English in Canada, South Africa, Australia, New Zealand and India*. London, Andrew Dakers, 1951, x 341 pp. //Chapter on 'Australian English' by E. H. Partridge, pp. 85-9; appendix on Australian English by A. K. Thomson.
       Reviews: E. B. ATWOOD, *American Speech*, Vol. 27, 1952, pp. 191-6.
              G. GRABAND, *Zeitschrift für Anglistik und Amerikanistik*, Vol. 1, 1953, pp. 216-20.
              R. I. McDAVID, *Studies in Linguistics*, Vol. 11, 1953, pp. 39-42.
              Randolph QUIRK, *Journal of English and Germanic Philology*, Vol. 52, 1953, pp. 280-2.
              E. ZELLNER, *Neuphilologische Zeitschrift* (Berlin and Hannover), Vol. 4, 1952, pp. 420-4.

030   PEI, Mario Andrew. *The World's Chief Languages* (i.e. *Languages for War and Peace*, 3rd ed.) London, George Allen and Unwin, 1949, 663 pp. //pp. 72-5.

031   QUINN, T. J. 'Is There a Place for Language Study?' *English in Australia* No. 6, 1968, pp. 51-64. //Linguistics and teaching of grammar, with reference to Australian schools and textbooks.

032   RAMSON, W. S. 'Australian and New Zealand English: The Present State of Studies'. *Kivung*, Vol. 2, No. 1, 1969, pp. 42-56.

033   READDY, C. A. South Queensland Aboriginal English: A Study of the Informal Conversational Speech Habits of Two Aboriginal Communities in the Area with Special Reference to Four Male Speakers of the 9-12 Age Group in the Closed Community of Cherbourg. B.A. (Hons.) thesis, University of Queensland, 1961.

034   RIDOUT, Ronald and CHRISTIE, L. H. *The Facts of English: Being a Reference Book Giving in Alphabetical Order the Literary and Linguistic Facts of the English Language as Used in Australia, and Elucidating What is Acceptable and What Unacceptable Usage*. Melbourne, Cheshire, 1963, 206 pp.

035   RUSSELL, George Harrison. 'The University of Sydney Australian Language Research Centre: An Introduction'. *Occasional Paper* No. 1, Sydney University ALRC, August 1964, 8 pp. //Includes short bibliography.

036   RYAN, John Sprott. 'Austral English and the Native Languages; Problems Confronting the Researcher'. *Zeitschrift für Mundartforschung*, Neue Folge IV, 1968, pp. 743-60.

037   SCHUCHARDT, H. 'Beitrage zur Kenntniss des englischen Kreolisch II: Melaneso-englische'. *Englische Studien*, Vol. 13, 1890, pp. 158-62.

038   SHAW, William. *The Land of Promise, or, My Impressions of Australia.* London, Simpkin, Marshall and Company, 1854. //Notes on slang, pp. 33, 49-50; London accent, p. 32.
039   TURNER, George William. *The English Language in Australia and New Zealand.* London, Longmans, 1966, xi 236 pp.
Reviews: A. DELBRIDGE, see *070.*
R. D. EAGLESON, *Notes and Queries*, NS Vol. 14, No. 1, 1967, pp. 38-9. See also *080.*
K. C. MASTERMAN, *Canberra Times,* 11 June 1966, p. 10.
W. S. RAMSON, *The Modern Language Review*, Vol. 63, 1968, pp. 697-8.
H. L. ROGERS, 'The Anzac Tongue?' *Australian Book Review*, Vol. 5, 1966, p. 199.
TIMES LITERARY SUPPLEMENT, 23 June 1966, p. 553.
R. W. ZANDVOORT, *Lingua*, Vol. 18, 1967, pp. 216-18.
040   WAKEFIELD, Edward Gibbon. *A Letter from Sydney, the Principal Town of Australasia,* ed. R. Gouger. *Together with the Outline of a System of Colonization.* London, Joseph Cross, 1829, x 222 xxiv pp.; London, J. M. Dent, 1929 (Everyman's Library), 256 pp. //'Corruption' of the language brought to Australia, p. 51.
041   WARD, Harvey E. *Down Under Without Blunder; Guide to the English Spoken in Australia with a Random Sample of Australian Words and Phrases and Translations of Some Australian Pronunciations.* Melbourne, Paul Flesch, 1967; Rutland, Vt., C. E. Tuttle, 1967, 59 pp.
042   WARD, Russel Braddock. *The Australian Legend.* Melbourne, Oxford University Press, 1958, x 262 pp.
043   WURM, S. A. 'Some Remarks on the Role of Language in the Assimilation of Australian Aborigines'. Linguistic Circle of Canberra, Series A, *Occasional Paper* No. 1, 1963, ii 12 pp.

II LEXICON

044   ACKROYD, J. 'Lingo-Jingo'. *Southerly*, Vol. 7, 1946, pp. 97-103. //Review of Baker, *052.*
045   ACLAND, L. G. D. 'A Sheep Station Glossary'. *The Press,* Christchurch, 1933; and in Acland, *The Early Canterbury Runs*, ed. A. Wall, Christchurch, 1951.
046   *ALL THE YEAR ROUND.* 'Australian Colloquialisms'. London, 30 July 1887, pp. 64-8. //Unsigned vocabulary.
047   AUSTRALIAN COUNCIL FOR EDUCATIONAL RESEARCH. 'A Speech Vocabulary of Australian Pre-school Children'. *ACER Information Bulletin,* Vol. 23, 1951.
048   A.W.G. 'Australianisms and their Origin'. *Lone Hand*, Vol. 4, 1908-9, pp. 114-16.
049   BAKER, Sidney John. *Australia Speaks. A Supplement to 'The Australian Language'.* Sydney, Shakespeare Head Press, 1953, 336 pp.
Review: R. G. HOWARTH, *Southerly*, Vol. 16, 1955, p. 228.
050   ——. 'Australian English'. *Australian Encyclopaedia*, 1958.
051   ——. 'Australian English'. Introductory Essay, *Standard Dictionary*, Funk and Wagnall's, 1965.
052   ——. *The Australian Language. An Examination of the English Language as Used in Australia, from Convict Days to the Present, with Special Reference to the Growth of Indigenous Idiom and its Use by Australian Writers.* Sydney, Angus and Robertson, 1945, xii + 425 pp.
Reviews: J. ACKROYD, see *044.*
A. CLUNIES ROSS, *Australian Quarterly*, Vol. 17, 1945, pp. 123-5.
R. I. McDAVID, *Studies in Linguistics*, Vol. 9, 1951, pp. 13-17.

R. J. MENNER, *American Speech*, Vol. 21, 1946, pp. 120-2.
N. PALMER and B. ELLIOTT, see *122*.
R. E. SPILLER, *Saturday Review of Literature*, Vol. 29, No. 3, 19 January 1946, p. 12.
R. M. WILSON, *Year's Work in English Studies*, Vol. 27, 1946, pp. 56-7.
R. W. ZANDVOORT, *Erasmus*, Vol. 2, 1948-9, pp. 335-7.

053 ———. *The Australian Language*. . . . Sydney, Currawong, 2nd ed., 1966, xiv + 517 pp.
Reviews: *AGE*, 8 October 1966, p. 22.
A. BURGESS, *Australian Book Review*, Vol. 5, 1966, pp. 215-16.
A. DELBRIDGE, see *070*.
THE ECONOMIST, 31 December 1966, p. 1400.
G. H. JOHNSTON, 'Something Personal—Words and Idioms of Australia'. *Sydney Morning Herald*, 20 August 1966, p. 19.
W. S. RAMSON, *Canberra Times*, 20 August 1966, p. 11.
TIMES LITERARY SUPPLEMENT, 14 November 1967, p. 1075.

054 ———. 'Australian Slang'. *Encyclopaedia Britannica*, 1950.

055 ———. A Dictionary of Australian Flora and Fauna. Typescript, Mitchell Library, Sydney, 1950.

056 ———. *The Drum. Australian Character and Slang*. Sydney, Currawong, 1959; reissue, Sydney, Angus and Robertson, 1960, 158 pp.
Review: A: DELBRIDGE, see *060*.

057 ———. 'The Influence of American Slang on Australia'. *American Speech*, Vol. 18, 1943, pp. 253-6.

058 ———. 'Language'. Pp. 102-30 in McLEOD, Alan Lindsay, *The Pattern of Australian Culture*. Ithaca N.Y., Cornell University Press, 1963, x + 486 pp.

059 ———. 'Language'. *Reader's Digest Great Encyclopaedic Dictionary*, Sydney, 1965, Vol. III.

060 ———. 'Language and Character'. Pp. 175-9 in HUNGERFORD, T. A. G. (ed.), *Australian Signpost: An Anthology*. Melbourne, F. W. Cheshire, 1956, xi + 308 pp. Reprinted in HESELTINE, H. P. (ed.), *Australian Idiom: An Anthology of Contemporary Prose and Poetry*. Melbourne, Angus and Robertson, 1963, xiii + 305 pp.; and in BAKER, S. J., *The Drum, 056*.

061 ———. *A Popular Dictionary of Australian Slang*. Melbourne, Roberston and Mullens, 1941, 91 pp.

062 BERNARD, John Rupert Lyon-Bowes. 'The Need for a Dictionary of Australian English'. *Southerly*, Vol. 22, 1962, pp. 92-100.

063 BRITTON, J. H. An Investigation into the Source Materials of the Australian Additions to the English Language. M.A. thesis, University of Sydney, 1938.

064 COLLINS, David. *An Account of the English Colony in New South Wales*. London, T. Cadell, jun. and W. Davies, 1798, xx + xxxviii + 618 pp. Suppl. vol. 1802; rev. ed. (abridged, ed. Mrs Collins) 1804; ed. J. Collier, Christchurch, Whitcombe and Tombs, 1910, 450 pp. //Port Jackson pidgin: I, 544.

065 COOKE, Elizabeth A., MacCALLUM, Susan E., and EAGLESON, R. D. 'Early Goldmining Terms and Popular Collocations'. *Occasional Paper* No. 10, Sydney University ALRC, December 1966, 27 pp.

066 ———. 'Fresh Evidence from Early Goldmining Publications 1851-1860'. *Occasional Paper* No. 9, Sydney University ALRC, October 1966, 28 pp.

067 CROWE, Cornelius. *The Australian Slang Dictionary, Containing the Words and Phrases of the Thieving Fraternity. Together with the Unauthorised, though Popular Expressions Now in Vogue with all Classes in Australia*. Fitzroy, Melbourne, Robert Barr, 1895, [vi] + 104 pp.
Review: *BULLETIN*, 17 August 1895. See also Baker, *053*, p. 16; Ramson, *130*, pp. 13-14.

068   *DAILY TELEGRAPH.* 'Australia Needs More Slang'. Sydney, 14 July 1936, p. 6.
069   DELBRIDGE, Arthur. 'Beating the Drum'. *Southerly*, Vol. 21, 1961, pp. 50-1. //Review of Baker, *The Drum, 056.*
070   ——. Reviews of:
        Baker, *Australian Language, 053.*
        Ramson, *Australian English, 130.*
        Turner, *English Language, 039.*
        Australian Literary Studies, Vol. 2, 1966, pp. 300-4.
071   DOWNING, W. H. *Digger Dialects. A Collection of Slang Phrases Used by the Australian Soldiers on Active Service.* Melbourne, Lothian Book Publishing Company, 1919, 60 pp.
072   DOYLE, Brian K. 'List of Current Underworld Argot'. *Australian Police Journal*, 1950.
073   EAGLESON, Robert Donn. 'Australianisms in Early Migrant Handbooks, 1788-1826'. *Occasional Paper* No. 2, Sydney University ALRC, October 1964, 16 pp.
074   ——. 'Australianisms in Early Migrant Handbooks, 1827-1830'. *Occasional Paper* No. 4, Sydney University ALRC, February 1965, 16 pp.
075   ——. 'Contemporary Evidence of the Connexion Between Word and Meaning'. *Notes and Queries*, NS Vol. 11, 1964, pp. 70-1.
076   ——. 'Convict Jargon and Euphemism'. *Australian Literary Studies*, Vol. 2, 1965, pp. 141-6. //See also Gunson, *091,* and Ramson, *135.*
077   ——. 'In Pursuit of Australian English'. *The Australian Highway*, Vol. 47, 1967, pp. 2-5. //The necessity for investigating the Australian English lexicon.
078   ——. 'Naming a Currency: A Study of Contemporary Methods of Word Creation'. *Southerly*, Vol. 23, 1963, pp. 264-70.
079   ——. 'The Nature and Study of Australian English'. *Journal of English Linguistics*, Vol. 1, 1967, pp. 11-24.
080   ——. 'The Ramifications of Australian and New Zealand English'. *Southerly*, Vol. 26, 1966, pp. 199-208. //Reviewing Ramson, *130*, and Turner, *039.*
081   —— and McKIE, Ian. 'The Terminology of Australian National Football'. Part I: A-C. *Occasional Paper* No. 12, Sydney University ALRC, June 1968, 24 pp.
082   —— and ——. 'The Terminology of Australian National Football'. Part II: D-O. *Occasional Paper* No. 13, Sydney University ALRC, September 1968, 27 pp.
083   ——. 'The Terminology of Australian National Football'. Part III: P-Z. *Occasional Paper* No. 14, Sydney University ALRC, January 1969, 26 pp.
084   EHRENSPERGER, C. 'Australianisms'. *Taalstudie* (Te Kuilenburg), Vol. 9, 1888.
085   FULLERTON, M. E. (Turner O. Lingo, pseud.). *Australian Comic Dictionary of Words and Phrases.* Sydney, 1916.
086   GARTH, J. W. 'Some Australian Slang'. *Australian Magazine*, November 1908, pp. 1249-52.
087   GREENWAY, John. 'Australian Cattle Lingo'. *American Speech*, Vol. 33, 1958, pp. 163-9.
088   GUNN, John Samuel. 'Can the Folk-song Enthusiast Help Language Research?' *Australian Tradition*, Vol. 1, No. 4, 1964, p. 6.
089   ——. 'The Terminology of the Shearing Industry'. Part I: A-L. *Occasional Paper* No. 5, Sydney University ALRC, April 1965, 36 pp.
090   ——. 'The Terminology of the Shearing Industry'. Part II: M-Z. *Occasional Paper* No. 6, Sydney University ALRC, June 1965, 40 pp. Review: R. W. V. ELLIOTT, see *018.*
091   GUNSON, Neil. '*Bushranger* and *Croppy*: A Footnote to "Convict Jargon and Euphemism".' *Australian Literary Studies*, Vol. 2, 1966, pp. 214-16. //See Eagleson, *076*, and Ramson, *135.*

092 HARDER, Kelsie B. 'Is *Finalise* [*-ize*] an Australian Coinage?' *American Speech*, Vol. 36, 1961, p. 239.
093 HARRISON, Tom. 'People: Wowsers'. *New Statesman and Nation*, 23 November 1946, p. 375. //Note on *wowser* and compounds.
094 HESLING, Bernard. 'Youse and Non-youse'. *Quadrant*, Vol. 1, No. 3, 1957, pp. 53-8.
095 HICKS, W. 'Australian Slang'. *Life*, 18 April 1952, pp. 15-17.
096 HODGSON, Christopher Pemberton. *Reminiscences of Australia, With Hints on the Squatter's Life*. London, W. N. Wright, 1846, [viii] + 368 pp. //Comments on Australian vocabulary.
097 HOLDEN, W. S. '*Bloody* in Australia'. *American Speech*, Vol. 35, 1960, pp. 236-7; cf. Baker, *053*, pp. 197-8.
098 HOWARTH, Robert Guy. 'The Great Australian Adjective'. *Southerly*, Vol. 8, 1947, pp. 34-6.
099 HOWITT, William. *Land, Labour and Gold; or Two Years in Victoria*. London, Longmans, Brown, Green and Longmans, 1855, 2 vols., xvi + 414, xii + 398 pp. //Comments throughout on vocabulary and swearing.
100 IREDALE, T. and TROUGHTON, Ellis. 'Captain Cook's Kangaroo'. *Australian Zoologist*, Vol. 7, 1925, pp. 311-16.
101 JOHNSTON, George Henry. 'This War is Evolving New Army Slang'. *Argus*, 15 November 1941.
102 JOHNSTON, Grahame. 'The Language of Australian Literature'. *Australian Literary Studies*, Vol. 3, 1967, pp. 18-27.
103 JOHNSTON, M. 'Aussie Dictionary'. *Aussie*, 18 January 1918, pp. 10-11.
104 LAKE, J. *A Dictionary of Australian Words*. Springfield, Mass., G. and C. Merriam, 1898. //Australasian supplement to *Webster's International Dictionary*.
105 LENTZNER, Karl. 'Australisches Englisch'. *Englische Studien*, Vol. 11, 1888, pp. 173-4.
106 ——. *Australisches Englisch*. Heilbronn, 1888. //Not seen. Refer to Ferguson, *Bibliography of Australia*, entry no. 11579.
107 ——. *Colonial English: A Glossary of Australian, Anglo-Indian, Pidgin English, West Indian, and South African Words*. London, Kegan Paul, Trench, Trubner and Company, 1891, xii + [iv] + 238 pp.
Identical edition: *Dictionary of the Slang-English of Australia and of Some Mixed Languages*. London and Halle-Leipzig, Ehrhardt Karras, 1892, xii + [iv] + 238 pp.
Review: W. SATTLER, *Englische Studien*, Vol. 16, 1892, p. 416; see also Ramson, *130*, pp. 14-16.
108 McKNIGHT, George Harley. *English Words and Their Background*. New York, D. Appleton and Company, 1923, x + 449 pp. //Comments on differences between Australian and American English.
109 MARJORIBANKS, Alexander. *Travels in New South Wales*. London, Smith, Elder and Company, 1847, viii + 268 pp. //Investigations of Australian swearing, pp. 57-8. See Ramson, *130*, pp. 36-7.
110 MAURER, David W. ' "Australian" Rhyming Argot in the American Underworld'. *American Speech*, Vol. 19, 1944, pp. 183-95. //An account of rhyming argot referred to as Australian by American criminals. In collaboration with S. J. Baker.
111 MENCKEN, Henry Louis. *The American Language; An Inquiry into the Development of English in the United States*. New York, Knopf, 1919, x + 374 pp.; New York, Knopf, 4th ed., 1963 (rev. Raven I. McDavid, jun.), xxv + 777 + cxxiv pp. //Ramson, *130*, p. 26: 'Brief notes on the character and affiliations of Australian English, (p. 378, 1919 ed.)'.
112 MITCHELL, Alexander George. 'Fighting Words!' *Salt*, 22 December 1941, pp. 34-6.

113   ——. 'A Glossary of War-Words'. *Southerly*, Vol. 3, No. 1, 1942, pp. 11-16.
114   ——. 'A Supplement of Australian and New Zealand Words'. In *Chamber's Shorter English Dictionary*. Australian ed., Sydney, 1952.
115   MORRIS, Edward Ellis. *Austral English, a Dictionary of Australasian Words, Phrases and Usages, With Those Aboriginal Australian and Maori Words which Have Become Incorporated in the Language and the Commoner Scientific Words that Have Had Their Origin in Australia*. London, MacMillan, 1898, xxiv + 526 pp.; republ. Detroit, Gale Research Co., 1968, xxiv + 526 pp.
       Reviews: *AUSTRALASIAN*, 22 January 1898, p. 217.
       BULLETIN, Red Page review, 18 December 1897.
       N. PALMER, see *121*.
       H. A. STRONG, 'Austral English and Slang', *University Extension Journal* (London), Vol. 3, 1898, p. 23.
       A. E. H. SWAEN, *Englische Studien*, Vol. 26, 1899, pp. 111-12.
       SYDNEY MORNING HERALD, 1 January 1898, p. 5.
       See also Baker, *053*, pp. 5, 16-18, and Ramson, *130*, pp. 16-19.
116   MORRISON, Hugh. 'Australian *Callithumpians*'. *American Speech*, Vol. 30, 1955, pp. 153-4.
117   *NEW YORK TIMES MAGAZINE*. 'Aussies' Own Talk'. 22 March 1942, p. 38.
118   ——. 'Slang Down Under'. 7 January 1943, p. 31.
119   O'BRIEN, S. E. and STEPHENS, A. G. Material for a Dictionary of Australian Slang, 1900-10. Typescript, Mitchell Library, Sydney.
120   O'MEARA, D. 'Australian *Cobber*'. *American Speech*, Vol. 21, 1946, p. 273.
121   PALMER, NETTIE. *Talking It Over*. Sydney, Angus and Robertson, 1932, [viii] + 154 pp. //Chapter, 'Austral English', pp. 38-43, discusses Morris, *115*.
122   —— and ELLIOTT, Brian. Review of Baker, *052*. *Meanjin*, Vol. 4, 1945, pp. 186-92.
123   PARTRIDGE, Eric Honeywood. *A Charm of Words: Essays and Papers on Language*. London, Hamish Hamilton, 1960, 190 pp. //Chapter on Australian English, pp. 113-31.
       Review: A. G. MITCHELL, *Meanjin*, Vol. 21, No. 2 (89), 1962, pp. 243-7.
124   ——. *Slang Today and Yesterday. With a Short Historical Sketch and Vocabularies of English, American and Australian Slang*. London, Routledge, 1933; 2nd ed., 1935; 3rd rev. ed., 1950, ix + 476 pp.
125   ——. 'Their Language'. Pp. 212-23 in BEVAN, Ian (ed.), *The Sunburnt Country: Profile of Australia*. London, Collins, 1953, 256 pp.
126   QUINN, J. 'Diggers Add to Dictionary'. *Sun* (Sydney), 26 August 1942.
127   RAMSON, William Stanley. 'Aboriginal Words in Early Australian English'. *Southerly*, Vol. 24, 1964, pp. 50-60.
128   ——. 'Australian Aboriginal Words in the OED'. *Notes and Queries*, NS Vol. 11, No. 2, 1964, pp. 69-70.
129   ——. *Australian English*. Canberra, A.N.U., 1965, 26 pp. //Commonwealth Literary Fund Lecture, A.N.U., 1964. Bound with G. A. Wilkes, *The Literary Career of J. F. Mortlock*.
130   ——. *Australian English. An Historical Study of the Vocabulary, 1788-1898*. Canberra, Australian National University Press, 1966, x + 195 pp.
       Reviews: N. DAVIS, *Notes and Queries*, NS Vol. 14, 1967, p. 279.
       A. DELBRIDGE, see *070*.
       R. D. EAGLESON, 'Early Strine'. *Australian Book Review*, Vol. 5, 1966, p. 181. See also *080*.
       A. P. ELKIN, *Oceania*, Vol. 37, 1966-7, pp. 318-19.
       R. W. V. ELLIOTT, see *018*.
       SCRUTARIUS, *Walkabout*, October 1966, p. 47.
       TIMES LITERARY SUPPLEMENT, 16 November 1967, p. 1075.

131 ——. 'A Critical Review of Writings on the Vocabulary of Nineteenth-century Australian English'. *Australian Literary Studies*, Vol. 1, 1963, pp. 89-103.
132 ——. 'The Currency of Aboriginal Words in Australian English'. *Occasional Paper* No. 3, Sydney University ALRC, December 1964, 16 pp.
133 ——. 'Early Australian English'. *Australian Quarterly*, Vol. 35, No. 3, 1963, pp. 50-8.
134 ——. 'Early Australian English: The Vocabulary of an Emigrant Mechanic'. I.e. Alexander Harris, author of *Settlers and Convicts*. *Southerly*, Vol. 25, 1965, pp. 116-30.
135 ——. 'Early Evidence for *Bushranger* and *Croppy*'. *Australian Literary Studies*, Vol. 2, 1966, pp. 295-8. //See also Eagleson, *076*, and Gunson, *091*.
136 ——. 'The English Language in Australia'. *The Teaching of English*, Vol. 13, 1968, pp. 49-63.
137 ——. An Historical Study of the Australian English Vocabulary. Ph.D. dissertation, University of Sydney, 1963.
138 ——. 'Primary Sources for the Study of the Vocabulary of Nineteenth Century Australian English'. *Australian Literary Studies*, Vol. 1, 1964, pp. 251-9.
139 ROTARIAN. 'Cooee This is Fair Dinkum'. June 1946, p. 36. //Unsigned article on 'curiosities of Australian English'.
140 RUDSKOGER, Arne. 'A Note on the Use of *She* for Inanimate Things in Australian'. *Moderna Språk*, Vol. 49, 1955, pp. 264-5.
141 RYAN, John Sprott. 'Isolation and Generation Within a Conservative Framework. A Unique Dialectal Situation for English'. *Orbis*, Vol. 15, 1966, pp. 35-50. //Vocabulary of Australian English, 1788-1850.
142 SCHONELL, Fred Joyce, MEDDLETON, I. C., SHAW, B. A., et al. *A Study of the Oral Vocabulary of Adults: An Investigation into the Speech Vocabulary of the Australian Worker*. Research Study No. 1, Faculty of Education, University of Queensland. Brisbane, University of Queensland Press, 1956; London, University of London Press, 1956, 176 pp.
143 SHARWOOD, John A. and GERSON, Stanley Harold. 'The Vocabulary of Australian English'. *Moderna Språk*, Vol. 51, 1963, pp. 2-10.
144 SHAY, Jack (pseud.). 'On Australian Slang'. *Bulletin*, Red Page, 17 December 1898.
145 STEVANS, C. M. (ed.). 'Supplement of Australasian Words'. *World's Standard Dictionary*. Australian ed., Auckland, 1915.
146 SYDNEY *Slang Dictionary: Comprising All the Slang Words and Phrases in Use in Sydney and in the Shadows of Life. Sporting, Stage, and Gambling Slang, Low Life and Flash Slang, &C. Together with Examples of Slang Phraseology, Showing How Hidden Conversation is Carried On . . . New Edition—Several Thousand New Words Added*. At head of title: 'The Detective's Handbook'. Bound with two articles on prostitution. Sydney, H. J. Franklin, [c. 1882], 16 pp. //See Ramson, *130*, p. 13.
147 TENCH, Watkin. *A Complete Account of the Settlement at Port Jackson in New South Wales, Including an Accurate Description of the Situation of the Colony; of the Natives; and of its Natural Productions*. London, G. Nicol, 1793, xvi + 212 pp.
148 VAUX, James Hardy. *The Memoirs of James Hardy Vaux Including a New and Comprehensive Vocabulary of the Flash Language*, ed. B. Field, London, W. Clowes, 1819, 2 vols., 248, viii + 228 pp.; ed. N. McLachlan, London, Heinemann, 1964, 315 pp.
149 WAUGH, David Lindsay. *Three Years Practical Experience of a Settler in New South Wales, 1834-7*. Edinburgh, John Johnstone, 1838, 74 pp. //Comments throughout on Australian vocabulary and slang. See p. 33.

III PHONETICS AND PHONOLOGY

150   A.B.C. WEEKLY. Varied comments and letters. 19-26 September 1942. //Includes comments by R. G. Menzies on 'the flat Australian voice'.
151   ADAMS, Corinne. The Intonation of Question and Answer in Australian Speech. M.A. thesis, University of Sydney, 1967, v + 270 pp.
152   AUSTRALIA. Commonwealth Office of Education. 'Sound Advice'. *English: A New Language*, Vol. 9, No. 2, February 1963, 31 pp. //Problems of English sounds in TEFL.
153   BAEYERTZ, C. N. Article on 'Errors'. *Sunday Morning Sun*, 23 June 1940.
154   BAKER, Sidney John. *Australian Pronunciation: A Guide to Good Speech*. Sydney, Angus and Robertson, 1947, 54 pp.
   Reviews: R. I. McDAVID, *Studies in Linguistics*, Vol. 6, 1948, pp. 46-7.
      H. M. SYMONDS, 'Standard Australian?', *Southerly*, Vol. 9, 1948, pp. 51-4.
155   ———. 'Pronunciation, Australian'. *Australian Encyclopaedia*, 1958.
156   BENNETT, George. *Wanderings in N.S.W., Batavia, Pedir Coast Singapore, and China.* . . . London, Richard Bentley, 1834, 2 vols., xvi + 440; viii + 428 pp. //Casual comment on 'very pure' accent, Vol. I, p. 331.
157   BERNARD, John Rupert Lyon-Bowes. 'An Extra Phoneme of Australian English'. *AUMLA*, Vol. 20, 1963, pp. 346-52.
158   ———. 'Australian Pronunciations and Australian Attitudes'. *Teaching of English* No. 15, October 1969, pp. 4-17.
159   ———. 'Length and the Identification of Australian English Vowels'. *AUMLA*, Vol. 27, 1967, pp. 37-58.
160   ———. 'On Nuclear Component Durations'. *Language and Speech*, in press.
161   ———. 'On the Uniformity of Australian English'. *Orbis*, Vol. 18, September 1969.
162   ———. 'Rates of Utterance in Australian Dialect Groups'. *Occasional Paper* No. 7, Sydney University ALRC, August 1965, 20 pp.
163   ———. Some Measurements of Some Sounds of Australian English. Ph.D. dissertation, University of Sydney, 1967, 920 pp.
164   ———. 'Towards the Acoustic Specifications of Australian English'. *Zeitschrift für Phonetik, Sprachwissenschaft und Kommunikationsforschung*, in press.
165   BOARD, Ruby W. *Australian Pronunciation. A Handbook for the Teaching of English in Australia*. Sydney Teachers' College Press, 1927, [v] + 6-31 pp. //Introduction, 'Australian dialect is drifting from . . . the best speech'.
166   BRADISH, C. R. 'The Australian Vernacular'. *American Mercury*, July 1954, pp. 72-4.
167   BULLARD, Audrey May and LINDSAY, Edith Dulce. *Speech at Work*. Sydney, Longmans Green, 1952, xii + 180 pp. //Manual in speech training for teachers in Australian schools.
   Review: J. A. McCALLUM, 'Australian Speech', *Southerly*, Vol. 15, 1954, pp. 191-3.
168   BURGESS, Oliver Neil. 'Extra Phonemes in Australian English: A Further Contribution'. *AUMLA*, Vol. 30, 1968, pp. 180-7.
169   ———. 'A Spectrographic Investigation of some Australian Vowel Sounds'. *Language and Speech*, Vol. 11, 1968, pp. 129-37.
170   COCHRANE, George Robert. 'The Australian English Vowels as a Diasystem'. *Word*, Vol. 15, 1959, pp. 67-88.
171   ———. 'loŋ [æ] in ostreiljən iŋgliʃ'. *Maître Phonétique* No. 124, July-December 1965, pp. 22-6.
172   ———. 'The Perception of Short Segments from Some Australian English Vowels'. *Zeitschrift für Phonetik, Sprachwissenschaft und Kommunikationsforschung*, Vol. 20, Nos. 1/2, 1967, pp. 81-8.

173 DELBRIDGE, Arthur. 'The Australian Accent'. *Hemisphere*, Vol. 7, 1963, pp. 14-16.
174 ——. 'The Australian Accent and Articulatory Merit'. *English in Australia* No. 4, 1967, pp. 20-6. See also entries *214, 215*.
175 DINNING, Hector William. *The Australian Scene*. Sydney, Angus and Robertson, 1939, xi + 225 pp. //The non-Cockney nature of Australian speech.
176 DORSCH, Theodor Siegfried. 'The Australian Accent'. In KEVIN, J. C. G., *Some Australians Take Stock*. London, Longmans, 1939, ix + 240 pp.
177 FLINT, Elwyn Henry. 'Intra-syllabic Pitch Movement in Communicative Australian English Utterance Morphemes'. *Proceedings of the Sixth International Congress on Phonetic Sciences*, Prague, in press.
178 FOWLER, Frank. *Southern Lights and Shadows; Being Brief Notes of Three Years' Experience of Social, Literary, and Political Life in Australia*. London, Sampson Low and Son, 1859, [iv] + 132 pp. //A lisp and sniffle in Australian speech, p. 38. See also Horne, *193*.
179 FRASER, John Foster. *Australia, The Making of a Nation*. London, Cassell & Co., 1910, xix + 299 pp. //Denies Cockney nature of Australian English, pp. 43-5.
180 FROUDE, James Anthony. *Oceana, or England and Her Colonies*. London, Longmans; New York, Charles Scribner's Sons, 1886, xii + 396 pp. //Pp. 84-5, the purity of Australian speech; its intonation is British, not American.
181 GARNSEY, Edward R. (Edward Kinglake, pseud.). *The Australian at Home. Notes ... Anecdotes ... Useful Hints, etc*. London, Leadenhall Press, 1891, 160 pp. //The colonial accent and Cockney twang.
182 GERSTAECKER, Friedrich. *Narrative of a Journey Round the World*. London, Hurst and Blackett, 1853, 3 vols., viii + 360, iv + 344, iv + 352 pp. //Irish brogue and Cockney dialect, Vol. II, p. 269.
183 GRAHAM, J. D. Consonant Phonemes in Brisbane English; An Auditory and Instrumental Study. M.A. thesis, University of Queensland, 1965.
184 GRIFFIN, David. 'Australian Accent'. (Letter) in *Sydney Morning Herald*, 17 August 1946, p. 2. //Accompanying editorial. Also further correspondence, 15 August (W.McF.), 19 August (W.J.C.), and 27 August (John W. Perry).
185 GUNN, John Samuel. 'The Influence of Background on the Speech of Teachers' College Students'. *Forum of Education*, Vol. 22, No. 1, 1963, pp. 18-41.
186 HANLEY, Theodore D. and ANDREWS, Moya Landsberg. 'Some Acoustic Differences Between Educated Australian and General American Dialects'. *Phonetica*, Vol. 17, 1967, pp. 241-50. //Duration characteristics.
187 HARDCASTLE, William John. Stress in Australian English. M.A. thesis, University of Queensland, 1968.
188 HARWOOD, Frank William. 'Quantitative Study of the Speech of Australian Children'. *Language and Speech*, Vol. 2, 1959, pp. 236-72.
189 HILL, Robert P. Early Australian Pronunciation—The Value of Manuscript Evidence. M.A. thesis, University of Sydney, 1967.
190 ——. English in Australia; A Survey of Some of the Manuscript Material in the Mitchell Library, Sydney. B.A. thesis, University of Sydney, 1957.
191 ——. 'Prospects of the Study of Early Australian Pronunciation'. *English Studies*, Vol. 48, 1967, pp. 43-52.
192 HOPE, Alec Derwent. 'Australian Speech'. *Southerly*, Vol. 7, 1946, pp. 241-3. //Review of Mitchell, *212*.
193 HORNE, Richard Henry (Hengist). *Australian Facts and Prospects*. London, Smith, Elder and Company, 1859, xii + 258 pp. //Reply to Fowler, *178*, on the sniffle in Australian speech, p. 67.

A Bibliography of Australian English

194   JAMES, George Lacon. *Shall I try Australia? or, Health, Pleasure and Business in New South Wales, etc.* Liverpool, E. Howell, 1892, iv + 290 pp. //Correctness of Australian English apart from '*ai* diphthong'.

195   JERNUDD, Björn H. 'A Listener Experiment: Variants of Australian English'. *Kivung*, Vol. 2, 1969, pp. 19-29.

196   JONES, Alexander Idrisyn. 'Australian Accent'. *Balcony, The Sydney Review* No. 3, Spring 1965, pp. 11-14. //Comment on Afferbeck Lauder, *Let Stalk Strine*, and Mitchell and Delbridge, *214*.

197   ———. 'An Outline Word Phonology of Australian English'. *Occasional Paper* No. 8, Sydney University ALRC, July 1966, 18 pp.
Review: see Elliott, *018*.

198   ———. *Phonetics: A Phonological Introduction.* University of Sydney, n.d. [126] pp.

199   ———. A Phonological-lexical Study of the Distribution of the Sounds [æ] and [æ:] in the Speech of Secondary School Children in New South Wales. M.A. thesis, University of Sydney, 1966, ix + 185 pp.

200   ———. 'Sydney Australian—A Seven Vowel System'. *Studies in Linguistics*, Vol. 18, Nos. 1-4, 1964-6, pp. 29-35.

201   LAYCOCK, Donald C. 'lɔŋ "ʃoht" vawlz in *əstrəljən* iŋgliʃ'. *Maître Phonétique* No. 126, July 1966, pp. 22-3.

202   McBURNEY, Samuel. 'Australasian South Eastern—A Comparative Table of Australasian Pronunciation'. Pp. 236-48 in ELLIS, A. J., *On early English pronunciation*, Vol. V (The existing phonology of English dialects compared with that of West Saxon speech). London, Early English Text Society, 1887.

203   ———. 'Colonial Pronunciation'. *The Press* (New Zealand), 5 October 1887. //See Turner, *228*.

204   McGUIRE, Dominic Paul. *Australian Journey*. London, Heinemann, 1939, xii + 396 pp. //Comments on regional differences in Australian speech, p. 47.

205   MARSHALL, Alexander James. *Australia Limited*. Sydney, Angus and Robertson, 1942, 118 pp. //Comments on non-Cockney nature of Australian accent. Quoted by Baker, *053*, p. 435.

206   MITCHELL, Alexander George. 'Australian English'. *Australian Quarterly*, Vol. 23, 1951, pp. 9-17. //Also subsequent correspondence: Vol. 23, 1951, pp. 115-16, objections, John McCallum; Vol. 24, 1952, pp. 77-81, reply, A.G.M.

207   ———. 'The Australian Accent'. *Quadrant*, Vol. 3, No. 1, 1958-9, pp. 63-70.

208   ———. 'The Australian Accent'. An address delivered to the Australian Humanities Research Council at its Fifth Annual General Meeting, Canberra, 8 November 1960. AHRC, *Fifth Annual Report*, Adelaide, 1961.

209   ———. 'Australian English'. *Southerly*, Vol. 1, No. 3, 1940, pp. 11-13.

210   ———. 'Australian English'. *Southerly*, Vol. 2, No. 1, 1941, pp. 35-7. //Letter to the Editor, in reply to 'reviewers of the pamphlet on Australian pronunciation, published by the [English] Association'.

211   ———. *The Pronunciation of English in Australia*. Lecture privately printed for members of the Australian English Association. April 1940.
Reviews: *BULLETIN*, Red Page, 11 September 1940.
      J. CLUNIES ROSS, *Australian Quarterly*, Vol. 12, 1940, pp. 114-15.

212   ———. *The Pronunciation of English in Australia*. Sydney, Angus and Robertson, 1946, 80 pp.
Reviews: A. D. HOPE, see *192*.
      A. L. McLEOD, *Quarterly Journal of Speech*, Vol. 42, 1956, pp. 207-8.

213   ———. *Spoken English*. London, Macmillan, 1957, [iv] + 238 pp.

214   ——— and DELBRIDGE, Arthur. *The Pronunciation of English in Australia*. Sydney, Angus and Robertson, rev. ed., 1965, xiv + 81 pp.
Review: see Jones, *196*.

215 —— and ——. *The Speech of Australian Adolescents*. Sydney, Angus and Robertson, 1965, xi + 99 pp.; + 7" 33⅓ rpm record.
216 MORRISBY, Edwin S. 'The Australian Accent'. *Manchester Guardian Weekly*, 12 February 1959, p. 7. //The effect of climate on lip-aperture.
217 MOSSMAN, Samuel. *The Gold Regions of Australia; A Descriptive Account of New South Wales, Victoria, and South Australia*. London, William S. Orr and Company, 1852, viii + [9]-194 pp. // 'Cockney drawl', p. 19.
218 NEW SOUTH WALES, Department of Education. Standing Advisory Speech Committee. *Speech Education. A Handbook for Secondary School Teachers*. Sydney, c. 1958, 121 pp.
219 NEW SOUTH WALES. Legislative Assembly. *Votes and Proceedings of the Legislative Assembly During the Session of 1856-7, Vol. II*. Education. Final report from the School Commissioners, 6 December 1855, Section 29. //'Vicious pronunciation'.
220 PEAR, Tom Hatherley. *Personality, Appearance and Speech*. London, Allen and Unwin, 1957, 167 pp. //Chapter on 'Australian English', pp. 106-8.
221 PLATT, H. A Comparative Study of the Phonetics of Australian English and German. M.A. thesis, Monash University, 1968.
222 RANSLEY, T. H. Problems of Speech in Spoken English in Our Schools. M.Ed. thesis, University of Sydney, 1950.
223 ROBERTSON, Margaret Anne. The Intelligibility of Australian English Vowels. M.A. thesis, Macquarie University, 1969, 426 pp.
224 SANSOM, Clive. 'Australian Speech'. *Quarterly Journal of Speech*, Vol. 39, 1953, pp. 470-6; *Speech News*, Vol. 105, 1951, pp. 2-5.
225 SHARWOOD, John A. and HORTON, Ivor. 'Phoneme Frequencies in Australian English: A Regional Study'. *AUMLA*, Vol. 26, 1966, pp. 272-302.
226 TRUEBLOOD, Thomas C. 'The Spoken English of Australasia'. *Quarterly Journal of Speech Education*, Vol. 6, No. 2, April 1920.
227 TURNER, George William. 'On the Origin of Australian Vowel Sounds'. *AUMLA*, Vol. 13, 1960, pp. 33-45.
228 ——. 'Samuel McBurney's Newspaper Article on Colonial Pronunciation'. *AUMLA*, Vol. 27, 1967, pp. 81-5. //See McBurney, 203.
229 WEAVER, L. A. The Significance of Speech Education in a Teachers' Training College. M.Ed. thesis, University of Sydney, 1954, vi + 292 + xxii pp. //Includes comments on Australian situations, and a survey of Wagga Wagga college students.
230 WOOD, Thomas. *Cobbers. A Personal Record of a Journey from Essex, in England, to Australia, Tasmania and Some of the Reefs and Islands in the Coral Sea, Made in the Years 1930, 1931 and 1932*. London, Oxford University Press, 1934, xiii + 256 pp. //Glossary. Comments on the non-Cockney nature of Australian English, p. 176.

IV MIGRANT VARIETIES OF AUSTRALIAN ENGLISH

231 ANDREONI, G. 'Australitalian'. *University Studies in History*, Vol. 5, 1967, pp. 114-19.
232 CLYNE, Michael G. Australian Migrant Language Studies: A Survey and View Towards the Future. Presented to Linguistics Society of Australia, Canberra, May 1968. Duplicated.
233 ——. 'Decay, Preservation and Renewal: Notes on Some Southern Australian German Settlements'. *AUMLA*, Vol. 29, 1968, pp. 33-43.
234 ——. 'Deutscher Idiolekt und deutscher Dialekt in einer zweisprachigen Siedlung in Australien'. *Wirkendes Wort*, Vol. 18, No. 2, 1968, pp. 84-95.
235 ——. 'Maintenance of Bilingualism'. *Australian Journal of Education*, Vol. 12, 1968, pp. 125-30.
236 ——. 'Migrant Languages in Schools'. *Babel*, No. 27, October 1964, pp. 11-13.

237 ——. 'Some Instances of Limitations on Speech Capability as Exhibited in German-English Bilinguals'. *Proceedings of 10th AULLA Congress*, Auckland, 1966, pp. 251-9.
238 ——. *Transference and Triggering; Observations on the Language Assimilation of Post-war German-speaking Migrants in Australia.* With a foreword by Hugo Moser. The Hague, Martinus Nijhoff, 1967, xi + 148 pp.
239 FORSTER, Kenneth I, and CLYNE, Michael G. 'Sentence Construction in German and English Bilinguals'. *Language and Speech*, Vol. 11, 1968, pp. 113-19.
240 FORSYTH, Elliott Christopher. 'Bilingualism in Australian Migrant Communities'. *Australian Journal of Education*, Vol. 12, 1968, pp. 113-24.
241 JERNUDD, Björn H. 'Foreign Language Broadcasting in Victoria'. *Babel*, Vol. 5, No. 2, 1969, pp. 24-5. //Comment on effect of foreign language broadcasts on migrant English.
242 JOHNSTON, Ruth. *Immigrant Assimilation—A Study of Polish People in Western Australia.* Perth, Paterson Brokensha, 1965, xviii + 289 pp.
243 ——. 'Language Usage in the Homes of Polish Immigrants in Western Australia'. *Lingua*, Vol. 18, 1967, pp. 271-89.
244 KOCH-EMMERY, E. 'Die Rolle der Zweisprachigen in heutigen Australien'. *Moderne Sprachen*, Vol. 7, 1963, pp. 52-60.
245 McCORMICK, C. A. 'Italian and Assimilation'. *Babel*, No. 26, 1964, pp. 2-4.
246 NIJENHUIS, J. G. J. *Het Nederlands in Australië; een aantal beschouwingen over het gebruik van de Nederlandse taal loor de immigrant.* Articles from *Dutch-Australian Weekly*, Dec. 1966—January 1967. Sydney, Dutch-Australia Publishing Company, 1967, 32 pp.
247 PAUL, Peter. Das Barossadeutsche—Ursprung, Kennzeichen und Zugehörigkeit. M.A. thesis, University of Adelaide, 1965.
248 RANDO, G. 'Influenze dell' inglese sull' italiano di Sydney'. *Lingua Nostra*, Vol. 29, 1968, pp. 17-32.
249 SHARWOOD, John A. Spoken English in Two Areas of Italian Settlement in North Queensland; An Analytical Study of the English Spoken by a Cross-section of Fifty First and Second Generation Informants in all Age Groups from Italian-speaking Homes in the Innisfail and Ingham Areas. M.A. thesis, University of Queensland, 1965. //Short title: The speech of the Italian community of Northern Queensland.
250 TARNAWSKI, L. L. K. The English of German-speaking Bilingualism. B.A. (Hons.) thesis, University of Queensland, 1961.
251 ——. The Aural and Oral Command of English of a Group of German-speaking Migrants in the Brisbane Area. M.A. thesis, University of Queensland, 1965.
252 ZUBRZYCKI, Jerzy. 'Immigration and Cultural Conflict'. *REMP Bulletin*, (The Hague), 1957, pp. 71-7.
253 ——. *Settlers of the Latrobe Valley: A Sociological Study of Immigrants in the Brown Coal Industry in Australia.* Canberra, ANU Press, 1964, xx + 306 pp. //Contains comment on the part of language in assimilation. See index, 'language'.

V PLACE NAMES

254 AUSTRALIAN BROADCASTING COMMISSION—Standing Committee on Spoken English. *A Guide to the Pronunciation of Australian Place Names.* Sydney, 1957, xviii + 147 pp.
255 BROOMFIELD, Fred J. *Australian Gazetteer.* Springfield, Mass., G. and C. Merriam, 1910. //Supplement to *Webster's New International Dictionary*.
256 COCKBURN, Rodney. *Nomenclature of South Australia.* Adelaide, W. K. Thomas & Co., 1908, 150 pp.

257 MARTIN, A. E. *One Thousand and More Place Names in New South Wales.* Sydney, N.S.W. Bookstall Co., 1943, [108] pp.
258 ——. *Place Names in Victoria and Tasmania.* Sydney, N.S.W. Bookstall Co., 1944, 107 pp.
259 MOORE-ROBINSON, J. *A Record of Tasmanian Nomenclature with Dates and Origins.* Hobart, Mercury Printing Office, 1911, 106 pp.
260 O'CALLAGHAN, T. 'Australian Place-names'. *Victorian Historical Magazine,* Vol. 7, 1919, pp. 186-91; Vol. 8, 1920, pp. 15-35.
261 QUEENSLAND PLACE NAMES COMMITTEE. Bulletins Nos. 1-11, March 1938-July 1941.
262 RYAN, John Sprott. *Papers on Australian Place-names.* (Collected for a Conference of Historical Societies, Lismore, N.S.W., 16-18 August 1963.) Armidale, University of New England Department of University Extension, 1963, 79 pp., 3 maps, bibliography.
CONTENTS: 1. Toward an Australian Place-name Society. Techniques to be Employed in a New-World Context. See *263.*
2. Australian Place-names—A Neglected Study.
3. Some Aboriginal Place-names in the Richmond Tweed Area.
4. Some Place-names in New England: The European Element.
263 ——. 'Toward an Australian Place-name Society. Techniques to be Employed in a New-World Context'. *Onoma,* Vol. 10, 1962-3, pp. 247-57.

AUTHOR INDEX TO THE BIBLIOGRAPHY

Numbers in italics indicate main entries for an author

A.B.C. Weekly, *150*
Ackroyd, J., *044,* 052
Acland, L. G. D., *045*
Adams, C., *151*
Age, 053
Alexander, D. H., *001*
All The Year Round, 046
Andreoni, G., *231*
Andrews, M. L., *186*
Atwood, E. B., 029
Australasian, 115
Australia. Commonwealth Office of Education, *152*
Australian Broadcasting Commission, *254*
Australian Council for Educational Research, *047*
Australian Encyclopaedia, 050, 155
Australian Language Research Centre, *002, 013, 014, 035, 065, 066, 073, 074, 081, 082, 083, 089, 090, 132, 162, 197*
A.W.G., *048*

Baeyertz, C. N., *153*
Baker, S. J., 044, *049, 050, 051, 052, 053, 054, 055, 056, 057, 058, 059, 060, 061,* 067, 069, 070, 097, 110, 115, 122, *154, 155,* 205
Baugh, A. C., *003*
Bennett, G., *156*
Bernard, J. R. L.-B., 002, *062, 157, 158, 159, 160, 161, 162, 163, 164*
Bevan, I., 125
Board, R. W., *165*
Bradish, C. R., *166*
Britton, J. H., *063*
Brook, G. L., *004*
Broomfield, F. J., *255*
Bullard, A. M., *167*
Bulletin, 067, 115, 211
Burgess, A., 028, 053
Burgess, O. N., *168, 169*
Cattell, N. R., *005, 006*
Chambers's Shorter English Dictionary, 114
Christie, L. H., *034*

A Bibliography of Australian English

Churchill, W., *007*
Clarke, J. W., *029*
Clunies Ross, A., 052
Clunies Ross, J., 211
Clyne, M. G., *232, 233, 234, 235, 236, 237, 238, 239*
Cochrane, G. R., *170, 171, 172*
Cockburn, R., *256*
Collins, D., *064*
Commonwealth Office of Education, *152*
Cooke, E. A., 002, *065, 066*
Crowe, C., *067*
Culotta, N., *028*
Cunningham, P. M., *008*
Daily Telegraph, 068
Davis, N., 130
Delbridge, A., *009*, 039, 053, 056, *069, 070*, 130, *173, 174, 196, 214, 215*
Dinning, H. W., *175*
Dixon, J., *010*
Dorsch, T. S., *176*
Douglas, W. H., *011*
Downing, W. H., *071*
Doyle, B. K., *072*
Dutton, T. E., *012*
Eagleson, R. D., 002, *013, 014, 015, 016*, 039, *065, 066, 073, 074, 075, 076, 077, 078, 079, 080, 081, 082, 083*, 091, 130, 135
Economist, The, 053
Education Department, N.S.W., *218*
Ehrensperger, C., *084*
Elkin, A. P., 130
Elliott, B., 052, *122*
Elliott, R. W. V., *018*, 090, 130, 197
Ellis, A. J., 202
Encyclopaedia Britannica, 054
Field, B., 148
Flint, E. H., *019, 020, 021, 022, 177*
Forster, K. I., *239*
Forsyth, E. C., *240*
Fowler, F., *178*, 193
Fraser, J. F., *179*
Froude, J. A., *180*
Fullerton, M. E., *085*
Funk and Wagnall's *Standard Dictionary*, 051
Garnsey, E. R., *181*
Garth, J. W., *086*
Gerson, S. H., *143*
Gerstaecker, F., *182*
Graband, G., 029
Graham, J. D., *183*
Greenway, J., *087*
Griffin, D., *184*
Gunn, J. S., 002, 018, *088, 089, 090, 185*

Gunson, N., 076, *091*, 135
Hanley, T. D., *186*
Hardcastle, W. J., *187*
Harder, K. B., *092*
Harris, J. K., *023*
Harrison, T., *093*
Harwood, F. W., *188*
Heseltine, H. P., 060
Hesling, B., *094*
Hicks, W., *095*
Hill, R. P., *189, 190, 191*
Hodgson, C. P., *096*
Hope, A. D., *192*, 212
Holden, W. S., *097*
Horne, R. H., 178, *193*
Horton, I., 225
Howarth, R. G., 049, *098*
Howitt, W., *099*
Hungerford, T. A. G., 060
Iredale, T., *100*
James, G. L., *194*
Jernudd, B. H., *024, 195, 241*
Johnston, G. H., 053, *101*
Johnston, Grahame, *102*
Johnston, M., *103*
Johnston, R., *242, 243*
Jones, A. I., 002, 018, *196, 197, 198, 199, 200*, 214
Kevin, J. C. G., 176
Kingslake, E., *181*
Koch-Emmery, E., *244*
Lake, J., *104*
Lauder, A., 196
Laycock, D., *201*
Lentzner, K., *105, 106, 107*
Lindsay, E. D., *167*
Lingo, T. L., *085*
McBurney, S., *202, 203*, 228
McCallum, J. A., 167, 206
MacCallum, S. E., 002, *065, 066*
McCormick, C. A., *245*
McDavid, R. I., 029, 052, 111, 154
McGuire, D. P., *204*
McKie, I., 002, *081, 082, 083*
McKnight, G. H., *108*
McLachlan, N., 148
McLeod, A. L., *058*, 212
Marjoribanks, A., *109*
Marshall, A. J., *205*
Martin, A. E., *257, 258*
Masterman, K. C., 039
Maurer, D. W., *110*
Meddleton, I. C., *142*
Mencken, H. L., *111*
Menner, R. J., 052
Menzies, R. G., 150
Meredith, L. A., *025*

Mitchell, A. G., *026*, *112*, *113*, *114*, 123, 192, 196, *206*, *207*, *208*, *209*, *210*, *211*, *212*, *213*, *214*, *215*
Moore-Robinson, J., *259*
Morris, E. E., *115*, 121
Morrisby, E. S., *216*
Morrison, H., *116*
Mossman, S., *217*
New South Wales Department of Education, *218*
New South Wales Legislative Assembly, *219*
National Identity Conference, *027*
New York Times Magazine, *117*, *118*
Nijenhuis, J. G. J., *246*
O'Brien, S. E., *119*
O'Callaghan, T., *260*
O'Grady, J. P., *028*
O'Meara, D., *120*
Palmer, N., 052, 115, *121*, *122*
Partridge, E. H., *029*, *123*, *124*, *125*
Paul, P., *247*
Pear, T. H., *220*
Pei, M. A., *030*
Platt, H., *221*
Queensland Place Names Committee, *261*
Quinn, J., *126*
Quinn, T. J., *031*
Quirk, R., 029
Ramson, W. S., 002, 003, 018, 032, 039, 053, 067, 070, 076, 080, 091, 107, 109, 111, 115, *127*, *128*, *129*, *130*, *131*, *132*, *133*, *134*, *135*, *136*, *137*, *138*, 146
Rando, G., *248*
Ransley, T. H., *222*
Readdy, C. A., *033*
Reader's Digest Dictionary, 059
Ridout, R., *034*
Robertson, M. A., *223*
Rogers, H. L., 039
Rotarian, *139*
Rudskoger, A., *140*

Russell, G. H., 002, *035*
Ryan, J. S., *036*, *141*, *262*, *263*
Sansom, C., *224*
Sattler, W., 107
Schonell, F. J., *142*
Schuchardt, H., *037*
Scrutarius, 130
Sharwood, J. A., *143*, *225*, *249*
Shaw, B. A., *142*
Shaw, W., *038*
Shay, J., *144*
Spiller, R. E., 052
Stephens, A. G., *119*
Stevans, C. M., *145*
Strong, H. A., 115
Swaen, A. E. H., 115
Sydney Morning Herald, 115
Sydney Slang Dictionary, 146
Symonds, H. M., 154
Tarnawski, L. L. K., *250*, *251*
Tench, W., *147*
Thomson, A. K., 029
Times Literary Supplement, 039, 053, 130
Troughton, E., *100*
Trueblood, J. C., *226*
Turner, G. W., *039*, 070, 080, 203, *227*, *228*
Vaux, J. H., *148*
Wakefield, E. G., *040*
Ward, H. E., *041*
Ward, R. B., *042*
Waugh, D. L., *049*
Weaver, L. A., *229*
Webster's International Dictionary, 104, 255
Wilson, R. M., 052
Wood, T., *230*
World's Standard Dictionary, 145
Wurm, S. A., *043*
Zandvoort, R. W., 039, 052
Zellner, E., 029
Zubrzycki, J., *252*, *253*

INDEX

Aboriginal English, 137-60
Aboriginal languages, influence of, 35, 43-4, 49, 96
Aborigines, 21, 34, 35, 39, 137-60
Accent, definition of, 4-5, 15-16, 26
Agriculture, occupational terms, 9, 37, 49, 59, 92-4
American English: influence of, 36, 42, 45-6, 53, 56-7, 73-5, 79-80, 82, 87, 88; parallel development, 1, 10-11, 34, 39-40, 43, 45, 46, 128, 190-2
Asian students in Australia: attitudes to Australian English, 210, 211; grammatical deviations, 217-18; lexical deviations, 218-19; linguistic difficulties, 203-8, 210-12, 213-20; phonological deviations, 213-17; socio-cultural difficulties, 203, 208-9, 210-12, 219-20
Australian Academy of the Humanities, vi
Australian English, relation to New Zealand English, v-vi, 25, 69-70, 72, 73, 76, 77, 78, 84-6, 87-90, 91-3
Australianism, definition of, 36, 50-4, 58
Australian Language Research Centre, vi, 59

Baker, S. J., 3-4, 33, 50, 55
Baylebridge, William, 190
Beach-la-mar, 105-6, 141
Bernard, J. R., 19, 21, 24, 25, 66
Bilingualism: in migrant communities, 123-8; Asian students, 203-20
Black-birding, 105
Brennan, Christopher, 188, 195
British English, 1, 4, 5, 6, 26; *see also* Standard English
British regional dialects, 36, 37-9
Broad Australian, 6-7, 17-20, 21, 25, 28-9, 126
Buckley, Vincent, 198
Bulletin, 34, 47

Clause rank, 172-6
Cockney pronunciation, 2, 72
Colloquialisms, 38, 43, 45-6, 49-67, 75-80, 87, 91, 192
Colonialisms, early condemnation of, 34

Compounds, formation of, 39-40, 41-2, 54, 55-6
Contextual meaning, 165
Convicts, influence of, 9-10, 38, 41
Criminal cant, 38, 46
Criticisms of Australian pronunciation, 1-4, 11, 13-14
Cultivated Australian, 6-7, 11-12, 17-20, 21, 23, 25, 28-9, 126

Dairy farming, 94
Daley, Victor, 194
Dennis, C. J., 38, 199
Dialects, *see* British regional dialects
Diminutives, 55, 76
Diphthongs: Asian students, 211, 213-17; Australian, 7, 12, 20, 22-4, 28-9, 126; German settlers, 131-2; New Zealand, 70-2, 88-90
Drawl, 7, 26-7, 72
Dried fruits industry, vocabulary of, 59-60
Dutch migrants, 124, 128, 134

Educated Australian, 6-7, 17; *see also* Cultivated Australian
English English, *see* British English
Extensions of meaning, 35, 39-41, 65-6

Fauna, naming of, 42-4
Flora, naming of, 40, 42-4, 81
Formal meaning, 165
Franklin, Miles, 192
Furphy, Joseph, 199-200, 201

General Australian, 6-7, 17-18, 19-21, 25, 28-9, 126
General English, 56-8, 86-7, 134
Generalisation, lexical, 9, 37, 39
German: in Papua-New Guinea, 107-8; influence of, 36, 46, 105-6, 115, 134; migrants, 124, 125, 128, 130, 131-3, 134
Grammatical description, 162-6
Group phrase rank, 176-8

Halliday, descriptive theory of, 164-6
Harris, Alexander, 34, 38, 44, 47

241

Historical development, 8-10, 24-5, 32-47, 69-70, 84-5
Homophones, in pidgin, 113-14
Hope, A. D., 45, 193, 196, 197, 198, 201

Immigrant minorities, 123-35, 203-20; influence of, 10, 21, 46, 72, 130-4
Intelligibility of Australian pronunciation, 13-14, 28-9, 211
Interference phenomena, 123-8, 144-5, 205-8
Intonation, 5, 26-7, 72, 88, 189, 214, 217
Inventiveness, see Popular attitudes
Irish immigrants, influence of, 9
Isolation, leading to historical development, 9, 33, 72
Italian migrants, 130, 133

Jones, Evan, 198

Kendall, Henry, 194

Land, terms relating to, 39-40, 42, 61, 73-5, 92-3
Latin influence on Pidgin, 115
Lawson, Henry, 199-200, 201
Lexical features, of spoken and written English, 181-5
Local expressions, 50, 64
London English, 25; see also Cockney pronunciation, Urban origins

McAuley, James, 196, 197, 198
Maori, influence of, 44-5, 80-2, 99-100
Maurice, Furnley, 196
Mining terms, 37-8, 45, 49, 58, 73
Mobility, of Australian population, 9-10
Money, terms for, 63-4
Morpheme rank, 180-1

Nasality, 3, 72
New Australians, teaching English to, 125, 127
New Zealand English, relation with Australian English, v-vi, 25, 69-70, 72, 73, 76, 77, 78, 84-6, 87-90, 91-3

Obsolescence, 38, 52, 62-4
Occupational vocabularies, see Agriculture, Dairy farming, Dried fruits industry, Mining terms, Opal-mining, Pastoral industry, Shearing terms, Sheep-farming terms, Timber terms
O'Dowd, Bernard, 190, 194
Opal-mining, 58

Papua-New Guinea English, vii
Paralinguistic features, 15-16, 26-7, 72, 88, 189, 214, 217
Pastoral industry, occupational terms, 9, 37, 41-2, 45, 49, 59, 92-4
Pidgin: Aboriginal, 35, 105, 115, 137-59; migrants, 129; New Guinea (attitudes towards) 108-9, (examples) 112, (its future) 118, (grammar) 116-17, (historical background) 105-9, (lexical influences) 115, (literature) 117-18, (orthography) 114-15, (phonology) 113-15; origins and definition, 102-5, 153-4
Pitch, 5, 26-7, 72, 88, 189, 214, 217
Place-names, 37, 55, 82
Police Motu, 106, 107, 108
Polynesian influence, on Pidgin, 115
Popular attitudes: towards Australian pronunciation, 1-4, 11, 13-14, 15, 211; towards Australian English, 33-6, 49, 50, 67; towards Pidgin, 108-11
Popular etymologies, 32, 95
Portuguese influence, on Pidgin, 115
Praed, Mrs Campbell, 199

Queensland English, influence of, 105-6, 152
Queensland Speech Survey, vi, 20-1, 142

Racing slang, 60
Rank, 165-6, 171-81
Received Pronunciation, 1, 6-7, 11-12, 25, 26-7, 70-2, 188-9, 210
Reduction, lexical, 9, 36
Regional variation: in Australian English, 7-8, 20-1, 25, 50, 58-9, 64, 88; in New Zealand English, 72, 91
Rhyming slang, 54
Rhythm, 5, 7, 26-7, 72, 88
Richardson, H. H., 192
Robinson, M. M., 193

Schools, vocabulary associated with, 94-5
Scottish immigrants, influence of: in Australia, 9, 37, 132; in New Zealand, 70, 71
Semantic description, 160-1
Semantic features, of spoken and written English, 181-5
Sentence rank, 171-2
Shearing terms, 58-9, 64, 92-3
Sheep-farming terms, 9, 37, 41-2, 45, 49, 59, 92-4
Simpson, R. A., 198
Slang: Australian, 36, 38, 47, 49-67; New Zealand, 75-80

Index

Slessor, Kenneth, 195, 196, 198
Spanish influence, on Pidgin, 115
Speech of Australian Adolescents, The, 5-7, 18-20, 88, 126
Speech perception, 16-17, 27-9
Spelling, of Pidgin, 114-15
Spelling pronunciations, 71
Spoken English, 161-85; description of sample, 167-9; differences from written, 169-70
Sporting terms, 60, 95-6
Standard English, 32-3, 36, 47, 70-2, 188-9, 210; *see also* Received Pronunciation
Standardisation of pronunciation, *see* Uniformity
Surfing terms, 60

Teaching English as a second language, 125, 127, 164, 205-8
Timber terms, 37, 56, 93-4
Torres Straits English: examples, 155-9; its future, 153-4; grammar, 145-9; historical background, 140-2; lexis, 149-52; phonology, 144-5
Transference, in migrant communities, 123
Triggering, 126-7
Trilling, Lionel, 190-2
Truncated rhyming slang, 54
Twain, Mark, 190-2, 199, 200

Uneducated Australian, *see* Broad Australian
Uniformity: of Australian English, 7-8, 10-11, 20-1, 58-9; of New Zealand English, 72
Urban origins, of Australian English, 9, 25, 36-47

Vaux, James Hardy, 38
Voice quality, 15-16, 26-7, 72, 88
Vowel sounds: Asian students', 213-17; Australian, 2, 7, 12, 18, 21, 22-4, 25, 28-9; German settlers', 131-2; New Zealanders', 70-1, 88-90; Pidgin, 113

Wallace-Crabbe, Chris, 196, 198
War words, 46, 57, 61-2
Welsh immigrants, influence of, 9
Wentworth, W. C., 193
White, Patrick, 188, 190
Word rank, 178-80
Working-class origins, of Australian English, 9, 36-47
World English, 56-8, 86-7, 134
Wright, Judith, 196, 197, 198, 200-1
Written English, 161-85; description of sample, 167-9; differences from spoken, 169-70

Yiddish, influence of, 134

Designed by Arthur Stokes

Text set in 10/12 pt Times Roman, and printed on 85 gsm Burnie Antique Wove paper by Halstead Press, Sydney

DATE DUE			
6/10			
GAYLORD			PRINTED IN U.S.A.